Modern Capitalism

*A systematic historical depiction
of Pan-European economic life from
its origins to the present day*

Werner Sombart

Modern Capitalism

*A systematic historical depiction
of Pan-European economic life from
its origins to the present day*

Werner Sombart

I: The Pre-Capitalist Economy

K A Nitz
ALBANY, NEW ZEALAND

The 2nd edition of
Der moderne Kapitalismus
first published in German
1916

This translation into New Zealand English
Copyright © K A Nitz 2019
All rights reserved

ISBN: 978-0-473-49650-0

Table of Contents

Translator's Note..9
Source Abbreviations...11
Foreword and Introduction..15
Foreword to the Second Edition..17
   Introduction..31
      Chapter 1: The Basic Facts of Economic Life...............33
         I. Satisfaction of Basic Needs....................................33
         II. Technology...35
         III. Labour and its Organisation...............................37
         IV. The Economy...43
      Chapter 2: The Diversity and Conditionality of the Economy....45
         I. The Diversity of Economic Life.............................45
         II. The Conditionality of Economic Life...................47
      Chapter 3: The Task of Economic Science......................51
         I. The Differentiation of Economic Science.............51
         II. The Principles of Economics................................52
         III. The Task of this Work..53
The Pre-Capitalist Economy..59
   Section 1..61
      Chapter 4: The Pre-Capitalist Economic Disposition.....63
   Section 2: The Age of Self-Sufficiency............................75
      Chapter 5: The State of the Material Culture of Europe during the Early Middle Ages................................77
      Chapter 6: The Village Economy......................................83
      Chapter 7: The Socage Economy......................................91
         I. The Distribution of the Manors and Monastic Lands.........93
         II. The Main Features of the Socage Economy.......97
         III. The Organisation of Work in the Socage Economy.........102
            1. Agriculture...103
            2. Manufacturing Production...................................108
               a) The Manufacture of Foodstuffs.....................109
               b) The Manufacture of Clothing........................110
               c) The Building Trade..114
               d) The Manufacture of Equipment....................116
            3. Transportation..120

Section 3: The Period of Transition..123
  Chapter 8: The Renaissance of the Exchange Economy............125
    I. The Exchange Economy and its Origin in Particular..........126
    II. The Development of the Exchange Economy in the
        European Middle Ages...127
    III. The Preliminary Stages of Professionalised Trading.......145
    IV. The Beginnings of Professionalised Trade........................148
    V. The Beginnings of Craftwork..151
  Chapter 9: Towards a Theory of City Formation.......................155
    I. The Concept of the City..155
    II. The Outline of a Theory of City Formation.......................159
  Chapter 10: The Origin of the Medieval City...............................163
    I. The Birth of Cities from Villages, particularly the Founding
        of Cities...164
    II. The Subjects of City Formation..171
      1. The Consumers..171
      2. The Producers...181
    III. The Objects of City Formation..186
      1. The Clergy..187
      2. Soldiers and Officials..189
      3. The Craftsmen...190
      4. The Traders...194
      5. Alms Recipients..200
    IV. The "Draw Towards the City"..200
Section 4: The Period of the Craftwork-based Economy.............205
  Chapter 11: The Economic Policy of the City..............................207
  Chapter 12: The Economic System of Craftwork.......................215
    I. The Concept of Craftwork..215
    II. The Overall Organisation of the Economy........................217
    III. The Task of the Craftsmen's Cooperative........................218
    IV. The Particular Nature of the Work of Craftsmen.............220
    V. The Professional Structure of Craftwork...........................221
    VI. The Order of Craftwork..221
    VII. The Inner Structure of Craftwork....................................222
  Chapter 13: The Conditions of Existence of Craftwork.............225
    I. The Population..225
    II. The Technology..226
    III. The Configuration of Selling Conditions.........................230

  1. Causes on the Demand Side...233
  2. Causes on the Supply Side..234
 Chapter 14: The Configuration of Goods Demand....................239
 Chapter 15: The Manner of Satisfaction of Demand.................247
  I. The Final Consumers..247
   The distant sale of goods during the Middle Ages...............255
    Wooden wares..258
    Skins and Leather..259
    Leather Wares..259
    Various Small Items..259
    Clothing and Finery...260
  II. The Producers..262
 Chapter 16: The Organisation of Manufacturing Work............265
  I. The Linking of the Producers with the Market..................265
  II. The Location of Manufacturing...265
  III. The Number of Manufacturing Producers and their
   Productivity..269
  IV. The Form of Economy...274
 Chapter 17: The Organisation of Export Manufacturing..........289
 Chapter 18: Trade as Craftwork..295
  I. The Extent of Business..296
  II. The Traders..306
  III. The Regulation of Pre-Capitalist Trade............................312
  Postscript to the Second Edition..320
Bibliography..327
End Notes..365

Translator's Note

Sombart's work contains several untranslated quotations from sources in languages other than German — most notably in Latin. I have followed a policy of retaining each of these in its original language followed in square brackets by a rough (sometimes very rough) and fairly literal translation so as to retain more of the feel of what it would be like for someone with a basic familiarity with these other languages to read Sombart's original text. I have also followed this policy with quoted passages of non-standard German (such as the Low German of the Hanseatic sources). All such translations are my own unless explicitly noted otherwise.

I have endeavoured to clarify the citations used by Sombart (particularly expanding his abbreviations), and have provided the additional bibliographic details with these references where possible (and occasionally provided a more recent work or translation to aid those wishing to investigate the sources). I have also tried to add bibliographic details where possible for direct quotations (not always indicated as such by Sombart!) which did not have a source cited. Where the many volumes of the *Monunenta Germaniae Historica* (see the abbreviations section) are referenced, I have endeavoured to check the passages copied and correct any inaccuracies (both in the text quoted and in the reference itself). I have also attempted this for many of the other references where the original work was accessible to me.

The formatting of glosses — used extensively throughout by Sombart to provide further detail and discuss the sources — has retained the smaller typeface as used in the German text, but with the addition of a vertical bar on the right-hand margin to help further distinguish them.

The extent of the footnotes in the original, and the addition of the translations of non-German passages, has regrettably necessitated the footnotes being moved to endnotes so as to aid the flow of the text on the page.

This volume incorporates the introduction and first book ("The Pre-Capitalist Economy") from the first half-volume of the first volume of the original work. The second book ("The Historical Foundations of Modern Capitalism"), which spanned both the half-volumes of the first volume of the original work will be in a second volume.

I wish to acknowledge the School of Languages and Cultures at Victoria University of Wellington, and in particular Richard Millington of the German Studies Programme, for their support and encouragement in the translation of Chapters 5 and 6 during 2011 as part of my studies there.

As always, I accept all responsibility for any errors in this translation.

Source Abbreviations

MGH Monumenta Germaniae Historica (http://www.dmgh.de)

SS rer. Merov.	Scriptores rerum Merovingicarum
SS	Scriptores
SS rer. Lang.	Scriptores rerum Langobardicarum et Italicarum
Staatsschriften	Staatsschriften des späteren Mittelalters
LL	Leges
LL nat. Germ.	Leges nationum Germanicarum
Capit.	Capitularia regum Francorum
DD O I	Diplomata: Otto I
DD O II	Diplomata: Otto II
DD L II	Diplomata: Ludwig II

Volume I

Foreword and Introduction

—

The Pre-Capitalist Economy

Foreword and Introduction

Foreword to the Second Edition

The second edition of the book *Modern Capitalism*, two volumes of which I hereby present half a lifetime after the appearance of the first edition, is outwardly *an entirely new work*, as can be gauged from a look at the contents. Scarcely a tenth of the earlier work has been reused, and this fraction of the old work also finds itself arranged for the most part in an entirely new logical framework.

If I have, as it happens, equally well retained the title (as little as I love it), it is in order to express that the essential problem whose treatment the work pretends to address has remained the same, and with it a series of fundamental ideas. Besides that, the new edition is, with regard to its content, a new work — as those who study it will observe after reading the first chapter.

I do not want to explain in this foreword what the new work undertakes to do in its new spirit — I have sketched the task that it presents from page 53 onwards of this volume. However, I would like here at the start of the book to give the reader two different pieces of information: about the significant differences that the new edition has compared with the first; and about the space in which I would like to place the scientific character of this book, or — which amounts to the same — about the standpoint from which I have observed the things in this book.

***

The *differences between this second edition and the first* are chiefly the following:

1. Materially the new edition has been considerably stretched. Whereas only a fraction of the historical development is contained in the first, this new edition attempts to give a picture of the entire economic development of the European peoples. Hence, I now begin my portrayal with the Carolingian period and lead it with special attention through the epoch of early capitalism (particularly that of the 16th, 17th and 18th centuries, which in the first edition was left almost entirely unconsidered) through up until the present.

Those lands from whose economic life I have primarily taken the material for my portrayal are Italy, Britain, Switzerland, Holland, Germany and Austria, whereas I have less often included Spain, Portugal, Scandinavia and Russia in the ambit of my observation. Naturally the Asian, African and American colonies of the European nations were considered where appropriate.

The distribution of material in the various volumes has similarly changed. The *first* volume now contains, aside from a conceptually grounded introduction, a portrayal of pre-capitalist economy and the historical foundations of modern capitalism[*], whereas the entire extent of the fully rewritten *second* volume is dedicated to the portrayal of economic life in the age of early capitalism. A *third* volume, to appear later, should then depict the fulfillment of capitalism in the age of high capitalism.

2. The second edition differs *in construction* from the first through its much more complex design. A symphony based on a stronger contrapuntal handling appears in place of an "extemporary discourse", and it expects of the reader a greater effort and immersion. The 20th chapter of the first volume[†] tries to give an insight into the, in parts complicated, melody. This new way of treating the material, doubtlessly also bearing the reproach of greater ponderousness and blindness, will save this book from the frivolous and thoughtless type of critic who gives judgment at the very start and dismisses the entire work with the observation that it is a

---

[*] [Tr.: volumes 1 and 2 of this translation.]
[†] [Tr.: volume 2 of this translation.]

book on the "Theory of Ground Rents" [*Grundrententheorie*] or such like.

On the contrary, I ardently wish that the deepest impression remaining with the reader after studying my work is of a lively feeling of the *huge wealth of problems* which is embodied in these words: the genesis of modern capitalism. It would be a special satisfaction to me if from now on it would be impossible for such a "development history" of capitalism to be constructed from first principles, like that just written by Fritz Gerlich, and be yet more impossible that a respected historian like von Below were to publicly award such frivolous undertakings with "the praise of a useful work".

If, in my recent writings, I have stressed with deliberate arbitrariness *one side* of capitalist development, so too was this method thoroughly under-appreciated. The wise heads shook and began to doubt the intelligence of an author who wanted to reveal as the origin of modern capitalism now the rents, tomorrow the production of rare metals, the next day the Jews, then luxury, then war. They did not notice at all, strangely enough, that with these it was a question of partial studies — they did not realise that I aimed with this spotlight method at nothing more than to focus the eye of the viewer each time on *one side* of the problem in order that he would be forced to occupy himself intensively for a while with that partial problem. Now I am weaving these individual threads together into a fabric and showing, not just something of mine which is already appreciated, but that yet more forces have had a share in the building of modern capitalism.

3. The second edition seeks *methodologically* to avoid if possible perhaps the worst mistake of the first (which in addition, it should be remarked in passing, no single critic deemed it necessary to rebuke — Max Weber alone has often pointed it out to me in private conversation), which is the inadmissible blending of theoretical and empirical considerations. This mistake made itself especially noticeable in the depiction of the crafts, but also came to light elsewhere with unpleasant frequency. I have now aimed at the separation of the theoretical and empirical parts in the treatment of each individual problem and have strictly carried out this dual consideration throughout the entire work, as I have sounded out

yet further on pages 54-55 in this volume. I place great importance on this innovation and hope that it has also helped our science in a methodological respect. With that I come to talk of the second point that I wanted to discuss in this foreword: the place of this work (and its author) in the various "orientations" or "schools" or "methods" of political economy.

***

Whoever in this day and age still knows no differently than to separate the orientations of our science into the "abstract-theoretical" and the "empirical-historical" schools will be at a loss opposite this work. For his best efforts won't succeed in assigning it to one of the two "schools" or "orientations" or "methods". But it is allowed of every work of the social sciences of our day that they want to take new routes. And that it is allowed is not too surprising, since every contrast between 'historical' and 'abstract' political economy has lost all sense and meaning for us, or at least should have.

If even today a number of one-sidedly gifted, younger political economists set something like a "theoretical" orientation on our science in conscious opposition to the research methods advocated by the "historical school", it is the result of arbitrary limitations on the concept of "theory" justified by nothing more than a certain traditionalism. This concept of "theory" has been limited to the cultivation of a quite restricted complex of problems — specifically to those problems that refer:

1. to the maintenance and further development of the conceptual scheme established by the so-called "classical writers" of our science; and

2. with the help of this conceptual scheme, to the "regularity" of phenomena (of rational mental processes) which has been established using the methods of abstraction.

Now nobody can give a higher estimate of the value of this so-called "theory", especially of the abstract-isolating procedure, than the author of this work. Anyone who undergoes the trouble of making a study will find this method used in countless places in this work: he reads for example chapter 33 of the first volume*, which was constructed entirely according to this procedure. But to now think that the nature and content of the social science of economic life, which one calls political economy or national economy (picturing the first part of such constructions as somehow independent from the part of this science under consideration), exhausts itself in these abstractions and isolations appears to me to be completely inadmissible. To assume that would be to call a man who only ever uses calculations for the load-bearing capacity, etc. of building materials a master builder, whereas this man is, however, only a part-worker. In the same way, the abstracting isolator in political economy is nothing more than a part-worker, and no better than his counterpart: the researcher who amasses facts. It appears obvious to us today that the union of both activities represents in the first place the fulfillment of scientific political economy — it is almost a triviality to establish that "theory" and "empiricism", like the form and content of these same objects, are related to one another. (What I mean is given with special clarity by a comparison of chapter 33 with chapter 35 of the first volume†: chapter 33 establishes by means of the isolating procedure the "conformity to natural laws" that prevails, in theory, between money value and price; and chapter 35 investigates, with the help of this schema, the actual relationship between rare metals production and price setting in a specific historical period.)

In addition, this concept is represented already by the leading heads of the older so-called "historical" school. It is the ruling concept today with all researchers of my generation who have helped to bring some life into our science. The older generation would not have used for themselves the tags of *either* "theorist" *or* "historicist". They were, just like, incidentally, the gifted representatives of the younger generation, all obviously "theorists" *and* "historicists". This work is also theoretical *and* historical.

Now it has been described as just a peculiarity of the research orientation of our time that in it the "theoretical" problems (as in other sciences, so in the social sciences) have once

---

* [Tr.: second half-volume, and third volume of this translation.]
† [Tr.: second half-volume, and third volume of this translation.]

more stepped into the foreground — one speaks really of a *"renaissance of theoretical interests"*. And one is right in doing so. Only, as far as our science comes into question, the word "theory" must not be understood in the narrow sense cited above. If that "theoretical renaissance" also means an advance or a revival for political economy, then the bearers of this advance are certainly not entirely all strong-willed men who are unswervingly upholding the standard of "abstract" research. Anyone who in the continuing development of the Ricardian formulae (which, as I once more wish to explicitly mention, I consider to be very useful and profitable — always provided that one remains consciously mindful of one's limited store of knowledge and above all that all abstractions and isolations only make sense in the framework of one economic system marked off according to its historical characteristics), anyone, I say, who sees the task of our science in the care and development of this conceptual framework, can — if he is gifted as well — perform undoubtedly useful work, but he is not an innovator, a life-giver, a reformer. He is, on the contrary, an imitator.

What one calls the theoretical renaissance of our time, which coincides with a philosophical renaissance, has another meaning entirely. Our age has become the philosophical, so far as questions are asked, more so than earlier, about the *"sense" of appearances* and about the "sense" of knowledge. But the sciences outside philosophy have become theoretical, and the social sciences too, in that, more so than earlier, value is being placed on conceptual rigour, on systematic comprehension of the materials, and above all on the synthesis of independent knowledge. I would actually like to see the distinguishing mark of our time in this *need for synthetic summing up* of scattered research results.

We feel the burden that the constantly increasing material is placing on our chest as an, in the end, unbearable pressure and look to free ourselves of this burden so life will be good. But that is not possible, if we do not want to turn away from all "science" and flee "up and away to a far-off land", unless we bring to life the dead material, unless we try to become its master by giving it life through the use of ordered and systematic categories. I would like this work to be seen as one such attempt of intellectual liberation, one that thus looks to the development of concepts and systems with special love in order, with their help, to master and give life to the material which several generations have amassed with tireless diligence.

Because it is an argument over terms, it is an idle argument as to whether the science expressed in this work (and, similarly, related works) is *"political economy"* or, rather, economic sociology, or something similar. It is correct that it is something other than that which some of the advocates of the Manchester School called political economy 50 years ago, in particular that discipline which, without being weighed down by historical or philosophical ballast, deals with the economic questions (that is, mostly the mercantile problems) of the everyday, that doctrine of common sense, that "science" of the market for the market, of real life for real life, that business doctrine that one can also describe as the political economy of the secretary of a Chamber of Commerce. Now, I am on the other hand some distance from drawing doubt on the high utility of such everyday lessons of the market. But, what I dispute categorically is this: that it is now the science of human economy in general. On the contrary, that political economy of the secretary of a Chamber of Commerce only increases by one the ever more numerous doctrines within the wide limits of the economic sciences. Next to it stands that very science which exists as the intrinsically central science of the sciences of economic life, which sets itself the task of ordering them in the greater context of human social life, and which would not be possible except on a historical-philosophical foundation.

We cannot possibly concede to the science which one calls political economy today being thrown back on the position which it had arrived at 50 years ago when the German masters, be it the so-called "historical school" or the so-called socialist orientation, began their work of reform whose basic results should signify an inalienable possession for us.

That my work does not serve as a specifically political or economic or socio-political *manifesto* should, firstly, not have to be explicitly stressed at all. It goes very well without saying.

It is a bad sign of our times, and reminds dangerously of American conditions, that one has begun to see also in the last decade in Germany that the representatives of our science are distinguishing themselves not according to their scientific methods and achievements, but rather according to their political opinions. If representatives of practical interests act in this way then it is not so easy to be cross with them on account of that, for they do not need to know as such what science is. But that the mischief is also spreading into scholarly circles is dangerous in the highest degree. I think that only unoriginal and, in their innermost being, unscientific spirits can arrive at the idea of asking, accordingly, for the opinion of a scientific personality as to how they should vote for something in the parliament, or whether they should be thinking "business-friendly" or "worker-friendly", or the like.

***

My characterisation of the ideas by which this work is governed being incomplete, I wanted to give in more than a few words the position that I am taking *opposite the historical research and the historians.*

In the circles of proper historians it is considered to be settled that this work, in the guise of the first edition, is an awful and mistaken book. And the historians were correct for the good part with their disparaging criticism. The first edition contained awful blunders in the details, and their entirely wild and impetuous form invited contradiction and the challenge of rejection by a severe school of established historians who had been habituated to painful meticulousness. I hope that a considerable portion of those errors which the first edition contained has been removed in this second edition.

But, I cannot concede to the historians that their disparaging criticism was justified in all its parts. What I have to reproach many of those very historians who publicly gave their opinions about my book with is not just the hostile tone of their criticism — although it would have been of more use to the affair if it had been avoided. Especially when the scholars regarded themselves so obliged to agree on the tone that their masters had struck. It almost amused me to observe how it belongs to the good custom of some universities that a young doctoral candidate who deals with a problem of economic history, often in a quite remote place of his pet work, cocks a leg at me, and declares that he "obviously" does not want to have anything to do with my views. (Which were, however, often very useful to the writing of his work.)

But that is, after all, not so important. More important is that many historians reject the kind of historical portrayal that is contained in my work (that is, the constructive, generalising aspects of my method) as unjustified. Against this view I would like to assert the following: obviously there are two possibilities for questioning the historical world, in that one asks either what has happened *once*, or what has *recurred*. The question about the uniqueness of events could probably be called the specifically historical, the other, about the recurrence of events, sociological — enough, they are both justified, and all historical writing serves both questions. Depending upon the object under consideration, sometimes one and sometimes the other will predominate. The most extreme contrasts will be depicted by biography and the history of social conditions. Both questions are also at home in economic history. There is also no either-or here, but rather only a both-and. It must be stressed that a profitable economic *history*, for that special reason, also requires an investigation of the particularities of historical-sociological research, not merely of the end products but rather right to the foundations. Only then, when some economic phenomena are established as being general (that is, those which are recurring), can we state with certainty where the particularity of the problem complex considered by us lies.

Now the particular nature of this work consists in that *the question of the generality of economic phenomena has been stretched right up to the outermost border of permissibility*. This border is the cultural area formed as belonging to the South and West European peoples who, since the mass migrations, have been the bearers of Europe's history. As far as this is relevant, the question is on the other hand specifically historical: there is only a history of *"modern capitalism"*, not a history of capitalism in and of itself. But, inside the just given cultural area, every peculiarity of the different nations has then been disregarded, and the question asked: which economic phenomena which lead to the origin of modern capitalism are common to *all* European nations? I regard this question as not only amply justified, but, as I have already said, the investigation of these general European features of economic development is the necessary prerequisite to examining, now with the prospect of a rich yield, the economic fates of narrower units.

It is not that my work would exclude the special research that would like to refer sometimes to an entire land and sometimes to a single village. In contrast, it makes it even more fruitful. Only now, since one knows what European economic history is, will the German, French, English, etc. economic histories be able to be written. Like the mathematician, who removes recurring letters in all variables and places them before a bracket so that he, instead of $ab + ac + ad$, writes $a(b + c + d)$, so too was I acting when I sought out from all the European economic histories (which are themselves each a product of European and national being) the European note and pursued it in their idiosyncratic organisation. Every historian *must* acknowledge this process, after careful consideration, as justified next to historical research in its narrow sense.

He must, admittedly, then make himself still clearer: that actually the solution to the problem, as I have myself presented it, makes the application of a scientific apparatus necessary — an apparatus which the historian does not care to use on the solution of what are to him common problems. This apparatus is the artful schema of a *systematic* science of the economic life. Only the basic *theoretical* comprehension of the entire stock of material knowledge makes it possible to uncover the general connections of phenomena. The history of the origin of modern capitalism can only be written by a fully developed *theoretically*, political economist who, above all, also knows about the economic life of the past. He can certainly also be a historian of the subject. But that he must be one is, especially in the circles of the older historians, unfortunately not yet generally accepted opinion. Otherwise it would not have been possible for a famous historical researcher, like Henry Pirenne, to give to his fellow historians of the entire world (at the London Historians Congress 1913) a lecture on the development phases of capitalism that gave evidence of an almost astounding naivety. All the laborious conceptual efforts of the past decade passed over this scholar without trace, and he confronted with the innocence of a child the problems with which we have struggled for a lifetime. This type of economic historian must die out, otherwise we will get no further. And that he already, as a matter of fact, half belonged to the past, is vouched for by the works of a few younger economic historians in various lands who are not ignoring the problems that we have thrown up, but proceeding from that point of view with pleasing zeal and expertise. I cherish the solid confidence that works like mine will also appear from the *rising generation* among the historians, not as useless and mistaken undertakings, but as a necessary completion of their own inquiries into economic history in the narrow sense.

***

Last of all, I must still mention a point of more peripheral interest: *my method of citation*. It was complained of by numerous critics (which would not be objected to in my book!) The objections which some have raised against it provide me with a welcome opportunity for briefly characterising my method of citation. First of all, with regard to the quantity of citations, I cite for some too much, so as to "burden" the work with too much "dead material". My reply to these critics is that I am not aware of having piled up "dead material", that I believe, rather, that each of my examples is vital. As the reader sees, almost all my citations are *primary sources*, also where they are cited from the treatment of the matter in the literature. I quoted only by way of exception the opinions of other researchers, not because I esteem them inferior, but because I would like to eliminate from a work like this all polemic, if possible, as it serves no purpose in my experience. But I need those source examples, often piled up in quantity and, if possible, in wording, in order to impress the exhibited phenomena on the reader's soul, and to have the particular case that I have set forth become an intensive experience for him. I could only make the extreme generalising tolerable by continually placing the most forcible pictures of reality before the reader's eyes. It is my endeavour to deduce the last generality from the most intimate particularity. For that I had to give a *quite* concrete conception in order to then *fully* establish the general features. But a certain high degree of material abundance was indispensable for it. That is why there is the frequently tiresome mass of citations.

I cite, according to the others, too little. That is, they miss in this or that place the reference to this or that work or source. I hold out to them that I was entirely conscious of not having a command of all the relevant literature. It is also hardly possible, in view of the quite extensive area of investigation. I am thankful to everyone who proved to me that I overlooked here or there an essential source (provided that it was apt to correct the result of my investigations on an important point). I feel that the procedure is petty where, with some, even renowned, critics, it was popular to complain if one named twelve works and had not also mentioned a thirteenth, probably entirely unimportant work that only the critic knew. Besides, completeness of the documentary sources on the stated problem, like those this work is based on, is also sometimes an unnecessary requirement for a compelling presentation of evidence.

Some will feel that it is a weakness of the book that I used *only printed* and not handwritten *sources* as well. I ask them to consider that this work could not have been written if I had lost myself in archival studies. Certainly it is correct that many points of European economic history still lie in the dark today, and that only archival research can clear them up. But, a clear overall picture has already been provided today on the basis of printed sources. And the attempt has to be made to give that picture first, precisely in order to make the later research more fruitful. That a wealth of new information is being produced already by the working through of today's printed source materials will, I think, be proven by a study of this work.

Then, as far as the method by which I cite is concerned, doubts were also heard as to whether I found my quotes myself and did not perhaps borrow them from other works. I note with regard to this that I have constantly felt that the *to a broad extent (also and particularly with historians!) popular* custom of copying other writer's citations, without noting this explicit borrowing, is a form of theft of intellectual property. Actually, one should always make it known when one owes the reference on a source location to someone else. But it is not feasible in the long run. What *absolutely* must be demanded of scientific decorum is that one verifies *every place* that one cites with one's own eyes (or with less accessible works have a schoolboy or a good friend look it up). This principle was also standard for me in the writing of this work.

Just such a deplorable habit, which is more and more becoming a habit in scholarly circles, is to give a *literature review* without knowing the cited works. With the state of our bibliographical technique today, it is not difficult to marshal arbitrarily long lists of books which certainly only make an impression of learnedness on the layman, while the initiate usually notices the mnemonics to which the list owes its origin. Such mischief should be controlled with the implicitly assumed rule of citing in a literature review no book whose usability for the defined purpose one has not sufficiently informed oneself of. Bibliographies are useful for the reader in my experience, especially for the beginner, only if they at the same time contain a sort of guide through the relevant literature. Hence, I have had it requested of me that I, where possible, include with each quoted work a quite short reference from which the reader receives a rough introduction to what it is about.

A few factual arguments with critics who complained about individual parts of my book are better undertaken in specific places in the text. The critics are very numerous who took such pains to especially go into my thought processes ... not. In the interest of the matter, I wish that their number would increase in comparison for this second edition. The majority of critics have left in doubt whether it lay in a shortage of goodwill or in their feeble understanding that they knew nothing at all of importance to say about the book. For it is a fact that they rejected it. I would like to write the words of old Goethe in their commonplace book:

> Against criticism you can neither protect nor defend yourself; you must defy them and they will gradually relent.[1]

Werner Sombart

It is a comforting thought that only seldom do the wells of life have their source where the critic dwells in the science, and no critic, not even the most spiteful, can destroy that which is lively in spirit.

Mittel-Schreiberhau, September 1916
Werner Sombart.

Introduction

Chapter 1: The Basic Facts of Economic Life

I. Satisfaction of Basic Needs

Like all living creatures, man must, in order to preserve his life, continually supplement his individual existence through the ingredients of material nature which he includes in his consumption and strives to adapt to his purposes. That man has stretched the circle of his needs out past the elementary needs of maintenance, and has created a new world of needs in "cultural needs", represents merely a difference of degree. The animal world also has an extraordinarily different set of needs as graded by quantity and quality.

Together with all living creatures, man is, however, also set with the necessity of devoting a great part of his vigour to the acquisition of that stock of necessities upon which his life depends. He must, because the nature surrounding him is brittle in relation to his need, look after the "fulfillment of his demand" — he must practice "the satisfaction of basic needs".

This satisfaction of basic needs, which is said to be a shared characteristic of all life on this earth, presents itself in a regular cycle that is grounded in the natural constitution of the needing being and of its consumption of necessities — objects of external nature are taken up and adapted to the needed purpose: the bird keeps feathers, and gets them ready for the nest, and it "builds" its nest. We call this first act *production*. The goods, after they are produced, are fed into their purpose (into consumption): the bird feeds the individual young with the regurgitated midges. That is, as we say, the act of *distribution*. Then the goods are used or consumed — the act of *consumption*, from which must then follow (out of necessity again) an act of production. Production ("generation") — distribution — consumption will constantly repeat themselves until the last life on this earth will have vanished.

We describe as (material) *goods* or tangible goods (in contrast to the purely intangible (incorporeal) goods) all objects of the external environment that are relevant to the satisfaction of basic needs. They are either already known as such (effective goods) or not, even though they already possess material suitability for finding a use in the satisfaction of basic needs — woollen threads could always serve the bird as building material, though it would only be "discovered", so to speak, in the bustle of cities. When material things serve immediate consumption, then we speak of consumer goods, when they serve for the manufacture of other goods, then they are production goods. We describe the former, after the method of Carl Menger, as goods of the first order and the latter as goods of higher (second, third, etc.) order.

All *production* or goods generation, as we somewhat pompously say, is based on us living entities making an expenditure of energy by means of which we form the materials or forces existing in the environment ("nature") in accordance with the purposes of our needs. Thus, in each act of production, labour and the environment necessarily work together. Hence, we can describe them as *factors of production*, the former as the personal and the latter as the material factors of production.

The external *environment* appears in each production process, firstly as working conditions, and secondly as objects of labour. In its first function, it creates the material conditions for productive labour, whether these conditions are given now either by nature — like the earth as location, the air as atmosphere, or the forces — or first manufactured in the form appropriate to the goals of production — like factories, roads, canals, or the wax cells of honeybees. An object of labour is that very thing on which the labour itself operates. It is also either found finished in nature, or is already a product in itself. In the first case we call the objects of labour raw materials.

II. Technology

The depiction so far has identified the components of the satisfaction of basic needs as they regularly recur in every form of satisfaction of basic needs — animal's as well as man's. Now the phenomena particular to the satisfaction of man's basic needs are to be considered with respect to what makes them economic phenomena.

The first phenomenon which distinguishes man's satisfaction of basic needs is that of man's own process for the production of goods (which always stands for all handling of objects, and also in particular the transport of goods); the use of which we justifiably call *instrumental technology* or, if we want to restrict the sense of this word, just technology in general.

We understand by technology, in the widest sense, all the processes to achieve a specific objective, and thus by material or economic technology all the processes for the production of goods.

The technical abilities are in particular:
1. The knowledge of the properties of our surrounding environment. This technical *knowledge* extends to the usability of the materials, the forces, and the development processes of nature itself.
2. The technical *capability*. This reveals itself in some cases merely in a specific method for the carrying out of activities. Of such methods, two in particular are to be stressed as especially significant: the dismantling of the entire activity into its individual components, which then appear as separate activities; and the amalgamation of material by which one and the same activity is carried out at the same time instead of one after the other on similar objects.

In other cases the technical capabilities develop themselves into an *instrumental technology*. By that I understand such a process by which the inducing of technological outcomes is attained by the use of some objects, or instruments. With respect to goods production, we describe these instruments as the *means of labour*, which are thus to be considered a third form of the environment's involvement with the satisfaction of man's basic needs (next to objects of labour and work conditions, which are peculiar to *all* satisfaction of basic needs). We can also call all the components of the material factors of production in a further sense the *means of production*, and distinguish as means of production in a narrower sense those among them that are already products of labour. I will speak in the following, where it is not specifically stated, of means of production in the wider meaning of the embodiment of all the material factors of production.

Precisely considered, the *means of labour* (according to the Marxian definition) is a thing, or a complex of things, which the worker shoves between himself and the objects of labour in order to have them operate as instruments of power on other things in accordance with his goals. We can differentiate active and passive means of labour. Marx describes the first as "the mechanical means of labour, whose totality can be called the skeleto-muscular system of production"[2]. They are work tools and machines which actively intervene under human control in the forming of the material anew, whilst the other category of means of labour plays a more passive role in production, serving as receptacles for materials and forces. These are the boilers, pipes, vats, barrels, baskets, jugs, etc. — those means of labour "whose totality can be described quite generally as the vascular system of production."[3]

A *work tool* is a means of labour that serves to support human labour (eg. a needle), whereas a *machine* is a means of labour that shall replace human labour, that thus does itself what in its absence a human would do (eg. a sewing machine).

> The extensive *literature* which is tied to my differentiation of work tools and machines does not lead me to make any changes. When one ascertains that the ideas of both means of labour were being framed (and had to be framed here) with regard to their usability for economic-scientific knowledge, then one probably cannot differentiate any other way than I did. For only with this contrast is the economically fundamental thing, the relationship to the activity of work, recognised as the principle characteristic of the concepts.

So the first, quite significant characteristic of the satisfaction of man's basic needs expresses itself in the use of means of labour. Man is "a tool making animal".

Not only in the superficial sense that (perhaps purely by chance) man makes use of the means of labour, and animals do not. Rather, in the deeper sense that the behaviour peculiar to man — a conscious action after purposeful ideas —

finds expression most distinctly in the use of work tools (that here stand for all means of labour and weapons), but also (which is yet more significant) in that according to every supposition this special humanness has rambled right up into the work tools. Then this made it possible, and then again necessary, for man, through the development of his purely intellectual abilities, to set himself up as lord of the earth.

III. Labour and its Organisation

1. Man lives by actively using his powers. Human activity differs (or is distinguished by us) from that of animals because it is action according to reason, ie. an action towards some goal. That human activity which serves purposes lying outside itself, we can contrast as *labour* with sport, which finds that purpose within itself.

> With that I am attempting to define the concept of labour according to purely objective characteristics. It only obtains the required clarity, it seems to me, when each insertion of subjective factors necessarily provides something particular and variable. The most travelled path with which to attain the concept of labour leads on the one hand to the travail over value judgments and on the other hand to usefulness. Every attempt to clearly establish both these categories must, however, fail simply because of their property as value judgments. Thus, by my definition, an activity like that which a thief expends in order to carry out a burglary is just as much labour, although it is (socially) harmful, as that trade which makes "no trouble" when it is only aimed at a goal lying outside itself.

We call its ability to produce a definite quantity of goods in a given time the *productivity* (or yield) of labour, and we call the amount of energy expended in a given time the *intensity* of labour.

2. All human labour is *social* labour. The problem of human labour is hence always (also) a sociological one.

All human labour is social in the sense that the labour of no man is possible without the work of another man. Human evolution could only have taken place within the bounds of a human community and today the work of the solitary man also rests on the work of all earlier races.

It has often been rightly stressed that when Robinson Crusoe was washed up without any property (which was not at all the full extent of the case, since he had rescued a garment or some other trifle) on the beach of an uninhabited island, he had, however, been given along the way the memory of much knowledge and many skills as indispensable equipment during his struggle for existence, and without that he would not have been in a state to build the life that he did. That is, a Robinson Crusoe is conceivable only as the artistic production of a culture thousands of years old. This concatenation of human labour over time thus always exists. The concatenation is either a purely intellectual one (corresponding to memory), or a material one mediated through the products of labour. Our labour also rests at any time on the work products of the past. The purely non-material concatenation of human labour over time is not an especially human phenomenon, but is general to all living things, whilst the material concatenation is actually almost exclusive to man. It is valid in a still higher degree for the other kind of concatenation — the concatenation in space. The success of a man's labour is always tied to the labour of others during his lifetime. In primitive conditions the labour of an individual is made possible through the cooperation or parallel labour of his comrades in the community in which he lives. Today the labour of individuals is tied to the labour of thousands, and thousands more still, whose labour products he makes his own by way of an exchange of products. It is only a degree of difference in the social character of labour when a specific labour is carried out in a spatial community by several people at the same time.

3. All human labour, since it is a social fact, exists under a specific *order*. For any methodical activity duly takes place as soon as several men are brought together with each other. The plan is objectified in the order. We speak, when we have the order of human labour in mind, of its *organisation*. The organisation of human labour is based on two — and only two — principles: those of *specialisation* and *cooperation*. Every other possibility for ordering human work in a different manner is only a subcategory of these two principles.

Whether one wants to describe these different possibilities with special expressions or not will be decided individually according to one's own inclinations. But, on the other hand, Willy Hellpach has suggested a quite broadly specialised nomenclature in the essay which he published in Vol. 35 of the *Archiv für Sozialwissenschaft and Sozialpolitik*[4]. The detailed expressions and the detailed differences say little to me.

They confuse me more than they give me clarity. Hence, I prefer to stay with the two categories of specialisation and cooperation which, as stated, include all conceivable possibilities of organising labour. The attempt to bring the objective difference of various organisational principles into some connection with the purely subjective relationship of human nature, or at all of human consciousness, or of human desires for or against performing labour appears to me to be quite mistaken. How a specific labour operates on men is entirely a (incidentally, psychological and not sociological) problem for themselves.

Under the term *specialisation* I understand that sort of arrangement which constantly allocates to one and the same worker identical, repetitive activities. The degree of specialisation can be extraordinarily different. It was an employment of the principle of specialisation when women first performed women's work and men men's work, and when blacksmithing or pottery was first carried out constantly by the same worker. And it is only an extended use of the same principle when a worker in the modern clothing industry sews her whole life long only horn buttons onto men's vests. It remains principally just the same, whether the partial activity that a worker carries out constantly arises from the horizontal or vertical division of the previously united, or to-be united, overall labour process — whether the separation takes place between metal-working shop and smithy, or between tannery and shoe-maker's shop. Finally, it is unimportant for the concept of specialisation whether the specialisation occurs between firms (which will be discussed next) or within a firm. In the former case, what we call specialised firms arise, among which there is again an extraordinarily multifarious hierarchy of grades, but within which no somehow fixed border is at all to be drawn for a specific differentiation.

The smithy as a whole is a specialised concern compared with the formerly widespread production of home industry surrounding it. The smithy is a specialised concern, after the metal-working shop separated itself from it, the tool smithy is within the thus specialised smithy again a specialised concern, the scythe smithy within the tool smithy, etc. It is of course admissible in historical deliberations to assume as given a certain degree of specialisation, and to describe those firms that demonstrate it as "full concerns", and all concerns only comprising parts of these full firms as "specialised concerns". We thus proceed with complete justification when we have made the processes of decomposition of the old "craftwork" clear to ourselves.

Cooperation is the working together of several people on a complete work that itself can only be defined by use in consumption or objectively. Cooperation *can* take place when the labour is not specialised, but it *must* take place when the work is specialised. For then it manufactures the necessary association of part workers.

It is evident then that cooperation and specialisation stand in the same relationship to one another — like in the organic world, or in the mathematical idea of integration and differentiation. Nothing of course stands in the way of also applying these descriptions to the organisation of human labour, provided that one remains conscious of the purely figurative meaning of borrowed expressions from other spheres.

4. If we think of the great phenomenon of human labour as the discharge of rational actions, then the thousand different individual actions appear bound to inwardly coherent units of activities through their dependence on a particular work plan. The world of labour thus organises itself in our thought in just as many uniformly arranged labour processes as work plans are available. We speak of firms when there is a higher degree of coherence with a persistent connectedness of individual actions to a whole. And we can more precisely describe *firms* as *events for the purpose of continued work activity*.

When a person performs labour alone, she forms the firm with her work activity alone, so a purely subjective plan is enough for the regulation of her activities and for the organisation and maintenance of the concern. This must necessarily objectify itself in an order as soon as several persons unite their labour to joint effect. For in order for the activity of the individual to then be adapted to the overall labour according to the plan, it must from the start be allocated to the right place, and at the right time, and only in the correct way. An order of the firm constantly arises thereby — it may be thought, spoken, written, printed; it may be silently agreed upon or expressly enacted; it may be autonomous or heteronomous for the individual organs of the labour process — it remains the same, enough that it is there.

The overall task of the configuration of a firm, we can say, is the appropriate fitting together of the individual factors of production into a whole through their correct distribution over time and space. The configuration of a firm refers to the following points in particular, in all of which the unity of the arrangement must be demonstrable in order that we may talk of *a* firm:

a) the *introduction* of labour processes — to which belongs power of disposition over acceptance, employment, and dismissal of workers in both quantitative and qualitative aspects as well as the power of disposition over the workplaces necessary for production, and over the required means of labour;

b) the *formation* of the labour process — ie. the determination of the site (where?) and the time (when?) that labour should be provided;

c) the *performance* of the labour process — ie. the care for the actual execution of the prescribed plan, for the staging of the work process according to instructions. In other words, the management must also be a unitary one which manifests itself outwardly in the identity of the leading supervisory organs[5].

What a firm is, is often asked and answered in very different senses. One will do best to see the unity of the firm also in the *unity of the order of a firm*. What brings about the unity can either be justified by the activities — objective or work unity — or stems from the arbitrary goal-setting of the labourers — subjective or purposive unity. The purpose can be a different one in *one* and the same labour environment.

> Now and then a different purpose of the *workers* and a different purpose of the *work* were considered in themselves; as the master builder can have for a purpose the earning of money, but the purpose of building is the house.[6]

In particular, it becomes a fundamentally important distinction in the capitalist economy, where the purpose of the workers and the purpose of the work always fall apart. I have previously called the unity created through the first purpose the economy, and that created through the second purpose the firm, and described the first unity as a community of use, and the second as a work community. It is better to create the generic term concern, and within this concept to distinguish an economic (or utilisation) concern from the labour concern.

5. The quite various *forms* that the concerns can assume will be best made comprehensible in their particularity when we always select as the distinguishing characteristic the special configuration of the factors of production, and certainly in the manner by which we seek above all to imagine the relationship of individual workers to the entire process and the final product. For every essence of the concern's organisation appears in the end in the particularity of this relationship to the phenomenon. The relationship of the worker to his work can be fundamentally a dual one: either effects and labour belong peculiarly to *one* individual, are his identifiable discharge, and only his activity in-person, and are consequently private and personal to himself (this is generally understood so far as it is a question of that labour which happens within the bounds of a concern); or effects and labour are the joint result (indistinguishable as individual labour from its independent parts) of many activities existing only as overall effects and overall work — and thus not personal, not individual, but rather collective and social. Accordingly, let the concerns be divided into the two groups of *individual* and *social* concerns, in which the product appears, respectively, as the work of *one* worker or of a totality of workers.

Of one worker — strictly, this is only taken to be the case in the *sole concern*. However, we will also allow to be counted as individual concerns those in which either a couple of workers are always performing a specialised work next to each other, or in which the principal worker is supported by a few lesser helpers — they are the *assisted concerns*. According to the count of workers employed (the only criteria that statistics know), the individual concerns belong to the category of "small" or "medium" firms, whilst the social concerns are mostly "large" firms.

We will distinguish amongst the large social concerns, particularly in industrial production, the manufacturers and factories.

I call *manufacturers* those large social concerns in which the essential parts of the production process are carried out by manual labour. I call *factories* those large social concerns in which the decisively important part of the production process is made independent of the shaping contribution of the worker, and is assigned to the lifeless body of an automatically acting system. The factory's special function is to translate into reality in the most complete and up-to-date manner the overcoming of the qualitative and quantitative limitations of individual workers that is enabled through the introduction of machinery and the scientific processes of chemistry into production. There is no room in it anymore for the development of individually personalised work[7].

The economic concern assumes special forms — I call them *forms of economy*.

IV. The Economy

Economics involves the satisfaction of man's basic needs. Therefore we will meet in every economy:

1. a specific *economic cast of mind*, with which I describe everything intellectual by which the individual economic activities are characterised — thus all the ideas of value, setting of goals, and maximisation which come alive in the people shaping the economy, whom we will call *economic subjects*. The economic cast of mind of the economic subjects is objectified in the *principles of economics*.

2. a specific *technology* — thus specific methods of proceeding which the economic subjects make use of in carrying out their objectives.

3. a specific *organisation of labour* — thus a specific order which underlies all individual economic transactions.

Chapter 2: The Diversity and Conditionality of the Economy

I. The Diversity of Economic Life

A glance at the reality of economic events in the present, and an examination of economic life in times past convinces us that man indeed economised at all times and in all places. In addition, it convinces us that a series of basic facts recurs in every human economy, just as in the same way we are convinced by the fact that the forms in which economic life occurs demonstrate extraordinary differences from place to place and time to time. A closer look and a short reflection teaches us that this diversity derives itself from the different organisation of the three basic facts characterising the human economy. We shall envision which possibilities exist for such organisations[8].

1. *The economic principles*. Differences arise first of all through the diverse goal setting of the economic subjects. However, we can distinguish in particular two significantly different sorts of goal setting. Man actually strives either for the acquisition of needed goods (ie. he seeks to fulfill his basic needs), or he strives for profit (ie. he seeks to acquire as large an amount of money as possible through his economic activity). In the first case, we say his actions are under the spell of the *principle of satisfaction of needs* and, in the second case, they are under the spell of the *profit principle*.

A diversity of economic principles further arises through the different possibilities for economic conduct. This is either *traditional* or *rational*. Traditional when it is based on an unthinking compliance with traditional rules; rational when it is based on the deliberate wish for a fundamental expediency of all transactions.

2. *The technology*. These differences are likewise particularly brought about through the contrast of rational and empirical procedures. When the bringing about of the technical end-result is the result of a consciously sensible consideration of expediency, we speak of a *rational* method, and this is based on the causal explanation of natural phenomena by a *scientific* method. By contrast, the technical procedure is based on a merely traditional and unthinkingly adopted craftsmanship, and so we call that method *empirical*.

3. *The organisation*. A motley diversity arises first of all when we imagine all possible arrangements and formations that are called into being by the organisation of the economy. This defines:

a) the manner in which the factors necessary for the production — *means of production and labour force* — are raised to productive activity. Whether, for example, the workers come to work as members of the family following the orders of the head of the family; or whether as strangers they are dragged there by force; whether they are induced to work by the state authorities in a society of free men; whether they arrange themselves as equal partners to a joint labour; whether they are sold as wares on a market, or recruited as assistants perhaps for payment in kind of taxes set by the authorities, etc.;

b) the manner in which the persons collaborating in the production *exert influence* on the organisation and its operation. The production manager is the economic subject here. But the relation of the production manager to the other participants in production can be extraordinarily diverse — from the most unrestricted despotism, to the freest democratic constitution. Here hierarchies of the leader to the led are conceivable and real;

c) the manner in which the product is *utilised*. Whether it is delivered to ordering customers for a consideration; whether it is consumed by the business of production; whether it is delivered to the feudal estate, or to the abbey; whether it is deposited in a state warehouse, etc.;

d) the manner in which the *participants share in the profits of production*. Whether not at all (one thinks of the vassal obligated to do labour for his lord); whether with a share of the profits; whether with a fixed sum (in kind or in money) independent of profits; whether the participation takes place in the way of silent agreement, or freely given explicit agreement, or official standardisation, or such like;

e) the manner in which the *work process is organised*. Whether in small or large firms, etc.;

f) the manner in which the *form of economy* is configured.

II. The Conditionality of Economic Life

A just as simple reflection leads us to the insight that the characteristic shape that economic life experiences is dependent upon the fulfillment of certain conditions — or, expressed in another way, that a particular economic life constructs itself on a number of mental and material, natural and artificial facts.

The conditions of economic life are either *homogeneous* or *heterogeneous*. Homogeneous phenomena are such as are favourable to the realisation of the dominant set of goals of the economic subjects. I call heterogeneous phenomena, in contrast, those which create obstacles for the achievement of the goals strived for by the leading economic subjects.

According to their own manner, our conditions are either *natural* or *artificial conditions*, depending on whether they are given to man finished by nature, or are first created by him.

Land and people are the two spheres within which natural conditions revolve.

Land can become decisive for the organisation of economic life through what the ground contains within itself — be it in plant nutrients or in minerals. It can become decisive through the climate, through its geographical position, or through its internal structure.

The *people* are certainly for the most part a construction of the human hand, and their ways must be appreciated in this respect as the cultural conditions of economic life. But they also represent a given of nature for every culture, and are also a (mightily effective) condition of nature. The population wins influence over the organisation of economic life from two sides: through applying their genetic constitution, worldview, leadership ability and temperament; and through the number of their relationships, which are expressed in density, age structure, and growth rate.

The "*cultural conditions*" of the economy are as diverse as there are expressions of culture. In systematic order, the following summary is given:

A. The conditions of *objective* culture: that is, of all culture that has its existence external to the individual, and whose duration outlasts an individual life because it is "objectified" in some object which tends to have only the meaning of a symbol — like say a flag or a statue of a monarch.

The objective culture depicts itself in a specific cultural property, which is:

I. *Material* nature. The material cultural property is constituted by the material goods available to the whole of a community of men.

II. *Spiritual* nature. The spiritual cultural property refers not only to some material goods — in its material substratum — but in addition to this also itself represents an intellectual property.

Such spiritual cultural property is of two sorts. It establishes on the one hand what I call the institutional culture and on the other hand the so-called intellectual culture.

1. The *institutional* culture (as we are able to say, for the sake of simplicity, instead of cultural property) exists in the domain of arrangements, organisations, and organisational systems which a people can make use of. They are objectified in constitutional documents, statutes, religious systems, factory orders, guild charters, toll rates, etc., from which men infer the directives which they possess for arranging their conduct with each other. We can distinguish within the entire institutional culture four large complexes in which the millennia have reflected and accumulated their experiences: a) the state; b) the church; c) the economy; and d) tradition.

2. The *intellectual* culture, as far as it describes a cultural property, is formed by all that non-material cultural property which goes beyond ordered arrangements of some sort. Here also belongs all possession of ideals, ideas of worth, aspirations, etc. It amounts to an essential part of the cultural possession of a people when a strong nationalism, or a deep

sense of religion, or a humanitarian worldview, or a mammonistic spirit is at home in it.

Besides the above, everything comes into consideration which one naturally thinks of when one speaks of the intellectual cultural property of a people — the products of science and of the culture with whose blessing it is able to be realised.

Here also belongs technical knowledge and technical capability, which are especially significant properties for the organisation of economic life.

Opposite this objective culture now is that which can be called:

B. *personal culture*, which can also be called individual culture. It consists in the utilisation of cultural goods by a living person. It is the "education" [*Bildung*] of this person himself — is his highest personal self, arises with him, through him, and dies with him. The individual culture is: 1) a *physical* one; or 2) a *mental* one. All training of the body through sport, etc., but also all cleanliness, all elegance of dress, and the like belongs to the physical, whilst the mental individual culture finds its expression in the moral, intellectual, or artistic perfecting of the individual. It is apparent that further cracks can gape between the objective culture and the subjective, and in particular that one and the same objective culture — eg. a certain property of scientific or artistic works — can be reflected differently in the culture of the individual. This can occur qualitatively — according to the various types of effect that the utilisation of cultural goods exerts on people — or quantitatively — according to the environment of the individuals who take part generally in the exhausting of the content of objective culture.

When we speak of the culture of a people, we think both of the totality of its (objective) cultural property and of the extent and character of the personal culture of the members of this people. Besides that there is then still a third, which we have in mind especially when we talk of the culture of a specific "period", and which is objective and subjective culture in *one* as it were, only existing and demonstrable in them, and yet a different culture next to them. It is:

C. the embodiment of all cultural phenomena which we combine in our spirit to a unity and equip with especially typical characteristics. One could call it perhaps the *cultural style* (of a period or a land), which we doubtless feel to be a unity even if it appears as such in nothing other than in the thousandfold disparate expressions of the objective and subjective culture of this period or this land. When we speak of the "culture of the Renaissance" in contrast perhaps to "modern culture", then it is the peculiar "cultural style" that we have in mind.

Reflection advises and history teaches that this special cultural style can also practice a large influence on economic life.

Chapter 3: The Task of Economic Science

I. The Differentiation of Economic Science

Originally, that is when economies were first made the objects of reflection, there was only a single "science" of economic life. That was the doctrine of domestic science, the economic, which was itself, however, called economy (οικονομια), and which we first see developing with the Greeks.

"We had thus found", said Socrates, "that domestic science is the name of a science and that it enables men to improve their household affairs. By household affairs we understood the overall capabilities; as such we consider that which is profitable to each one for the conduct of his life, profitably appearing to us in the end as that which one finds usable."[9]

The οικονομια included both the care of a father for his family's livelihood and the care for his own livelihood — the orders that he gives in order to breed sheep, press wine, and spin wool; his decisions on the raising of children and treatment of slaves; his purchases and sales, as well as possible contracts, and all the activities performed (the ploughing and harvesting, the spinning and weaving, and the storage and distribution).

The science of οικονομια had the task of being a good advisor to the good patriarch in all these obligations of his.

But that was also still the opinion of the cameralists in the sense of cameralism, in which everything should have been taught that a good administrator had to know — how to breed pigs, how to populate the lands, how to keep the royal household in order, and how to make industry and trade prosper.

The solution of the old trade associations, the ever more skilful organisation of economic life, led to the formation first of all of a range of skill instructors, to whom the task fell of dealing exhaustively with particularly difficult parts of the satisfaction of basic needs in order to convey a reliable knowledge of the subject to the practical person. All the arrangements which had condensed into the "law" were discussed scientifically in the jurisprudence. All technology — be it that of agriculture, of material processing, of goods transportation, or of commercial and industrial management — was allocated to the thorough treatment of special "technological" sciences.

Thus finally a residue of the old economic science remained which was not jurisprudence and was not technology, and we describe this residue as national economy or political economy or economics. Its object is best described negatively — the object of economics (or however else one wants to name the science) is the satisfaction of man's basic needs so far as these are not dealt with by the doctrines of law or the various other doctrines. We can state positively that national economy is *the doctrine of economic systems* (see below). With that the principles of this science have been sketched out.

II. The Principles of Economics

1. Since the satisfaction of man's basic needs is a social phenomenon, the science that it has as a whole for its object is a *social science* — all its concepts must, after the technical sciences are discarded, take a social scientific cast.

2. If one wants to think of the economy and apprehend its phenomena scientifically, then one can only conceive of it amidst an already existing historical environment, thus as a specifically formed historical arrangement. That economics is a *historical* social science is a priori to it. Thus all concepts of economics are also "historical categories". What one has contrasted to these as "economic categories" were not social scientific but technological concepts (capital = means of production). These are only admissible as auxiliary concepts.

3. The foundational concept of national economy is the *concept of the economic system*. By that I understand a spe-

cifically mannered way of economy — that is, a specific organisation of economic life within which a specific economic disposition prevails and a specific technology comes into use. In the concept of an economic system, the historically conditional character of economic life collapses into a conceptual unity. All remaining economic concepts are organised on this general or basic idea.

4. The *scientific methods* which economics operates will be different depending on the type of economic system that is being investigated. But there will always be three distinct viewpoints which are placed under consideration:

a) the *theoretical* — the conceptually pure capture of all phenomena and their connections;

b) the *empirical-realist* — the discovery of the actual organisation of economic life and its mutations in the sequence of time, with the help of "theoretical" knowledge.

The concept corresponding to the concept of the economic system, in the empirical-realist approach, is that of the *economic epoch*. By that I understand a historical timespan in which a specific economic system, or more precisely the economic manner appropriate to a specific economic system, *predominated*.

c) the *political* — the orientation of all phenomena to an ideal, and the measurement of the means and ways which serve towards the attainment of the ideal.

III. The Task of this Work

This work is created in accordance with the principles developed above, and has set itself the task of portraying in a genetically systematic way the economic life of the European peoples from their beginnings to the present day.

With that I observe the following:

1. "*From their beginnings*" — that means from the time when the economic life of the peoples who had taken possession of Europe after the mass migration began to grow anew from its own root — from about the time of the Carolingian era.

2. "*The economic life of the European* (particularly South, West, and Central European) *peoples*" — so far as, it must be added, it is uniformly shaped and proceeds uniformly. The

posing of the problem was thus aimed at the highest possible universal in the economic phenomena, and not at the distinguishing features from land to land. Both problems posed — that about the agreements and universals, and that about the differences and distinctive features (which can be described as sociological and historical) — are obviously fully justified. They are not mutually exclusive, rather they complement each other. Next to the countless treatments of the economic history of individual regions, this work signifies the first attempt at a pan-European economic history.

3. "*In a genetically systematic way*" is how European "*economic life*" should be depicted. That means the following. That each individual phenomenon of economic life is oriented to the currently prevailing economic system. The concept of the economic system, and accordingly that of the economic epoch, conduces to the ordering of all the monstrously large materials, which were only able to be mastered with the steady assistance of both these foundational concepts.

Thus the various economic systems which had predominated in the eleven centuries from 800–1900 had to be deduced and first of all described in conceptual purity (using "ideal types"). The economic systems described in such a way are:

a) self-sufficiency in its double form: as farming, and as manorial/monastic* self-sufficiency;
b) craftwork; and
c) capitalism.

These three economic systems correspond to the three economic epochs which have followed one after the other in the last millennium in Europe. To depict the actual form of economic life in these three epochs is the real task of this work. It has undertaken the attempt to describe for the first time the *economic manner*, whereas hitherto, apart from narrowly restricted monographs, all comprehensive so-called economic histories were nothing more than the histories of the eco-

---

* [Tr.: I have endeavoured to consistently translate the terms *grundherrlich* as manorial/monastic, *Grundherrschaften* as manors/monastic lands/estates, *Gutswirtschaften* as landed estates, *Grundherr* as lord of the manor, and *Gutsherr* as estate owner.]

nomic systems. Neither the works of Cunningham, nor of Levasseur, nor of Inama-Sternegg, nor of Kowalewsky are in any way fundamentally different from legal histories. This work attempts, however, to show how the satisfaction of basic needs was shaped in reality, and how the course of economic events played out in reality. This work would like to bring into lively view what the farmer and the manorial/monastic lord, the craftsman and the businessman thought, wanted, did; and how their individual actions fitted together with the wondrous object of the general, social economy. The problem to be solved consisted in placing a "wealth of visions" before the eyes of the reader, in having him experience intensively the immense wealth of individual phenomena, and yet keeping for him at all times a clear overall view of the whole, in giving him the certain feeling that he can give himself over safely to the consideration of the thousand details, to run without danger, to get lost in the chaos of actualities. Procuring this certainty for him is served, on the one hand, by the generally strictly executed alignment of all phenomena to the currently prevailing economic system and, on the other hand, by the double treatment performed in detail on each problem: the abstract-theoretical and the empirical-realist. Of what I also speak of throughout this work — whether of craftwork or capitalism, of the development of cities or wealth, of the development of prices or markets, of the money or barter economies — the reader, when I treat the objects for the first time, is always groomed for the empirical depiction of the realities by a theoretical construction of the complex of phenomena. I hope that this method, used here for the first time, will prove fruitful.

4. To have the economic life in its various configurations come to *life* was the goal that I set myself in this work. Thus in particular, the method that Mephisto already mocked, but is unfortunately still in vogue, had to be avoided:

> Anyone who wants to discern and describe the living,
> Seeks first to drive out the spirit...[10]

In point of fact, it was my fervent desire to not destroy by my investigation the "spiritual ties" that hold together all living economy, but to show them directly in their concentrated force. Hence, I have taken pains to consult in particular the spirit which governed each specific economic epoch and out of which the economic life in that epoch was formed, and also taken pains to trace it in its effectiveness. It is a basic idea of this work that in each of the various periods a different view of the economy prevailed, and that it is the spirit which gives itself a shape appropriate to the times and thereby creates the economic organisation. This basic notion, which is already found in the first edition of this work, was developed even further and made into the leitmotif of all my explanations.[11] As I understand it, I will yet have opportunity to explain it often.

5. But the spirit is not all powerful on earth. In order for it to form life after its own image, specific *conditions* must be fulfilled. A large part of the depiction in this work is devoted directly to the proof of these indispensable conditions for the realisation of economic ideas. Since, as we know, the shape of economic life is conditional on the shape of the overall remaining culture, the explication of the conditions of economic life leads into all the branches of civil and intellectual life, and contributes significantly to the giving of life.

I have depicted the conditions of a specific economic manner in one case (with craftwork) systematically, and in another case (with capitalism) genetically. A decisive weight has been laid on this genetic portrayal in the main part of this work depicting the origin of modern capitalism.

6. With this type of investigation, a specific *structure* of the historical sequence of events will arise unforced as of its own accord. One will find in empirically definable periods that the power of an economic principle, and of the economic system corresponding to it, is as good as unlimited. In others, however, new economic principles look to struggle for recognition within the bounds of the prevailing economic system. Expressed differently, each new economic principle must attempt first of all to gain acceptance within the bounds of an existing economic system. It will create for its realisation economic forms whose shape is still defined fundamentally by the particular nature of the economic order generated from another economic principle (that prevailing at the time), and is capable only gradually of shaping the entire economic life

after its own spirit. From the standpoint of the *new* economic system, this epoch, in which the new economic principles are operating within the bounds of the old order, is its *early epoch*. From the standpoint of the old economic system, it is the latter's *late epoch*. In between lies the *high epoch* of an economic system, in which the spirit of only *one* economic system arrives at a pure development. The following investigation is based on this scheme of a genetic approach applied to empirically specified economic periods.

General Literature

There is, to my knowledge, no work which traverses the same paths as this one. One will most probably encounter similar thoughts in Gustav Schmoller's *Grundriss der allgemeinen Volkswirtschaftslehre*[12] and Karl Bücher's *Entstehung der Volkswirtschaft*[13]. But a systematic portrayal of the historical course of the economy in the various lands lies in both works correspondingly distant from their plan. Such a portrayal was, until now, only undertaken within the scope of national boundaries. The most well-known *"economic histories"* of the most important peoples are: William Cunningham's *The Growth of English Industry and Commerce*[14], Emile Levasseur's *Histoire des classes ouvrières et de l'industrie en France*[15], and Karl Theodor von Inama-Sternegg's *Deutsche Wirtschaftsgeschichte*[16]. These three works, if they also, as I have said, depict histories of the economic *order* rather than economic *life*, are each in their own way excellent achievements. Today they have become obsolete for the most part in the questions they ask, their methods, and their conceptual development. Fully at the heights of today's research stands, in summarised depictions, the distinguished sketch of Rudolf Kötzschke, *Grundzüge der deutschen Wirtschaftsgeschichte bis zum 17. Jahrhundert*[17].

The work of Maxime Kowalewsky, *Die ökonomische Entwicklung Europas bis zum Beginn der kapitalistischen Wirtschaftsform*[18], does not contain what the title claims [the economic development of Europe up to the beginning of the capitalist economic form] — it is a *pure* legal history into the fundamental agricultural conditions, besides being likewise restricted to within national boundaries.

The Pre-Capitalist Economy

Section 1

Sections

Chapter 4: The Pre-Capitalist Economic Disposition

Sources and Literature

A *literature* hardly exists that busies itself with the problem of the historically specific spirit in economic life. Of note are the critics who concern themselves with the relevant chapters of the first edition and whom I will quote occasionally. Apart from myself, only Max Weber, in his essay "Die protestantische Ethik und der 'Geist' des Kapitalismus" [The Protestant Ethic and the 'Spirit' of Capitalism][19], has dealt with the theme independently. A number of critical remarks arise again in this work.

A depiction, like that attempted here, therefore has to rely exclusively on the utilisation of the *sources*. I want to observe in advance the following on their nature and value.

The sources needed to grasp the meaning of the spirit in economic life flow profusely for anyone whose eyes are first of all open to the problem. Here too there are direct and indirect sources of knowledge. The economic actors themselves convey direct experience of the economic spirit to us through their utterances. Such as:

1. Self testimonies can be of casual nature: conversations, written communications, etc., or they are ordered systematically: in autobiographies, testaments, "reflections", and the like. But the possibilities for winning insights into the psyche of economic actors are more numerous via detours. We can thus summarise these possibilities as indirect sources of knowledge. Coming into consideration here are:

2. The "works" of the economic agents in their widest sense, those in which its spirit was thus reflected as it were. I am thinking of:

   a) the general organisations that manage them, such as village establishments, factory concerns, and transportation enterprises;

   b) the technological works, such as the fitting out of workshops, organisation of the means of labour, layout of railways, of irrigation, and of canals and harbours, etc.;

   c) the special arrangements for the carrying out of economic objectives, such as accountancy;

   d) the welfare arrangements;

   e) the tempo of development; and

f) the rhythm of economic life, such as quick reorganisation, quick extension of the economic body, and likewise other things.

3. Legal norms, such as regulations over the right of free self-determination, over competition, over advertising, over price-setting, and over charging interest, etc.

4. Ethics, whether of religious or secular origin. To this one can also add all critical expressions, such as satires, polemics, and suggestions of reform, etc.

5. Reflections of the time:

a) in public opinion, eg. recognition of the various professions (trades!) by the collective, or within particular classes (acquisition of positions in the nobility!);

b) in literature, art, and science, eg. the portrayal of types, and the constitution of popular "trends".

6. The social position of individual groups of the population to one another, such as peaceful coexistence, hostile attitude (such as the worker to the firm), patriarchal relationship, and business regulation.

7. The organisation of politics, in which the view of the economy broadcasts itself in the particulars, such as power politics, or free trade and the like.

That the value of the evidence to be inferred from these sources is very diverse is quite clear.

The self testimonies (1. above) are in particular very rare and hence not very fertile. If need be, they can certainly become of quite large significance for the correct understanding of a state of affairs. Mostly they must certainly be read between the lines. That is especially true with all systematic expressions of the remembered sort. In the autobiographies or memoirs of some preeminent businessmen (of which there are a whole series) the authors always represent themselves naturally as wholly selfless men, only serving the public good, and to whom money-making was the last thing they wanted entirely. Some are also honest about it, and they of course give us the best information. Also to be considered is the fact that we have such systematic self testimonies mostly only for quite preeminent men, whose larger than life natures must thus be traced back to the average measure if we want to generalise their achievements and insights.

Of the remaining sources, the most reliable are the "works" of the economic subjects (2.). They at least never lie.

The sources named under 3. and 4. are very important, but especially dangerous to use, so that there are researchers who absolutely do not want to have them regarded as sources of knowledge for a specific factual configuration of the objects, in this case of the "spirit" of a period. Thus many critics reproached me at the time for attempting to derive the line of thought of medieval craftsmen from guild orders, or even from criticism and suggestions of reform, like some of the reforms of Emperor Sigismund. I observe thus the following on these types of sources and their usability.

Chapter 4: The Pre-Capitalist Economic Disposition

The mistake which is commonly committed is not that one wants to scoop knowledge from those sources but rather that one wants to scoop false knowledge. One will not want to inform oneself from the penal code about the spreading of the types of thefts, nor from the laws governing trade and industry about the organisation of worker relationships in the past. But what one can learn very well from them is the average opinion of theft and worker protection prevailing in our time. Of course the view laid down in the legislation or expressed in the polemical literature (applying similar rules) is "out of date" and does not correspond to the "zeitgeist" anymore. Then one will have that to establish. In particular by the hand of hostile utterances. A not overly stupid history writer of our time will have to indeed infer for example from the middle-class literature that in Germany a considerable number of people still think in a craftsmanlike spirit. He will have to establish, however, that the basic view of our time, as it comes to light in the authoritative literature, and as it asserts itself decisively in legislation and government, is a different capitalistic one. Conversely our opinion about the "spirit" that governs medieval economic life has to be that indeed there were certainly daily countless actions and thoughts, like those stipulating moral norms and establishing legal norms, that contravened the craftsmanlike view; towards the end of the Middle Ages they will have occurred more and more. However they were still just transgressions. And the "zeitgeist" (5.) condemned them. The zeitgeist felt them to be transgressions. And nobody dared to justify these transgressions. Or is there a single authoritative statement during the entire Middle Ages that would have dared to defend the *Ôte toi que je m'y mette* [get out of the way, so I can take your place] principle, individual self-responsibility, or the unrestricted pursuit of profit?

Before the arrival of capitalism, the living man stands in the centre of all endeavours and all concerns. He is the "measure of all things": *mensura omnium rerum homo*. But as a result, the stance of man towards the economy is also already fixed — it serves human purposes like all other works of men[20]. Thus, that is the fundamentally important consequence of this conception, that the point of departure of all economic activities is the demand of men, that is, his natural demand for goods. However many goods he consumes, as many must be produced; however much he spends, as much must he earn. First the expenses are given, after that the income defines itself. I call this type of management an *expense economy*. All pre-capitalist and pre-bourgeois economy is expense economy in this sense.

Demand itself is not characterised by the arbitrariness of the individual, but rather it has assumed in the course of time a specific size and nature within the individual social groups which is now seen as permanently given. It is the *idea of the maintenance of your social standing* which governs all pre-capitalist economic management. What life had evolved in slow development then receives by the authority of law and morals the consecration of fundamental acceptance and regulation. In the edifice of Thomistic teachings the idea of maintenance of your social standing constitutes an important fundamental. It is necessary that the relationship of men to the external world of property is subjected somehow to a restriction, a standard — *necesse est quod bonum hominus circa ea (sc. bona exteriora) consistat in quadam mensura* [it is necessary that the good of man consists in that measure (ie. external goods)]. This measure constitutes the maintenance of your social standing: *prout sunt necessaria ad vitam eius secundum suam conditionem* [as they are necessary for the way he lives his life].[21]

One's upkeep should be befitting one's station. It will thus be variously large and variously natured within the various classes. Here two strata whose conduct of life typifies the pre-capitalistic existence stand out distinctly from one another: the lords and the mass of the people; the rich and the poor; the feudal lords and the farmers, craftsmen, and shopkeepers; the people who lead a free independent life without economic labour, and those that earn their bread by the sweat of their brow, the working men.

Leading the life of *a feudal lord* means living life to the fullest, and having a full life; it means spending your days at war and at the hunt, and around the merry circles of the happy tippler, wasting the nights with dice, or in the arms of beautiful women. It means building castles and churches; the display of pomp and splendour at the tournaments, or at other festive opportunities; pursuing luxury as far as one's means allow it, and more besides. The expenses are always greater than the income. It must then be taken care of that the latter expands accordingly — the steward must raise the taxes of the farmers, the landlord must increase the rent, or one seeks (as we will yet see) the means to cover the deficit from outside the circuit of normal economic means of acquiring property. The feudal lord despises money. It is dirty, just as all gainful employment is dirty. Money is for spending

Chapter 4: The Pre-Capitalist Economic Disposition

there:[22] "usus autem pecuniae est in emissione ipsius" [the enjoyment of money is in the discharge itself][23].

As the secular lords lived, so too did the spiritual lords through long periods. Leon Battista Alberti sketches a clear picture of the conduct of the feudal life of the clergy in Florence during the 15th century, which may be considered to be entirely typical of all life of the rich in pre-capitalist times, when he says the following:

> [The priests] want to surpass all others in the display of pomp and splendour, want to have a great number of well-tended and beautifully decorated steeds, want to appear publicly with a great entourage, and from day to day are escalating their tendency towards doing nothing and their bare-faced depravity. Although fate throws great means into their lap, they are yet always dissatisfied and, without a thought to saving, without economy, they plan only on how they can gratify their fired-up desires. [...] Income is always lacking, the expenses are always greater than the ordinary income. So they must seek to snatch the deficit from elsewhere [etc.][24]

For the great mass of people it was also necessary in pre-capitalist times, since one only ever had limited means at one's disposal, to bring expenses and income, and demand and supply of goods into a lasting ordered relationship to one another. This certainly also occurred here with the same pre-fixing of demand, it being a traditionally fixed given and worth gratifying. That led to the *idea of sustenance* which gave its stamp to all pre-capitalist economic organisation.

The idea of sustenance was given birth to in the forests of Europe by the tribes of the young nations as they settled. It is the thought that each farming family should be given as much farmland, as much arable land, as much share in the common pasture and the common forests as they need for their livelihood. This complex of production opportunities and means of production was the old German '*Hufe*' or holding, which, as we will yet see, experienced its perfect formation in Germanic villages, but it is also found in accordance with its basic idea in all settlements of the Celtic and Slavic peoples. The basic idea is that the type and extent of the individual economy is determined by the type and extent of the requirements that are assumed as given. The economy is subordinate to the principle of satisfaction of needs, as I have called it.

The idea of sustenance was then transferred from the rural ideological sphere to manufacturing production, to trade and transportation, and ruled over the spirits in these economic spheres as long as they were organised like craftwork. We will also be examining that in detail.

Someone objected to me, when I had earlier already developed similar ideas, that it is entirely wrong to assume for any period that men had limited themselves to satisfying only their livelihood, to having only their "sustenance", to fulfilling only the traditional needs appropriate to their nature. Rather it has been part "of the nature of men" in all times to earn as much as possible, to become as rich as possible. I still dispute this today just as resolutely as before, and maintain today more decidedly than then that the economic life indeed stood under the principle of satisfaction of needs in the pre-capitalist period, that farmers and craftsmen sought their sustenance and nothing further. The objections raised against these opinions of mine, so far as anyone has attempted to absolutely justify them, are primarily two, both of which are however invalid:

1. There would always have been *individual* craftsmen striving out from under the framework of "sustenance", widening their businesses, and chasing profits with their economic activities. That is correct. It proves however only that there are always exceptions to the rule, and these exceptions also confirm the rule here. The reader recalls that which I have said about the concept of the "predominance" of a certain spirit. At no time has only *one* spirit reigned.

2. The history of the European Middle Ages teaches us that a strong addiction to money has also prevailed to a wide extent among the trading peoples in all times. That I also admit. And I will in the further course of this portrayal have something to say about this growing addiction to money. But I maintain they were not capable of shaking the spirit of pre-capitalist economic life to its foundations. It is rather again direct evidence in favour of the spirit of the pre-capitalist economy, which turned away from all pursuit of profit, the spirit *that strove to gratify all delight through work, and all avarice outside the nexus of goods production, the transport of goods, and indeed the great share also of the trade in goods*. One runs into the mines, one digs after treasures, one does a lot of alchemy and all sorts of magic arts in order to obtain money, one lends money out against interest *because* one cannot acquire it in the framework of the everyday economy. Aristotle, who recognised most deeply the nature of the pre-capitalist economy, hence quite appropriately sees the acquisition of money beyond the natural needs as not being proper to economic activity. Wealth in cash serves just as little towards economic goals. The οικος [house] on the contrary provides

Chapter 4: The Pre-Capitalist Economic Disposition

for the necessary upkeep, whereas money is only suitable for extra-economic "immoral" use. All economy has measure and limits, the acquisition of money none.[25]

When we now ask which spirit corresponding to these guiding principles shapes the management of the farmers and craftsmen, then it is enough that we recall *who* the economic subjects were who performed themselves, or had a few assistants perform, *all* the labour which took place — the leading, organising, planning and execution. They are simple average men with strong instinctive lives, strongly developed emotional and sentimental qualities, and just as meagrely developed intellectual powers. Imperfections of thought, deficient mental energy, and deficient mental discipline occur with the men of that time not only in the countryside but also in the cities which through many centuries were still large organically grown villages.

It was the same men whose meagrely developed intellectualism we also observe in other areas of culture. Thus Keutgen once remarked very subtly of the style of law creation in the Middle Ages: "It was only a question of a shortage of mental energy, which is commonly recognised with our older law records, that proceeded from men not being used to intensive mental effort [...] I am reminded only of how surprisingly sketchy in the consideration of the different areas of legal life our older municipal laws proved themselves."[26]

An analogy to that in the sphere of the economy is offered by the meagrely developed sense for the calculation-like, for the exact measuring of magnitudes, for the correct handling of figures.

Corresponding to this shortage in calculative sense on the other hand is the purely qualitative relationship of the economic subject to the world of goods. One does not produce (to speak in today's terminology) just exchange value (which is definitely purely quantitative), but rather exclusively goods for consumption, thus qualitatively different things.

The work of the genuine farmer, just like that of the genuine craftsman, is a solitary work of creation — in quiet contemplation he abandons himself to his activity. He lives in his work like an artist lives in it, he would like most of all to not relinquish it to the market at all. Under the bitter tears of the farmer's wife the beloved mottled cow is fetched from the stall and led to the slaughtering block; the old man struggles over his pipe bowl that the trader wants to buy from him. But when it comes to the sale (and that must at least constitute the rule with ties of economic trade) then the produced good should be worthy of its creator. The farmer like the craftsman stands behind his product; he cares for it with the reverence of an artist. From this fact is explained, for example, the deep dislike of all crafts for forgery, or even surrogates, for cast work too.

However with pre-capitalist economic men the energy of the mind is now just as little developed as the energy of the spirit. It expresses itself in the slow tempo of economic activity. In particular and first of all they sought to keep it at bay as much as at all possible. When you can "celebrate", you do so. They have mentally something like the same relationship to economic activity as the child to school teaching — they certainly do not undergo it if they do not have to. There is no trace of a love for the economy or economic labour. We can deduce that from no less than the known fact that in all of the pre-capitalist period the number of feast days in the year was enormously large. Hartwig Peetz gives a nice overview of the numerous holidays which still took place in the Bavarian mining industry during the 16th century. Accordingly in various cases there were:

of 203 days	....	123 holidays
of 161 days	....	99 holidays
of 287 days	....	193 holidays
of 366 days	....	260 holidays
of 366 days	....	263 holidays[27]

And you did not hurry yourself with the labour itself. There exists no interest at all in that something was produced or accomplished in a very short time, or that very much was produced or accomplished in a defined period. The length of the period of production is characterised by two factors: by the demands that place the work on a good and solid footing, and by the natural needs of the working men themselves. The production of goods is an activity of living men who "find complete expression" in their work; they follow therefore the rules of these hot-blooded personalities just as the growth

Chapter 4: The Pre-Capitalist Economic Disposition

process of a tree or an animal's act of procreation receives direction, goal, and extent from the inner necessities of those living beings.

Just as with the tempo of labour, human nature with its demands is also the sole authority with the putting together of the individual acts of labour into a profession: *mensura omnium rerum homo* [the measure of all things is man] also applies here.

To this in-person style of economic management there is its corresponding *empiricism* or, as someone has recently called it, its *traditionalism*. Empirically, things are managed traditionally; that is, they are done just as it was handed down, just as one learnt, just as one is used to doing it. With the decision about a resolution or action, one does not first look forward to the aims, one does not ask exclusively about their appropriateness, but rather one looks backward to one's models and patterns and experiences.

We must recall that this traditional behaviour is by all means the behaviour of all natural men, and that it definitely predominated in all areas of culture during the early period of human existence. The grounds for this are to be sought in the nature of men themselves, and they all take root lastly in the strong tendency of the human soul towards inertia.

From our birth onwards, perhaps already before, we are pushed by our surroundings, which stand opposite us as a convenient authority, into a particular direction of abilities and wants — all communications, lessons, acts, feelings, and opinions of our parents and teachers are accepted by us offhand to start with. "The less developed a man is, the more he is subjected to this power of the model, of tradition, of authority, and of suggestion."[28]

In the further course of human life a second power is now joined to this power of tradition: the power of habit, which has men always preferring to do what they have already done, and what they consequently "can", and which also holds them thus on paths which they have already hewn.

Tönnies[29] defines habit very nicely: wishes or desires arisen from experience. Originally indifferent or unpleasant ideas become themselves pleasing through their associating and blending with originally pleasing ones until they finally enter into the circulation of life and into the blood as it were. Experience is practice, and practice here is the formative activity. Practice, at first hard, becomes easy through being repeated many times, makes uncertain and vague movements certain and definite, and develops special organs and stores of strength. But at the same time the active man is again and again caused to repeat that which has become easy to him — that is, to stay with the once-learnt, to be indifferent, even hostile to innovation, in short to become traditionalist.

A moment arrives, which Vierkandt rightly points to, when the individual as a member of a group in its endeavours, in order to prove himself as a worthy member, tends especially to the cultural goods marking this group. On the other hand, this has the effect that the individual does not in principle aim at the new, but rather seeks to bring the old to perfection.

Thus the original man is pushed into the paths of the existing culture through diverse forces as it were, and through them his whole mental culture is influenced in a particular direction:

> The aptitude for spontaneity, initiative, and independence, which is small anyway, is lessened still more in accordance with the general proposition that talents are only able to develop in proportion to their continued use, and wither away in the absence of such.[30]

All of these individual features of pre-capitalist economic life, as well as of pre-capitalist cultural life in general, find their inner unity in the basic idea of a life based on inertia, and the effect of living in close juxtaposition. The highest ideal of that time, as the wonderful system of St Thomas Aquinas investigated thoroughly to perfection, commemorated the individual soul reposing in itself and rising from the core of its existence to consummation as an organic component of living humanity. All the demands of life, and all forms of life were fitted to this ideal. Corresponding to it is the fixed organisation of men in specific professions and positions, which are all looked on as of the same value in there mutual relationships to the whole, and which provide the individual with the fixed forms within which he can develop his individual existence to perfection. Corresponding to it are the

Chapter 4: The Pre-Capitalist Economic Disposition

guiding ideas which underpin economic life: the principle of satisfaction of one's needs, and the principle of traditionalism, both of which are principles of inertia. The main feature of pre-capitalist existence is that of secure ease, as is characteristic of all organic life.

Section 2: The Age of Self-Sufficiency

Chapter 5: The State of the Material Culture of Europe during the Early Middle Ages

If Emperor Charlemagne had wanted in the manner of Goethe to collect the impressions made upon him during his journeys and his military campaigns in the land of the Sorbs, on his way to Rome or to Roncevall, if he had wanted to create a picture of the way of life of the people whom he had become acquainted with, in particular their material existence and its foundations, I believe it would have looked strikingly uniform. It is true that the people on the Elbe lived in round villages and ploughed their rectangular fields with the scratch plough, whilst at the mouth of the Rhine tribes settled in nucleated villages and ploughed their long strip fields, laid out in a colourful patchwork, with the mouldboard plough. It is also true that they lived on solitary farms on the Weser, in western France, in the valleys of the Alps and elsewhere, whilst on the other side of the Alps they lived close together in town-like villages built wall to wall. But that was only the surface — as it were, only the external form of their way of life. The inner essence of their culture did after all exhibit more commonalities than differences. At least quite specific essential features can be identified in the material conditions of existence of that period which give it a strong imprint, and contrast distinctly with earlier and later epochs, provided that we don't tighten the temporal bounds all too narrowly and take a few hundred years — for example, the eighth, ninth and tenth centuries — as the basis for our consideration.

The general character of material culture therefore was similar in all parts of Europe during that time. That means in particular that the culture was primitive and bore a purely rural imprint. No city, and no civic life existed in the wide empire of the Frankish emperor. This is beyond doubt for that area into which Roman culture had not advanced; however, it also holds true for the lands previously belonging to the Roman Empire. The Roman towns in the prosperous lands along the Rhine had almost disappeared as early as the fourth century. In 311 Eumenius depicted the countryside of Burgundy and Lorraine as uncultivated, dirty, silent, and dark, and even the military roads as having fallen into disrepair[31]. And this panegyrist, who was perhaps exaggerating, is joined by another contemporary writer who informs us that the region of the Rhine valley contained no towns[32]. Worms and Mainz were destroyed in 406[33], whilst the Roman towns on the eastern banks and at the mouth of the Rhine had already collapsed in the fourth century[34].

Architecturally we need not think of these towns as completely razed, although the buildings must have often been destroyed as well. The temple and amphitheatre in any case became popular quarries from which the abbots fetched the building material for their churches and monasteries[35]. However for some towns it can be shown that the Roman walls remained intact[36], and some building work in such places has remained up to our time. The important thing is that culturally, that is above all economically, the towns had as good as vanished. For during the Carolingian period the people living inside the walls, where these remained standing, were the same as those living outside them: arable farmers. "There is no reason to assume that there were different demographic conditions in the Bishops' seats and the fortified places than in the country [...] it was the same community in the mark as in the country"[37]. This also explains the origins of the terms *Megunzan Marca* [Mark of Mainz], *Marca Wormacia* [Mark of Worms], *Marca Bingiorum* [Mark of Bingen am Rhein]! For an Arab travelling through Germany in the 10th or 11th century, Mainz was still a town, part of which was inhabited, the remaining area cultivated[38].

In 845 the historical centre of Strasbourg — the old Argentoratus — was still partly uninhabited. It is reported that

Chapter 5: The State of the Material Culture of Europe during the Early Middle Ages

the monastery of St Stephen was founded there "right in the midst of rubble and ruins."[*]

The Roman forts along the Danube from *Batava castra* [Passau] to *Sirmium* [Sremska Mitrovica], including *Vindobona* [Vienna], had also fallen into ruins[39].

The conditions in the other Roman colonies, and even in Italy itself, would not have been much different[40]. Here centuries of atrophy had gradually stripped the towns of their character. The municipalities had long ceased to be indispensable centres of commercial life, of capital formation, or even marketplaces. Since the later Roman imperial times they had been "basically only bleeding cups in the interest of the state's administration"[41] across the empire. With the downfall of the Roman Empire this function also fell away, accelerating their disappearance as architectural phenomena. The long Gothic wars, and especially the invasion of the Lombards, finished them off. We read that the Lombard princes razed the towns they conquered — Padua, Cremona, Mantua, the towns from Luni in Tuscia to the borders of the Franks, and many others. King Rothari, just like King Agilulf,

ad solum usque destruxit
[always razed to the ground][42],

expugnavit et diruit
[assaulted and razed to the ground][43],

murus civitatebus supscriptis usque ad fundamento distruens, vicus has civitates nomenare praecepit
[demolishing the wall of the city, even undermining the foundations, he had these cities called villages][44].

Rothari "had them called villages", which in an economic sense they had already been for a long time — places of residence for an arable farming population. This applies however not only to the Germanic areas of conquest, where the agrarian character of the new culture certainly emerged most distinctly (I will speak further of this), but even the forts of

---

*   [Tr.: not referenced by Sombart.]

the Byzantine governor were inhabited by the landowners, who had since the seventh century become the primary authorities there, and in the forts which had been erected on the sandy islands of the Venetian coast it was surely no different[45].

The countryside itself was quite thinly settled. The few villages, hamlets and farms were separated by wide stretches of desolate land consisting of swamp and forest in which wolves lived in packs of hundreds[46]. Italy was a picture of devastation. The drainage and irrigation works were in such disrepair that drought and swamps dominated where fields had previously flourished (a land reliant on such an intensive agriculture as Italy suffers doubly under neglect, let alone despoliation):

> desolata ab hominibus praedia atque ab omni cultore destituta; in solitudine vacat terra, nullus hanc possessor inhabitat;* [...] hac in terra, in qua nos vivimus, finem suum mundus non iam nuntiat, sed ostendit

> [farms empty of men and moreover destitute of all inhabitants; the land is empty in the wilderness, no one dwells in possession of this [...] in this land in which we live, the world doesn't announce it's own end but reveals it] (!)[47].

Similarly Paulus Diaconus speaks of the "spatiosa ad habitandum loca, quae usque ad illud tempus deserta erant" [spacious places to dwell in which were deserted up to that time.][48] Swamps stretched across the deserted fields and malaria broke out in their train[49]. In other places the trees and shrubs struck out roots again forming those mighty forests reported in the sources of that time, in the countryside of Benevento, Regio Emilia, Modena, Pavia, Bologna, Parma, Ferrara, Verona (here lay the "immanis silva Nogariensis" [enormous forest of Nogara, south of Verona]) and other places[50], in most of which no trace of forestation remains today.

---

*   [Tr.: cf. "Benedicti Sancti Andreae monachi chronicon" in MGH SS (Vol. 3, § 10, 699).]

Chapter 5: The State of the Material Culture of Europe during the Early Middle Ages

Much land lay fallow in Spain when the Spanish Marches were annexed to the Frankish crown[51]. Enormous forests also existed in France[52] and Germany[53] — as is well established.

In short, it hardly needs to be stressed that the settlement was extremely thin.

Unfortunately we have no way of establishing the population density of that time even approximately. But the evidence cited above, considered alongside a whole series of existing statistical and topographical studies[54], leaves no doubt that the population figure was very low.

Chapter 6: The Village Economy

Literature

The following sketch of the village economy of the European Middle Ages is largely based on the picture drawn in the research now known as the "older" school. The men to whom we owe most of this work are von Maurer, Landau, Guérard, Meitzen, Inama-Sternegg, Lamprecht, Gierke, and Seebohm. Since I have essentially drawn my portrayal from the writings of these researchers, I have not meticulously cited all my documentary sources. Their views have been critiqued several times in recent decades, particularly — to name only the most important representatives of the "new" school — by Caro, Wittich, R. Hildebrand, S. Rietschel, J. Reichel, Thévenin, Fustel de Coulanges, Tamassia, and finally by Dopsch. What these critics have said cannot yet be fitted, even with the best of intentions, into a unified picture. Hence I have declined to enter into the argument in detail as it leaves undisturbed those key features of the old *village economy* that are of primary interest to us here. This will remain so, as far as I can see, even if the "new" school should be proved right in all questions. For whether the holdings were at one time commensurate or not, whether they and the marks were an autonomous or manorial/monastic formation, alters nothing of what seems to me to be the fundamentals of the economic organisation of the medieval village: economic autonomy, satisfaction of needs essentially through self-sufficiency, and private economy in various degrees partially integrated into a communal economic organisation.

Now how did *economic life* constitute itself in this environment? In what ways did the people of those centuries secure their livelihood?

We can clearly distinguish two different types of organisation in the economic structure of that time, which we will now consider one after the other: the farming economy in the village communities, and the socage [*Fronhofwirtschaft*]* economy in the manors and monasteries.

---

*   [Tr.: *socage* is a tenure of land held in return for specified and certain services.]

The peoples of Europe (to the west of the Russian border) had settled a considerable time before the epoch under consideration here. This is true not only of the descendants of the ancient civilisations. Since the first centuries A.D., the Teutons had also resided in fixed settlements and practised arable farming; since the Slavs' migration into areas vacated by the Germanic tribes, they had likewise made the transition to a settled way of life; and finally (around 600) the Celts in Ireland had gone from being nomads to arable farmers. The great migrations of peoples had ended several centuries earlier. The agrarian practice of Europe had begun to stabilise and to develop within the fixed forms which it had acquired with the final settlement of the cultivators of the land.

As I have already indicated, these settlement forms had been quite diverse and — considered quite superficially — European agrarian practice was highly varied, especially as different nationalities, and different peoples, had settled one after the other in the same area, often enough with lasting effects on the configuration of settlement.

As we know[55], only quite small stretches of Europe had been settled by single tribes: Low Germany between the Elbe, Weser, the Central Uplands, and the North Sea was the only purely Germanic land; and Ireland was the only purely Celtic land. Across all other regions various peoples passed, depositing their culture like geological strata.

The settlement of Europe was in essence a question of the various national settlement types of the Latins, Celts, Teutons, and Slavs. The territory of Europe was divided among them. Up to the epoch which we have in view, Germany was settled by Slavs as far as the Elbe, in the remainder it was partly German, partly Celtic. France and Great Britain displayed a mixture of Celtic and Germanic settlement forms, whilst south of the Alps — in as far as there were no longer remnants of the original settlement — the Roman division of the land into centuriae* existed alongside Germanic village settlement[56].

A detailed description of the four national settlement types is not within the scope of the task I have set myself here. I

---

* [Tr.: rectangular plots of about 133 acres/54 hectares.]

Chapter 6: The Village Economy

content myself rather with a short sketch of the main features of the various settlement forms, and refer the reader to the work of Meitzen for further detail.

Slavic settlement was based on household communities. The farmers lived in round villages, on whose periphery the individual farms were situated. The estates associated with these individual farms radiated out from the villages, and each farm was a single undivided unit.

Celtic settlement was based on the clan. Settlement was on isolated farms. Each farmer owned a piece of land with the farmhouse or hamlet at its centre.

Germanic settlement had a cooperative basis. The farming community lived in irregular nucleated villages. The arable land of each farming family lay strewn in various places in so-called *Gewanne* or open field furlongs. This is the origin of the term *Gewannendorf*.

Latin settlement occurred in town-like villages, in which stone houses stood wall to wall. The centuriated settlement of the Roman colonies was distinctively laid out in regular rectangles of around 200 jugera.*

For my purposes the important thing here is to demonstrate that, although the types of settlement were so extraordinarily diverse in their appearance, the agricultural economies at that time were, in their essence, very similar in the north and south, east and west. They in any case displayed a very large number of features in common which can be attributed partly to "the nature of the thing"[57].

As we know, if we want to grasp some social construct such as a specific economic system in its organic unity and particularity, we have to look for the *principal idea* which has led to its emergence and which it continues to contain.

The principal enduring idea is in turn nothing other than the leading interests of the dominant social circles internalised as a coherent system of thought.

What defined the basic underlying form of European tribal settlement could only be the striving of members of a nomadic tribe to secure their own existence in the face of in-

---

* [Tr.: a juger was a Roman measure of area typically about ⅔ of an acre or about 0.3 hectare.]

creasing land shortages and the increasing encroachment of rich livestock owners. It was the idea of "sustenance", as this striving was later named.

Let us consider the objective conditions of economic activity in that early period in which settlement took place:
1. land was indeed insufficient for a nomadic economy, but more than enough for extensive arable farming;
2. technology was quite primitive both for arable farming and livestock breeding, as well as for industry and transportation;
3. the population was negligibly small, and people were still bound fundamentally to their kinship groups.

Under these conditions it was inevitable that striving to realise "the idea of sustenance" would lead to an economic structure of the kind which we actually observe occurring among the European peoples in their infancy.

The work of settlement was accomplished in an area which had been the joint possession of a group of nomadic families related by blood and used communally up to then. The economic focus was transferred from livestock breeding to arable farming. To this end each family was allocated — permanently or temporarily — a piece of land for its exclusive use large enough to sustain its cultivators and to utilise their labour capacity, which was aided by a plough team. Ideally the field allotments were commensurate in size and quality. In many places the possession itself was called *pflug* [plough], *aratum*, plough-land or alternatively *possessio familiae*, *terra familia* or quite simply *familia*.

This basic idea — that each farming family receives a plot of land suitable to its needs and its labour capacity — recurred regularly with all peoples. It was implemented most meticulously in the German structure of land holding; but in fact, although "the (Celtic) hamlets were farm estates of unequal size," they were "thought to be of like productive potential sufficient for the sustenance of a farming family"[58], which is why, for example, in French documents we find the expression "mansus"* also used for holdings. And the same holds for the Dzedzin estates† of the Slavs.

---

* [Tr.: passive participle of the Latin for chew or eat.]
† [Tr.: дзедзін estates were passed down from grandfather to grandson.]

Chapter 6: The Village Economy

In all forms of settlement, often a considerable part of the total area of farmland remained as common property excluded from allocation to individual families: the commons. This part of the village farmland served then as the foundation for communal economic activity, mostly as pasture for livestock. This can probably be attributed to the conditions of that time only allowing for communal livestock farming. This rudimentary livestock farming in turn was matched by a similarly rudimentary state of arable farming. We may assume that the first field systems used after settlement were a quite rough alternation of crops and pasture or at best a quite rudimentary one-field system.

The sense of belonging among the members of a farming community had its roots in original kinship and in the emotional attachment arising from this, leading to the development of a "community" in Tönnies's[59] sense. This found economic expression in the self-sufficiency of the community as a whole and the interdependence of individual farming families. As trade with outsiders was as good as non-existent. To begin with there was no perceived need for paths between the separate villages. The community's entire existence was bounded in the narrow circle of village farmland. As each individual family wanted to be self-sufficient on its own clod of earth, the principle governing production was necessarily the satisfaction of its own basic needs.

The *principle of satisfaction of needs* governed the claims of individuals to the community's resources. Each member of the community was able to draw on them to the extent required to meet particular needs (at least originally), only without being permitted to sell anything.

The same principle defined the range of end-products: popular edible crops, spun yarns, etc.

The same principle provided the motivation for the help farmers offered each other unquestioningly in all earlier times.

The same principle also forced every family to engage not only in agricultural production but also in *the manufacturing of goods*. It goes without saying that this was mostly provided for within each farming economy. Cottage industries in the farming economy have continued up to our time, as will be discussed further later in this work. House building, the manufacture of clothing, tools, and jewellery, and the baking of bread have certainly always been branches of self-sufficient rural economy. In addition, whatever ironwork the farmer had need of — nails, horseshoes, etc. — he produced himself from iron ore that he found nearby and forged into iron in simple smelting furnaces known as bloomery furnaces[60]. Where greater investment was demanded, the community as such took responsibility for construction. This applied to the (water) mill[61], but also to the smithy[62]. Finally, from early times there must have been individual specialists in the villages who carried out the necessary technical tasks for others. The most important among these were the two original forms of rural trade, the smith and the cartwright[63]. However they were not originally independent craftsmen but rather occupied a type of community office, and would be supported by the community in return for their commitment to perform all required smith or cartwright tasks free of cost. Remnants of these occupations persist up to the present day, generally in the somewhat altered form of so-called estate craftsmen on large properties, but also here and there as village craftsmen.

It goes without saying that this restrictive lifestyle was reflected in a restrictive legal system. The community of blood-related villagers opened only slowly to newcomers, and only slowly did individual farming families win free power of disposition over their field allotments. And where, as in the German nucleated villages, the fields of the individual farmer lay "in a jumble" with the others, the community practised a strictly regulated type of economy, over whose form — that is, the compulsory rotation of crop and fallow — individual farmers had no power of influence.

There is no doubt now that the original form of farming economy sketched above was preserved in its basic features throughout the centuries right up to the Carolingian period. What had in essence changed was the following: *affinitas*, or kinship relations, must have made way increasingly for *propinquitas*, or neighbourly relations, as the villagers related by blood were interspersed over time with foreign-blooded elements. Above all, an already quite strong differentiation in the conditions of ownership had become more pronounced. The old owners of holdings had begun to disappear, and their place was being taken by larger farmers or share farmers. And the tenant farmers — the cottarius, cotsettle, cotters and crofters of the English sources — were already appearing next to the owners of holdings.

But the spirit of the old farming economy had certainly remained the same — as it would for another 1,000 years — and the structure of the economy had not undergone significant changes either. We know after all that the three field system, which would go on to influence the rural economy right through the Middle Ages and up to our time, did not begin to spread before the end of the eighth century[64].

However, perhaps the economic life of the Carolingian period would not have been so uniformly configured throughout Europe, as it was in practice, if it had been dominated exclusively by the rural economy. For notwithstanding the many traits we have been able to demonstrate that these economies had in common, they always adhered to the characteristics of the various national forms of settlement. Rather, what lent a high degree of uniformity to European economic life of that time was the second estate which has already been mentioned: the socage economy on the manors and monastic lands, which in fact displayed almost no differences from Sicily to Scotland, from the land of the Sorbs to the Spanish Marches. This will be addressed next.

Chapter 7: The Socage Economy

Literature

In recent years the *literature* over manors and monastic lands and their economic structure has swollen enormously in Germany and particularly also in foreign countries. A bibliography of the *English* literature over the English manors is found in Nathaniel J. Hone (1906, 312 ff.). This book is itself a vivid description of distinct aspects of manorial/monastic life in England which it happily supports with old pictorial illustrations. Compare also Paul Vinagradoff (1905; 1908). The mostly monographic literature of the *French*, *Italians* and *Germans* is found reflected in the newest and most extensive portrayal in the German language, the work of Alfons Dopsch (1912a). Of the later literature, see the good work of Heinrich Pauen (1913). (The manor first developed from the 12th century.)

Although I wrote this section about the socage economy eight years ago now, the newer research, particularly the work of Dopsch, has not caused me to make any changes. To my delight I can establish that I agree especially with the work of Dopsch on many points, to the extent that a historian and a political economist can have absolutely the same "views".

That applies especially to the first volume, in which the incorrect approaches of previous researchers (particularly Inama-Sternegg's) are put right on the basis of an interesting critique of the sources. I assess the worth of the *Capitulare de villis vel curtis imperii*[*] exactly the same as Dopsch — I am able to leave my remarks on it unaltered.

It is different with the second volume, in which Dopsch wishes to go ahead "constructively". Here our ways part. In particular because our basic conceptions of the task of history writing are sharply opposed. I readily admit that the source material produced by Dopsch is richer than in any earlier complete portrayal of that period (up to the chapter on industry, which is conspicuously poor). But this material is still not a history. In order to become a history, Dopsch would have to investigate it thoroughly in the light of a "theory". And the writer quite energetic-

---

[*] [Tr.: A manorial edict of Charlemagne, c. 812, issuing detailed instructions over the management of Crown lands. See MGH Capit. (Vol. 1, 82 ff.)]

ally rejects just that. His principal enthusiasm is directed at the fight against "theorists", in particular against the "political economists" — Inama-Sternegg and Bücher. And there begins his mistake. Had he fought the wrong and bad theories of those men — and the "theory" of Inama-Sternegg is actually sincerely bad, in particular because it is *not* a (unified) theory, that of Bücher is at least capable of improvement — then it would have been very deserving of thanks if at the same time Dopsch had also placed a theory of his own against theirs. Instead he wants to have absolutely nothing to do with "theory" — and nevertheless he wants "to construct"!?

I want to set forth here once and for all my point of view with regards to the argument between "theorists" and "historians".

Let us make the following clear. Only one of two things can obtain: either the historian contents himself with being our labourer, ie. placing the source materials at our disposal so that *we* do the "constructing", or instead they construct themselves. In the latter case they must however have a design, and this design is just that which they contemptuously call "theory". This theory has two distinct aspects:

1. a system of clear unambiguous *concepts*;
2. a *schema* according to which the individual facts are fitted together into a whole — in our case, this schema supplies the idea of a particular economic system.

Anyone who does not have at their disposal both these intellectual prerequisites cannot "construct". If he nonetheless undertakes an ordering of the facts, then a misfortune will occur. Unholy confusion will arise, which is worse than the mere provision of material which another clearer and more systematic hand may then fit together into a unity. As little, for example, as someone should write military history who speaks of a professional militia, just as little should someone be permitted to write economic history who confuses an estate dependent obliged to provide trade services with a wage worker (in the sense used by Bücher) (Dopsch 1912a, 2:154), or who speaks of "barter capitalism" (sic) (Dopsch 1912a, 2:52) and deals with price formation and credit processes under the rubric of "the money economy" (Dopsch 1912a, 2:§ 12).

Such truly grotesque ideas then emerge as the Carolingian bans on usury and interest being enacted in order to protect the public from a "monopolistic forcing up of prices by capitalism" (sic) (Dopsch 1912a, 2:275). Of course, without "capitalism" it does not tally now with any epoch. When money lenders charge high interest for consumer credit, the lords of the manor drive up the prices for the essential foodstuffs: "capitalism" is quickly there. It was already thus in the Carolingian period. The evidence for "capitalism" is now expected with the old Germans in the time of Tacitus. "There the expert is astonished and the layman is surprised" is all you can really say against such "theories" (they are certainly "theories", just antiquated and bad). No — so long as the historians are writing "economic history" with such completely insufficient knowledge and training, an understanding is not possible. One of the very small number of historians of note who proceeds differently is Georg von Below, whom we thus also argue with happily and easily any

Chapter 7: The Socage Economy

time. I cannot fail to quote here the golden words which von Below provides in his newest work about the requirements for the profitable writing of history, and which I underlined point for point. They possess their weight because they are spoken by one of our foremost historians, since we "systematisers" are continually shoved aside as eccentric "theorists" when we say similar things. Von Below's accomplishments pertain to the history of law, but they of course apply exactly the same to economic history:

> Quite certainly it is the privilege and duty of the historian to warn of arbitrary legal constructions, that is, constructions undertaken without consideration of the source material. The juristic view, furthermore, is obviously not the only permissible view of the past. If we only want to set forth the old legal conditions, then we are only in a position to do so with the tools of jurisprudence. "Legal history deals with juristic questions and must consequently also answer juristically" (von Amira). For legal history, "there remains material lying dead which it cannot gather dogmatically" (Brunner). — My claim lies merely in that a historical portrayal should take in all elements of our century's learning, and that hence the historian in his labours also has that neatness, precision, and clarity of ideas to point to which we simply desire today from all depictions. [...] I myself have several times already dispensed my opinion *that sharpness and clarity of concepts are themselves in no way enemies of genuine historical research*. (1914a, 1:107 ff.) [My emphasis.]

When will the "economic historians" finally make this conception of their prominent colleague their own? Thus, it is not at all the contrast between "political economists" and "historians" which divides myself and other political economists from most of the economic historians of the older school. There are also writers of history who approach the study of the past with our assumptions, and — I would not like it left unsaid — on the other hand there are enough "political economists" who in vagueness of concepts are a match for any representative of another science.

***

My opinion of the work of Dopsch does not stand apart — quite similar results come from the historic point of view in Paul Sander's answer (1914) to a "correction" which Dopsch bestowed (1914) upon Sander's review of his book (1913b).

I. The Distribution of the Manors and Monastic Lands

That the "manors/monastic lands", along with the specific economic structure developed on them — the "socage economy" which practised the greatest influence of all on the entire cultural development of the peoples, but in particular on the organisation of their economic life — was a phenomenon common to the European peoples during the Middle Ages, is disputed by no one today.

At issue is only (1) the meaning of the "manors/monastic lands" (in the sense of immunities with their own ("estate") law) for the development of constitutional law (whether municipal law originated from estate law or from common law; whether the rights of townsfolk passed through estate law, and gradually ascended from dependency; whether the guilds were based on estate law or on common law, were of dependent or of free origin, etc.). *These questions are of course completely eliminated from our view.* Likewise, (2) the other problem, which is especially brought into consideration by Gerhard Seeliger (1903), is what effects the manors/monastic lands exercised on the personal legal status of people living in their domains (Seeliger holds, so I believe, the correct point of view that "even within the manor/monastic land, the free element amongst the population did not disappear, it even abounded from time to time" (1903, 196)). Similarly, I leave open (3) what spatial extent the manors/monastic lands possessed — that is, in what quantitative relationship did the land taken up by the manors/monastic lands stand to the free farmland during the first half of the Middle Ages. Undoubtedly the assumption, commonly encountered in the past, that there were *only* manors and monastic lands in the 10th and 11th centuries was an exaggeration. This was maintained by Seebohm, Ashley, et al., whose extreme views have, however, since been corrected by the investigations of Vinogradoff, Earle, Round, Maitland, Pollock, et al. Likewise, Flach, et al. have verified the continued existence in France of free farming communities next to manors/monastic lands. Strangely, Ludo M. Hartmann now holds the old point of view again for Italy (1900, 2.1:40 ff.; 2.2:15 ff.).

I have already stated that the organisation of the manorial/monastic socage economy had a quite uniform cast in the various lands of Europe. As a matter of fact almost the same picture always appears to us — as will yet be shown in detail in the process of my depiction — whether we look at the constitution of the abbeys of Bobbio or Farfa, or the possessions of the Patriarch of Grado, or of the Bishop of Ravenna in Italy; or those of the abbeys of Saint Germain-des-Près or de la Sainte-Trinité de Tiron, or the abbeys of Clairvaux or Corbie or St Remi in France; or those of the monastery of St Gallen in Switzerland; or the abbeys of Prüm or Weißenburg, or the domains of Charlemagne or of the abbots of Reichenau or Fulda or Lorsch or Werden on the Ruhr, or the possessions of Count Siboto von Falkenstein in Germany; or those of the

Chapter 7: The Socage Economy

abbeys of Ramsey or Malmesbury or Worcester or Peterborough in England; or of the abbey of St Trudo near Liege.

All this is well-understood in so far as the organisation of estate production, distribution, and consumption as a complex of life circumstances is a question of the concrete configuration of the technical-economic process. Other aspects of the manors/monastic lands demonstrate great diversity in comparison:

1. the political position of the lords of the manor in the country;
2. the private legal status of the farmer or labourer, which demonstrated all possible nuances from pure slave relations in the old Roman sense in a few parts of Italy, to the complete personal freedom of the *socmanni* [sokemen, tenants] and *alodiarii* [freeholders];
3. the ownership rights of the farmers, which likewise provides a quite variegated picture where absolute ownership appears next to short-term leases, hereditary leases next to socage [*Livellarbesitz*], emphyteusis* next to share-cropping style circumstances, often varying regionally, and often next to one another on the same manor/monastic land.

The plan of this work does not just allow for, but virtually calls for leaving aside all these differences and considering the concrete phenomena alone.

I want to describe economic life. And here we should reemphasise that the legal forms, at this earlier time in which the formal law was not nearly so vital as tradition and custom, had only a peripheral meaning for the arrangement of life. The bustle at a manor/monastery or in a village of the 10th or 11th century was absolutely not defined by the more or less free legal status of the people doing business. It all ran together in a colourful mess from the *ingenui homines* [free-born men] to the *servi* [slaves, servants], and the system of rights and obligations established itself quite independently of this difference. If a family had its own clod of earth then it was basically quite incidental for their life whether they were *ingenua* or *serva*, whether *terrae adscripta* [tied to the land] or *potebat ire ubi voluerit* [free to go where they want]; whether they held the property as *beneficium* [benefice], as *precarium* [revocable lease], as *colonia partiaria* [share-cropping], as hereditary lease, or as something else. The only important things for them were:

1. how much they handed over from the harvest;
2. how many days in the year they had to labour on the lord's land; and
3. whether they actually remained on their clod of earth from generation to generation.

---

*   [Tr.: A real right, susceptible of assignment and of descent, charged on productive real estate, the right being coupled with the enjoyment of the property on condition of taking care of the estate and paying taxes, and sometimes a small rent. *Webster 1913*]

It is instinctive to ask where that surprisingly great similarity originated from. The answer usually given to this question consists in referring to the general source of the medieval form of the manors/monastic lands: the Roman estates, and the levelling influence which the Christian Church practised. I hold this explanation to be simply insufficient, believing rather that there is a third factor to be taken into consideration in the formation of the medieval manors and monastic estates. It is, for my part, the "nature of the thing", as the facts of the case can unfortunately be described, that phenomena like those observed here must appear under specific conditions with a certain necessity. It is in any case an established fact that we also encounter the manorial organisation in quite different cultures — in particular, however, those peoples who created the history of the Middle Ages had for a long time produced quite similar objects before there was any talk of a Roman influence. What Tacitus tells us of the Germans[65] already contains in its core the manorial form of economy of the Middle Ages.

One will surely come to the conclusion that the spread of the manorial/monastic organisation in Europe during the Middle Ages was materially helped by the similar structures which were already strongly developed in the tribes. That the form of the manorial system attained its full development during the last centuries of the Roman Empire is of course sufficiently known[66]; likewise the connection which exists between the Roman and medieval manor has often been the object of investigation.[67] But even the role which the Church played in the development and spread of this form of economy has been made clear.[68] We know that not only did the Church, and later the conquering tribes, appear in the territory of Roman culture simply in the place of the Roman possessors, but that, particularly in the other parts of Europe, direct influence by representatives of the Church was spreading the same type of economy.

The *Benedicti Regula monachorum** (Benedict 1895) was becoming of great importance — which I will have the opportunity to speak of later. The administrative principles of the mother-monasteries were applied from the start at the founding of monasteries. Thus it has certainly

---

*   [Tr.: Monastic rule of St Benedict.]

been traced how the abbey of Werden's organisation was patterned on the *Benedicti Regula monachorum* by its first two principals, Ludger and Hildigrim, who had both lived in Monte Cassino (Kötzschke 1901, 103 ff.). The influence then went on and on from one monastery to another, be it through transfer of the order, or be it through the exchange of individuals. Thus the directive of Wala for the abbey of Bobbio in northern Italy (Hartmann 1904b, 129 ff.) was obviously influenced by Adalhard's *Statuta antiqua abbatiae S. Petri Corbeiensis* (Guérard 1844, 2:306 ff.). That the abbots of the monasteries were frequently "transferred" between quite distant stations is well known. Thus in the middle of the ninth century, Prüm received one of their most significant abbots, Markward, from the abbey of Ferrières (see Hontheim (1750, 185 note) cited in Lamprecht (1885, I.1:79)). The famous building plan which was drawn up in 820 for the rebuilding of the abbey of St Gall was of Italian origin (see Julius von Schlosser (1889)).

II. The Main Features of the Socage Economy

When we now ask, however, what the essence of the new economic system which came into the world with the manors and monasteries consisted of, then we can say first of all, describing quite generally, that it was the economic structure which created a class of wealthy people for the purpose of having their demand for goods fulfilled by other workers in independent enterprises.

As this is not the place for the depiction of the genesis of this economic system, we can thus also refrain from describing the *origin* of this new class of leading economic subjects and their wealth which consisted essentially in their power of disposition over a vast estate and the labour force necessary to its cultivation.

It must suffice to name the most important causes leading to the origin of the medieval great estates.

The causes were:

1. the annexation of larger pieces of the Marches by the princes at their becoming settled (thus even before the migrations);

2. the occupation during the mass migrations by the kings, and the further allocation of this crown and state land, and of both the entire extensive great estates in the Roman territories, and the Marches in the old areas of settlement;

(The actual continuation of Roman ownership also occurred — thus the settlers on the Venetian sea in the sixth and seventh centuries, who came from the threatened cities on dry land, were the families of tribunes who brought with them their *servi* [slaves, servants] and *coloni* [tenant farmers], and transplanted their manorial relationships

directly in the lagoons. See the "Chronicon Venetum quod vulgo dicunt Altinate" in MGH SS (Vol. 14), and also Hartmann (1904a, 434 ff.).)
> 3. the quite widespread submission of fee simple owners to clerical and secular leaders;
> 4. the progressive winnowing out of land from the mark and the commons;
> 5. the acquisition of land through securities and purchase (made easier in common law at an early date);
> 6. unwarranted, specious, and violent occupancy which remained unchallenged and became ownership through customary title.

Rather, we will turn our attention immediately to the new economic subjects themselves: to their efforts, to their needs, to the spirit with which they were filled when they were constructing the economy on a new foundation, as well as to the economic organisation itself which they created.

Thus, first of all, who were the *"new" men* to whom a large part of the management of the economy had already passed, and a growing part was about to pass; and what distinguished them from the only economic subjects known till then, the farmers living in village communities?

The men who, after the fall of the Roman empire, raised themselves up out of the great mass of their comrades bore, as one knows, a character that was part spiritual, part temporal. They were the pious, solitary monks, and the dignitaries of the Church; they were the kings and princes, and those of the free who had a war-ready following at their disposal; and they were those vassals who were provided with land by their masters as remuneration for their services.

It was common to all these men that they possessed assets and also sufficient income to not have to be economically active themselves. They could live as a leisured class, and wanted to. The *artes sordidae* [vulgar crafts] were avoided. They filled their life with other things: with military service or priestly service; or they spent it in solitary leisure, or in the happy circle of intimates with merry feasts and meditative thought, at the hunt or with play. They led a seigneurial life. Only the monks, especially in the quite early Middle Ages, reached often for the spade or the axe in order to clear the forests and acquire a livelihood for themselves with the work of their own hands on the newly developed land. But they were then simply farmers and not "lords" like their successors in later centuries.

Chapter 7: The Socage Economy

We must imagine that the dimensions of the individual manorial/monastic possessions, and therefore the unearned income which the lord of the manor obtained, were quite varied. From the small knight who had command over the yield of two or three villages[69], there was every gradation of wealth right up to the temporal and spiritual magnates who had at their disposal the yield of entire lands[70]. Doubtlessly there were a great number of lords whose income went far beyond the customary needs of a family. Indeed, this category of large landowners probably constituted increasingly the normal type of lord. What did this prosperous lord of the manor start doing with the surplus of his revenues?

Primarily he was surely intent on widening the circle of persons who, far from the troubles of earning a living, took part in the consumption of his income jointly with him or in dependence on him. The temporal lords created their own court. In particular, however, they created a retinue of war-ready men, because a contingent ready to serve was demanded by the king, and because they considered it necessary for their own security or for the development of their own power. The spiritual lords, whose surroundings developed often enough into considerable farm holdings, were intent on increasing the servants of the church or the inmates of the monasteries, or taking care of the livelihoods of the poor through alms.

But along with this mere expansion of the horde of consumers went the endeavours to improve their lifestyle and to refine their needs. With the temporal lords, the impulse for pageantry arose, and gradually also the sense for a prosperous and luxurious lifestyle, which was soon cultivated by women in particular[71]. With the abbots and bishops, the striving began to not only furnish their church or their monastery richly and magnificently to the glory of God, but also to give their own life a worthier content through material and intellectual comforts. We probably have the clergy in particular to thank for the refinement of culinary delights.

The striving to meet the purposes of demand reliably and amply provided the leitmotif for the management of the entire economy of the manorial/monastic lords. As an edict of Charlemagne expressed it:

Et qui nostrum habet benificium, diligentissime praevideat, quantum potest Deo donante, ut nullus ex mancipiis ad illum pertinentes beneficium fame moriatur, et quod super est illius familiae necessitatem, *hoc* libere vendat iure praescripto.

[And those of us who have favour should provide most diligently, as far as it can be the gift of God, in order that none of the dependents by the favour extending to him die from hunger, and as far as it is above the necessity of a household, the *latter* may sell freely as prescribed by law.][72]

And if we also observe during the Middle Ages the unmistakable endeavour of the manorial/monastic lords to increase their fortunes, ie. their landed property, then this striving was always based on the wish to be able to meet the present purposes of demand even better, even more extensively, to have at their disposal as a consequence more people, to have more dependent farmers, to win influence over more souls. Or else to display more splendour, or to furnish the beloved church more richly. Saying it in the terminology I have coined: *the principle of satisfaction of needs remains the regulating principle in the manorial/monastic form of economy*[73].

The management of the economy itself was now defined quite peculiarly by a series of external circumstances.

The fact arose, first of all, that in many cases a greater number of people led a communal life and so wanted to form a *large unitary consumption economy*. That was so in the immediate environment serving the seats of the temporal and spiritual princes, but also in particular in the religious communities of monks (which had existed since the founding of the Christian Church), and later the theologians outside the orders as well. The transition of the clergy to the communal life had been carried out from the sixth century[74].

The occasional endeavours in this direction, which we observe during the sixth and seventh century, were then systematised and generalised in the eighth and ninth century by the spread of the rule of Chrodegang and Aachen. In 760 Chrodegang, Bishop of Metz, had drawn up a rule for the clergy of his cathedral church after the model of St Benedict and the

Chapter 7: The Socage Economy

Canons Regular of the Lateran, the basis of which framed the rules of communal life. The rule spread rapidly, and its trend was strengthened by state legislation — even the capitulars of Pepin and Charlemagne prescribe the communal life whose most avid exponent then became Louis the Pious. Then around the year 817 at the Synod of Aachen, he had the *Regula canonicorum* passed. It was modelled on that of Chrodegang, and demanded of the clergy universally that they live, eat, and sleep communally in an assigned house. The entire labour of the clergy as incorporated into a *vita communis* at a church was called a chapter, and these chapters — spreading in the ninth century over the entire Christian world — represented a new important type of large consumption economy whose meaning for the development of economic conditions during the Middle Ages, as it appears to me, must not be made light of.

Unfortunately the sources offer us no clues at all for establishing the number of these large centres of consumption. We can only infer their extent in individual cases from a few pieces of statistical information which we find strewn here and there in the sources. These admittedly refer almost exclusively (so far as they are reliable) to large monasteries, thus the largest centres of consumption (excepting probably the royal palaces or a few archdioceses). In the abbey of Corbie[75] around the year 822, the number of mouths to be fed daily amounted to no less than 300 and seldom more than 400. The considerate abbot estimated the number of loaves of bread to be baked daily (according to the principle: "omnis substantia nostra, quae per ministros nostros dispensanda est, semper magis volumus ut supercrescat, quam deficiat" [all our substance which is to be distributed by our servants is always of greater volume so as to overflow rather than run short])[76] at 450 (from 15 mills), and the number of pigs consumed annually at 600. The abbey consisted of several separately administered departments:
1. the hostel for pilgrims, etc;
2. the chapter where 150 *provendarii* (the novices and employees) received their upkeep; and
3. the actual abbey.

In the English abbey of Peterborough at the beginning of the 12th century, there were 100 individuals to be catered for: 40 *servientes* [subordinates], and 60 "monachi ad plenum victum monachorum" [monks according to the full way of life of monks][77].

Echternach had a complement of 40 brothers in the year 885; Prüm boasted (in the 10th century) a total complement of 186, St Maximin one of 20 heads; Fulda around the year 920 possessed 180 inmates; and Lambert tells of Hersfeld already having early on a total of 150 monks[78].

But what was of great consequence for the decision on how production was to be organised was the fact that labour capacity in manifestly sufficient quantity and suitability was not available for an economy in the manner of Roman imperial times, certainly not even to create a manorial/monastic economy in the grand style. Perhaps the leaders of the new economic units would also have lacked the necessary technical knowledge to head a complicated large enterprise.

Furthermore, it should be kept in mind that there was, of course, likewise no mention of a class of professional and independent industrial producers — ie. craftsmen — somehow worthy of the name. The idea of an economy aimed at a market-like satisfaction of demand was thus ruled out.

In the end, the management of the economy had to be advanced on quite separate tracks, in that the landed property of all the manors and monasteries was a so-called dispersed possession [*Streubesitz*] — that is, it did not exist in an enclosed area, but lay strewn over wide stretches, often distributed across many villages in which a few holdings belonged to the lord of the manor, with different lords having land in one and the same village. This only changed when the lords were having their own land cleared and settling entire villages.

Thus we come to the peculiar organisation that we call the socage economy, which now looks as follows.

III. The Organisation of Work in the Socage Economy

To a large degree, the entire demand for goods arising from within the manorial/monastic consumption economy

Chapter 7: The Socage Economy

was fulfilled by the output of its own capabilities in the course of self-sufficient production. That is, the socage economy was fundamentally an economy of self-sufficiency like the farming economy, but differing from it significantly in that the circle of people unified in *one* economy included countless foreign (and very foreign) elements — which is why I call this type of economy extended self-sufficiency.

1. Agriculture

We now look first of all at how the production of foodstuffs and organic raw materials — ie. *agricultural* production — played out. Here we encounter the surprising fact that this was carried out for the most part in the same farming enterprises which we know already from above. The lord of the manor's right of ownership to the soil did not in any way change the form of the enterprise in most cases. Economically it manifested itself in nothing else but the obligation of the farmer to pay out part of his production yield to the lord of the manor. The latter's burden thus consisted primarily only in collecting that tribute. He entrusted this task to specific persons — called stewards or *villici* — of whom he placed one (which was probably the rule) in each village, particularly in those villages in which farmers obliged to pay tribute to him resided. It was often probably one of the farmers themselves when it concerned small amounts which had to be collected; or it was even one of the smaller lords furnished with several holdings who had the function of collection to exercise. The places to which the farmers had to deliver their tribute were called *Fronhöfe* in Germany; *rectorium* [governors' places], *dominicalia* [masters' places], *dom. dominicata* [masters' houses], etc. in Italy[79]; the administrative area of a *villicus* was called *fiscus* (= *terre* [soil]) in France[80]. The tribute consisted of all the products of the field and the stalls — grain, cattle, poultry, honey, wax, wool, wine, etc. — and was allotted partly taking into account the specific nature of the individual farms.

Extraneous to the economic structure were:
1. the rights of farmer to the land — whether it was his own or whether it belonged to the property of the lord;
2. the legal title which obliged the farmers to pay tribute; and

3. the personal legal status of the farmers.

According to the new findings, it appears as if the "free contractual relationships", among them also share-cropping, already played a greater role in the Carolingian period than one tended to assume previously[81]. Share-cropping, incidentally, is with respect to its innermost being a "self-sufficient" form of exploitation[82].

The *villicus* now discharged the products delivered to him to the manor or one of the manor-houses, where they were consumed. On large manors/monastic estates, the delivery was divided across the entire year so that each place of collection had to procure the entire supply for the manorial/monastic upkeep for a specific series of days — the provision of services on such a day was called *servitium*, which is already mentioned in the *Capitulare de villis vel curtis imperii*. On the large manors/monastic estates there were even intermediate instances between the central office of the manor and the individual stewards — provostships, headed by provosts or praepositors. Thus, for example, the dominion of Count Siboto von Falkenstein (in Bavaria) was organised into four provostships to which a greater number of manor-houses or stewardships belonged[83].

But the farming economy was only one of the sources from which the agricultural production flowed into the consumption economy of the lords of the manor. Another part stemmed from the manorial economy which the lord of the manor had his officers manage on his own land. This part of the manorial/monastic estate cultivated under its own direction was called *salland*, also *terra dominica, indominicata*; in England, the lord's demesne, and in Anglo-Saxon *thanes*.

That all lords of the manor during the Early Middle Ages managed their own production economy has recently been doubted from knowledgeable sides: Werner Wittich (1901; 1906, 77). Wittich assumes that there were also "small lords of the manor [...] who lived in the main from the tribute of their dependents settled on a few farms." I find that to be improbable, and believe that the reasons which Heck cites against Wittich's opinion are conclusive. See Philipp Heck (1900), and further under the named article. Dopsch (1912a, 1:287) also agrees with him now. In addition, it appears to me, a number of reasons grounded "in the nature of the matter" also speak against Wittich's hypothesis, which Wittich himself, incidentally, only gets straight to a lesser extent.

Chapter 7: The Socage Economy

A special investigation should be made some day over the extent of the demesne. The depictions to-date only ever deal with this important question in passing. Even what Inama-Sternegg (1889, 25 f.) teaches in that respect is unsatisfactory. I believe that many mistakes are made in the previous assessments. Primarily because it is difficult to distinguish in the sources sharply between the demesne and, on the one hand, the ownership of holdings by a simple *villicus* tilling by association, and, on the other hand, the administration area of a steward or provost. Thus, for example, Lamprecht (1885, I.2:756 ff.) as well as Inama-Sternegg (1879, 2:161) seem to me to go astray when, for the size of the demesne, Lamprecht for his district in the Carolingian and Ottonic periods, and Inama-Sternegg also for the 10th to 12th centuries, only estimate one holding, and also when Lamprecht calculates for St Maximin at the close of the 12th century an average of only 26.5 morgens*, for Rupertsberg about 30 morgens, and for Trier 50 morgens. Against that speaks the quite wide-ranging details on magnitude in the endowment documents of the 8th, 9th, and 10th centuries, especially in Lamprecht's area of investigation (cf., for example, the Mittelrheinisches Urkundenbuch (Beyer 1860, 1:No. 52, 58; No. 59, 66 f.; No. 63, 71 f.)), but above all on a number of grounds of pure logic. It seems to me that here there is a case of confusion between estate lands and stewardships (the *mansi indominicati* [stewards' houses] were in most cases only collection points). Conversely, one would, I believe, attain too high a figure if one attempted to identify from Guérard (1844) the average *terra indominicata* [land under stewardship] allotted to a *fiscus* as the size of the estate lands (one would then have to assume an extent of the individual estate area of 250 ha., or around 1,000 morgens†). There were potentially several estate farms in the area of governance of a *fiscus*. Safe calculations underlie the following details on magnitude. The demesne of the main farm Friemersheim belonging to the abbey of Werden amounted towards the end of the 9th century to 607½ morgens (inclusive of 12½ so-called *Bedemorgen*) (Kötzschke 1901, 13). There were 119½ contributing holdings, which Kötzschke in my opinion rightly estimates at some 30 morgens, so that an obligation-bound farming land of 3,645 morgens follows — the demesne relates to the holdings in the ratio 1 : 6. (The "studies" of Kötzschke belong among the best that have been written over manorial/monastic organisation in recent times — the author has *perception*.) I myself work out, for example, for the abbey of Prüm an average of 92.4 Prussian morgens (Beyer 1860, 1:No. 135, 142 ff.); for the abbey Lorsch 165 morgens, for Fulda 122 morgens; for the abbey of Weißenburg (13th century) 362 morgens (Zeuss 1842, 273 ff.); for the English abbey of Ramsey, it amounts to 300 acres and above (Hart and Lyons 1884, 1:405, 490). Seebohm (1883, 137) assumes, for the average manor of the 10th century, the magnitude of the home farm itself at 9 *hidae*, that of the farmland at 21 *hidae* (1 *hida* = 6 *virgata*; 1 *virgatum*

---

* [Tr.: a morgen is a measure of area equal to approximately 0.4 ha.]
† [Tr.: This should be closer to 610 morgens at 1 morgen = 0.4 ha.]

= 24 acres). Cf. also Philipp Heck (1906, 354). Heck himself assumes for the smallest category of "lords of the manor" a demesne of "considerably more than 30 morgens" up to 240 morgens. In my opinion rightly. And now Dopsch (1912a, 1:233 ff.) arrives at quite similar results. Dopsch represents the view that a master's estate [*Dominikalgut*] and self-sufficiency (Dopsch means manorial economy [*Gutswirtschaft*]) do "not fully" correspond. The reasons with which he defends this view do not always seem convincing to me. In particular, I am not persuaded by the weight of his main argument, which is that the sources also speak of *mansi indominicati* and of demesne holdings. Why should they not? The land of the lords, which we — in this I agree fully with Dopsch — must think of in most cases as scattered holdings, was fashioned though in all village settlements from a structure of land holdings made up of scattered individual strips, which obviously also lay intermixed with the land of the small farmers. How should they be described other than with the expression "demesne holdings"? It seems to me that the entirely erroneous idea still haunts people's heads that a manorial economy in the Middle Ages means an estate on a consolidated area or also only by necessity with its own personnel and equipment. It will be shown that that in no way constitutes the rule.

The demesne was worked from the manor [*Fronhof*] outwards under the management of the steward. The extent of this self-sufficiency seems to have fluctuated. The rule was surely the extent of a large farm, that is, the operation of three or four holdings.

The *workforce* with which the manorial economy was pursued consisted in part of single servants and married day labourers, who (but surely not regularly?) lived themselves on the estate and either worked a small property to obtain their livelihood, or received a fixed concession from the lord — not much different than the contractually bound worker of our large estates up to the present. At the same time, the private legal relationships of these estate workers were variously configured. In Italy they seem to have been kept not very different from the slaves of antiquity.

These estate workers are the *servi* and *ancillae* (or *praebendarii, servi cottidiani*) of the *German* sources (Beyer 1860, 1:No. 41, 46; No. 84, 90), "ut servi vel ancille coniugati et in mansis manentes" [namely married servants or maids and residents of the manor] (Das königliche Staatsarchiv in Stuttgart 1849, 1:92); who received no *beneficium, unde vivit* [benefice from which to live], "qui hoc non habuerit, de dominica accipiat provendam" [those who will not have this may receive produce from the master] ("Capitulare de villis vel curtis imperii" in MGH Capit. (Vol. 1, 82 ff., § 50)); in the *Italian* sources, they are called "*massarii*" = *servi mass.*, see the inquisitions of 862 and 883 for the abbey of Bobbio (Hartmann 1904b, 50 ff.); *cotsetles* in England, which already according to the *Rectitudines singularum personarum* either received a fixed concession or the morgen in the fields, a share of the earth's bounty [*Erdrusch*] or of other profits, or one or several head of cattle in the lord's herds as consideration for their output. (The Saxon text of the *Rectitudines* originates from the 10th century; the Latin translation from the 11th century, published in Thorpe (1840, 1:433–41), and in a special edition from Heinrich Leo (1842) with an interesting, but not faultless introduction.) Whether the '*mancipia*' [slaves] which, for example, the "Fragmenta ampliora Polyptychi Sithiensis" mentions (Guérard 1844, 2:397), belong to this category of dependent servants, as von Maurer (1862, 1:355) assumes, is doubtful to me. *Mancipia* often stand in contrast to *familia — cum familiis et mancipiis* [with household and slaves]. (Lamey 1768, 1:§ LIV, 100; § LXIV, 113).

In the inventory of the Villa Asnapium, 17 wooden houses are found on the farm with just as many rooms and ample furniture. They were surely the residences of the estates day labourers? ("Breviarii rerum fiscalium Caroli Magni" excerpts and translations in Guérard (1844, 2:§ 18, 301); and in Meitzen (1895, 1:603 ff.).)

If, from the sources[84], the picture of a strongly differentiated workforce in the 9th and 10th centuries already confronts us, one will not have to mistake this offhand for an image of reality. One has all too often committed the mistake of reconstructing from the *Capitulare de villis vel curtis imperii* the conditions of the manorial economy in the Carolingian period. But one must not forget that in such assignations, or in enumerations of all possible cases like the law books contain, even super-real ideal images crop up.

The second group of workers which the lord or the steward had at his disposal were the farmers from the village who were *obligated to provide compulsory labour*. This arrangement that, economically apart from independent farmers (though legally of an absolutely different quality), used a part of its workforce for the cultivation of the manorial/monastic lands (be it in the form of ploughing services if they had use of their own team, be it in the form of providing hands if not[85], or be it in the form of "head services"[86]) was handed down to the Middle Ages from the Roman world. In any case, it spread during the Middle Ages over all Europe, and indeed in an almost completely consistent shape and guise. When the monk Cesarius in the 13th century was glossing the Prüm book of benefices, he could make the remark in the chapter of farmer obligations, "Quomodo mansionarii debent iugera dominica, arare, seminare, colligere, et in orreum deducere suo tempore, et sepem facere, ac triturare, fere omnibus patet" [In that manner holders of benefices are responsible for the master's jugera, ploughing, sowing, harvesting, and taking it into the barn at the right time, and building fences, likewise threshing, nearly extending to everything][87]. An in-depth description of the obligated services recurring everywhere is thus surely superfluous more than ever today[88].

The obligations of the farmers bound the farming economy with the manorial economy in the most intimate way. We thus only properly visualise the economic structure of the Middle Ages when we consider the manorial and monastic economies to be ranged within the commoners' village economy of which they formed an integral component. Where compulsory rotation of crop and fallow existed, the lord's land was subject to it just as much as the farmers' land; the lord's herds were driven together with the farmers' herds onto the common meadows; and often the lord of the *curtis dominicalis* (the manor) was obliged to keep the breeding stock which could be used by the entire village's herds[89], etc. Even where the lord of the manor called new settlements into life on his own land, in most cases a sort of village community was created into which the manorial economy voluntarily entered.

2. Manufacturing Production

Most depictions abandon us right here with the description of what we usually call *manufacturing activity*, hence I consider it my task to report somewhat in-depth about the organisation of the manufacturing work within the scope of the socage economy. The sources present an overabundance of material for it, which has, strange to say, only been processed to a very small extent.

As a rule, when it concerns the manufacturing activity on the manors/monastic estates of the Early Middle Ages, one makes do with enumerating the familiar lists of those professions of which Charlemagne in the *Capitulare de villis vel curtis imperii* declared that they shall be represented at all his manors. But with that, one then makes the thing somewhat too simple. For one would doubtlessly obtain a quite false picture of the manufacturing organisation of those centuries if one tried to transfer the "craftsmen" listed plainly in the *Capitulare de villis vel curtis imperii* to all manors/monastic estates[90]. That is inadmissible for more than one reason. First of all, it must in fact be considered that that list depicts a programme which will in no way have arrived at a strict implementation. Not even on the imperial domains, as is made known to us by the inventories which we possess from the time of Charlemagne himself[91]. And then the organisation of the imperial estates must not be equated offhand with the smaller or middling manorial estates. Furthermore, one will have to distinguish between religious and secular establishments. Decisive for the organisation of manufacturing activity was the fact that the female hands were missing in the former (mostly, not always!) Finally, one must consider quite specifically the large monasteries in which a portion of the monks were themselves active in manufacturing.

In the following, I want to attempt to consider the stated differences where feasible and to project an image of the normal — or, better, what recurs everywhere roughly the same — conditions of manufacturing production on the manors/monastic estates.

Thus it follows now in particular that the demand for manufactured products was also (exactly like for the agricultural products) satisfied by an interoperation of the particular (manorial) economy with the farmers in the village[92]. We best create ourselves a clear picture of the ingenious system of manufacturing production which thereby arose when we aspire to bring to mind the production process compartmentally in its individual steps.

a) The Manufacture of Foodstuffs

The farmers delivered the *bread* to some extent in a condition ready to use[93], after they had previously had the grain ground in the village mills and baked the flour in their own baking ovens (?). But that was in any case not the rule on the continent. On the contrary, it seems absolutely to have been the normal case that the farmers just delivered the grain or (the miller) the flour[94], but the lord had the bread produced in his own bakehouses. A 'bahchus' (and from here even in anticipation might be mentioned: 'bruhus') seems to have belonged to the buildings of every half-respectable manor[95]. Most lords of the manor probably possessed their own mills early on as well[96], if they chose not to assign to the village mills the milling and crushing of a certain quantity of grain as an obligation[97]. Farmers were employed[98] in the mills or the countryside belonging to them; in the bakehouses (and brewhouses), either day labourers were steadily employed for concession, or position holders performed it in rotation[99].

That the demand for *beer* was fulfilled in a similar way to the demand for bread is already evident from the preceding depiction. Only that malt (*bratsa*) was just delivered instead of grain or flour. The *wine*[100] and, in the southern lands, the *oil*[101] were obtained quite similarly. *Salt* had to either be purchased (as I will yet show in a suitable place), or likewise be produced by the lord of the manor in his own saltworks[102]; or it was raised as payments in kind from farmers' saltworks, or as customs duties[103].

b) The Manufacture of Clothing

To begin with, "textile industries" and tailoring will be considered — those trades which clothe us with woven material. We find them organised on the manors/monastic estates in quite various ways, without being able to give a reason why in individual cases one or the other form has been chosen. In particular, either the entire production process, from the first handling of the raw flax or wool to the finished objects of use (pieces of clothing or adornment), is undertaken on the farm — a single farming family might have performed all the separate tasks one after the other — or the production might lie with various farming families. In any case, we find the finished object of use immediately passed by the obligated farmer to the lord of the manor.

The *'femoralia'* [trousers], which the monks of the abbey of Prüm wore, were (still in the 13th century) sewn by the wives of the farmers after the material (linen) had also been produced by them, as Cesarius shares with us:

> mansi nostri tenentur annuatim camsiles facere. Camsil enim est lineus pannus, de puro lino compositus, habens in longitudine VIII vlnas et in latitudine duas, que femoralia tenentur femine hominum nostrorum suere, et camerario conuentus, ita consuta [...] debent representare.

Chapter 7: The Socage Economy

> [our holdings are obliged annually to produce shirts. Shirts are of course composed of linen cloth, pure linen, having a length of eight cubits and width of two, and the women of our men are obliged to sew the trousers, and must manifest them to the chamberlain of the abbey] (Beyer 1860, 1:145 note 5)

The wives of the farmers in the area of the abbey of Fulda had the following to deliver to the monastery: *mappae* (altar cloths?), *mensales, mensalia* (table cloths?), *lodices* (other cloths), *tunicae, pellicia,* etc. From the urbaria of the abbey (9th–11th century) in Schannat (1729, 1:26 ff.). We find 'Tunicae ad opus ecclesiae' (thus mass garments?) also amidst the tribute in the "Reginonis Abbatis Prümiensis Chronicon" (Beyer 1860, 1:143 ff., § 135).

Sometimes too, industrious nuns performed the work which otherwise fell to the farmer's wives. Thus the monastic women of St Andrea had a garment of goat's wool to deliver, originally to the King's court in Florence, later to the Bishop. The nuns of Or San Michele had a 'laboratorium' in which they (with their maids) wove. The abbot of Nonantula, as overlord of the monastery, placed the duty on them of manufacturing annually from wool, which he would send through his envoys, five pieces of heavy material. See the references in Davidsohn (1896b, 1:91). If you view the convent of nuns itself as a 'manor', then the form of the satisfaction of demand belongs to the type to be discussed next.

It might be recalled that 'vestes' [garments] were delivered by the bonded farmers of the Germans already in the time of Tacitus (1903, 12, § 25), as the entire peculiar combination of farming and manorial economy with the production of manufactured wares is probably of specifically German origin.

Or else (and it was probably the rule, as the frequent mention of this case in the sources implies): the farmers delivered only the finished *fabric* (of linen or wool)[104]. Be it that they used for this production raw materials which they had themselves produced and processed[105], or be it that they received the raw materials from the lord[106]. The latter materials would have then been delivered as payments in kind by other farming concerns, or produced on the estate.

On the manor, of course, in all the cases in which the farmers delivered the finished items for use, no manufacturing activity was in general performed. When the farmers, however, delivered only the fabric, it must on the lord's estate surely still have been frequently improved, and always processed further into clothing, etc. We may assume that the *tailoring work* was performed in the rule by the women of the house together with their maids. Where a female workforce was absent, as in the chapters and monasteries, tailors were kept especially for the production of clothing. No monastery was surely without its own tailor's workshop[107].

Where was the cloth *fulled*? Surely in the manorial fulling mills which were found in any case on the larger estates[108].

Where was it *dyed*? Also at the manor? It is indicated by the fact that the lord of the manor provided himself with dyes, be it through purchase at the markets, like the monks of St Germain, be it through obliging the farmers to deliver it[109].

But the 'tintor' is also expressly named in the sources as a manufacturing worker in the manor (abbey!)[110].

Now finally, however, a third case was possible: that the overall production of clothing (from the first handling of the raw materials onward, or at least the spinning and weaving) lay with the manorial concern. That surely occurred often in particular on the larger secular manors, for which reason here the number of busy maids in the house proper became so great that special spaces had to be assigned for them. They are the ominous *gynaecia**.

> *Gynaecia* are seldom found mentioned in the sources; understandably, since they were commonly missing from the religious estates. But we also encounter them there; if indeed not on the main estates, then on the larger stewardships. Thus on that manor Leer belonging to the abbey Werden an der Ruhr, there were, during the 11th and 12th century, regularly seven women occupied with the wool work, for whose upkeep specific amounts were set aside (Kötzschke 1901, 80). The depictions are based almost always only on the places referring to it in the *Capitulare de villis vel curtis imperii*; likewise for the best depictions which come from the pen of von Maurer (1862, 1:241 ff.). But there were also manifestly *gynaecia* on other large secular estates, like there are still *gynaecia* on every feudal estate today. See, for example, the documents over the donation of Count Eberhard to the monastery Mosbach in the year 728, in which it states: "de mancipio nostro scopulicolas† quas in genicio nostro habuimus plus minus numero quadraginta" [we had plus or minus forty among our slaves or the girls which are in our gynaecium] (Feudrix de Bréquigny and La Porte du Theil 1791, 1.1:458). The gynaceum of the Stephenswert estate contained 24 women who produced clothes and leggings. Cf. the *genecéo puellarum* on the estate of

---

* [Tr.: gynaeceum = the part of a large house exclusively allocated to women]

† [Tr.: *scopulicolas* = *seu puellas* (Levison 1902, 386)]

Count Egbert in Flanders in the 10th century, in MGH SS (Vol. 15, II, 583, line 2).

But in religious establishments (monasteries!), we also meet manufacturing workers who practised the initial processes of weaving, for example, processing the wool[111].

Were, in this case, the *spindles* delivered by the farmers? I am doubtful whether those named in the Prümer Urbar (Beyer 1860, 1:170, § 135) as 'linum fusa XXX' and 'de lino fusa XXX' signify linen spindles, or a spindle full of linen thread.

The second great area of clothing manufacture, which concerns the clothing of feet with tanned leather, dissolved into the two main branches of *tanning* and *shoemaking*. Both production processes seem to have taken place within the framework of the landed estate. At least, no single case has become known to me in which farmers would have been obligated with the delivery of leather or shoe-work. In contrast, we often find tanning facilities mentioned on the larger manors/monastic estates[112], and just as commonly a shoemaking workshop or at least a pair of shoemakers.

A quite illustrative picture of the various manufacturing facilities on a large manor, amongst which are found a fulling mill, a flour mill, and a tannery, is given by the already mentioned description which we find in the works of the venerable Bernard (1839, 2.2:2529–2534). Since they are little known – I have only hit upon them in a solitary embodiment, in H. D'Arbois de Jubainville (1858), where excerpts are reproduced in French translation – I want to place the main points in the original text here. The description comes from the pen of a contemporary and was written down in the 13th century; it is kept very 'poetic' and seeks to avoid the dryness of the enumeration of individual buildings by grouping them all about the stream which (an arm of the Aube) flows through the monasteries courtyard:

> Fluvius [...] primum in *molendinum* impetum facit [then] eum [...] ad se *fullones* invitant, qui sunt molendino confines [...] graves illos sive pistillos sive malleos dicere mavis vel certe pedes ligneos [...] alternatim elevans atque deponens gravi labore fullones absolvit [...] tot ergo volubiles rotas rotatu rapido circumducens, sic spumans exit ut ipse quasi moli et mollior fieri videatur [...] excipitur dehinc a *domo coriaria* ubi conficiendis his quae ad fratrum calceamenta sunt necessaria operosam exhibet sedulitatem. Deinde minuatim se et per membra multa distribuens singulas officinas officioso discursu perscrutatur, ubique diligenter inquirens, quid quo ipsius ministerio opus

habeat: *coquendis, cribrandis, vertendis, terendis, rigandis, lavandis, ruscendis* [...]

[The river [...] makes a charge into the *mill* [then] the *fullers* entice it to themselves, who are neighbours of the mill [...] you prefer to play either that heavy pestle or mallet or even certainly the wooden treadles [...] the fullers by turns lifting and putting down complete the heavy labour [...] now many whirling wheels spinning in rapid rotation, thus foaming it goes out like meal and looks smooth [...] it is followed after that by the *tanning house* where the making of the shoes for the brothers are essential [and] they exhibit painstaking dedication. Next it sinks and distributing the individual workshops through many arms, the discourse of work is studied, seeking diligently everywhere what the work of the ministry itself needs: *to be cooked, to be sifted, to be transformed, to be threshed, to be watered, to be washed, to be cut down* (?)]

c) The Building Trade

When the lord of the manor wanted to build, a quantity of raw materials and workers were at his command on his estate to begin with. He found the wood in his forest, the sand and the stones in his sand and stone quarries, the straw in his barns. "Unskilled" workers were found sufficiently among the servants, or the day labourers of whom one or another was, however, a learned mason or (which was more important for the earlier period) skilled carpenter. We meet in the sources the *cementarius* [mason] as well as (still more commonly) the *carpentarius* amongst the workers resident at the manor. The latter was originally not only a carpenter, but also a cartwright[113]. The missing workers, when they were not kept amongst the lord's own staff, as well as the missing material were again provided by the farmers.

We find the following obligations and tribute mentioned:
1. construction of a lime kiln, and the fetching of the necessary material for it — the staves, rods, wood, and limestone;

How a lime kiln was erected has been told to us in a very descriptive way again by Cesarius, to whom we owe surely the most information about the organisation of the socage economy. The place deserves again to be placed here in full (Beyer 1860, 1:151 note 1, § 135):

sciendum est, quod dominus abbas quolibet anno si vult ad edificationem ecclesie, calcis furnum potest facere, et ad hoc omnes curie citra Kile tenantur eum iuvare. Curia enim de Denesbure et Hermansbanyde, adducent palos et perticas ad tunicam furni sepiendam. Omnes alie curie de Oslihc adducent

Chapter 7: The Socage Economy

truncos laudabiles et magnos, quilibet mansus adducet IIII truncos, quorum quilibet habebit XVI pedes in longitudine, et duos et dimidium in grossitudine (latitudine). Curie autem alie, sicut Rumersheym, Sarensdorpht, et Valmersheym, adducent lapides calcis, quilibet mansus carratas XVI.

[he is skilled, whom the master abbot, for the edification of the church, is willing to let live through the year wherever he pleases, he is able to make a lime kiln, and for this all the manors on this side of Kile are obligated to be helpful. Namely the manors of Denesbure and Hermansbanyde bring palings and rods to the apron for enclosing the oven. All the other manors of Oslihc bring praiseworthy and large trunks, one holding brings four trunks, of which one was 16 feet in length and two and a half in thickness (breadth). The other manors also, like Rumersheym, Sarensdorpht, and Valmersheym, bring slaked lime, one holding 16 cartloads.]

(N.B. what mass!) In addition, this lime kiln obligation was mentioned: "ad furnum calcem de petris carradas V" [five cartloads of rocks for the lime kiln] (Lamey 1768, 3:212).

2. building or renovation of the house[114];
3. building the walls, maintenance of fences, etc.[115];
4. roofing workers[116];
5. delivery of building wood[117];
6. delivery of bricks[118];
7. delivery of wooden battens and shingles for the wooden roof[119];
8. delivery of millstones[120].

Of course, only the common wood and framed constructions, probably very primitive during the Early Middle Ages, were produced in this way. When it concerns the erection of a palace or church from stone, one must have aimed to shackle to oneself one of the few artisans and craftsmen who had obtained that art of building in stone. These artisans dwelt during the building period at the manors of the great clients who solicited them from one to the other. Thus the King of the Picts, Nechtan, requested from the Abbot Ceolfrid (710):

architectos [...], qui juxta morem Romanorum ecclesiam de lapide in gente ipsius facerent

[architects [...] who made according to the custom of the Romans the church of stone in their nation][121].

Thus the Bishop of Salzburg sent master masons (*magistros murarios*), smiths, and carpenters for the building of churches[122]. Or one set the official administrative organisation in motion, and had the rare materials necessary for building delivered through the agency of officialdom. Thus Pope Hadrian entreated King Charles in the year 768 that he would like the 2,000 lb of tin which he needed for the roofing of St Peter's, having every 100 lb raised through the Counts[123].

These professional construction workers will have been in part obligated — but, to perhaps a greater extent, they were surely freely wandering artisans. As such, we will encounter them once more later.

What the individual lord of the manor desired from his vassals as an obligated service was imposed by the king on the clients as a public levy: the production or maintenance of royal palaces, churches, and other public buildings, bridges, and roads. The residents were obligated first of all. In a report of Emperor Louis II (in MGH Capit., Vol. II, §212–213, 84–88) (from 850), the disrepair of the named buildings was lamented, each person was required with compulsion to work, and they were not to be released from the place and their position until they had carried out their share. We see here the remnants of the Roman *munera publica*.

d) The Manufacture of Equipment

The manufacture of equipment encompasses every trade not contained in the three groups named above, thus in particular the trade for the manufacture of tools and weapons (smiths and cartwrights), as well as that for household equipment (other than those already named, we have coopers and potters).

These trades were now surely practised as a rule by farmers who were obligated to the lordship to provide service or payment in kind. Only a proportionally small part of the production fell within the ambit of the estate itself — the sources report without break the deliveries of finished commodities by the farmers.

Italy: The estate Luliatica of the abbey of Bobbio delivered five ploughshares (Hartmann 1904b, 64). In a document from the year 907, a bondman of the monastery Nonontola was obligated with the annual delivery of 15 sickles (Baudi di Vesme, Desimoni, and Poggi 1873, 730,

Chapter 7: The Socage Economy

No. CCCCXXII); in the inventory of St Julia's in Brescia, we encounter the deliveries of sickles, iron forks, axes, and ploughshares (Baudi di Vesme, Desimoni, and Poggi 1873, 706 ff., CCCCXIX).

Germany: At the beginning of the 12th century, the abbey of Corvey collected in payments in kind: "[...] quinquaginta frustra (!) de cultellis, de rasoriis, de forcipibus" [fifty items of knives, razors, and tongs] (Kindlinger 1787, 2:116, No. XVIII § 11). — The farms each delivered (in the 13th century) a "securis et achia" (hatchet and axe) to the abbey of Weißenburg; in addition, individual holdings were encumbered with "opus fabricandi vomeres ad tria aratra et malleos cementariorum" [work building blades to the three ploughs and the masons' hammers]; "idem opus persolvit hugo de fabricca in colle" [Hugo of Fabricca offers the same work on the hill](that is the smith from the mountain!); "item oggerus persolvit vomerem" [likewise Oggerus paid off a ploughshare] (Zeuss 1842, 273 ff.). Other holdings in the same area delivered the wine barrels, "in autumno vascula [...] ad vinum" [in autumnal barrels of wine] (Zeuss 1842, 278). — A little cottage which possessed *quartalem I* [one quart] delivered a pan to the abbey of Prüm (Beyer 1860, 1:169).

The laity on the manors/monastic estates of North-West Germany delivered household equipment (Wittich 1901, 297 ff.).

France: 22 *mansi ingenuiles* [holdings of freemen] delivered 30 mattocks in the region of the abbey of St Germain (Guérard 1844, 1:731); a *villicus* delivered eight axes, the inhabitant of half a holding six lances; the same, six javelins; the craftsman Hadon paid the contribution for half a holding with his products (Guérard 1844, 2:149). — A farmer of the abbey of St Bertin delivered 12 bottles (?) and 100 small bowls (?), see the "Fragmenta ampliora Polyptychi Sithiensis" (Guérard 1844, 2:400, § 13). *Autlemarus servus* [the vassal Autlemarus] and his wife belonging to the yeomanry [*Colonenstand*] in Nova Villa rendered annually, amongst other things, six pieces of wooden cutlery, three wooden rims, and seven wooden torches (Guérard 1844, 2:143, § 64).

Or we learn of general obligations for the provision of specific work — for all smith, all cartwright work, etc. — which was allotted to a corresponding property of the lord.

England: "Faber (de Wermouth tenet) XII acras pro ferramentis carucae" [The smith (resident at Wermouth) [receives] 12 acres for iron ploughs]; "Faber (de Queryndonshire tenet) XII acras pro ferramento carrucae fabricando" [The smith (resident at Queryndonshire) [receives] 12 acres for iron ploughs needing to be made]; "Faber I bovat pro suo servicio" [The smith [receives] one cow for his services]. From the Boldon Book, cited in Seebohm (1883, 70). The *carpentarius* stands in the same relationship in the English sources. Cf. also Hale (1865, 56a), cited in Ashley (1896, 1:62 note 111). The cartwright in South Brent has a plough and a harrow to make from wood which he delivers himself, in addition to helping the farmers with the manufacture of their wagons. The smith has ploughs to manufacture conjointly with the cartwright, and also specific horses of the lord (a riding horse and a

117

draught horse, an "aver" [work horse]) to provide with horseshoes. When a horse dies, he receives from it the skin for his bellows. He finally has the reapers' sickles to sharpen in the hay harvest, for which he receives an acre of meadow in Chalgrove. In Winterborne, he has the vats in which the cheese is prepared to repair and provide with iron bands. For that he receives a lamb and a fleece, and a cheese which is made before John the Baptist's feast day, in addition to a bowl full of butter for greasing his bellows (Hone 1906, 73).

Germany: The holding, "quod pertinet ad fabrile opus" pays only 12 d., the rest pay a contribution of 24 d. per head. See the donations of the Bishop Megingod in support of the church of St Martin in Münster (10th century) (Beyer 1860, 1:339, No. 287).

Here also, surely, belongs the *Reginhardus* **tornator** *apud* [the turner Reginhardus at] Veldern (at Utendorf, Pinzgau), which with other small properties of Count Chunrad von Sulzau (around 1150/60) is relinquished to the foundation of Berchtesgaden, and taken in fee against tribute obligations (Muffat 1856, 320, § CXLI); cf. F. V. Zillner (1890, 2.1:154).

France: "mansos unde carpentas exeunt" [the holdings from where the carts leave] (from 682) (Guérard 1840, 28, No. 9); "preter illam terram unde opera carpentaria exeunt" [besides that land from where the works of the cartwrights leave] (from 721) (Guérard 1840, 47, No. 27).

In addition, there will of course also have been work of the same sort carried out by those resident on the estate, the "estate craftsmen", as we would say. We quite commonly encounter the *estate smith* and the *estate cartwright* on the manors[124].

But *cooperage* appears to have also been performed on the manor. The obligation of some farmers for the delivery of barrel staves and barrel hoops is indicative of it. I think that was the case for those manors/monastic estates which practised a lot of viticulture. Here, of course, the production of "vasa magna ad vindemiam valde necessaria que appellantur 'buden'" [large vessels extremely necessary for grape gathering which are called 'barrels'][125] also belongs to the office of cooper.

Should the named trade have been carried out without disruption, be it by the farmers, be it by the estate people, then the necessary raw materials and semi-finished products must have been present. Their procurement created no difficulties when it involved wood, or clay, or lime. It was quite another thing though where *iron* was processed. Here a difficult problem existed: how could you obtain this material. The problem was solved in three different ways.

Either the lord of the manor bought the necessary iron at the markets. This case does not concern us here.

Or he set up himself a small ironworks on the land of his estate[126].

Or (the sources speak of it the most frequently) he laid the delivery of iron as an obligation on his farmers. He could naturally only do that when bog iron ore was found in the region, which the people processed into iron in the most primitive way[127].

The iron was then given further on to the farmers obligated with the blacksmith's work, when it did not find its use in the workshops of the estate smith[128]. The same applies to the charcoal required for the forging process, which the holdings of charcoal burners probably had to deliver.

***

The manufacturing life on the manors/monastic lands was fashioned in this way perhaps in the great majority of cases. It displays, I believe, only immaterial changes during the long time from the forming of the manors/monastic estates to deep into the Middle Ages — up to the 12th and 13th centuries. There can be no talk, as far as I can see, of a "dispersal" of any of the existing large economic operations on the landed estates. These operations did not exist anywhere in reality, except perhaps on a few royal domains and a quite small number of large monasteries. As a rule, it always involved a small landed estate which also contained manufacturing activity, and which in its essential content, I would like to say, has barely changed up to our own times. Next to it, the germ of an independent manufacturing life developed, under the influence of the manor/monastic estates, within the villages which solidified (as we will see) gradually into towns.

Here for the time being, it should still be pointed out that the primitive manufacturing activity, as it was practised as a rule on the manors/monastic estates, had worked its way up in a few places already during the Early Middle Ages to high *artisanal achievements*.

One knows that the monasteries were its seat, and that artistic and industrious monks were actually the preservers and admirers of the old Roman manufacturing techniques. They were the architects of that time; they fostered glass painting, enamelling, the art of engraving, the art of jewellery, organ making, the art of weaving[129], gold beating, and gold spinning[130]. And vying with the monks were artistic princes of the Church like Abbot Bernward, later Bishop of Hildesheim.

> He himself was well versed in much art: "nec aliquid artis erat quod non attentarit" [nor was he unskilled in any other that he attempted] and erected workshops in his palace where numerous workers worked on the metals — he himself visited every day: "inde officinas ubi diversi usus metalla fiebant, circumiens, singulorum opera librabat" [hence the factory, where metals of diverse use were being worked, circulating, swung in the work of individuals], from Tangmarus, *Vita Sancti Bernwardi* cited in Labarte (1864, 1:146).

But the arts and crafts may have flourished also on some secular manors. Thus, we are told of the artistic daughter of Wichmann, Count of the district [*Gau*] Hamalant, that she outdid almost all the women of the land in the making of sumptuous clothes. She had at her disposal a bevy of skilled assistants whom she had gathered to herself[131]. Thus, we hear of silk weavers which the Norman Kings of Sicily maintained (12th century)[132].

3. Transportation

Just like the activities of agriculture and manufacturing, the *transportation* by water and by land was organised and brought to fruition by the lords of the manor on the basis of socage obligations. Yes — it applies to transportation that it often had to be induced first of all by the lords of the manor as a special economic function. Goods production was known, even if in an essentially simpler form, even before the manorial/monastic organisation of the economy. Transportation over distance, in contrast, has no place in the framework of the original farming economy where all goods were consumed in the place where they were produced. The necessity for transportation between locales only emerges with the manors/monastic estates whose properties were often lying far apart, and emerging with it by the way, as Meitzen has rightly stressed, was the necessity of developing a network of routes between the individual places. The required transportation capacity was now, as stated, placed on the individual farmers as an obligation, thus giving them the impulse to train as professional mariners or carters, who we then, in the next economic epoch, encounter in the framework of the exchange economy's organisation. Here only a few sources from which the transport obligation is evident will be noted.

In the *French* urbaria are found as obligations, the duty:
1. to provide wagons to transport grain and wine, etc.;
2. to provide horses for journeys; and
3. to provide boats, where transport must take place by water.

See the documents in Guérard (1844, 1:§§ 411 ff.).

Germany: The formulae read "Navigium facit" [He provides a ship] (Beyer 1860, 1:155), "scaram facit cum nave" [he is obliged to provide a ship] (Beyer 1860, 1:182), "scaram facere debent in navi, usque ad Covelenze, vel quantum in IIII dies possunt ambulare" [they are obligated to serve on ships right up to Coblenz, or are obliged to be able to travel for four days] (Beyer 1860, 1:196), and similar in the "Reginonis Abbatis Prümiensis Chronicon". Of the 120 manors which the monastery possessed, 30 rendered the 'scara', which is itself the transport obligation, according to the compilation by Imbart de la Tour (1896, 77 ff.). In the Lorsch Codex, it states:

> item serviles hubae XXX, quarum unaquaeque [...] servit, sicut ei praecipitur, cum navi & aliis instrumentis
> [likewise Huba has 30 servants, each of which [...] serves, just as they are ordered with ships and other equipment] (Lamey 1768, 3:210, No. MMMDCLXXI); or,
> octava [mansa servilis] non solvit [...], sed navigat
> [the eighth [servant of the holding] does not pay but sails] (Lamey 1768, 3:192, No. MMMDCLX).

In the Weißenburg Codex:

> unusquisque [...] cum navi per ordinem pergere [debet] aut ad frankenvort aut ad lidrichesheim
> [each had to continue with the ship in order either to Frankfurt or to Littersheim] (Zeuss 1842, 277);
> et illi XIII qui vinum solvunt cum suis carr, infra magonciam et wormaciam, et frankenvort pergere debent
> [and those 13 who deliver wine, must continue with their carts further to Mainz and Worms, and Frankfurt] (Zeuss 1842, 278).

Likewise, there is a ferry service obligation (Lacomblet 1840, 1:95, No. 153).

Italy: On the possessions of the abbey of Bobbio, the *massarii* [mace-bearers (?)] of Sorlasco:

> colligere olivas in Garda et trahere oleum et ferrum cum anona domnica de Sorlasco usque Placentia
> [to collect olives in Garda and carry oil and iron with the year's produce of the lord from Sorlasco and Piacenza] (Hartmann 1904b, 86, and table 55 in Anhang V).

That is, from one property of the abbey to another.
For *England*:

> et idem faciet averagium apud Bristoll' et apud Wellias per totum annum et apud Pridie et post hokeday apud Bruggewauter cum affro suo ducente bladum domini, caseum et lanam et cetera omnia quae sibi serviens praecipere voluerint [...] Et debet facere averagium apud Axebrugge aut ad *navem* quotiens dominus voluerit [...]
>
> [and he will do the same on average at Bristol and Wells all year round and the the day before and after Hoke Day at Bridgewater with cart horses taking his master's corn, cheese, and wool, and all the other things they will have wanted them to take in service [...] And that he must do on average to Axbridge or by *ship* as many times as the lord will want] Smirke (1849, 203), cited in Seebohm (1883, 57).

Section 3: The Period of Transition

Chapter 8: The Renaissance of the Exchange Economy

Sources and Literature

For I. below: Karl Andree (1867, 1:23 ff.), surely was the first to depict in context the "silent trade". Fundamental for most later work is Otto Schrader's *Linguistisch-historische Forschungen zur Handelsgeschichte und Warenkunde* (1886). The drawing in of observations of primitive cultures fetched from travellers delivers surprising information. It is discriminatingly assembled in the works of Josef Kulischer, of which one published in German (1899, 305 ff.) collects the results of the earlier studies. Valuable too is the article by Sartorius von Waltershausen on the origin of trade in Polynesia (1896, 1 ff.). The same applies to the thorough processing of the subject by Maffeo Pantaleoni (1899).

For II. below: we possess sufficient source material to establish the fact of a continuous goods trade during the Early Middle Ages. See Schulte (1900), and *the works named in it on p. 69 in note 1*. To those, I add important works appearing in recent years: Varges (1903); Bugge (1906); Schaube (1906); and Dopsch (1912a, 2:180 ff.).

Unfortunately, the necessary schooling in political economy is missing from most of the writers of the history of trade, so that one rarely learns more than the facts of the trade laws from the books. But even in establishing these, it does not work without precise knowledge of the economic world. Thus we encounter all too commonly a misinterpretation of symptoms useful in themselves for the history of trade, like, for example, *customs duties*. Certainly a customs duty is an important clue to ascertaining the movement of goods, the sort of goods moved, etc. Only one must not always deduce from the fact of a customs duty the presence of a goods trade, let alone a professional *commodity trade*. The sources instruct us that duties were also raised on those goods which (without being somehow exchanged or even traded) were relocated within the manorial/monastic estate's own economy. Thus the Capitular of 805 in MGH LL (Vol 1, § 13, 134) expressly mentions that *no* duty shall be raised when:

> sine negotiandi causa substantium suam de una domo sua ad aliam ducunt, aut ad palatiam, aut in exercitum

> [without the purpose of trade, they move their own resources from one house to another, or to the palace, or into the army].

Thus these goods will also have had duty paid in other cases. — On the other hand, customs duties can be direct proof for the spread of a non-exchange-based organisation of the economy, in particular when they are, by virtue of the duties raised, *duties on natural produce*. These play a large role during the entire Early Middle Ages. See for the 8th century, Pardessus (1843, 2:501) (duties for Corbie); for the 9th century, the "Leges portorii" in MGH LL (Vol. 3, 480); further still perhaps, the "Charta Bosonis de Monasterio Dervensi" in Guérard (1844, 2:347) (salt duties); Hartmann (1904b, 77) (duties on salt, pepper, cinnamon, glue, etc. on the Po); for the 10th century, the duties on natural produce which were raised on the alpine passes, in Schulte (1900, 1:68); but also even for the 11th century, the time of Henry IV, see the duties roll for Coblenz, in which bronze kettles, metal basins, wine, cheese, goatskins, buckskins, fish, wax, swords had duties raised on them (Beyer 1860, 1:1:467 ff., No. 409).

I. The Exchange Economy and its Origin in Particular

An exchange-based (or trade-based) organisation of the economy is present everywhere that the demand for goods of several economic concerns is satisfied in a way that the one concern takes produce from another concern voluntarily in exchange for an equivalent, and consumes it. It includes practically all forms of economy that are not fundamentally self-sufficient. It can just as well be based on barter as on the exchange by means of money, that is, it can be barter or "money" economy; it can base itself on craftwork or capitalist foundations.

There was a time when one thought economics and exchange were synonymous — humanity took its development from the progress of exchange; and trade was a component of all human economy, just like production or consumption. Exchange was not (as we call it today) a category of economic history, but a category of elementary economics. We now know that roughly the opposite is correct — that humanity probably developed trade only relatively late, and that it in any case needed a prolonged process of development before men were accustomed to "exchange" something with others, that is, in particular, before they lost the suspicion that others (strangers!) might want to betray them with the reciprocal offering. The saying "anyone who has a desire to exchange, has a desire to betray" is even today used amongst our children[133]. But we also know the forms in which this education in trade was accomplished, if we are permitted to infer from the customs of today, or from primitive peoples living a short while ago, the foundations of primitive times. Then the peculiar form would have been the so-called silent *trade*, as Herodotus already described it to us as an experience which the Carthaginians shared with him, and as it has been correspondingly observed in our own time in the trade with numerous primitive peoples; be it that these exchanged goods amongst each other, or be it that they wanted to enter into trade with Europeans.

II. The Development of the Exchange Economy in the European Middle Ages

There can be no talk of an "origin of the exchange economy", in the original sense, with the European peoples during their historical period. Only of individual tribes in the extreme north-east of Europe (on the Siberian border) do we learn that they operated the form of "silent trade" in their traffic with western traders[134]. Apart from that, we may assume with certainty that the three largest tribes, Celts, Slavs, and Germans, once we have tidings of them, had already accustomed themselves to the exchange of goods, even by means of money[135], whereas understandably in the region of the Roman culture, a highly developed, centuries-old trade existed when the northern tribes took up residence in it[136].

Certainly during the Roman Imperial Era, a strong retrogression into conditions of self-sufficiency took place[137], which probably continued for centuries after the downfall of the Roman Empire until it reached its extreme point between the 8th and 10th centuries[138]. Notwithstanding that more or less strong trading connections existed at all periods during the Middle Ages, the self-sufficient economy was supplemented in every century by the sale and purchase of goods and services[139]. If I thus describe the period perhaps up to the end of the first millennium A.D. as the Age of Self-Sufficiency, then that is to be understood in the sense which I ascribed to this linguistic usage in the introduction. It shall mean that economic management was aimed fundamentally at the principle of self-sufficiency, that this depicted the economy's governing idea, its spirit — that is, that the striving of the economic actors was directed primarily at the satisfaction of demand in their own economic concern, and that exchange with other economic concern formed a secondary phenomenon which was not able to alter the overall character of economic management.

I chose the title of this chapter correspondingly. One cannot talk here of the origin of the exchange economy in the European Middle Ages, but only ever of its reinvigoration, its *development*. The seeds are present. Now we will follow how they developed into the vigorous plants which already stood before us in the 13th and 14th centuries.

Belonging to those forces which were constantly pushing for an expansion of trade are:

1. *the professional traders* who beset Europe from the Orient, be it to obtain in trade, particularly in the north and east of Europe, valuable products of the countryside like amber, sumptuous pelts, etc.[140], or be it to dispose of the products of the Orient (jewellery, clothes, etc. — of which will yet be spoken). We must just never forget when we follow the path of European life in the Middle Ages, that Byzantium and Baghdad lay in the East — two centres of the highest culture, from which emanated impacts on the 'barbaric' (or foundering in 'barbarity') Europe which surely had some common features with those which today return again from our cultural centres to the East, or to the regions of the primitive African or Asian peoples.

2. Besides that, continuing to work in silence were the forces which awoke the tendencies in each of the still so vulgarly ordered, *farm-like self-sufficient economies* for their transformation into forms of life proper to the exchange economy. The possibility always existed of producing surpluses which in bulk, when the original communal idea had lost its force[141], represented convenient objects for sale[142]. To these farm surpluses produced in the case of especially favourable harvests were now added, surely more and more frequently, steady surpluses, or already better production yields of defined specialties whose creation a farm had to perpetually deal with:

Chapter 8: The Renaissance of the Exchange Economy

honey, wax, wine, fowls (see Hænsa-Thorir!). Here belong also the farmers washed up on inhospitable coasts, who plunged into fishing and sometimes into the fish trade[143] or the salt trade[144], and thereby supported the development of the exchange economy considerably.

In both directions — both that of the occasional production of surpluses and that concerning specialty products — the tendency towards the dispersal or at least the limitation of self-sufficiency was now strengthened by a process which was carried out with the greatest persistence right into the centuries in which our interest is especially directed. That process was the differentiation of the size of farming estates. To the extent that, on the one hand, large farming estates formed with more than one holding, the probability of a purely quantitative surplus of foodstuffs grew; but to the extent that, on the other hand, the property shrunk to half and quarter holdings, or even to the possession of plots, the necessity was established of either producing valuable agricultural specialities (perhaps practising beekeeping) or obtaining a living in another way (perhaps by manufacturing activity). (That the local trade nurtured in specific places was frequently the nucleus of an exchange-based form of economic organisation is even verified in more than one example in the sources.) With that, of course, the increase in population is also an important fact to draw into consideration.

3. Now it can be subject to no doubt at all though that the formation of the exchange-based form of economic organisation during the Middle Ages would not have been carried out anywhere near as quickly as was actually the case, if a third factor had not also influenced the development in the same direction — the *manors/monastic estates*.

The economic concerns of the lords of the manor must have from the beginning of their existence had a strong leaning towards other economic concerns. At first *as a seller*. It was extremely probable that the size of the consumption economy, particularly with the rich estate owners, did not grow in the same ratio as the extension of the property and with it the tribute in natural produce of the farmers. The more so with the latter if it involved specialty products. Here was the wine which streamed so abundantly that a spacious monastery cellar was itself incapable anymore of holding it; here was the salt which the manorial saltworks delivered in heaps. Where would one have started with it? "Such a quantity of wine and salt stream into the monastery from its farms that it became directly necessary to sell the surpluses," the admirable Cesarius teaches us again[145]. We see wine-making districts hence turning onto the path of the exchange economy especially early, the more so as in them the growers also produced surplus production in their operations especially early on. Already in the 9th century, the Latin poet praises the residents of Strasbourg for not having to drink all the home-grown wine themselves, since it would otherwise look bad in the town — the Alsatian wine soon formed a primary component of the Cologne trade. Here was the wool which particularly on the English manors represented an important product in all periods[146], and which had of course to be sold if they did not want to carry out the spinning and weaving at scale themselves. Here was the cheese. Where would Count Siboto von Falkenstein have begun, and even if he liked to gather about himself such a stately band of martial servants, with 9,694 cheeses a year[147], and the Tridentine canons with 14,000 cheeses[148], if they did not sell them? Here was, however, also the grain which one could not bake all into bread oneself[149], even if hundreds of men were to be sated.

Thus it is not astonishing to us when we frequently hear of instructions which would regulate the sale of surpluses in the socage economy.

> The Statuta antiqua of the abbey of Corbie (in 822) specifies that the tithe of the distantly lying villas should not be brought to the monastery (but sold?); from the nearer lying estates, however, a second tithe shall be purchased. The tithe of the gardens shall, where it is carried out profitably, be sold: "quae rationabiliter venundari possunt, venundentur aut contra denarios aut contra annona (!), et ad portarium deferatur" [what can reasonably be sold is sold either for money or else wheat (!), and is carried to the porter]. Of the cattle tithe, only the pigs shall be consumed; in contrast, the foals, the calves, and the kids shall be sold or bartered straightaway or after two years: "portarius eos non servando, sed [...] venundando vel commutando, ad utilitatem hospitalis, prout ratio docuerit et melius potuerit, eos convertere studeat" [the porter does not need to serve them, but [...] needs to sell or barter in exchange for the use of a guest room, as a method he pointed and was able to do better, he busies himself exchanging] (Guérard 1844, 2:325–326, § IX; 332, §§ XII–XIII). Well known are the value-taxes for grain etc. which

Chapter 8: The Renaissance of the Exchange Economy

were already enacted by Charlemagne. See, for example, the resolution of the Frankfurt Synod from the year 794 in Fagniez (1898, 1:48-49, No.88).

The Edictum Rothari (from 643) in MGH LL (Vol. 4, § 234, 58) gives the authority to the "Servus massarius" [Servant mace-bearer (?)]: "de peculio suo, id est bove vacca cavallo simul et de minuto peculio" [from his own private property, his ox, cow, and horse together, and from his small things], to sell: "quod pro utilitatem casae ipsius est, quatinus casa proficiat, et non depereat" [where this is for the benefit of the cottages, so that they benefit the cottage and they are not lost]. "Et sunt in Chama manentes XIII, qui reddent de sirico libras X, et de ipsis in Papia ducitur, et ibi venundabitur ad solidos L" [And there are 13 resident in Chama, who will render 10 pounds of silk, and it is taken to Papia, and is sold there for 50 gold coins] (Baudi di Vesme, Desimoni, and Poggi 1873, 726, No. 419). In the *Capitulare de villis vel curtis imperii* in MGH Capit. (Vol. 1, 82 ff.) it states:

in § 33, 86: "quicquid reliquum fuerit exinde de omni collaboratu usque ad verbum nostrum salvetur, quaetenus secundum iusssionem nostram aut venundetur aut servetur" [anything that will be left over afterwards from all who always work together is made safe on our word, or sold or kept after at our command];

in § 39, 86: "quando non servierint ipsos [ie. ova et pulli] venundare faciant" [when they are not kept, they (ie. eggs and chickens) are put on sale];

in § 65, 89: "Ut pisces de wiwariis nostris venundentur et alii mittantur in locum, ita ut pisces semper habeat; tamen quando nos in villas non venimus, tunc fiant venundati et ipsos ad nostrum profectum iudices nostri conlucrare faciant" [The fish from our fishponds are sold and others put in their place, so that it always has fish; but when we do not come to the estates, then he sells them and for our success makes a joint profit].

The thought always recurs, first to provide for the demand, what *remains*, sell!

But still more frequently, we see the lords of the manor enter the markets as *buyers*. Understandably, since they had money income not only from the proceeds of their own produce, but also from early on in the form of *monetary tribute* which they received from the farmers.

The farmers' monetary tribute was probably never completely absent at any time during the Middle Ages. One encounters it in the sources in every century. That it occurred in the 5th century in Gaul[150], because it could *still* be raised in that time and in that region, is not so momentous as that it confronts us everywhere in the 8th and 9th centuries.

For the sake of example, in the 8th century: in *Italy*: the abbey of Farfa among others (Kowalewsky 1901, 1:388, 411); in *England*: see

Kowalewsky (1901, 1:538); in *Germany* (Trier): see the "Fragmentum Chartae Leodoini" (Guérard 1844, 2:341).

In the 9th century: in *Italy* (Bobbio): see Hartmann (1904b, 58); in *France*: for the abbey of St Germain-des-Près, see Guérard (1844, 1:892 ff.); for the abbey of St Remi de Reims, see Guérard (1853, XLVII); for the abbey of St Bertin, see Guérard (1840, 199–200, § XXV; 201–202, § XXVII; 203–204 XXIX; and passim); in *Germany*: for the abbey of Prüm, see Lamprecht (1885, 2:143); and for the abbey of Weißenburg, see Zeuss (1842, 273).

The sums which flowed from the farmers' contributions in cash into the exchequers of the lords of the manor were not even always tiny. According to the sources just named, I have made the following compilation. The incomes amounted in present-day (1916) currency with the abbeys to:

Bobbio	... ca. 100 marks
Prüm	... ca. 6,000 marks
St Germain	... ca. 10,000 marks
St Remi	... ca. 12,600 marks

The fact of this proportionately high cash income, to which the incomes from the sale of their own produce were yet to be added, would make it a priori probable that the lords of the manor made purchases. We now have, however, enough testimonies which turn this conjecture into a certainty, as the following selection will prove.

Firstly the numerous duty privileges, which were meted out to the religious estates for their ships or carts or mule trains, again speak a distinct language, the more so when we learn that it, for example, concerns salt boats; or if the talk in the duty privileges is expressly about procurement; see, for example, the letter over freedom from custom duties which Prüm received from King Pepin (Beyer 1860, 1:23, § 18), in which it states:

> ubicunque infra regna nostra homines ipsius monasterii pro verilitate vel stipendia monachorum in quacunque civitate vel porto negotiandi porrexerint [...] hominibus suprascripti monasterii qui pro necessitate eorundem monachorum discurrere videntur.
> [everywhere within our realm, men of that monastery, for the service or the pay of the monks, offer that needing to be traded in every city or port [...] the men of the above monastery are seen to run about for the needs of those same monks]

Similar expressions are common: the monks of the abbey of St Germain shall be permitted to move everywhere free of custom duties: "tam ad luminaria comparanda vel pro reliqua necessitate" [as needing to be

Chapter 8: The Renaissance of the Exchange Economy

acquired in the light or for the remaining needs], from the diplomata of Charlemagne of 779 in Bouquet (1840, 5:742, § XLV). Also, in another context, the sources speak often enough directly about the purchases of the lords: St Gallen sent its *itinerarius* to Mainz "pro pannis laneis emendis", see MGH SS (Vol. 2, 97). (We already find foreign cloth in the 8th century in the abbey St Bertin: "drappos ad kamisias ultro marinas, quae vulgo *berniscrist* vocitantur" [shirts of cloth from overseas which are commonly called *berniscrist*] (Guérard 1840, 66, No. 47).) Insufficient needs shall have been supplemented through additional purchase: "si vero hoc ei non sufficit (ie. humlo), ipse vel comparando, vel quolibet alio modo (!), sibi adquirat" [if however this is not sufficient for him (ie. the hops), it either needs to be acquired, or is purchased wherever, only elsewhere (!)] (Guérard 1844, 2:333, § XV). In the deeds of donation, the specific use for a money gift is occasionally stipulated — it is gifted "argenti solidos, X ad pisces emendos, ad pastum unum fratribus ibidem exibendum" [10 silver coins must buy fish, one for pasture of the brothers from that place] (Beyer 1860, 1:116, § 110) (from the year 868). The four people whom we shall encounter on the way from Helmstädt to Brunswick[*], shall fetch home fish as "return freight" — "quod cum frumento et insuper 6 sol. piscium emi potest plaustro suo reportabunt" [they brought back on their wagon what fish could be bought with grain and also six gold coins][†]. For suchlike, also see the "Ansegisi Capitularium" in MGH Capit. (Vol. 1, Liber I, § 117, 410):

> *De thesauris ecclesiasticis.* Ut singli episcopi, abbates, abbatissae diligenter considerent thesauros ecclesiasticos, ne propter perfidiam aut negligentiam custodum aliquid de gemmis aut de vasis vel de reliquo quoque thesauro perditum sit, quia dictum est nobis, quod negotiatores Iudaei necnon et alii gloriantur, *quia quicquid eis placeat possint ab eis emere.*
> [Of the church treasures. When individual bishops, abbots or abbesses contemplate carefully the church treasures, not because of perfidy or somewhat negligent custody of gems or of dishes or of other things besides, they permit ruin of the treasures, because we have been told how Jewish traders and also others are famed because whatever gives them pleasure they can buy from them.]

Or we learn from anecdotes, which the sources hand down to us, about the purchases which the lords tended to make. Most well-known is the nice little tale of how Charlemagne played a prank on his sycophantic courtiers when he compelled them to put on their silk garments, freshly purchased from Italian traders, for a hunt through the undergrowth of the damp forests, and thereby of course consecrated them to their demise. Less well-known is another joke which the same king played on one of his ecclesiastical lords, whom he had buy from a

---

* [Tr.: see p. 135.]
† [Tr.: source unclear.]

Jewish trader (who was brought in on it) for a sinful amount a mummified mouse caught in Aachen as a precious relic. Both anecdotes are charmingly recounted from the sources (Monachus Sangallensis) by Gustav Freytag (1867, 1:323 ff.).

We may also deduce from the wares which we find traded regular purchases by the lords. We see the monks of Corbie buying local and foreign spices in Cambrai (Guérard 1844, 2:336); whereas the Parisian monks join with others in the — famous in its time — commodities market of Quentovic on the northern French coast to buy honey, madder, spices, etc. (Guérard 1844, 1:786 f.). Cf. also Otto Fengler (1907, 91 ff.).

In the custom duty rolls of the 8th and 9th century, the following were written down as merchandise: gold, silver, gems, weapons, clothes, wax, steeds, slaves, in short objects which only the rich lords could purchase. See, for example, Edictus Rothari (from 643) in MGH LL (Vol. 4, 48 [?]); Sicardi Principis Pactio (from 836) in MGH LL (Vol. 4, 216–221); Karoli Magni Capitularia in MGH LL (Vol. 1, § 11, 142); Leges Portorii (from c. 906) in MGH LL (Vol. 3, 480 ff.); Capitular of 805 in MGH LL (Vol. 1, § 7, 133) with the well-known text, "ut arma et brunias non ducant ad venundandum" [they may not lead to offering weapons and armour for sale], namely to the "hereditary enemy". Published also in Fagniez (1898, 50, No. 90). In the dialogues of Aelfrid, the following were listed as imports: crimson, silk, jewellery, ivory, gold, coloured material, dyes, wine, oil, beer, tin, glass, and sulphur. See Thorpe (1834, 101), cited in Gibbins (1897, 45).

Finally the graves also speak a distinct language. The grave finds from the Merovingian period, even in Germany, show an abundance of objects of jewellery which "distinguished themselves as the products of foreign industry and the tradition of trade" (Lindenschmit 1880, 2:381 ff., 2:437). That merchants brought objects of jewellery from "overseas" to Europe is also handed down to us in other ways. Thus, the Lex Visigothorum in MGH LL nat. Germ. (Vol. 1, Liber XI, Titulus III, 404) states "de transmarinis negotiatoribus" [from overseas traders] sold the gold and garments "vel quelibet ornamenta provincialibus nostris" [or any of our provincial ornaments].

And when we encounter the ships on which the authorised agents of the lords took the cargos of grain to market, or the wagons or mule trains which the farmers were obliged to provide, which likewise headed for the marketplaces, then we will also find it of course.

The ships of the churches and monasteries, which were granted freedom from custom duties and tribute by the emperors, are — more so in Italy — a phenomenon often recurring in the sources: for *Italy*, see the numerous documents in Hartmann (1904b, 87), and Schaube (1906, 37 ff., 72 ff.); for *Germany*, in Inama-Sternegg (1879, 1:440), and Beyer (1860, 1:23, No. 18); for *France*, in Guérard (1844, 1:789).

These ships probably served especially often to bring home the purchased goods (salt!). But we may assume that they, if somehow possible, went out loaded up. That this in any case occurred, the sources

Chapter 8: The Renaissance of the Exchange Economy

verify for us: in the year 861, Louis II permitted an authorised agent of the monastery of Brescia to trade free of *ripaticum* [river tolls] and sales duty: "quocumque cum *propriis* mercimoniis negotiando perrexerit" [whoever carried out trade with *their own* merchandise], in MGH DD L II (§ 32, 132).

We find the obligated farmers of the abbey of St Remi de Reims (9th century) on the way to Châlons (80 km), St Quentin (70–110 km), and Aachen, that is, the places where the monastery's grain found its market. It was sent either on wagons harnessed with oxen, or on asses: "duos asinos in Veromandense" [two donkeys to Vermandois] (Guérard 1853, XXVI, XXVII, XXIX). Four obligated farmers of the monastery Helmstädt had 9½ *maldaria** of grain to transport "ad vendendum in Bardewik" [to sell in Brunswick], see Behrends (1834, 33), cited in Inama-Sternegg (1879, 2:372 note 1).

But the manors/monastic estates were not only thereby turned into fosterers of the exchange economy in that they themselves were involved in the market. They were also turned into a *catalyst which brought the self-sufficiency of the farmers to a dissolution more rapidly* than it would otherwise have happened. The single fact of the monetary tribute which they demanded from the farmers suffices in order to see that. For, obviously, as soon as a farm is obliged to make regular monetary payments, it must seek to obtain a monetary income through the sale of its produce.

Then even the development of the manorial laws of prohibition took effect on mills, cloth fullers, bakeries, breweries, etc. in the same terms. We find particularly frequently bound with the obligation to serve only the lordly establishment the direct prohibition of undertaking the milling, baking, brewing, fulling, etc. in one's own house[151]. An economic exchange nexus was thereby formally enforced on the farmers, and it would surely merit the trouble to delve even closer into the connection between the development of laws of prohibition and the forming of an exchange-based form of economic organisation. Wherein how far the lords compelled the farmers to visit the markets through their interest in high market incomes would also immediately be tested.

Finally I can also conceive that the manors/monastic estates pressured the farmers into the exchange economy by the sponsorship of specialisation of production. The more an ob-

---

* [Tr.: a *maldarium* (also *multrum*) is a medieval dry measure equal to four bushels.]

ligated farmer was required by the lord to deliver particular specialities of an agrarian, or especially even of a manufactured nature, then the more he had to feel the ground of self-sufficient independence swaying under his feet, and the more it became in his interest now to profit thereby from the specialties which he commanded by dedicating himself exclusively to them, and by and by dropping off to other persons by way of sale what the lord did not desire as tribute from him.

Also embedded within the manorial/monastic organisation as such lay the tendency to blast apart its own and the farmers' self-sufficiency. Hence that the process of dissolution must have been carried out, if also slowly, steadily with the growth of the manors/monastic estates. That it was suddenly and dramatically carried out from perhaps the 11th century, so that the European Middle Ages in the short period of one or two centuries passed over from a fundamentally self-sufficient form of economic organisation to a fundamentally exchange-based form is owed to the conjunction of a series of special circumstances and explained perhaps in the following way.

We can establish first a series of transformative measures by the lords (which were in part again mutually dependent):

1. The farmers' tribute in natural produce was transformed into *monetary tribute*.

We have already established the effect which this transformation must have exercised on the farming economy — the farmer was compelled into selling.

2. The old *administrative system of the manors/monastic estates* was *dissolved*. The stewards (*villici*, bailiffs) became leaseholders of the demesnes or manors on which they had previously sat as merely the lord's administrators, or even to leaseholders of the farming estates whose tribute they had previously only collected.

3. The farming estates were likewise variously freed from the old relationships of serfdom, and subjected to *freer forms of leasing*.

The exchange economy did not need to experience any advancement by this development in itself if, in particular, the lease payment was also paid hereafter in natural produce, as was the case, for example, in some areas of north-western

Chapter 8: The Renaissance of the Exchange Economy

Germany[152] and Italy[153], where share-cropping was practised in the form of grain lease [*Getreidepacht*]. Only that a greater surplus above their own demand was created (through the introduction of their own interest), and with it the sale of agricultural products became at the same time both possible and necessary. Moreover the reform of the system of administration was surely combined in the majority of cases with a transformation of the tribute from natural produce to money.

The processes described here took place with great uniformity in all the countries of Europe and have been clarified fairly well by the research. From the extensive literature, I want to mention only a few works which seem to me to provide especially good information.

Overall depictions for *Europe*: Samuel Sugenheim (1861) (partially dated). Kowalewsky (1901).

In *France*, the transformation shall have started already in the 9th century, and was essentially complete in the 12th according to Flach (1893, 2:87 ff.). But "villications" continued naturally to exist, particularly on the great monastic possessions where the autonomous administration only dissolved in the 13th century. See H. D'Arbois de Jubainville (1858, 309 f.).

In *England*, the decisive transformation was taking place according to Seebohm (1883, 75) between Liber niger (1125) and Hundred Rolls (1279); according to the editor of the *Registrum sive liber irrotularius et consuetudinarius prioratus Beatae Mariae Wigorniensis* (Hale 1865), only between the middle of the 13th century and the *Valor ecclesiasticus* of 1534. That is surely not right in this generality. Ashley (1896, 1:§§ 3–4), whose source is in essence the just named *Registrum*, places the transformation of natural produce into monetary tribute at the beginning of the 13th century. Even in England, the reform will have been carried out earlier on the secular manors than on the religious estates. The manufacturing services were also probably detached in England earlier than anywhere else. In the sources of the 12th and 13th century, they are already very rare. Meitzen (1895, 2:132) shares this view, extending it even to all tribute and services. Cf. also Kowalewsky (1901, 3:164 ff.). In the Cartularium Monasterii de Rameseia (13th century), for example, the *agricultural* service obligations are still fully intact. Cf. also G. F. Steffen (1901, 1:174 ff.); R. M. Garnier (1892, 1:214 ff.).

In *Italy*, we may surely place the start of the described transformation in the 11th century or even earlier. See, for example, the documents of the monastery of St Francis at Ripa from the beginning of the 11th century in Kowalewsky (1901, 3:352). Apart from that, compare also, in addition to the literature named in note 153, with G. Bianchi (1891, 51 ff.), where the older literature is handled.

The developments in *Belgium* are depicted by Brants (1880).

For *Germany*, first in consideration is the depiction in Lamprecht (1885, 1:620 ff., 947; 2:587 ff.), and Inama-Sternegg (1879, 2:167 ff.,

204 ff). From the later appearing literature are highlighted: Wittich (1896, 312 ff., 317 ff.), and Meitzen (1895, 2:139 ff, 599). Extraordinarily instructive is the depiction in Kötzschke (1901, 133 ff. and elsewhere).

For the *Austrian* lands, in particular, see A. Dopsch in the introduction to his publication of the "Landesfürstlichen Urbaren Nieder- und Oberösterreichs aus dem 13. und 14. Jahrhundert" (1904, CXII ff., CXC ff., CCXI ff.). Also here in Austria is the later decline of the religious estates. "Here appears in Werden what had reached its conclusion with the royal estates." Dopsch proves that the development in Austria in the 13th century progressed just as far as in the other German territories (1904, CXCI).

These transformations obviously originated from the conscious will of the lords. This will is explained firstly and above all by the need to increase the profits from the land and to be able to use these profits freely, especially for the procurement of valuable consumption goods. Thence the preference for the monetary form. The striving for increased monetary returns was again the consequence of a general appreciation of the comfortable, magnificent, or luxurious conduct of life as we are able to observe it in the 11th and 12th centuries generally in Europe — an expression of the newly awakened spirit which we will often see at work in other directions.

This tendency of the upper strata, even the clergy, towards "secularisation", as we can quite simply express it, was now supported by a serious of external circumstances which partly owe their origin to that tendency, and partly are traced back to other causes. The most important are the following:

1. The *increase in wealth* which was undoubtedly making itself felt from the 11th century, and particularly strongly in the 12th century. The times had become more peaceful. The plundering had stopped. The wastelands were enlivened by settlers who settled down most of the time on manorial land. *Agricultural* labour became more productive. From the second half of the 12th century, the intensity of cultivation rose (in western *Germany*) through the transition to the tending of more specialised cultures; from the middle of the 12th century, the terraced cultivation for vineyards, and a little later the breaking in of meadows, became a common form of reclaiming land[154]. The agricultural land was gradually tilled better — with three and four ploughings. The fertilising became more intensive. One began with the cultivation of feed crops[155].

Chapter 8: The Renaissance of the Exchange Economy

In *Italy*, vines and olives were planted again[156].

In *England*, the clearings follow quickly after each other from the 12th century; the three field system advances quickly from at least the end of the 12th century[157].

From *France*, we hear similar news. That, in any case by the end of the 12th century, the double ploughing of the winter fields had been naturalised is confirmed for us by the sources[158].

In the lowlands of the Rhine, in *Holland* and *Flanders*, an agriculture of moor and marshlands prospered, which was carried by countless colonists from these stocks into the countryside of the Elbe and deep into the East[159].

The *manufacturing* work, however, became more productive, in particular in consequence of the advancing specialisation. Nothing is known of ground-breaking changes in technology. But the increasing specialisation suffices undoubtedly to raise manual skills, as well as the efficiency of the likewise naturally specialised means of production, so much in their effects that the productive success became noticeably greater.

2. The more and more frequent and tightening *relations with the Orient*. It is well-known that it was they which loosened the worldly disposition, provoked the delight in the comfortable and magnificent conduct of life as it were; that they first showed how one could use the growing riches to one's own advantage.

3. The dissolving of the *vita communis* in the chapters and abbeys. This was beginning in the chapters already in the 10th century, then attempts were made again and again to arrest it (ascetic reaction against the "secularisation" of the clergy in the 11th and 12th centuries!), but in the 13th century it is an accomplished fact[160]. One can associate it with the general turn to a more secular valuation of life. The wish for a freer conduct of life met with the wish to enjoy the rich income over which the chapters had disposal more than it facilitated the "canonical" simple lifestyle. To these commonly operative causes, the following special causes are added with the bishopric chapters. In the 11th century, in part even earlier, the bishops had divided their dioceses into various districts, and allotted these to the clergy of the bishop's church. The canons

139

of the cathedral thereby had become archdeacons, high officials of the church, and had obtained a special position before all the clergy of the diocese. But that became a primary cause for the destruction of their monastically simple way of life — for high officials of the church, it became impossible in the long run to live like monks[161]. The transformation of the way of life, however, consisted in that the daily delivered rations were transformed into a fixed annual income, furthermore that from then on, in contrast to before when the prebend essentially consisted of prepared meals and drinks, the canon was delivered unprepared natural ingredients which he had to sell, and, in increasing measure, money. Every canon now had his house — his *curia* — and the possession of the house came with its own staff of servants, and above all with its own economy which was *a priori* tailor-made to inclusion in the trade of the markets. The development of the numerous cathedral chapters was carried out similarly[162]. This dissolving of the *vita communis* helped naturally to speed up the dissolving of the old state of villication.

A similar reshaping was experienced by the organisation of the monasteries and abbeys, and indeed apparently from the same causes. From the 10th and 11th centuries, the abbots "secularised" — the "abbeys transformed more and more at the time into imperial institutions with worldly, political aims"*. The life goals, and the life conduct of the abbots to whom the pursuit of these goals fell, separated from those of the monks — their princely holding court distanced itself from the simple monk's household. Thus it naturally resulted in a partitioning of the monastic estate between the abbot and the convent — the individually important offices of the monastery were endowed with special incomes with which they maintained the brothers, whilst other estates remained reserved for the abbot, and served to defray his princely expenses. All with the simultaneous transformation of services into fixed tribute. "Thus there were now, instead of the originally singly administered monastic estate, several clusters of estates separated from each other, and each was administered by itself."†

---

* [Tr.: quote-marked but not footnoted by Sombart.]
† [Tr.: quote-marked but not footnoted by Sombart.]

Chapter 8: The Renaissance of the Exchange Economy

But also within the monastery, a transformation was being carried out: the monastic life was becoming strongly individualised; "the benefice-like character of positions in the monastery was taking shape"[163]. Some monasteries, the abbey Werden an der Ruhr, for example, were transformed in the end into cathedral chapters, and the cathedral chapters themselves frequently assumed in the course of time the character of sinecures for the younger sons of the upper and noble classes, in which cases, they were quite secularised[164].

Thus, also from here, incentives developed for the extension of the exchange and trading relationships.

4. The fact that in the 10th and 11th centuries, the *production of precious metals*, particularly the extraction of silver, was reinvigorated[165]. From the end of the 10th century, the openings of the silver mines began which were directly most important for the Middle Ages (gold played no economic role during that period): in Silesia, in the Harz Mountains (Goslar, Klausthal), in Saxony (Freiberg), in Carinthia, in the Salzburg area, in Bohemia, in Alsace, etc.

Since I ascribe to the production of precious metals a great significance for the origin of capitalism, I treat it at length where I describe how the "preconditions" of capitalism were fulfilled. The production of precious metals was, however, also an influence on the path of development of the pre-capitalist economic life, and especially played a not insignificant role in the transformation of the economy of self-sufficiency into the exchange economy. Hence, a mention must already occur in this place. And here firstly that very effect of an increase of the supply of precious metals shall be pointed out which likewise expressed itself in a "secularisation" of the conception of life: the rapid enrichment, which is always bound up with a sudden increase in gold and silver production, awoke and enlarged the desire for money, increased the attractions of wealth, and heightened the general valuation of money possessions. We learn from the earliest periods how an opening up of rich mines has always released the same core dispositions.

But now also, in the complex of problems present before us, the importance of an increase in the production of precious metals exceeds the power of these dispositions in as much as it can be proved that the entire transformation of the social organisation could not have succeeded without it.

If we want to clarify, however, the role which the increase in the production of precious metals played in this transformation, we must apprehend correctly a few economic concepts, respectively revised, which we require urgently for the assessment of the connections which come into question. In many heads in fact — particularly the historians' — the concepts of *self-sufficiency* and *barter economy* on the one side, and of *exchange economy* and *money economy* on the other side run together, whereby a terrible confusion occurs. Self-sufficiency and barter economy are just as different as exchange economy and money economy are, and self-sufficiency and money economy are not opposites, nor are barter economy and exchange economy, but rather only self-sufficiency and exchange economy, and money and barter economy are opposites. We have in the course of this portrayal, I think, made clear enough what the former mean. The expressions money and barter economy, by comparison, can only have the meaning that money economy describes a type of economy in which, alongside consumption goods, a money good appears, whereas barter economy is conducted without it. If a money good now exists, in so far as some good is used to estimate, measure, and express the value of the other goods, then it is evident that for the presence of money, no exchange-based form of economic organisation is required, if perhaps both the term used for money and the money good itself only manifest themselves with the placing of fines, and the raising of taxes, etc. Even if, for example, in the framework of a manorial/monastic organisation, the tribute was transformed into money, or if custom duties were captured in money instead of wares, though all these changes signify a transition from the "barter" to the "money" economy, they in no way also necessarily signify a transition from self-sufficiency to exchange-based economic relations. On the other hand, an exchange economy can exist in peaceful harmony with a barter economy. For the exchange can take place without the mediation of money, the lease payments can be assessed in terms of the produce of the land instead of money, the wages of labour can

Chapter 8: The Renaissance of the Exchange Economy

be paid in foodstuffs — all in the midst of a fundamentally exchange-based form of economic organisation.

If one must sharply distinguish the concepts of self-sufficiency and barter economy, exchange and money economy, then it can be conceded that the self-sufficient form of organisation and the money economy stand in a certain relationship of interdependence — monetary relations bring into being or demand a dissolution of self-sufficiency, and produce or solidify exchange-based relations, just as vice versa the exchange economy develops by itself tendencies towards the use of money.

If we keep these connections distinctly before our eyes, we are now able to also realise where *the significance of the production of precious metals rests for the transformation which took place here of self-sufficiency into the exchange economy*. An increase in the supply of precious metals caused:

a) firstly, the substitution of other money goods by gold and (in this case) silver, thanks to the technical advantages adhering to these goods. Only with the introduction of precious metals as money did this become so durable, high-value, and mobile that it could be used for the exchange of goods over distance, which it thereby first made possible. The same applies to a corresponding, that is, as far as it became a professionalised practice, progressive specialisation of productive activity. A certain supply of metal money was thus necessary so that these pre-conditions of an exchange-based form of economic organisation were fulfilled, and this form had a scope for development which was larger the greater that supply was.

But the increase in the supply of precious metals — at least in a stage of economic development like that which Europe had reached in the 10th and 11th centuries, that is, in a period in which the common people have passed the period of learning, and already value precious metals in essence as money goods — had the effect of immediately undermining self-sufficiency, that is, of promoting the exchange economy. And it thereby primarily had the effect that:

b) in specific places in the land, a demand was produced for goods which were to be be acquired through purchase, so that they thus had to be produced for exchange. Now, in a state of affairs like that in which the men of that epoch found themselves, this demand was directed first to such goods as came from economically more advanced areas and which were brought in the course of distant trade to the less developed regions — these were the goods of the Orient. But, in the course of time, the demand of the producers of precious metals, growing from nothing, prompted in their own land a production for sale.

It now came about that through a more abundant flow of precious metals:

c) a series of monetary relations were created, which on their part again fostered the exchange-based form of organisation. I mean the transformation of payments of natural produce into money payments (or even their relief through payment of a lump sum), of payment in kind into money wages, of custom duties from natural produce into money, and the inception of money taxes. All of the obligations for monetary outlays contained in these measures assumed with necessity the presence of a minimum threshold of money goods, and could be imposed all the more easily, the more metal money came amongst the people — the preceding exchange economy thus again made possible the money economy. When this, however, was now executed in the way conceived here, then it naturally fostered again the exchange-based economic relations — those obliged to pay in money were compelled to become sellers, and those who were qualified to receive money payments were placed in the position of becoming buyers, as we have already established in another place.

It may finally be recalled that the increase in the money supply in consequence of the raised production of precious metals created still other monetary relations, or was suited to develop them at scale, which added on their part again directly or indirectly to the destruction of self-sufficiency. I mean:

d) the formation of money lending, which occurs in these centuries, and which added in good part to the dissolving of feudal society and the self-sufficient form of organisation suited to it. Since I will speak yet in another connection explicitly about it, a closer examination can be spared at this point. I want still to at least mention here that also:

e) the significant introduction of troops paid with money, the "soldati", which wrenched apart the bonds of the self-sufficient economy, was tied to the assumption of a preceding strong increase in the production of precious metals.

***

All those tendencies which pressed for the transfiguration of economic life into an exchange-based form of economic organisation, however, now experienced an enormous strengthening through that event in which, in another respect, a momentous significance resided:

5. through *the development of cities*. I will speak in the following chapter explicitly about cities, their genesis and their growth, as they are actually (not perhaps the child, as some surely believed, but) the mother of the exchange economy and of the craftsman-like order of economic life which was built up within them. Here I must, however, dwell for a moment on the reorganisations which the structure of society experienced through the developing exchange economy, and must first reveal a few things about the bearers of the new economic structure — about traders and craftsmen.

III. The Preliminary Stages of Professionalised Trading

Exchange economy does not yet mean trade, nor does it yet mean craftwork. That is, the individual economic concerns can be tied by the bonds of exchange (with or without the mediation of money), without intermediation (trading, mercantilistic) or manufacturing (craftsman-like) activity being practised professionally by particular groups of the population. The manufacturing activity can be paired with the agricultural, as certainly formed the rule in all the beginnings of exchange economy during the European Middle Ages; and the "mercantilistic" function could be practised by the producers themselves. That is also surely the normal case in the beginnings of exchange-based forms of economic organisation, at least where it concerns localised exchange. What farmers, estate owners, and craftsmen had to exchange amongst themselves in the narrow scope of the countryside has been exchanged right up to our time by them themselves — without the intermediation of a trader. But we also learn that in the early periods of the Middle Ages, the goods were sold across wide distances by the producers themselves (or their agents).

We see the craftsmen going with their products to distant fairs (of which I have yet to speak in another connection). We encounter the small salt shippers from Venice and Commacchio on the rivers and the coasts of Italy. We meet the monks on the way to far-flung marketplaces[166] and become acquainted with representatives of the churches and monasteries who are employed explicitly to mediate the intercourse of exchange for their institutions, and hence are described directly as 'merchants', 'negotiatores', without of course representing thereby anything else but business officers of the chapters and monasteries[167].

And often enough, when we read in the sources about the movement of goods and even about 'mercatores', it will concern the marketing of their own products; more often perhaps than we were formerly inclined to assume. But we know today at least that we must not translate 'mercator' as 'merchant' everywhere in the texts of the Middle Ages, that the word rather signifies just as often the visitor to the market who has produced their own goods[168].

But even when the mediation of goods exchange had already developed into the performance of a special category of person adjoining the producers, we must not suggest offhand that this constituted professionalised trade. Interpolated between this and the immediate exchange of goods by producers and consumers, there are in point of fact two other stages of development, which we can describe as *preliminary stages of professionalised trade*. These stages are the trading of stolen goods, and the opportunistic trade [*Gelegenheitshandel*].

The *trading of stolen goods* is the twin brother of theft. It consists of the selling (mostly professionally) of wares which were neither produced nor purchased by the seller, but were acquired by violence. One can in this case also speak of a one-sided trade. As is known, the seminal field of activity for the trading of stolen goods is the sea, where it has been practised

Chapter 8: The Renaissance of the Exchange Economy

professionally as piracy for thousands of years, as the most spirited treatise of the pirate trade has taught us:

> Two ships alone with us took,
> With twenty we return to port.
> And what great matters we have done,
> That by our lading men may see.
> The spirit frees the ocean free,
> Who knows there what bethinking is!
> A speedy grip there only tells,
> We catch a fish, or catch a ship,
> Then straight upon the fourth we seize,
> Then badly goes it for the fifth,
> If one has power, one has right.
> You ask for the *what?* and not the *how?*[169]

That all trading peoples were familiar with the trading of stolen goods before and alongside the professional trade is just as certainly a matter of fact as it is proven that the European Middle Ages made no exception to the rule, and even the most recent times must have reckoned piracy still to be a universally distributed convention.

The words "lucrum" and "gain" originally meant nothing but booty or spoils (Schrader 1886, 59). Over the universality of the trading of stolen goods at primitive stages of culture, see Schrader (1886, 68 ff.); and Kulischer (1899, 318 f. and elsewhere). Much material, although not always sifted, is contained in Andree (1867, 1:314 ff.). Cf. also Letourneau (1897, 95 ff., 335 ff.). In all earlier times, piracy was seen as a thoroughly admissible, not even dishonourable profession. Well-known is the recognition of the pirates' association (επί λείαν) by the Solonian laws as well as by the treaty between Chalaeum and Oeanthia in Locris (Goldschmidt 1891, 27). I will yet speak about the trading of stolen goods during the Middle Ages and modern period in another connection. See Chapter 39 in a subsequent volume. The psychological necessity of theft as a type of variation of possession preceding exchange has been developed in a subtle way by Georg Simmel (1900, 53 ff.). A poetic glorification of theft can be read in the Bedouin novel "Anthar", translated from the Arabic by Terrick Hamilton (1819).

A second preliminary stage of professionalised trade, but one which occurs more frequently than that just mentioned, is that form of goods exchange which I call *opportunistic trade*. This is distinguished by it already being a two-sided exchange, that is, it rests on the purchase of wares for the purpose of sale, but still lacks the professionalism needed for the full essence of trade. The trading activity is, on the contrary, practised incidentally at this stage, a sideline as it were, by arbitrary persons (who are not themselves the producers of the traded wares). Opportunistic trading is also an occurrence spread over all primitive cultures (the trade of chiefs!), and plays in the European Middle Ages especially a significantly greater role than previous depictions of medieval trade would imply. As I believe I will be able to prove in this work in another connection.

An especially important form of opportunistic trade is that which can be called *seasonal trade* — the trade which farmers in particular practise alongside their agricultural activity. I believe that this cross between trade and agriculture in the Early Middle Ages was at least as common as that between manufacturing and agriculture[170].

IV. *The Beginnings of Professionalised Trade*

Now, one would undoubtedly be mistaken, however, if one also wanted to deny for any period of the European Middle Ages the existence of *professionalised merchants* or at least established persons who were sharply distinguished from the other classes of the population. The sources, even for the Early Middle Ages, often enough place the 'negotiatores' in a conscious contrast to the other residents of a place[171]; and the privileges which were also bestowed on the 'negotiatores' in particular in the Merovingian and Carolingian periods — in virtue of which they received a (personal) right from the king, to which they were subject in all parts of the realm — make the assumption probable that in that period already a special class of professional traders were in existence.

Who were these traders of the Early Middle Ages? More to the point, what was their origin?

One can say in summary that in their beginnings, for the most part, they were *foreigners*. Ahead of other nations were the *Syrians*. The *negotiatores syrici* formed, up to the end of the 7th century, the link between Asia and Central Europe. "Up to this day, such an innate zeal for business resided in the Syrians, Martian says in his explications of Ezekiel, that they traverse the entire earth for the sake of profit; and so great is their lust for trading that they strive to acquire riches everywhere in the Roman Empire amidst wars, murder and manslaughter."[172]

After them came the Jews, who must not be put on a level with the Syrian merchants as Kiesselbach does. Even they had become "foreigners" in all the lands of Europe after they had stopped being considered as *cives Romani*[173]. The mention of the Jews in the sources of the Merovingian and Carolingian Empires in the almost stereotypical form of "vel Judaei vel ceteri ibi manentes negotiatores" [Jews or other merchants abiding there] is so common[174] that we may assume offhand a strong proportion of Jews in the trade of that time.

Apart from the Jews: in *Italy*, Arabs, Libyans, Africans[175], and Greeks[176]; in *Spain*, North Africans[177]; in *northern Europe*, the same peoples and also Italians[178]. London was called in the 8th century "multorum emporium populorum" [emporium of many nations][179]. Likewise Paris[180]. The talk in the sources of the Early Middle Ages is of the "transmarini negotiatores" [overseas traders][181]. In Bremen, we find in the 11th century "negotiatores, qui ex omni terrarum parte" [the merchants who [had come] from all parts of the earth][182].

But we hear also early on with regard to northern peoples that they actively took part in trading, though admittedly the sources do not betray to us whether they did so as professional traders or only as opportunistic traders.

Thus we meet in the 9th century at the Danube markets "Sclavi, qui de Rugis vel de Boemanis mercandi causa exeunt" [Slavs who come for the merchandise of Rugii or Bohemians], to exchange here horses and slaves for wax and other things[183]. We meet Russian merchants from Kiev, Chernihiv, and Pereiaslav in the 10th century in Constantinople, to which they had travelled on the Dnieper, bartering furs, wax, and slaves in exchange for silks, material woven with gold, wine, morocco leather boots, and spices[184].

And certainly the local inhabitants were soon joining the foreign merchants to the extent that their individual lands were economically advanced. The nascent cities already encountered everywhere a stock of local traders of whom the sources also give information occasionally from much earlier periods[185].

We would be able to imagine easily what sort of *business concern* these "large merchants"[186] were in the time before cities on the strength of our knowledge of the entire character of economic life, even if the sources did not put such abundant material in our hands as they do.

There were small freeloaders, 'market visitors', as are regularly found today at the fairs of the small towns; pack bearers, pedlars who moved with their packs, their mules, or their carts from village to village, from manor to manor, as they do even today in isolated mountain regions; small boatmen like those that have long died out on our rivers, compared with whom the boatman Wulkow* is a great shipowner.

That there was no settled trade before the inception of cities is surely not to be doubted. Trade at markets and fairs (about which I will share some more in further course) had been the rule since the 8th and 9th centuries. Previously the *pedlar trade* had formed the rule, but it also continued to exist of course alongside the market trade: "omnium negotiatorum sive in mercato *sive aliubi* negotientur" [let all the merchants trade whether in markets *or in other places*] ("Capitulare de disciplina Palatii" from 809, in MGH LL (Vol. 1, § 2, 158)) also testifies "source-wise" to its existence.

A Russian document even calls the Gotlanders plying their trade in Novgorod in the year 1190 "varyag" (Bugge 1906, 250). The word 'varyag' (ВАРЯГЪ) still exists in Russian; it means "a wandering trader, pedlar, or purchaser".

The means of transport on land were the cart or the mule (for example, "cum carris et saumariis" [with carts and beasts], from "Diplomata Ludovici Pii Imperatoris" of 831 in Bouquet (1840, 6:572, § CLXX), cited in Guérard (1853, 1:787)), or their own backs (slaves, etc. — see above page 149 — "*de onere unius hominis* massiola una ... solvere cogantur" [they are compelled to release ... the burden of one man with one massiola†], from MGH Capit. (Vol. 2, § 6, 251)), or (if somehow possible) the *boat*. The trade was a river trade to the extent anyhow that the circumstances allowed it. Hence, already early on, the striving of estate owners for river ports: see the numerous examples in Imbart de la Tour, loc. cit., 76. The predominance of river trade is attested by the use of 'port' and emporium as synonyms in early medieval *England*: Maitland (1907, 195 f.); cf. 'portus' in *Flanders* (poorter?), Pirenne (1898, 57, 75).

Transport by sea in that period is discussed in-depth (unfortunately admittedly, from a predominantly technological viewpoint) by Walther Vogel (2008).

---

*   [Tr.: Wulkow is a character in Gerhart Hauptmann's play "The Beaver Coat".]

†   [Tr: massiola = unit of currency = a twelfth of a gold solidus]

Chapter 8: The Renaissance of the Exchange Economy

We should also be able to create a distinct picture of the extent of that early medieval trade with the help of the facts already provided. It was of course tiny. The following details confirm the correctness of this assumption "source-wise".

The riverboats were usually crewed by three men: "de unaquaque navi legittima, id est quam tres homines navigant" [with regards to every proper boat, that is, sailed by three men] (from "Inquisitio de Theloneis Raffelstettensis" in MGH Capit. (Vol. 2, § 7, 251)). It fits with these scales when we hear that one fastened the boats to posts which were first driven in for this purpose each time, see the privilege from Berengar II and Adalbert (22 September 951) in Baudi di Vesme et al. (1873, No. 595, 1019); or that one carried them over land for a bit to avoid rapids (when navigating the Dnieper), see Bugge (1906, 247).

In a trade agreement which a Byzantine emperor concluded with Russian merchants (10th century), the latter were permitted to sojourn for a month in Constantinople. But no more than 50 merchants were permitted to come at any one time, and *none were permitted to purchase silk fabric for more than 50 gulden*. See Bugge (1906, 246).

V. *The Beginnings of Craftwork*

And what does it look like with regards to the manufacturing 'craftsmen' in the epoch being examined here, that is, up to the inception of the cities? Were there free craftsmen in the sense of independent producers of manufactured goods?

I fear that we will never receive a satisfying answer to these questions. In any case, quite new and formerly unknown sources have been revealed. The material which we possess today allows for all sorts of interpretations.

We see quite clearly how the manufacturing workers on the manors/monastic lands gradually developed into independent craftsmen; how they at first were only permitted to use a portion of their manpower to work for the public at large in return for payment (as per the statutes of the Leges Burgundionum[187]); how then working for themselves became more and more the primary thing, and only defined work was still to be carried out for the lord within limited bounds (as per statutes of the older Strasbourg municipal laws*); until in the end even these obligations without consideration were being dropped or bought from the lord. The interest of the lord in the manufacturing services of his dependents died out, and was superseded by the interest in an active market trade.

---

* [Tr.: not footnoted by Sombart.]

But whether there had always been "free" craftsmen alongside the manor's manufacturing workers (who in large part, as we have seen, sat in the village) is something we can only conjecture[188]. *In favour* speaks the consideration that there were also manufacturing workers in the villages, already even in the time of the common people's freedom [*Volksfreiheit*], and that certainly not all villagers or village inhabitants were enmeshed in the manorial/monastic nexus. *In favour* speaks a certain probability (nothing more!) that, at least in Italy, residues of the Roman craftwork were preserved into the Middle Ages. The best aficionados of the Italian Early Middle Ages assume it[189] (the sources are silent from the 7th to the 11th centuries!). The same applies to those Roman cities outside Italy. *In favour* speaks the existence of nomadic manufacturing workers who could not possibly have been dependent in any way on a lord. The researchers whose specialty is the "Origins of Craftwork" should focus their attention on these "nomadic craftsmen". If in general between 500 and 1000 a "free" "craftwork" existed to an appreciable extent, then it was certainly in the form of the nomadic craftwork whose main representatives will surely have been the building craftsmen. I refer for the time being to the following places in the sources:

"Edictus Rothari" (from 643) in MGH LL (Vol. 4, 33, §144): "si magister comacinus cum collegantes suos cuiuscumque domum ad restaurandam vel fabricandam super se placito finito de mercedes susciperet" [if the master of masonry with his associates receives payment to restore or build any house above the acceptable limit]. For which, compare the comment which Muratori makes to this law (1739, 1.2:25), and T. Hodgkin (1895, VI:191).

"Liutprandi Leges De Anno VIII" Cap. 18 (from 713–735) in MGH LL (Vol. 4, 115, § 18): "si quis ad negotium peragendum vel *pro qualicumque artificio* intra provincia vel extra provincia ambolaverit et in tres annos regressus non fuerit" [if they go to carry out any task or *any kind of business* inside or outside the province and have not been back in three years]. Documents of Otto I: "quanticumque negotiatores *vel artifices* seu et Frisones apud Worm. urbem advenissent" [whatever traders *or craftsmen* and Frisians arrived in the city of Worms]*. (Here the talk, however, can also be of craftsmen who bring their products to Worms; nevertheless it amounts to the same — if they could come (from

---

* [Tr.: not footnoted by Sombart. Cf. MGH DD O I (165, § 84).]

Chapter 8: The Renaissance of the Exchange Economy

wherever) to Worms, they must have possessed freedom of production, have been "free", and have been craftsmen.)

The manufacturing workers whom Charlemagne employed in his constructions were surely also free nomadic craftsmen, at least in part: "Ad cuius [basilicae] fabricam de omnibus cismarinis regionibus magistros et opifices omnium id genus artium advocavit. Super quos unum abbatem cunctorum peritissimum ad executionem operis [...] constituit. [...] Providentissimus igitur Karolus quibuscumque primoribus [...] praecepit, ut opifices a se directos omni industria sustentare, et cuncta ad opus illud necessaria subministrare curarent. Qui vero ex longinquis partibus advenissent, commendavit eos praeposito domus suae [...] ut eos de publicis rebus aleret et vestiret" [In order to fabricate [the basilica], he summoned all the masters and workers of all the crafts of that kind from across the region. One generally expert abbot was appointed over them for the execution of the work. Most prudently then, Charlemagne gave instructions for whoever was in charge to direct all workers to maintain activity and to care for the supply of all that was necessary for that work. But for those who might arrive from remote parts, he committed the command of his own house, while he clothed and fed them on the public purse.], from "Monachus Sangallensis Gesta Karoli" in MGH SS (Vol. 2, Lib. I, 744, 745, §§ 28, 31).

The following account of the building of the abbey Hyde in Hampshire, which I not seen turned to account anywhere yet, also seems especially instructive to me — the construction took place in the year 902, and was described as follows by the chronicler:

> Artificibus itaque plurimis et operariis coadunatis, jactisque fundamentis, coeptum opus quotidie certatim acceleravit, et in duobus annis, quod mirum est dictu, et difficile videtur, perfecit. Rex autem magnam pecuniam, et largis diversarum specierum donis, in argento et auro, sancto patri obtulit. [Therefore, many craftsmen and labourers gathered and erected the foundations, vied with each other to accelerate the work that they had begun, and in two years, which is remarkable to say, and which appeared difficult, they completed it. Now the King offered up a lot of money, and a large variety of gifts, in silver and gold, for the Holy Father.] (Edwards 1866, 81)

Then: artists and workers were hired externally, and paid with money. They could not have been just manufacturing workers under an obligation. This place seems to me to better than some others at showing the presence of a "free" (nomadic) craftwork in the 9th century. That it adhered within quite defined bounds is self-evident. But there it was very probable. And that became significant for the entire further course of history.

Chapter 9: Towards a Theory of City Formation

I. The Concept of the City

At first sight, it seems almost as if the word "city"* describes quite explicitly an entirely specific phenomenon. At least, a clearly delineated picture arises in our minds when we here the word — the picture of a settlement of many people in houses and streets, if possible surrounded by walls and battlements, a settlement which contrasts sharply with the "countryside", and which is described on the map with a more or less large spot. Perhaps the image of Nuremberg as Albrecht Dürer drew it for us. But when we look more precisely, when we attempt to say in words what we mean by a "city", that is, when we attempt to put down sharply and explicitly the *concept of the city*, then we will very soon be aware that it is not at all so simple. We note that the features of the city concept are in no way fixed. Not in daily linguistic usage, but also not (or rather still much less) in the sciences.

Just to mention a few examples from the literature over the nature of cities in the Middle Ages: von Maurer's definition, "cities are walled villages", may be the most widespread, which connects with that well-known saying of the Middle Ages, "townsfolk and farmers are separated by nothing but fences." Another scholar protests against that: "The decisive characteristics of a city are not given by walls and moats, nor by the number of inhabitants, nor by the blossoming of trade and commerce. The city council, freely elected by the towns-

---

* [Tr.: "Stadt", which can translates as either town or city, and so references to "city" should be read as town/city, as appropriate.]

folk and endorsed by the appropriate higher authority, is the sure sign of the German city entering into its full blossoming. The town seal symbolises, no less than the walls, the legally recognised, organised difference between city and country."[190]

The same thought appears somewhat differently coloured in Kallsen[191]: "The characteristic thing about a city is not the separation of a place from the surrounding countryside by an enclosing wall, but the special life growing in the shelter of the wall, based on independent municipal association."

The city is a place to which market rights are bestowed; "the city is a market settlement", says the representative of the theory of market rights.

Still others desire that several features coincide to form the concept "city": a place must be fortified and it must be the centre of a castle[192]; it must be fortified, pacified, in possession of the *usus negotiandi* [custom of trade] and be a corporation of public law[193]. "The city has a market [...] It is surrounded by a fortification. It forms a special area of jurisdiction [...] It possesses greater independence in community affairs and a greater wealth of community facilities [...] than the country communities [...] It is finally, with respect to the public [...] benefits and duties, privileged over the countryside [...] The granting of privileges is in general the characteristic of the medieval city"[194].

Johann Heinrich Gottlob von Justi defined the city very nicely in his work *Staatswirtschaft* (1758, 1:491, § 477): "A city is a connection of associations, families, and individual persons, who live in a protected place with one another under the supervision and direction of a *policeycollegii*, which is called a city council, or of other persons authorised for the management of the policing institutions, so as to ply with greater profit, effect, and contiguity such commerce and forms of sustenance which are required immediately, as well as for the need and comfort of the land, than would be obtained by the combining of the overall level of sustenance in the countryside." Justi then analyses his definition as follows: a city must be "protected" (by nature or artifice) in such a way "that the access can only occur at a few places expressly determined for that purpose, which one calls gates, because the policing institutions necessary as the primary means for the

Chapter 9: Towards a Theory of City Formation

end goal of cities cannot occur in a different shape." (1758, 1:493, § 478)

The following more recent definitions of the "city" are arranged against that as examples. From the International Statistical Congress: "cities are places of residence of more than 2,000 inhabitants", a definition which the official statistics in most civilised lands adhere to today; from the Prussian cities ordinance of 1853: "all places represented in the provincial assemblies in the status of cities"; by an inspired American: "a city is a place which possesses a university"[195]; from a young legal historian: "the city is the local settlement form of the large social circle"[196]. In the most comprehensive, newer writing which is dedicated to the problem of city formation and claims to tackle it from the viewpoint of "sociology", the city is defined as follows: "une société complexe dont la base géographique est particulièrement restreinte relativement à son volume ou dont l'élément territoriale est en quantité relativement faible par rapport à celle de ses éléments humains" [a complex society whose geographical base is particularly limited in volume or whose territorial element is relatively small in comparison with that of its human elements][197].

There shall also be people who talk or write about "cities", and about what is connected with them, without undergoing the trouble of sharing with us their opinion over what they stipulate as understanding by a "city".

Who is right now?

One could be tempted, with regard to the obvious ambiguity of the concept "city", to fight with those who abstain entirely from a definition. If only so much mischief had not been wreaked in the literature over the nature of cities, but particularly in that over the history of the medieval city, by conceptual ambiguities. We will have to decide thus, whether we like it or not, on a specific concept. But which?

I think, first of all, that we will determine at once that the answer to what is to be understood by a "city" will turn out differently according to whether the features are given to us from another place or created by us first. The former is the case when we want to practise the art of law, interpret specific documents, or the like. Of course, we have only to ask then: what is a "city" in the sense of the law of ..., or what in the sense of documents (for example, in the eastern Elbe region of Germany during the 9th and 10th centuries, what does *urbs, civitas, oppidum*, etc. mean here?). Here the settling of the definition is an art of interpretation. The concept obtained by the science of interpretation may be described as an *analytic* concept.

But it is quite something else when we form the concept itself by assembling arbitrary features and coalescing them into a unity. Then no city is there before we did not think it[198]. One can call the concepts issuing from this procedure quite generally *synthetic* concepts. Their "correctness" is decided only by the aim — they are correct when they are expedient. But it is apparent now that there can be quite many aims which a concept like the "city" has to serve. The aim can be a *practical* one — for example, that of giving designations to a country coachman if he should travel into the "city"; or that of apprehending the population of a land statistically according to specific features and the like. Or the aim can be a *scientific* one — that specific connections of human society, especially of human history, shall be clarified. Then it thus concerns under what point of view one contemplates the history of a period — whether under one of military history, art history, intellectual history, legal history, economic history, or some other. For each of these manners of contemplation, a special concept of "city" is established whose "correctness" is only decided by the wealth of knowledge which its sculptor reveals to us from historical life with its help.

Thus the solution is that anyone who practises economic history will have to establish an *economic concept of the city*. More obviously, it will have to tell us what we must understand by a city if we want to recognise and appreciate the economically significant conditions around this phenomenon. I define a city *in the economic sense* as a larger settlement of people who rely for their livelihood on the products of other people's agriculture work[199]. The special economic colouring of this concept becomes immediately clear if we compare it with other concepts of the city — perhaps the architectural or the legal or the statistical or some other.

Chapter 9: Towards a Theory of City Formation

A city in the economic sense can very well be a village in the administrative sense — Langenbielau perhaps in the present; Kempen up to the year 1294[200].

A village in the economic sense does not become a city when it is fortified, like perhaps the "vici in modum municipiorum" [village in the municipal manner] of Roman Africa, of which Frontin speaks, which were usually called *castella*, that is were just villages equipped for defence[201].

It no more becomes a city if a market is held in it or even market rights bestowed on it.

A village also, however, does not become a city in an economic sense even if it were ten times a city in the administrative sense. The countless "villages" which were "raised to cities" in the Middle Ages by the granting of municipal laws[202] naturally remained economically what they had been up to then: villages.

Finally, the economic concept of the city also distinguishes itself from the statistical. That is, large numbers of "agglomerated" living persons. We must learn not to look on the giant "cities" of Oriental antiquity, like Nineveh and Babylon, as cities in the economic sense[203], just as we must not award the large communities of old India, the likes of Calcutta[204] or modern Tehran and similar settlements[205], with the character of a city.

II. The Outline of a Theory of City Formation

But now obviously the depiction of the genesis and nature of the "city" is formed quite variously according to whether it concerns this or that "city". Obviously when, where, and why a place was bestowed with municipal laws or received a city council is different from when, where, and why it received a collar of walls and towers; when, where, and why a market was erected there is different from when, where, and why a university arrived in that place; and when, where, and why thousands of farmers joined together at a point which forms a city in the statistical sense is different from when, where, and why a city arose in the economic sense, that is thus, when, where, and why a greater number of people settled on a patch of land, who had to live from the products of other people's working of the soil.

When we pose the question of the genesis of the city in an economic sense, then we must, I think, answer it in two respects.

Firstly, where did the people without crops or acres of land come from to form the city, and what brought them to join together into a civic settlement. That is the question as to the causes which led to an uprooting of populations rooted to the soil; the question as to the causes which moved the individuals to become townsfolk. But secondly (and especially), it is incumbent on us to explain how it became possible (economically) that such peculiar settlements could form which were estranged from all natural manners of existence. To find the answer, we must first keep in mind for the present that a city lives from the surplus of the land, so its living conditions and its scope for life are thus dependent upon the extent of that surplus production which it is able to draw to itself[206]. This fact can be illustrated perhaps in its details by the following:

1. The size of a city is conditioned by the size of the production from the area for its upkeep and the extent of its share in it, which we can call excess production.
2. For given sizes of the area for its upkeep and given (by the degree of fertility of the region or the state of the agricultural technology) totals of production, its size depends on the extent of the excess production.

Hence, for example, under otherwise equal conditions, the cities in despotic states with a high coefficient of exploitation of the country folk will be larger than in those lands with a democratic constitution.

3. For given sizes of the area for its upkeep and given extents of excess production, the size of the city is conditioned by the fertility of the soil or the state of agricultural technology.

Hence, fertile lands under the given conditions can have larger cities than infertile lands[207].

4. For given extents of excess production and given yields of the ground, the size of the city is conditioned by the extent of the area for its upkeep.

Hence, for example, the possibility of larger trading cities, and the possibility of larger capital cities in larger realms.

5. The extent of the area for its upkeep is conditioned by the degree of development of the transport technology.

Chapter 9: Towards a Theory of City Formation

Hence, under the given conditions, sites on rivers or by the sea affect the expansiveness of the city favourably[208] and, in a land with paved roads — again under the given conditions — the cities can be larger than where there are only dirt roads, and in a land with railroads, larger than where there are only paved roads.

In addition, we will have to be clear that there are among the "city-founding" men two sorts who are intrinsically different from each other. Such as those who, by virtue of some power, some wealth, or some activity, are capable of autocratically drawing in the products of the land required for their upkeep, and perhaps also for the upkeep of other people. They are the actual *founders* of cities; the subjects of city formation; the active, or original, or primary city builders. Thus a king who makes profits in the trade with *foreigners*; a craftsman or industrialist who sells manufactured products *away from home*; a writer whose writings are bought *out before the gates*; a doctor who has *clients in the countryside*; a student whose parents live *in another place*, and who lives off "stipends" from his parents, etc.

They are the people who live and let live.

Letting live the other residents of cities who are not able to provide from their own power the necessary means of sustenance (I want to say the product of the land), but who only partake in those of the primary city builders. We can describe them as *fillers of the cities*; as the objects of city formation; as passive, or derivative, or secondary (tertiary, quaternary, etc) city builders. They are secondary city builders when they obtain their upkeep immediately from a primary city builder — the cobbler who makes boots for the king; the singer who sings him his songs; the innkeeper at whose place the lord dines; the jeweller from whom the merchant buys jewellery for his beloved; the theatre director to whose theatre the craftsman goes; the bookseller who delivers the books for our writer; the hairdresser who shaves our doctor; the landlord from whom the student rents his room, etc.

When another townsman now "earns" again from a secondary city builder, then this townsman is a tertiary city builder, etc. When we take an arbitrary case: a waiter drinks a glass of beer in a restaurant, the restaurant owner lives off

161

him, the brewer off the restaurant owner; the waiter pays with tips which a doctor paid him; the doctor has customers in the city, e.g. an actor; the actor receives his fee from the earnings of the theatre director; these originate (for this small part) from the theatre tickets which a professor took; the professor draws his salary from the state — here alone does the original city builder appear, the tax-raising state; all others are derived city builders. In general, all tradesmen, all merchants, all liberal professions which satisfy the demand of the townsfolk themselves are never founders of cities, but rather fillers of cities[209]. The clear insight into the contrast of these two entirely differently placed groups of the civic population is the necessary assumption for every understanding of the genesis of a city.

This itself is a historical phenomenon, and it receives its special stamp from the particular configuration of the circumstances of the time. It is a task of the historian to explain from these the origin of the historical city. It is thus to discover the special causes of the time which separate the masses of people from the soil; to reveal the special motives of the time which unite people into a civic settlement; to establish the special conditions of the time under which the founding of cities takes place; to describe and interpret the special types of original and derived city builders at the time. That I would like to attempt in the following for the medieval city.

Chapter 10: The Origin of the Medieval City

Literature and Sources

This is an attempt to explain the origin of the city in the European Middle Ages as a real phenomenon of social life. Approaches are found especially in the *regional historical research* in many cases. But by and large, the enormously comprehensive literature for the medieval history of cities has gone out of the way of the problems posed here. It has — in conformity with the old psychological law that a movement to the side follows the tiniest resistance — almost exclusively turned towards the question of the origin of the *constitution* of the city. Understandably, since the sources most beloved at the moment, namely the charters, point in this direction. Next to these, the other sources from which one could have learnt much more for that vital phenomenon, the "city", have been as good as entirely neglected. Only a few researchers have turned the *cartographic method*, which has provided such rich booty for the settlement history of the countryside, onto the city. In *Germany*, except for a few regional historians like H. Ermisch for Freiburg in Silesia, and F. Haagen for Aachen, J. Fritz and A. Püschel in particular have helped themselves to their advantage; in *England*, Raymond Unwin and H. Inigo Triggs. Far too few have utilised the *chroniclers*. If anything, one can learn from them the external conditions under which cities arose. Noteworthy beginnings have been made in the utilisation of the *statistical material on population and wealth* which can also give us information in a roundabout way about the origin (since social structure) of the medieval cities. Of special value here are the numerous recently published investigations regarding the *history of the churches and monasteries* in the cities.

There is no point in making note here of individual works from the literature on the history of cities. Where I refer to a writer, I will name him in his place. Apart from that, I refer to a few critical *overviews* of the newer evidence in this literature — thus that of K. Uhlirz in the *Mitteilungen des Instituts für österreichische Geschichtsforschung* from Volume 7 (1886) and onwards (he has in fact covered far more than 100 works); further, see those of J. Ziehen in the *Zeitschrift für Kommunalwissenschaft*, Vol. I, No. 1 and 2 (1914).

When one seeks for a special reason why in the great mass of books which have been written in the last generation about medieval cities so little is contained about the real life phenomena, one may find it in the circumstance that many authors *believed* they were talking about the origin of cities, whereas they were actually speaking about the origin of the constitution of the city. Thus they did not sense the gaps at all which their portrayals left. Which may, on the other hand, explain why the correct posing of the problem remained hidden from them.

This connection manifests most distinctly with the representatives of the so-called theory of market rights, that is, those scholars who have the "cities" of the Middle Ages "arise" from a market settlement. Since a very real phenomenon is obviously described here as the cause of the origin of cities, the semblance is aroused as if this theory has directly given an economic and thereby very realistic explanation. Thus, for example, von Below (1892, 14) judges that the theory of market rights is surely from the standpoint of economic history correct because it envisages the origin of the *existence* of the city, whereas he engages it from the standpoint of the history of the constitution. The matter is now such that the economic history standpoint from the theory of market rights is absolutely untenable. Wanting to explain cities economically from the markets is similar to proceeding like Uncle Bräsig*, who is known to have deduced "hardship from poverty". The causal connection is surely the inverse to what the theorists of market rights assume — cities don't arise because markets are held (or even because market privileges have been dealt out!), but markets are held because cities have arisen or are arising. The markets have contributed not just nothing, but absolutely nothing at all for the genesis of *cities*. As with that determination, of course, nothing is conclusive in the question of what meaning the granting of market rights perhaps has for the origin of the civic *constitution*.

My own depiction will only indicate where the problems lie, and how one could probably master them. They can in no way be treated conclusively.

I. The Birth of Cities from Villages, particularly the Founding of Cities

One can be doubtful whether, in general, there were cities (in the economic sense) during the European Middle Ages. In any case, they did not, at any period, "arise" within a short timeframe like perhaps an American city arises. Rather they grew one and all in a process of reshaping from villages, most probably stretching over centuries, slowly and organically (without exception from villages — in the economic sense!)

---

* [Tr.: Uncle Bräsig is a comic character in Fritz Reuter's novel *Ut mine Stromtid* (1905).]

Chapter 10: The Origin of the Medieval City

How slowly the reshaping of villages into cities must have taken place, we can observe from the fact that even the largest cities (to remain silent of the entourage of medium and smaller ones) carried within themselves even in the High and Late Middle Ages strong traces of country or agricultural towns, that is, of half-civic settlements in which a part of the population still engaged in agriculture, and thus had not actually become townsfolk.

A lively picture of the village-like character of the medieval cities is created by Gustav Freytag in his *Bilder aus der deutschen Vergangenheit*:

> Whoever enters the city in the morning certainly encounters the city cattle first. For even in the great cities of the realm, the citizens engage in farming on meadows, pastures, arable fields, and vineyards of the city's land; most houses, even distinguished ones, have cattle stalls and sheds in the narrow courtyard. The beat of the thresher is still heard near the town hall in 1350 in Nuremberg, Augsburg, and Ulm; not far from the city walls stand barns, every house has its grain store and commonly a winepress [...] The cows trot in the lanes of the city, a shepherd leads his flock with his dog on the nearby heights; even in the city's forest, the cattle graze [...] The pigs travel through the house doors into the houses, and search for their unclean sustenance on the way. On the arms of the river which leads through the city, the cattle have their swims [...] The mills are not missing either; in secluded places, great heaps are dumped [etc.][210]

I believe that no part of this picture is false, and that what Freytag says here about the large German cities of the High Middle Ages applies in a similar way to the Italian cities, at least up to the 12th century, as well as for the English and for all medieval cities.

The facts have been established so often "source-wise" that it is unnecessary to mention individual documents. I refer the reader for *Germany* to the summary depictions in von Maurer (1870, 2:176 ff. and elsewhere); von Below (1889, 22 ff.); cf. von Below's other work (1905, 38 f.); W. Varges (1893, 163 f.). Also Emil Michael (1897, 1:129 f.) has collected a number of references. I also add, for Salzburg in the 14th century, F. V. Zillner (1890, 2:234); for Lübeck in the year 1300, Hoffmann (1889); Pauli (1847, § 47, 130-131); for Cologne in the 16th century, J. Greving (1904, 11). In the 13th and 14th centuries, every "civic" activity, like, for example, the building of walls, was interrupted in the cities by agricultural work (Lamprecht 1885, 2:523). The deepest insight into the economic structure of the medieval (medium-sized) city is provided to us still by Karl Bücher (1886). See for the question discussed here, for example, the portrayal on pages 260 ff., which is surely the most rigorous which we possess.

That in the *Italian* "cities", certainly still in the 11th and 12th centuries, agriculture was a very important branch of occupation is shown by the evidence with perfect clarity. See, for example, for Mantua, Pisa, and Cremona (11th and 12th centuries), the source evidence from Muratori (1739, 4:13, 16, 20, 23), cited in Bethmann-Hollweg (1846, 129 f.). In addition, see the source documents in Max Handloike (1883, 108 ff.). We may conclude with confidence that one or two centuries after that time strong agricultural interests were also still represented in the Italian cities. "The *negotiatores* were also resident and even the small property owners demanded the pasture lands" (Hartmann 1904b, 112).

We have enough witnesses of the *English* cities who provide proof that they bore entirely the same character as the German, namely the half-civic. For the time of the Domesday Book, see particularly F. W. Maitland (1907, 203 and elsewhere). But, that "even long after the Conquest the agricultural element prevailed in English boroughs far more than is commonly supposed", is suggested by the very cautious Charles Gross (1890, 1:4), where he also presents us with an abundant selection of literature and source evidence. Even in London, we encounter still in the 13th century the breeding of pigs, and even oxen. See Ashley (1896, 1:74 & 117), who draws on the Lib. Albus XLI –XLII.

> The activity of the townsfolk was not confined to their special craft or trade. In harvest time they poured out of the towns into the country. When the king dismisses his parliament in the middle ages, he sends the nobles to their sports, the commons to their harvest, and makes no distinction in his directions between knights of the shire and burgesses. So, we are told, the long vacation in the courts and the universities was extended from July to October, in order that such persons as followed the pursuits of law and letters might have ample leisure for the all-important work of the harvest. It is true that the aggregate of the town population was not of much account in the mass of the rural folk, and for the purposes of the harvest. But beyond doubt the land in the immediate neighbourhood of towns was better dressed and more heavily manured than that at a distance from any considerable centre of population, and the spare hands from the town were welcome to the larger proprietors. (J. E. T. Rogers 1884, 122).

Cf. also the same author's *History of Agriculture* (J. E. T. Rogers 1866, 1:252), and Mrs. J. R. Green (1894, 171).

Chapter 10: The Origin of the Medieval City

Recently an abundance of material has also been compiled for all the lands, and it may complete the sources and depictions mentioned by me. See R. Maunier (1910, 72 ff.).

The so-called *"founded cities"* — that is, the "cities" that are suddenly called to life artificially by a sovereign or lord, as we see arising in completely consistent forms in the east of Germany, in Bohemia, in France, and in Spain from the 12th century — are no exception to this rule that all medieval cities grew slowly from villages in a development lasting centuries. One has here in particular obviously been deceived by the sign on which 'city foundation' stood, and believed that these founded cities involved "artificial settlements of traders and craftsmen"[211]. This idea is downright adventurous. It could never have arisen if one had even just for a moment placed the question (which lies in the centre of these meditations) of what such a settlement would live off? Especially in the most desolate parts of the land, for example, in the "depopulated land of the Wends"[212] where Lübeck was "founded". One puts oneself in the position of such a colony, even today, in an amply settled land — from where would they find their clientele, since nobody desires the land? One envisions the hardship an individual cobbler or baker or shopkeeper has who newly moves into a small town or a village. And think now, that was the Middle Ages! It is a terrible delusion which reigns over many of the shrewdest historians that acts of law can create life. This belief has also given occasion to the claim which we have encountered already above, that a market or even a market privilege can give rise to a city. One thinks, for example, "the market right limited to a specific weekday was unable accordingly, as it appears, to contribute in the same way as an unrestricted right to the blossoming of a commercial settlement"[213]. It is the old Prussian principle which Germany is only now about to discard — that the decree creates the life. That the merchant at first needs customers and not privileges lies outside this way of thinking. And thus the superstition also arose that, in the Middle Ages, the depopulated lands were covered with a network of cities in the economic sense (for they would surely have been "settlements of traders and craftsmen") — the so-called "founded cities" in Germany, the *villes neuves* in France, etc. And when all the sources expressly state this simultaneously, in indisputable interpretation, then the researcher cannot say anything about it other than that the authors of the "sources" were either insane or that they wanted to play a joke at the expense of the German professors of the 19th and 20th century.

Now it is, however, completely incomprehensible to me how one, with respect to the overwhelming wealth of evidence which implies the opposite, could ever even arrive on the strength of the sources at that odd view that in the 11th and 12th centuries *cities* (in the economic sense) were "founded". The sources instruct us rather, as clearly as one could only wish, that in all cases what was "founded" was only what had a point in being founded: namely villages. With the addition of a few shopkeepers and craftsmen, for all that I care. That applies even in the great majority of cases to the "founding" of a "market settlement" in connection with an already existing city, let alone then with the founding of cities in the open fields. We must imagine those "city foundings" as a sort of Roman colony with centuriated assignments — the well-known square street plan in the newly founded villages even allows the thought to arise that the Roman military colonies god-fathered the medieval "city foundings". If we do not want to assume that the square form is the natural one for regular settlements. Why only the village is divided like a chessboard according to the way of the Roman colonies, and not also the open fields (as far as we know), is something we are able to explain faultlessly with reference to the particular nature of the German plough (which also gained currency probably in southern France and Spain, where we come across the same chessboard "cities", through the German tribes; or are the open fields also divided into squares there?). The massive "square" in the middle of the village-city, which incidentally at the outset also mostly possessed an "emporium" — thus perhaps a shed for the setting down of loads, or for putting carts, etc. — was obviously laid out so large as to serve as a place for driving the cattle which, in the desolate regions in which the settlements commonly arose, had need of greater protection than elsewhere. We may assume that the stalls and barns of the farming settlers originally lay around the square, whereas the few craftsmen were established in the side roads later named after them.

Chapter 10: The Origin of the Medieval City

What then do the sources reveal, that is, the charters by means of which the rights and privileges for the settlement in a specific place were conferred to a *locator* [lessor] or to a group of settlers?

Now, in the main, they transfer to the colonists who shall "found" the new city *a large, mostly very large area of open fields with all that pertains to it*, particularly the common meadows and the common forest. That thus at least a strong group of farmers *also* settled in the "founded city" may be put beyond doubt by the sources. And that is in the main. That, however, the so-called founded cities involved essentially village-like settlements is proved by the fact that from collectively about 300 foundings known to us in eastern Germany, only about 30 have progressed above the level of a small agricultural town[214]. But these thanked their development, as is easily proven, to the presence of the city-building forces also active in other cities, of which there will be more said in the further course of this depiction.

Here are a few arbitrarily selected examples from the sources:

Lübeck (founded 1165) received from Henry the Lion, with the mark already gifted to him by Count Adolph II, "all the villages laid before the city and containing the serfs". According to Detmar's chronicle of 1165 (Der historischen Kommission bei der Königlichen Akademie der Wissenschaften 1884), cited in Pauli (1847, 10–11), which incidentally itself has Lübeck arise as a "trading colony" (!).

Stettin receives 100 + 30 holdings (Blümcke 1884, 90). The holding only amounted to 30 morgens* — a stately area of open fields! But 150, 200, even 300 holdings were also added as donations to the new "cities" (Fritz 1894, 26).

Especially instructive is the founding charter for *Frankfurt an der Oder* (issued by Margrave Johann of Brandenburg, printed in Gerken (1775, 6:563); excerpted in Klöden (1845, 1:):

1. The Margrave transfers the establishment (*constructionem*) of the city to Godinus von Herzberg.
2. The Margrave transfers to the city the property of 124 holdings of pasture and arable land, and specifies that of the 104 holdings intended for cultivation, a *vierding*† in holding payments is to be paid annually. In addition, he commands its 60 holdings on the other side

---

* [Tr.: see footnote on p. 105.]
† [Tr.: a *vierding* is a term for a coin which is a quarter of the value of a larger denomination.]

of the Oder, in so far as they are cultivated, to be likewise subject to payment. The remaining land is commons.

3. Buyers and sellers are freed from duties with small purchases; whoever brings wares *to* the city, pays duty; whoever *buys* wares with cash, pays no duty.

4. The Margrave reserves in the market hall and at the annual fairs a *pensio* of 3 pfennigs from every 'stand'. The remaining earnings from the stands in the emporium (thus probably through the letting to the hawker women) flows to the city; likewise the earnings from facilities which the city may create for the use of the market.

Thus, we are clearly confronted by the image of a village which shall develop according to the possibilities into a small agricultural town. The 164 holdings are the secure foundation; the 'market facilities' are the hopes of the future.

The clearest view in the world of the "city foundings" is provided to us, however, by the *Bohemian* charters, whose content the excellent work of Julius Lippert (1896) has disclosed to us. Bohemia under the reign of Ottokar II, as is generally known, had, by this man himself and countless lords spiritual and temporal who sought mutually to compete for the fame of being a "founder of cities", been covered with a network of German settlements which we describe as "city foundings". With *none* of these foundings, however, did the assignment lack a large area of village fields, even if the new "city" itself was attached to an already existing city. Thus is the case with Prague, Pilsen (168 holdings), Budweis (received the villages Plawen and Malšic), Glatz (60 holdings), Aussig (26 holdings), Nimburg (Neuenburg an der Elbe) (117 holdings), Melnik (72 holdings); similarly with Trübau, Landskron, Chotzen, Aupa, Trautenau, Leitmeritz, etc. Only when a village found a secure living elsewhere, as for example the inhabitants of Kolin (Köln an der Elbe) who lived off the delivery of wood to nearby Kuttenberg, could the agricultural activity be somewhat restricted. But even in these cases, the precautionary "founders" equipped the new settlers with agricultural land (Lippert 1896, 2:42 ff.).

But that now even the quite similar city foundings in *France* — the *villes neuves* of the 11th century, the "bastides" of the 13th century in southern France — as well as in *Spain* were never put into motion without the assigning of sufficiently large open fields to the settlers is proved to us likewise more than sufficiently by the newly processed sources. I refer, for Spain, to the collection of sources by P. de Bofarull y Mascaro (1851); for France, to J. Flach (1893, 2:165 ff., 325, 334, 343 ff.), to whom I also owe my awareness of the previously named source; as well as to the special investigation of A. du Bourg (1882, 250 ff.). See in particular p. 272 f. The new inhabitants of the cities even had to perform agricultural obligations for the lord! (Du Bourg 1882, 268).

If one wants to create a picture of the founding of colonial cities, one must bring to mind the process with the origin of the (old) American cities (Andrews 1894).

I will give henceforward as schematic as possible an overview of the structure and manner of development of cities in

Chapter 10: The Origin of the Medieval City

the Middle Ages, and begin with an analysis of those elements which I have described as the city builders or subjects of city formation.

II. The Subjects of City Formation

1. The Consumers

Anyone who wants to correctly understand the medieval city must above all learn to recognise that the great majority of these cities — and certainly all the significant ones — were almost purely consumption cities during the first century of their existence. So that understanding their genesis thus means comprehending how a consumption city is able to grow under the conditions offered by the Middle Ages.

I call a *consumption city* that city which does not pay for its subsistence (as far as it obtains it from without, that is, from the surplus production of agricultural work) with its own production because it does not need to. It obtains this subsistence rather on the strength of some legal title (taxes, rents, or the like) without having to provide equivalent value. "It obtains" means naturally that a number of persons obtain, and they thereby become the founders of this city. The strange quirk of the consumption city thus consists in that its founders are those consumers, its 'fillers' by contrast all work for them, and receive thereby a share in the pool of consumption. The original, primary city builders are consequently the consumers, the derived secondary (tertiary, etc.) are the producers. The consumers are in this case the independent ones, the people with their own vigour, whereas the producers are the dependents whose possibility for existence is defined by the size of the share which the consumer class will allow them from its pool of consumption. (To understand the word "dependency" correctly: naturally, everyone is fundamentally in every society dependent upon everyone if one means by it that nobody can dispense with the other without decreasing their purpose in life.)

In order that consumption cities arise, it is in particular necessary that a larger pool of consumption is amassed in one place which is sufficient for consumption there. The pool of consumption can be brought together by one (or a few) massive consumers, or by a greater number of middling or small consumers — a king can found a consumption city just as well as 1,000 pensioned generals. But now, who were these consumers in the Middle Ages? Surely for the most part rulers who lived off taxes, and lords who lived off the rents from the land. By which it is to be remarked that the boundary between ruler and lord in the sense used here was fluid — the tax-raising prince was at the same time a large estate owner, hence also obtaining revenues from his own land which were represented as land rents. A sharp division between royal estate and state property had not yet occurred.

I now see in the Middle Ages an initial group of important cities arising as *residences* of princes, both temporal and spiritual. They are those in which the lord, who everywhere forms the cell of the medieval city (for God's sake, not in the sense of constitutional law! As if I have not finally made clear that I apprehend my concepts economically to the extent that I make no special remarks on it. One should leave me in peace now, and cease with the unbearable melody over the 'royal law [*Hofrecht*] theory'!), those in which the lord (I say), who everywhere forms the cell of the medieval city, grows into the greater prince, into the ruler in the sense that he augments his revenues from ground rents with revenues from taxes. That is a long-winded process, and the formation of cities in these cases proceeds accordingly just as slowly and stepwise.

The cities which this concerns are thus the seats of bishops[215] and archbishops, of counts, dukes, margraves, princes, and kings.

The seats of temporal and spiritual lords are very commonly found in one and the same city, which thereby experiences a double preferment. Thus the bishop's cities of northern Italy were the same as the seats of the Dukes of Lombardy and later of the Frankish Counts: Vicenza, Verona, Brescia, Bergamo, Milan, Pavia, Parma, Piacenza, Modena, Mantua, Turin, and others[216]. Likewise in Germany, the "civitates" of the Carolingian period were also the seats of the regional counts [*Gaugrafen*] and the courts of the counts[217]. That the important "Palatine cities" in Germany were also bishop's seats is well known, just as of course that the great metropolises of England and France were. In Hamburg, for

Chapter 10: The Origin of the Medieval City

example, the Archbishop and the Duke of Saxony resided there in the 11th century[218]; in Florence, the Margrave of Tuscany and the Archbishop[219]; in Amsterdam, the Bishop and Lords of Amstel[220]; in Ypres, the Bishop and the Counts of Flanders[221], etc.

Often enough, one may say, where it was generally possible, in particular in the old cultural region, the norm was for the residences of the medieval princes to lie in the region of the cities that had already been inhabited by the Romans. One has drawn the conclusion from it that the significance of medieval cities was somehow defined by their Roman past. Because they had been "seats of civic life" at that time, they had now become so again. That is certainly false. The Roman cities had long lost their significance as cities, as we have already been able to establish elsewhere*, when new civic life developed in the Middle Ages often in the same places. Especially in the Roman colonial lands, the cities were nothing more than garrisons and the residences of governors. At the moment when the legions and the governors withdrew, the cities collapsed into nothing. Not the tiniest thing linked the essences of Roman and medieval cities *internally*; it is the thoughtless empty phrase of "commerce and trade" which was "preserved" in the Middle Ages. That *externally* cities also flourished in the Middle Ages in the same places where cities had stood in the Roman Empire has its foundation in two facts:

1. that the Church prescribed that the bishop's seats should be erected in "cities" (*civitates*); and
2. that the ruins, particularly the remains of the walls, offered a good foundation for the fortifications on which, as is known, one focussed one's attention with the "founding" of cities. Hence they especially came into consideration as strongholds, of which the talk will be the same.

How large the significance of the residence was for the rise of the medieval cities, we will first be able to grasp (so far as it can even be accounted for in detail) when we become acquainted with the fillers of the cities who obtained their livelihood from the revenues of the resident lords. Here I would

---

* [Tr.: see Chapter 5.]

like, however, to bring attention to two symptoms from which the outstanding significance of the princely residence for the development of cities in the Middle Ages may be decided.

That is firstly this: that flourishing cities suffered a heavy loss when, for example, the bishop's seat was removed from them[222]. Secondly, the significant fact that the size and wealth of cities frequently stands in a direct relationship to the sphere of power and dominance of the princes residing in them. In other words, the medieval cities are larger, the larger (and richer of course) the area is of which they are "capitals". Where we early on observe centralising tendencies by the princes of the land, we also first find cities of a greater scale. Where in general during the Middle Ages it does not concern the larger "realms" and "capitals of the realm", no very large cities are present either.

Hence we see large cities growing earlier in southern Italy (Palermo, Naples) than in northern Italy; in Austria (Vienna) earlier than in the rest of Germany[223]; in France (Paris) and England (London) earlier than in Flanders and Brabant. That will not astonish anyone who once realises what significant incomes the English and French kings, for example, already obtained in the Early Middle Ages. Thus the revenues of the English King shall already have amounted under Henry I (thus at the beginning of the 12th century) to 66,000 pounds, that is perhaps 5,850,000 marks in present-day (1916) currency[224]. But even the incomes of the rulers of Upper and Lower Austria who were resident in Vienna amounted in the 13th century to 35,000 Viennese pfennigs, so perhaps 100,000 marks in present-day (1916) currency[225]. When one considers that the turnover of wares of a significant Hanseatic city in the high Middle Ages amounted to 1–3 million marks in present-day (1916) currency, if one computes this entire sum to external trade, and if one assumes a (very high!) average profit of 20% from the turnover, then the total profit, which represents thus the pool from which a civic population could be nourished, would be perhaps 200,000–600,000 marks in present-day (1916) currency. One can consequently say that the solitary King of England sustained with his revenues in the year 1100 ten to thirty times as many people as Lübeck or Tallinn in the 14th century.

Chapter 10: The Origin of the Medieval City

Next to these large, royal consumers, a number of more middling and smaller drawers of ground rents who were also able to form a sizable pool for consumption joined together now in the medieval city. I am thinking firstly of all the *churches* and *monasteries* which, as one knows, to some extent disposed of quite significant incomes. If one were now to begin to write the economic history of the medieval cities, then one would have to strive to determine the amounts of these incomes. I mention for the sake of example the following:

1. St Thomas's chapter and St Peter's chapter in Strasbourg together had an income (in the 15th century) of 2,374 marks, or 33,000 marks in present-day (1916) currency[226].
2. In the year 1487, the religious establishments (parish churches, chapters, monasteries) in the St Columba church district of Cologne possessed 159 tenements which delivered a rent yield of about 2,830 marks[227] (a quarter of the total rental yield in this church district).
3. The tithe which the churches of Cologne received in the 14th century totalled around 300 marks[228], their incomes amounted thus to around 3,000 marks, that is around 150,000 marks in present-day (1916) currency (should that not still be reckoned as being too low?).

In order to be able to establish to some extent numerically the share of the spiritual lords in the building of the medieval city, one must then also be informed more precisely than we have been up to now about their number. According to what we know, we can for the time being say with certainty only so much as that this number must have been correspondingly very high. What we possess in the way of detailed information makes it indubitable[229].

In *Florence*, 80 bells were already tolling at the end of the 12th century (Davidsohn 1896b, 1:732).

Over the great number of clergymen in particular during the Middle Ages, see Lamprecht (1885, 1.2:846).

An overview of the inventory of churches and chapters in 15 *German* cities is given by A. Püschel (1910). For *Vienna*, see Anton Mayer (1897). For *Strasbourg*, K. Achtnich (1910, 6 ff.).

In the 13th century in *Paris*, the names of 96 churches and monasteries are handed down to us (in the roll of taxes from 1292). See the compilation of the editor H. Géraud in the *Collection des documents inédits de l'histoire de France* (1837, 624–26).

With regards to the monasteries especially, we know that they grew in strength with the size of the cities, were protected by their walls against predatory attacks, and placed their seat in them, particularly also as the chroniclers tell us, in order to get the bones of the saints and the relics to safety from the pillaging of enemies. Evidence for *France* in Flach (1893, 2:331). For *Germany*, W. Arnold (1854, 2:162 ff.), has with evidence established the transfer of important monasteries into the cities dealt with by him, whilst he proves that since the 13th century most monasteries have been founded at the outset in the cities. If that was also predominantly the case with the "poorer orders" — Franciscans, Dominicans, and Augustinians — then we may assume that even they possessed in most cases estates in the countryside, thus drawing rents. For example, "a St Clare or Franciscan monastery was founded in 1282 by the patrician Humbert zum Widder and his wife Elisabeth zum Jungen in Mainz. They gifted all their estates, incomes, and powers in the eleven villages of Weiterstatt, Astheim, Bubenheim, Flersheim, Nierstein, Nackenheim, Zornheim, Spiesheim, Odernheim, Partenheim, and Alsheim to the monastery [...] which soon became even more propertied by further gifts" (Arnold 1854, 2:175). According to the information in the same source, there were in the 13th century eight monasteries in Worms, ten in Mainz, six in Speyer. About the monasteries in Vienna, see H. von Voltelini (1913, 25 f.); about the abundant estates of the religious institutes of Vienna in the countryside, see the same (1913, 48 f.). The monasteries of Vienna were founded to increase the magnificence of the city, according to R. Müller (1900, 155 ff.). About the monasteries in *London*, see W. Stanhope (1887).

Next to the churches and monasteries, the *religious orders of knights* also became significant for many German cities, erecting in them their own benefices, and, with their well-known wealth, being able to draw their considerable rents into the cities and deliver them for consumption[230].

The religious rent-collectors were now joined by the secular rent-entitled. I want first to mention at least in passing one category of original city builders who are surely not entirely without significance for many cities (Bologna, Paris, Oxford) — I mean the *schoolboys*[231] and *students*[232] who drew their "stipends" from outside the city. They certainly kept themselves from their own pocket and, in addition, kept many a *caupo* [innkeeper] and many a *puella* [girl].

That the cities of the Middle Ages, the more so in the first century of their existence, were extremely rich in *temporal 'lords'*, that is, persons who resided at a court, in a castle-like dwelling, a castle, a *torre* [tower] within the city walls, and possessed property outside which they either had worked by bonded farmers under their own direction, or which they had

Chapter 10: The Origin of the Medieval City

leased, or from which they raised interest — over that surely no difference of opinion reigns. And that alone is the phenomenon whose representation occupies me here. Whereas I let it remain to be seen what origin the land ownership of these lords had, and what class character they had — whether free, ministerial, landed nobility, or city nobility. For all these distinctions are irrelevant to the question which occupies us here. Here the only fact of significance is that in the medieval cities rent-entitled persons were resident in large numbers. Unfortunately, we do not possess for any city (as far as I know) numerical determinations over the quantity and the property of the temporal lords who settled in the cities — the best investigation has probably been undertaken for Florence. And here at the beginning of the 1180s, 35 "torri" [towers], that is, castle-like dwellings of manorial families prove[233] that "the real number may have been three times as great"[234].

And these great landowning families, who were certainly very numerous in the larger cities, became now city builders on account of the sum of their rents. That is what I wanted to direct the reader's attention to since I could otherwise offer him nothing new with these findings.

Only I still want to add two things in order to animate the picture somewhat.

Firstly, when drawers of ground rents, who lived in the city, were city builders (of which nobody who has read my explanations may doubt anymore), then it is obvious that a city will be larger and richer, the higher the ground rents which arrive in it for consumption. Thus, it will be larger and richer, the more the individual rent-collectors obtain in revenues, or the more rent-collectors conglomerate in the city.

In other words, the level of the rural ground rents which were consumed in the city depended on the power of attraction which a city was capable of exercising on the large landowners in the countryside on the one hand, and, on the other hand, on the fertility of the areas which were in the power of disposition of the original civic or later urbanised landowner. One must take note, more than has occurred up to now, that for the development of cities in the Middle Ages (for the reasons mentioned), their so-called trade situation was far less of a determinant than the fertility and density of population of their countryside. Here lay the head start which nature had already provided for Italy and Flanders; for the countrysides of these were already likened to a luscious, well-tended garden early in the Middle Ages. One must read the descriptions of the Flemish countryside in the *Phillipide*[*] to get the correct understanding of the early blossoming of the cities of the lower Rhine. One must also note, for example, that the Flemish coastal cities like Nieuport, Ardenburg, Dam, and even Bruges arrived at affluence much later than the inland cities like Ypres and Ghent. But of course the prerequisite for the utilisation of those favourable natural conditions was that the excess production of the countryside could be consumed in the city, and for that the inclusion of the lords within the ambit of the civic population was required. But this took place in various lands to quite different extents. Why will not be discussed here. One will be allowed to assume that the influence of the Roman, predominantly civic culture exercised an essentially determining influence. For that reason probably, there was in Italy[235] a strong tendency in the landed nobility for voluntary urbanisation, and a stronger concentration of large rural landowners in the cities everywhere outside Italy where the Roman Empire had left behind its traces — stronger in the Rhenish and southern regions of Germany than in the inhospitable lands of colonisation in the north and east. But it may also have been helped decisively by other circumstances. Thus, in England, a specific arrangement of constitutional life like the law of succession brought about early on a propulsion of the younger sons of the high nobility into the cities, as well as a fusion of the gentry with the bourgeoisie. In Italy, the confining of the landed nobility in the cities by force played a large role[236]; in Flanders and Brabant, the development was similar[237].

In the same period in which the Italian communes ensured the agglomeration of many rent pools in their walls through the *inurbamento*, the German cities threw the nobility out the gates.

---

[*]   [Tr.: not footnoted by Sombart. Most likely a reference to Guillaume le Breton (1841).]

Chapter 10: The Origin of the Medieval City

The municipal laws of Freiburg, Hamburg (1120), and other cities forbade the nobility from residing in the city — the municipal law of Freiburg specifies "nullus de hominibus vel ministerialibus ducis vel miles aliquis in civitate habitabit" [none of the people or officials of the duke or any soldier will reside in the city] — at the same time as the mighty Genoa had sworn in the Margrave Alderamo (1135), the Counts of Lavagna (1138), and other greats of the countryside — "ero habitator Janue per me vel per filium meum et tenebor adimplere sacramentum compagne" [I will be resident in Genoa by myself or with my son, and I will be bound to perform a sacrament in common] — and at the same time as a small city, like Treviso, during one year (1200) numbered over 60 landed, in part powerful and rich gentry who had acquired civic rights[238].

One would almost like to say that it is no wonder that with these dissimilarly configured politics, Freiburg became Freiburg, and Genoa became Genoa. In any case, no doubt may exist that, when the larger or smaller agglomeration of the large landowning class comes very much into consideration as a strongly determining factor in the development of the city, a great part of the differentiation which the history of the cities also displays to us here is to be traced back to the different arrangement of the circumstances which now engage us. This simple realisation had also already been obtained by the observers in the 16th century: "pleraeque Italiae urbes augustiores et majores sunt urbibus Galliae aut reliquae Europae idque quoniam nobiles Italiae urbes inhabitant" [most of the Italian cities are more stately and larger than the cities of Gaul or the rest of Europe, and this is because the nobles of Italy reside in the cities] is said by the best theorist of the city to date[239]. These days, one no longer sees such simple connections.

The second comment which I wanted to make over this point about the formation of cities through the agglomeration of land rents is the following.

There must have been in the Middle Ages a period — I think it is in the 10th and 11th centuries especially — in which a *sudden* agglomeration of rural estate owners took place at separate places. These places are the fortified, or about to be fortified places, or places designated as points of defence, thus as *fortresses*; and the obtainers of land rents, and thus the city builders coalescing at these points in greater numbers, are the *milites* [soldiers], are the garrison of defenders whom one pulled in for the defence of those places which were soon to develop into cities. They became, as far as I can tell, an important factor in the origin of the city. For they all of a sudden obtained a larger scope of livelihood for numerous folk. So that one could also say that the medieval city (not only in a fortification-architecture conception, but also — and directly — in an economic conception) in many ways grew as a fortress city, more correctly as a garrison city, for the walls and the castle did not nourish its population, but the *milites* who lay in the castle and pulled in the pool for consumption did. For the *castrenses* [military], the *castellani* [lords of the castles], and the *milites* were of course men owing fealty to some estate — the castle fiefs — and who thus brought the rents of these estates for consumption into the city where they were garrisoned.

A very illustrative depiction of the economic position of the *miles* is given by "Widukindi Res Gestae Saxonicae" in MGH SS (Vol. 3, § 35, 432).

The controversy tied up with this position is whether the *milites agrarii* [farming soldiers] were militarily obligated farmers or servants of the king. See D. Schäfer (1905), and compare with H. Delbrück (1907, 3:93 f.). Irrelevant for the connections highlighted here is page 109 f. The main thing is that "ceteri [...] octo seminarent et meterent frugesque colligerent nono et suis eas locis reconderent" [eight men sowed and reaped, and the ninth gathered the crops, they stored them at their place] (Delbrück 1907, 3:109).

Up to now in the general economic history of the medieval city, the city is treated as a garrison only incidentally, and also mostly from the point of view of constitutional history or topography.

I refer for the time being to the following writings in which the constitutional law, fortification, etc. sides of the problem of the medieval fortress are highlighted.

Germany: Inama-Sternegg (1879, 2:99 ff.); E. von Loeffler (1881); S. Schwarz (1892); G. Köhler (1893); W. Varges (1893, 163 ff.); S. Rietschel *(1905)*; C. Kissel (1907). In addition, the general works can of course be consulted, in particular the enormous collection of material by von Maurer.

For *Bohemia* especially, see J. Lippert (1896, 2:169). All Bohemian cities of significance were regional fortresses [*Gauburgen*].

For *England*, Maitland (1907, Essay I, § 9, 172-219) gives an account of a quite similar structure to that which Germany possessed in its castle charters. The strongest fortress in the land was London. In it, the garrison also played a salient role in constitutional history (as indeed was usual in most larger cities everywhere). When the Confessor sent a letter to London, he addressed it to the Bishop, the Portreeve, and the *burh-thegns* (those are thus precisely the three salient city builders!) (Maitland 1907, 191 n.1). The Lord Mayor of London is called in the oldest Anglo-Saxon sources *wiegerêfa* [commander of the town].

France in general is dealt with in Flach (1893, 2:79, 330 ff.); Champagne in particular by Réné Bourgeois (1904). The same structure as in England and Germany: "Le domaine propre [i.e.. du comté de Champagne] était [...] divisé en Châtellenies ou Prévôtés qui avaient chacune pour chef-lieu le principal centre de population, poiut spécialement fortifié, où se trouvait une forteresse qualifiée de château à l'exclusion des autres forteresses du même district. Les Prévôtés des comtes de Champagne étaient en 1152 au nombre de vingt-huit, dont les chefs-lieux sont aujourd'hui situés dans six départements" [The proper domain [i.e. of the Counts of Champagne] was divided into castellanies or provosts, each of which had its principal centre of population, specially fortified, where there was a fortress known as a castle to the exclusion of other fortresses of the same district. The provosts of the counts of Champagne numbered, in 1152, twenty-eight whose chief places are now situated in six departments], and see the lists that follow (Bourgeois 1904, 19).

For *Belgium*, see, for example, A. Wauters (1878, 209). All Belgian (large) cities were garrisons from the 10th century: Cambrai, Utrecht, Liege, Brussels, etc. (Pirenne 1905).

For *Italy*, the works of regional history are to be referred to. We are naturally best informed about Tuscany and Florence — the city was like "a large and populous castle which stood to the surrounding district in a very similar relationship as the individual castles stood to their boroughs" (Davidsohn 1896b, 1:331). But Gregorovius (1859) also contains much material.

2. The Producers

A city is barely conceivable in which a part of the population does not preserve itself and others by manufacturing or commercial activity, that is thus (as we know from the previous chapter) that it procures for itself the means of subsistence through exchange of its own output externally. Even in the Middle Ages, these ingredients were never completely missing from a city. It is time that we recall these ingredients, and learn to comprehend them one after the other in their particular natures.

The work of the cities for the surrounding countryside will be mentioned here first. That is, the production of manufactured objects for the farmers, and the delivery of foreign imported articles to them. We call a city whose inhabitants lived predominantly from this traffic with the surrounding countryside a country city, also a marketplace. In the Middle Ages, this type of city will have existed doubtlessly to an even greater extent than today; it will have been the spots of 500 to 1,000 inhabitants in which in addition strong agriculture was practised like today, and which thus remained lifelong small agricultural towns. These were the vast majority of those 270 "founded cities" in the east of Germany, for example, of which we have already learnt. Even in the large cities, those thus of which we especially think when we speak of cities, an *exchange with the farmers* (and still more with the lords) *of the surrounding area* took place, and a part of the population (craftsmen and shopkeepers) will have lived off it. One must not imagine though that these sales to the countryside were overly extensive — the economy of self-sufficiency was still distributed too strongly, and the state of culture of the rural population was not high enough. One must not think perhaps that this exchange between country and city would have formed the lifeblood of the medieval city. There can be no talk of the farmers purchasing, perhaps with the amount which they received for selling their products at the weekly markets to the townsfolk, of them now purchasing manufactured and foreign products. Rather the greater part of the cash receipts probably wandered into the pockets of the lords in the country and city, and *these* purchased from the cities' craftsmen and traders their wares with the money from the obligated payments (or the receipts from selling the natural produce delivered to them). And so, when they lived in the city, the lords lived off them and not off themselves.

The *international trade* may have had somewhat greater significance for some of the medieval cities. But one must also not have exaggerated ideas of its city-forming power.

The trading city has the idiosyncrasy economically that it draws its livelihood in small sums from a very wide circle[240]. And this idiosyncrasy of its existence places narrow bounds on the expansion of the pure trading city. There have never been quite large, purely trading cities, and there cannot be, for either the transport technology is still so little developed that the expansion of trade can only be a tiny one[241], or instead, with more developed transport technology, the rate of

Chapter 10: The Origin of the Medieval City

profit of trade is correspondingly so low that quite enormous quantities of goods must be turned over to leave behind an appreciable amount of value in the hands of the merchants as profit and thereby sufficient material for the sustenance of the city's population. The lay person — and most "theorists" who have written about the formation of cities are lay persons in terms of economics — does not tend to get straight in his own mind that not even a sparrow in the city can live from the stream of goods which passes through that city, it is as though the bird pecks its food out of the grain or pea sacks. What it comes down to alone is surely the amount of value in whose respect the merchants acquired a right by their moving the goods through their city, it is that "which is caught", which is "earned", it is the trading *profit* in one word, and it tends as is generally known to stand in reverse proportion to the amount of value traded. When it is relatively high (as in the Middle Ages), then the turnover is low. And how small it was in the Middle Ages, we will yet see. Thus even in the trading metropolises, only ever a small part of the population could have lived from "trade". If we assume an average income of only 100 marks in present-day (1916) currency for the Lübeck of the 14th century, and a rate of profit of 20% of the turnover (!), the trade even in Lübeck would only have sustained perhaps 6,000 people[242].

The production for export remains to be mentioned as a factor in the formation of cities. So far as it comes into consideration, it allows the development of the norm of the *industrial city*. And it certainly also already existed in the Middle Ages, doubtlessly also on the basis of a manufacturing production in the narrow sense (that is, of the finishing of material). Here cities which produced a manufactured specialty will certainly have been able to sustain with this a few hundred people, in a few cases thousands — Milan with weapons, Nuremberg with its "Nuremberg ware", Constance with its fabric, Florence with its cloth. But those are all just exceptions. And the development of these industries fell mostly in the later period of the Middle Ages, so that they barely come into consideration for the first development and expansion of the city.

Specific products of the land (or sea) which the city lay alongside acquired importance for the beginnings of the city's existence earlier on. I am thinking of the salt cities[243], the (silver) mining cities, the wine cities, and the herring cities. But I must again warn about overrating the city-forming power even of these sources of income.

Let us look at one of the first and most significant mining cities of the Middle Ages, the silver city of Freiberg in Saxony.

It began to develop around 1185. And indeed rapidly, as is understandable. "The same causes which in our time allowed the mining districts of California to develop populous cities overnight, also united settlers from all regions in the valley of the Münzbach stream; the new settlement grew thence very quickly, and had soon reached the size which it would then preserve for centuries."[244] And the result? In the year 1259, Henry the Illustrious* ceded the "fimum qui colligitur in foro" [the collection of any dung in the market] to the benefit of the hospital, from which we can conclude, firstly, "that his wealth was not tiny", and secondly, that the city cattle camped at night in the market. (Certainly it could also be conceivable that the dung originated from the cattle driven up for slaughter?) Admittedly, Freiberg became in the course of the Middle Ages the *largest* city in Saxony. But what does that mean? It had 379 house plots and consequently at most 4,500–5,000 inhabitants[245]. Thus the mining of this first silver city of Germany was never itself of overly strong impact.

Only one factor, as far as I can see, played a considerable role with the development of medieval cities alongside the accumulation of land rents. It is the *money dealing*, the banking business or usury, as one may decide in the individual cases. Of it and its significance, I will advise in yet more detail in the further course of this depiction. Here I only want to point out that the instinctively correct valuation of usury as a factor in forming cities surely itself explains the effort of some civic lords, who were concerned for the prosperity of their cities, to induce Jews to join the settlements. Thus Bishop Rüdiger says in the opening of the Speyer privileges from the year 1084: "cum ex Spirensi villa urbem facerem, putavi milies

---

* [Tr.: Henry III, Margrave of Meissen.]

Chapter 10: The Origin of the Medieval City

amplificare honorem loci nostri, si Iudeos colligerem" [when I made my house outside the city of Speyer, I thought it would enlarge the honour of our place a thousand times if ever Jews gathered there][246]. Nevertheless even the money dealing will have had a substantive influence on the population count for only a few large cities, and will have taken a backseat in most cities behind the city-forming power of the direct obtaining of land rents by the civic lords. How superior the latter's significance for the medieval city must have been is shown by the few indications which I have made in the previous pages. This impression of its preponderance is strengthened when we examine some of the larger cities of the Middle Ages for their economic character. We find then that pure "industrial cities" (like Freiberg) remained quite small, but that in every city of over 10,000 inhabitants an agglomeration of massive consumers took place. Whether it be Venice or Florence, Genoa or Milan, Basel or Strasbourg, Nuremberg or Augsburg, Lübeck or Hamburg, Bruges or Ghent, Ypres or Liège, Paris or London, Vienna or Prague, we always encounter in these cities one or several resident princes, kings, margraves, dukes, archbishops, bishops, etc.; an overwhelming crowd of religious institutions; and a very large number of temporal lords. Certainly, the share which these elements had in the formation of the cities cannot be verified quantitatively, but that they were the salient, determinant city builders is extraordinarily probable:

1. on the grounds of a general consideration of the facts;
2. by the afore mentioned fact that they were not absent in any significant city of the Middle Ages;
3. by the observation that where they were found together, every time a larger city also arose; and
4. by the other observation that where they were absent, an eminent city never arose in the Middle Ages.

But if someone would still like, despite all that, to doubt the correctness of my thesis that the medieval city was especially, and at least in the first period of its existence, a consumption city, and thus had the mass of land rents (and taxes) accumulated in one place to thank for its development, then he will, I believe, be freed of his doubt when he views the objects of city formation in the Middle Ages, those secondary, tertiary, etc., and so derivative city builders who, quite strictly speaking, first filled the cities. The talk shall from now be of them.

III. The Objects of City Formation

I divide the fillers of cities into two groups, direct and indirect breadwinners. The direct breadwinners are those who are in the service of the city builders, and are paid for services which they provide them, thus are maintained by them — here belong the domestics in the widest sense; the courtiers, but also the officials of the king or the bishop; finally also the entire clergy: priests, monks, etc. Indirect breadwinners are the independent craftsmen and traders who make manufactured products for the city builders or obtain goods from foreigners.

Unfortunately, as far as I know, there is again a lack of a somehow usable overview of the numerical extent of these different groups of the medieval population, for even the exceedingly valuable counts which Bücher has made for Frankfurt am Main still provide no solid clue, quite apart from Frankfurt not giving a typical picture of the larger medieval city (about which we are first and foremost preoccupied), as well as the late period to which Bücher's findings apply not being authoritative anymore for the origin of the medieval city, which is what we are occupied with here.

Since I lack the inclination and leisure for the investigations which are necessary here to form a statistical and sufficiently solid judgment over the share of individual social groups of the medieval city in its overall size, but especially to establish how many fillers of cities, in particular the indirect breadwinners, obtained their livelihood from this or that category of original city builders (I do not doubt for a moment on the basis of my own studies that these investigations are feasible), the following explanations are only a sort of outline, a basic design, a guidepost to be considered as hints for future research (just as my statements over the origin of civic wealth in the first edition of this work fell on such fertile soil).

Chapter 10: The Origin of the Medieval City

1. *The Clergy*

The chronicler reports to us that "Eo tempore [...] Unwanus archiepiscopus metropolem Hammaburg renovavit, clerumque dispersum colligens, magnam ibidem tam civium quam fratrum adunavit multitudinem" [At the time that [...] Unwanus, Archbishop of the city of Hamburg, renewed the dispersal of gathered clergy, in the same place as large a number of brothers had assembled as townsfolk][247]. And that will be hardly exaggerated, at least with what concerned the brothers. For the impression which we receive from every description of a medieval city is that it must have been black with frocks and cassocks. One only has to envisage that the greatest share of the churches and monasteries which we encounter in the large cities today already existed in the Middle Ages when the city comprised perhaps the tenth part of its present-day area. One must walk perhaps on a Sunday in the cathedral quarters of old, Catholic cities, when the priests cross the street in mobs, when a priestly vestment disappears into every house, to create an approximate idea of the everyday appearance of a medieval city in which a bishop or archbishop has his seat. The sources instruct us also that in some cities, for example Passau, the old city was inhabited exclusively by the bishopric or monastic community, whilst the free inhabitants were only resident in the suburbs[248].

Who were they all then! First the priors, the canons, the *clergé primaire* — the cathedral chapter, the provosts and deacons of the cities chapters, the abbots of the respectable monasteries, etc. But then also the entire mob of lower clergy, the domestics etc., the *vicarii* [vicars], *mansionarii* [sextons], *portionarii* [portioners], *capellani* [chaplains], in short everyone who did not belong to the chapter, but were employed instead primarily for the choir service and for the performance of other religious functions.

We possess at least a few figures to be able to create for ourselves an idea of the large *number of the religious population*. Certainly the statistics mostly concern only the higher clergy and the later Middle Ages. But even these numbers are valuable because they provide us with a clue for estimating accordingly the number of total clergy, at least approximately.

The tallies for the positions of the members of the cathedral chapters are known to us from a later period[249]. Thus, for example, each cathedral chapter had:

Würzburg:	24 "domini" (members)	28 "domicelli" (younger members)	= 52
Mainz:	24	17	= 41
Cologne:	23	16	= 39
Bamberg:	20	14	= 34
Trier:	16	24	= 40
Speyer:	15	12	= 27

That was only for the higher clergy of the cathedral chapter — the chapters of the collegial chapters then show similar numbers.

In Strasbourg in the 15th century, 116 prebendaries and chaplaincies existed at the cathedral for the lower clergy, 26 at St Thomas's, 31 at St Peter's[250]. According to the estimates of Kothe[251], there were in Strasbourg in the 14th century 343 male clergy and 626 nuns and beguins [*Beghinen*]; thus perhaps 1,000 persons — that will have been easily a twentieth of the total population. The Strasbourg diocese had towards the end of the 13th century over 800 non-cloistered priests, not counting the numerous monks[252]. The number of chapter members in the cathedral chapter in Liège amounted in the 13th century to 60[253]. According to the census of 1449 in Nuremberg, which at the time had around 20,000 inhabitants, the pastoral and monastic clergy "together with their servants" totalled up to 446 persons, whereas Bücher calculates for Frankfurt at the end of the 15th century, for a population half as large, a head count in the religious households of the city of 390–450[254], which was about 5% of its total population at the end of the Middle Ages. In the imperial city of Ulm, there were at the beginning of the 16th century 93 benefices[255]. Münster in Westphalia had (towards the end of the 16th century) 213 monastic inhabitants and 373 non-cloistered clergy with appendages, thus 596 clergy next to 10,600 inhabitants[256].

An interesting statistic of the clergy in the Middle Ages, the most encompassing and most precisely detailed of those known to me, is shared by W. Stubbs in his constitutional history for a few English cities[257]. According to it, the number of ordained persons numbered:

In the city of:	acolytes	subdeacons	deacons	priests	total
Cirencester (1314)	105	140	133	85	463
Worcester (1314)	50	115	136	109	310
Cambden (1331)	221	100	47	51	419
Worcester (1337)	391	180	154	124	849

They are quite imposing figures which, however, apply only to small and middling cities, and thus permit an inference of the impressive army of clergy in the larger bishop's cities. That these in fact filled up a not inconsiderable part of the city by themselves may not be doubted according to all that we know and are able to conclude.

The clergy now retained though on the other hand a number of servants. After the dissolution of the *vita communis*, as we have already seen, every member of the chapter moved into his own house, his *curia*. The possession of one's own house, however, gave cause for more domestics. We encounter in the sources the diverse types of servants which were in the service of the prelates: cooks, key custodians, cellar masters (*serviens cellarii*), etc.[258]

In addition to that, the lower officials and servants of the chapter remained themselves in force: the *ecclesiastici*, *subsacristae* [sacristan's assistants], *camerarii* [chamberlains], and *scutellarii* [storeman?]; the gatekeepers, *pulsatores campanarum* [bell-ringers], *portitores aquae* [water carriers], etc. In the Halberstadt cathedral chapter[259], 3 *ecclesiastici*, 1 *subsacrista*, 4 *camerarii*, and 1 *scutellarius* are mentioned; of the lower domestic charges, at most 12, in one case 24.

2. Soldiers and Officials

We are even less well informed about the size of these categories of secondary city builders.

That the number of '*scutarii*' [guards] was not very small, we may at least assume with certainty for the larger cities. Rietschel assumes that the 1,000 shields which the Magdeburg castle commander had at his disposal[260] possible represented the garrison[261]. That would be quite enormous. That would already be a sight like perhaps Potsdam and Metz offer today, where one stumbles over the military people. But that in any case the castle commanders had a "strong troop of soldiers" at their disposal is certain[262]. Otherwise, for example, a fight, as occasionally arose between the common people and the military people, would not have caused such a scandal — such a *clamor ingens* [unnatural clamour] — in a city like Strasbourg that they tolled the bells of the city[263].

And the *civil service*? Did they not also represent a considerable body? They were essentially formed of the ministeriales*. Von Below, to whom these people have provided so much grief already, would like most of all to banish them from the cities. "Most cities exhibit within their walls barely one ministerialis", he suggests[264] in his fury against the Lex familiae [*Hofrecht*] theorists. That probably goes — even viewed from a purely "constitutional history" perspective — a little too far. But that *officials* of the temporal and spiritual princes lived in the royal cities, and that they might now have had the class character which they wanted, von Below will also not want to deny. Where else but in the adjacent surrounds of their lord would the numerous dignitaries have resided of whom the sources tell us?[265] Thus, there will have been a quite stately staff of courtiers and "civil servants" in the medieval city[266]. We are, admittedly, even less than with the clergy, unable to say definitively how many there were.

3. The Craftsmen

We need not doubt that among the craftsmen, who later accounted for such a large component of the civic population, there were from the beginning such as who put their labour at the disposal of the farmers in the village-like cities just as it had been done earlier in the villages, or who turned their products to account in the surrounding areas of the city, or even went with them to distant fairs and markets, thus (in summary) that among the craftsmen in the medieval city, original city builders were present from the beginning. Perhaps those wandering craftsmen, or those whom we saw already

---

* [Tr.: *Ministeriales* were feudal administrators who were gradually assimilated into the nobility.]

Chapter 10: The Origin of the Medieval City

travelling to Worms in the 11th century, belong to this category of manufacturing producers.

But that they accounted for only a small part of the civic craftsmen, particularly in the first centuries of civic development, that they hence carry only a tiny weight for this itself, seems to me to be certain with respect to the overall character of the early times of the cities. I mean that not only general considerations, but also the few sources which give us some information about the first phases of craftwork, lead us to the assumption that the majority of craftsmen formed a group around the lords resident in the city; that they received commissions from the latter; that they thanked the latter alone for the possibility of living as free citizens.

This issue manifests itself especially clearly where the estate owner founding the cities is a solitary monastery; at least we can distinguish here a few especially lively descriptions from the sources. But the course of events was essentially the same everywhere, just as it is handed down to us for Bury St Edmunds in England, for the abbey of Tiron in France, and for Zweifalten in Germany — where we can follow precisely how a number of craftsmen settled around the monastery so as to work for it.

Domesday informs us about the origin of Bury St Edmunds in the following way:

> In the city where St Edmund is buried, the Abbot Balduin kept at the time of King Edward 118 men to provide for the monks' necessities of life. The city was previously worth 10 marks*, now 20. Now the city encompasses a larger area of land, which at the time [the time of King Edward] was still ploughed and sown. Located there in total are: 30 priests, deacons, and clerics; 28 nuns and poor brothers. The craftsmen number 75: bakers, brewers, fullers, shoemakers, tailors, cooks, doormen, servants, and these all serve the abbot and the religious brothers. Now 342 residences stand there on the ground of St Edmund where at the time of King Edward it was still agricultural land.

This description could with small adjustments (instead of abbot, put bishop, king, margrave, knight or the like) be repeated for all medieval city foundings.

---

* [Tr.: a mark was a former English unit of currency worth 13 shillings and four pence.]

Furthermore, we do not want to forget that in the socage form of economic organisation, a number of manufacturing workers had already been active in the service of the lord, and were now indeed properly "independent" producers, but economically their existence derived from the manorial/monastic estate just as before.

In particular, however, this consideration seems to me to affirm my conception that the *nature* of most specifically civic craftsmen, even in the early times of cities, allows only the contemplation of an employment under the authority of the civic lords. All that was produced beyond the scantiest thing (and where the now developing civic craftsmen were active directly in its production) could only be paid for by the lords. Sure enough also by those who resided in the countryside. And to the extent that the sales took place to the latter, the craftsman was an original city builder.

But we must not forget though that (the more so in Italy and the Netherlands, but frequently also in the other lands) precisely the most important and richest lords — in particular the spiritual and temporal princes, almost all affluent churches, etc. — had their seats in the cities. Only the knights often sat outside the city in a lonely castle in the countryside. And their demand for manufactured products could quite certainly be discarded in comparison with the demand from the orders of all the lords and sovereigns in the city itself.

We can now, however, prove conclusively for one branch of commerce which was especially important for the development of civic craftwork that it could only have unfolded in the shadow of the manorial/monastic estate. I mean the building trade.

Engaging in building and founding cities were, for the times when the cities first boomed meaningfully, almost identical concepts: "Magadaburgensem aedificare cepit civitatem [...] Nam urbem hanc [...] et acquisivit atque construxit" [They began building the city of Magdeburg [...] Thus this city [...] they acquired and built.][267].

The walls were now admittedly probably often enough erected by the surrounding farmers who had the obligation of performing this work[268]. But permanent workers were surely also thereby enlisted[269]. And when it now applied to building

Chapter 10: The Origin of the Medieval City

within the walls, then in any case free craftsmen must have been called for: "Acquiescente abbate, circumquaque invitati sunt artifices et cimentarii, cesores lapidum et alii operarii"[For the resting Abbot, carpenters and builders, masons and other workers were invited from all around][270]. They were certainly well-paid workers for whom now again a number of bakers, butchers, cobblers, tailors, etc. must have been active in contesting for their livelihood.

But now, who was building in the cities of the 10th, 11th, and 12th centuries? Building in such a way that they needed that staff of learned construction workers? Yet none other than the lords; among them particularly the churches. Church building was one of the most important processes for agglomerating population, that is, for forming cities, in the Early Middle Ages.

If we see the 11th century precisely as that in which the cities developed the most rapidly, then that is quite certainly not in the least part thanks to the circumstance that in this century almost all of the larger cities developed a buoyant construction sector, first and foremost naturally for the erection of monumental religious buildings. It would be going too far — and is not necessary either, since we possess a series of proficient works which spread a bright light over these processes[271] — to verify in what salient quantities church building was fostered everywhere in the 11th century.

The 11th century is also the period in which, in many cities, powerful, active, and often enough splendour-loving princes of the Church led the regiment to whom demonstrably we are especially to thank for the constructional growth of the city. I name at random Adalbert of Utrecht, Notger of Liège, Poppo of Trier, Hildebrand of Florenz, Adalbert, Bezelin of Bremen, Godohard of Hildesheim, Meinwerk of Paderborn, Aribo of Mainz, Pilgrim, Hermann of Cologne, Arnulf of Halberstadt, Werner, Wilhelm of Strasbourg, Burchhard of Worms, and Benno of Osnabrück. These and the others of their type are the fathers of civic craftwork.

What was found in the way of stately buildings even in a city like Paris in the 14th century was, apart from the public buildings, the palaces of the lords. "What large and beautiful hotels there are in Paris", Jean de Jeandun cries out, describing Paris at the beginning of the 14th century, "Some belong to the King, the counts, the dukes, the knights and other barons, others to the prelates. All are large, well built, beautiful and magnificent. By themselves alone, and apart from the remaining houses, they could form a wonderful city"[272].

4. The Traders

The birth of the traders, the *negotiatores*, emerges from the lap of the manorial/monastic estates even more clearly than the craftsmen.

The present "reigning" conventional opinion is admittedly a different one. According to it, the "merchants" shall have in fact actually been the "founders" of the medieval cities, and the latter shall have in fact actually developed from "market settlements". I have already expressed my objections to this "theory", and would like to add here a few more remarks to those made earlier, from which shall arise the reason why I hold to be erroneous this explanation of cities arising from markets.

Have, as I would like to ask first, the representatives of that view ever conceived what significance a "market" *can* have, from the viewpoint of settlement history, for the agglomeration of masses of people at one point in particular?

Whether annual fair, monthly market, or weekly market, it is all the same. The bare fact that at one point a market is held — that is, that people are periodically present there who buy and sell — does not give a single person the opportunity to settle where the market takes place. At the moment in which the market stalls are dismantled and the market visitors move away, the place is again made desolate. A periodic market at which buyers and sellers from all lands unite is really a hindrance for the development of a lasting settlement like that which a city portrays. One could thus say with greater justice that a city arose where one stopped holding markets, arose *because* one stopped plying market-like trade at one point, *because* the traders became settled and now consumed the profits from trade more than before in one place. That is, however, overly sharpening the formulation of the idea and exaggerating to the other side. A kernel of truth is hidden in the "theory of market rights" (also from the economic viewpoint), and I will strip it out forthwith. For the present, I want only to show that, in the way it is usually represented, it stands all the real relationships on their head.

To place in view the real progression of the thing as faithfully as possible, we will do well to bring to mind quite clearly once more the state and conditions of existence of trade in the period of self-sufficiency, so as to be able to then trace from there the further development up to the city.

Thus, in the 8th and 9th centuries, the peddling, which had naturally formed the first stage in the development of trade, passed quite rapidly into the *market trade*. The conferring of market privileges which was quite common in this period is suggestive of that[273].

How must we now imagine the existence of the traders who from then on moved to the markets, instead of from villa to villa?

If they were resident abroad, then they surely constantly went for a specific part of the year on the journey and visited in sequence several neighbouring marketplaces in a row, to then return after three or four months to their distant homes. If the traders were from not so distant lands, then they may surely have visited the market from the village in which they lived, and returned home afterwards, where they probably then took up the agricultural work again which had been seen to by the wife and children in their absence. For they surely did not move around the markets? The traders thus had their hearths at various points, and came together only at specific times into caravans[274] to obtain mutual protection during the crossing of desolate lands from market to market. In the same way that storks gather into long phalanxes when they strike off for their homeland. For when the market journey was at an end, one said farewell at the crossroads, and parted with a "Until we meet again next spring!"

At the marketplaces thus, the traders met, arriving individually or in caravans. How they dwelt here for the few days which the market lasted, we can trace quite precisely with the aid of the sources.

They held their wares for sale in market stalls (*stationes*), of which occasionally several were incorporated in a sort of covered market[275] in which the merchants then obtained individual stands. The market stalls or covered market were erected by the lords, and hired out for the time of the market to the traders[276]. Frequently the bonded farmers were obligated with the erection of the market stalls[277], when the market did not take place between the houses of the farmers themselves. It was in particular (we learn of England)[278] the custom here and there that the farmers had to give up their houses for the period of the market for the storing of the wares.

The market stalls of course stood *before* the gates of the castle, monastery, etc.[279]

In addition to for their own lodging for the night, one probably also erected sheds and stalls for the traders' carts and mules, or they themselves erected larger buildings[280] in the manner of the caravanserais which we encounter even today in areas of extensive trade. (From them developed surely then the Hanseatic trade offices [*Stahlhöfe*], the *fondaci* [warehouses], etc.)

As long as the traders lived in this way, they do not of course come into consideration as either fillers of cities or founders of cities. No more than the 200,000 Kirghiz and Afghans who offered their wares for sale during the months of July and August in the 6,500 stalls in Nizhny Novgorod would thereby form the city of Nizhny Novgorod.

The decisive step, that is, the one significant for the history of cities, was first taken at the moment when the market visitors decided one beautiful day not to move on anymore, but rather to offer their wares constantly at their *stationes*, to get their wives and children to join them, and to build themselves a little house behind the stall. Thus the *statio* [station, outpost] grew in time to a *mansio* [home] — a process which we can follow distinctly in the buildings of many cities[281]. It thus became significant that the traders A, B, C, who had been domiciled in the villages X, Y, Z and had regularly frequented the market in M, now moved from X, Y, Z to M as their permanent residence. Or perhaps, later, moving from M, where they did not cover their costs as they had hoped, to N[282]. That then gave filling for the cities developing in M or N which had thus stopped being just marketplaces for our friends A, B, C, and became their place of residence.

Chapter 10: The Origin of the Medieval City

And now the writer of the history of the existence of medieval cities would see himself placed before the main part of his task. He must namely attempt to conduct the verification of *why* the permanent settlement resulted, and why it resulted *here* and not elsewhere. We are for the time being reliant on conjectures or more correctly on the not entirely to be disesteemed "wellspring" of our rational consideration. That some "market privileges" prompted our small trader to build himself and his family a little house behind the market stall may be correct here and there. It will usually not have been the reason for his decision. For he enjoys his most valuable privileges — the market peace [*Marktfrieden*], personal rights, etc. — precisely as a market visitor, which is why he does not need to settle in London permanently. And *privilegium* here, *privilegium* there. As long as he found no buyers for his wares, the most wonderful *privilegium* was of no use to him. In particular, the most wonderful *privilegium* could nonetheless heave no customers from the soil. And *these* — as it shall often be repeated — were surely even in the 11th century already the merchant's only interest. When he had them, he did at a push without *privilegium*; when he did not, all the King's letters were of no use to him[283].

Why thus did he decide to erect his residence permanently in the place which he had up to then only visited in passing? Obviously because he said to himself that here in London, in Bruges, in Strasbourg, there are now so many consistent takers of his wares that he can risk opening up his shop for a greater part of the year than before in this one place (he will have offered his stuff somewhere else for another part of the year just like before). Or he told himself, thus, that he can earn with the sales to the locals just as much as when he wandered about ten places to all the fairs and markets. Perhaps he will sell somewhat less in it, but he thinks he will save appreciably in expenses. He also obtains time which he can dedicate to the care of his small property, which was entirely neglected before by his absence.

Theoretically formulating what the small trader has just reasoned, the settling of the *negotiatores*, and thus the development of a "market settlement", became possible when the agglomeration of consumers in one place had reached a correspondingly high degree.

When it had reached that, and *by what way* it could only have arrived at it (in the great majority of cases) in the Middle Ages, we know as being by the accumulation of a sufficiently large pool for consumption from taxes and rents. In other words, the *negotiatores* formed a market settlement in one place, and thereby helped that place create a civic appearance more rapidly, because at that place as many estate owners were already now resident as had been at ten different places previously.

Whereas a small tailor previously needed to haul around six fairs the six pieces of Flemish cloth which comprised his annual turnover, and sold at each and every fair to a chapter, or a bishop, or a count one of the six pieces; he now sold all six in London — two to the King, one to the archbishop, one to the portgreve, one to Westminster Abbey, and one he cut out for a pair of soldiers or minters. Thus arose what one tends to describe with the proud name of "merchant city" — that is, a settlement before the gates of a governing city in the place where the market was formerly held — a few stalls, a few little houses next to them where the traders' families now resided; and next to them a few taverns and craftsmen's stalls, for the "merchantry" must themselves also be provided for. A small mob of poor urchins who ate in deepest subservience the bread of the proud masters who were enthroned on the other side of the river in their palaces, their curia, their towers. As Flach (for Narbonne in the 11th century) describes very nicely:

> Les négociants, les changeurs, les banquiers, les armateurs habitent près du port dans le bourg, toute autour de la Porte Aiguière et dans les maisons construites, suivant l'usage du moyen âge, sur le pont qui la reliait à l'autre rive. Ils ne peuvent evidemment rien entreprendre contre la formidable citadelle qui les domine, ils n'ont que les droits que l'intérêt bien entendu des seigneurs leurs laisse ou qu'ils acquièrent à prix d'argent. [Traders, money changers, bankers and ship owners live near the port in the village, around the Aiguière gate, and in the houses built, according to the use

Chapter 10: The Origin of the Medieval City

of the Middle Ages, on the bridge which connected it to the other bank. They can obviously not undertake anything against the formidable citadel which dominates them, they have only the rights which are left to them of course after the interests of the lords or which they acquire by money.] (Flach 1893, 2:268 f.)

Or as one of the prettiest sources which we possess for the history of cities in the Middle Ages tells us (it concerns the castle of Balduin Bas-de-Fer, Count of Flanders, son-in-law of Charles the Bald):

> Post hoc ad *opus seu necessitates illorum de castello* ceperunt ante portam ad pontem castelli confluere mercemanni, id est cariorum (?) rerum mercatores, deinde tabernarii, deinde hospitarii pro victu et hospicio eorum, qui negocia coram principe, qui ibidem sepe erat, prosequebantur, domus construere et hospicia preparare, ubi se recipiebant illi qui non poterant intra castellum hospitari; et erat verbum eorum: "Vadamus ad pontem"; ubi tantum accreverunt habitaciones, ut statim fieret villa magna, que adhuc in vulgari suo nomen pontis habet, nempe *Brugghe* in eorum vulgari pontem sonat. [After this they came to the work or the needs of those from the castle, of the merchandise flowing past the gate and over the bridge of the castle. That is, the beloved stuff of merchants. Then of shops, then of inns for their food and entertainment; and those acting on behalf of the lord, in which place there was a fence, were accommodated; houses were built and lodgings prepared where those who could not lodge in the castle were received; and their motto was, "I could go to the bridge". Where so much habitation has accrued that they would then make a large city, which took the name of the bridge, which being Bruges sounds like bridge in the common tongue.][284]

"Ad opus seu necessitates illorum de castello" [the work or the needs of those from the castle] — in these words is contained the entire meaning of medieval civic history, at least in its beginnings.

The well-known remark of Pirenne, in which he summarises his conception of the origin of medieval cities, must thus be reversed exactly into its opposite if it will bear reckoning with the facts. Pirenne suggests: "Les villes sont l'œuvre des marchands; elles n'existent que par eux" [Cities are the work of merchants; they exist only by them](Pirenne 1895, 70). It should rightly read that the cities of the Middle Ages are (economically) the work of the obtainers of ground rents and taxes; the "merchants" only exist through them.

5. Alms Recipients

That their number in the medieval cities must have been significant, we can conclude from the fact that one of the tasks of the monasteries consisted in the care of the poor and infirm, and that particularly in the later centuries of the Middle Ages, endowments were made from secular riches, be it from humane, be it from religious grounds, for the upkeep of needy persons, particularly women. Here the beguinages[285] are to be recalled which were established in most cities in considerable numbers.

It is not known to me that a numerical census of alms recipients has ever been attempted for a city[286].

IV. The "Draw Towards the City"

Up to now the discussion has only been of the interests of the original city builders (thus predominantly the lords) in the origin of a city as well as of their (economic) possibilities. In order that the city could now in reality grow, the objects of city formation also had to be engaged. A history of cities thus demands the verification of which series of motives moved the people filling the cities to settle within the walls of the city.

A portion of them already were sitting from before in the place where the city arose — the entire corps of domestics in the widest sense, all the "fratribus et ecclesie" [brothers and the church] (and of course also the other lords) "cottidie in propria persona servientes" [the everyday personal servants]; also the manufacturing workers who had worked for the lords and were now gradually (as we have seen) developing into in-

Chapter 10: The Origin of the Medieval City

dependent craftsmen. They and their offspring formed the stock of city fillers.

To them were then added the fluctuating elements, so far as they were settled — I am thinking here perhaps of the free wandering craftsmen of whom we receive tidings.

But a very considerable part of the civic population was, as we may conclude with certainty from the abundant evidence, formed by immigration from the countryside.

Unfortunately, the fact that this immigration took place and that it must have been relatively strong is about all that we know about it[287]. We must guess most things; only a few things let themselves be verified by sources.

In order for an immigration from the countryside to take place as a mass phenomenon, two lines of specific circumstances must meet — the countryside must reject (repel), and the city must draw in (attract).

What put the people off staying on the land during those centuries which especially come into consideration for the first inner consolidation of the cities seems primarily to have been the following:

1. The great insecurity which had set in, especially during the 10th century, had as a consequential phenomena the invasions of plundering peoples and an associated proliferation of native knights. The most detailed description of these conditions is found in Volume 2 of Flach's work, which ascribes a formidable significance to this insecurity in the countryside (for the development of France). But even in other regions, the general sign of the times around the year 1000 is obviously insecurity[288]. Hence also the building of walls.

2. The obligated services in some regions. Thus, at least, a monk reports to us expressly of the secular lords whom the bonded serfs ran away from to seek refuge at the abbey: "cum multos haec possideat aecclesia, qui semet ipsos *propter afflictionem et multitudinem* servitutis, qua durissime premebantur a propriis dominis, in ius nostrum coemerint causa quietis, e quibus alii ruriculae, alii vinitores, quidam panifici, sutores, fabri sunt ac mercatores artiumque diversarum vel operum executores" [the church perhaps takes possession of many of them, who themselves desire on account of the affliction and great servitude which was pressed extremely hard by

particular lords, that they acquire rightfully our state of peace, and of them some are peasants, others vineyard workers, some bakers, shoemakers, craftsmen, and even diverse and skilled merchants or even executors of work][289].

The fact that numerous bonded serfs really established themselves in the cities suggests that they had at least had enough of their obligations; just like our landless villagers [*Insten*] today with their day-labouring on estates.

3. Here and there, from the 12th century, the displacement of farmers [*Bauernlegen*] — that is, the confiscation of independent farming positions — seemed to be popular. These displaced farmers saw themselves being deprived of their possibilities for existence on the land[290].

4. We must, for the period from the 9th to the 12th centuries and beyond, at least in some lands, reckon upon a greater increase in population[291], whereby a surplus of population was created which the army of those migrating from the countryside helped strengthen. They either vanished into the newly settled regions or presented themselves as material for filling the cities.

We now know in substance what made these into points of attraction for those pushed out of the countryside — it was in particular the possibility of obtaining a livelihood for oneself and one's family without possessing land, and the possibility of establishing a secure existence. And indeed in a state of freedom.

This ideal of freedom seems to have exercised an attraction at least as powerful as the prospect of security and gain. We know that the cities did their own thing to obtain or preserve the freedom of the immigrants whom they desired. In all lands, it became a principle of municipal law that the air of the city made people free, that the bonded (under defined, very simple conditions) was extracted from the persecutions of his lord[292].

Thus a preference for the life in the city which was no longer founded in the end on individual cases may finally have been implanted in the rural population from the interoperation of all the circumstances. This then became a "*prejudice*" and produced a general surge towards the city, the

Chapter 10: The Origin of the Medieval City

same "draw towards the city" as we see again so powerfully in effect 1,000 years later in our own time.

***

In these cities whose rise we have been following, a new, idiosyncratic economic life now unfolded, which became of prime significance for the subsequent development of European culture. Two forces created it. The interests of those small craftsmen's existences which we saw camping in the market stalls or in the small wooden houses which were stuck to the palaces of the rich lords like swallows' nests to the mountain.

And the interests of the city itself.

If we want thus to understand what it meant for the economic life in a medieval city, and especially of what sort the new structures were which arose there, then we will have to first of all clarify in what direction the interests of the two creative factors were moving — I want to tell what spirit animated them, and what ideal did they have in their minds and for whose realisation their striving was directed.

The final aims of the one are simply established, for what the city as a whole wanted, what its statutory organs wanted, is put down in the guiding principles of civic policy. We will familiarise ourselves with these first of all.

Section 4: The Period of the Craftwork-based Economy

Chapter 11: The Economic Policy of the City

> And thus the city, according to the Aristotelian description and according to the idea which underlies its natural guises, is also a self-sufficient household, an organism living collaboratively. Whatever its empirical origin may be, according to its being it must be seen as a whole, in relation to which the individual cooperatives and families of which it consists find themselves in essential dependence. Thus with its language, its customs, its beliefs as it is with its soil, its buildings and stores, it is a persistent thing which outlasts the changes of many generations and begets partly from itself, partly through inheritance and education of its citizens' houses, essentially the same character and manner of thinking ever anew.[293] (Tönnies 1887, § 18)

With these true words, Tönnies opens his beautiful meditations over the being of the city in itself, the πολις. And with the same words should every treatise over the city of the Middle Ages and its particular nature also be begun.[294]

In fact, in these words lies enclosed the clue to that idea alone from which the true being of this strange structure of the Middle Ages, which we call the city, can be comprehended — to the idea of community, which we impart not only to the things whose discovery we are concerned about, and which thus appears in this instance not only as a philosophical aid to our contemplation, but rather portrays the central point from which everything that happened in the medieval city received life, because as an energetic idea it filled the souls of the inhabitants and certainly those who intervened decisively in the formation of civic existence.

As wondrous as this phenomenon is, it is vouched to us by thousandfold testimony as indubitable historical fact that that strange mixture of people which, as we have seen, coalesced in the city of the Middle Ages was gripped by the same strong idea of community, of belonging together, of similarity to each other, of strangeness towards all that lay outside before the gates. Secular and religious, princes and beggars, rich and poor, patricians and plebeians, free and unfree, farmers and craftsmen were enclosed by that bond of an inwardly experienced feeling of unity and community which had formed the first human groups, which had lent the tribe, the village its life. A great number of people were again sensible of being an organic unity; many felt themselves to be members of a family; the consciousness of belonging together was so strong that it overwhelmed all the dissolving, disintegrating powers within, and lead everyone to common action, to united behaviour towards the outside world.

The entirety of measures which we tend to describe as *the policy of cities* thus also flowed like a natural current from this feeling of community. This strong consciousness of unity manifested itself in it, as it were. Whether it was the lords of the city in the beginnings of civic development, whether later the patrician families, whether finally the plebeian guilds, from which these measures originated, they were always filled by the same spirit; they were always sustained by the naive egotism of these small groups of men who were sensible of being a unity and were determined to prevail as a unity against the entire outside world, which meant for them the foreign. The foreigners towards whom one felt no obligations, whom one endeavoured to make subservient as objects of their own discretion; the foreigners whose envoys one met with suspicion because one again expected nothing good from them.

The basic idea from which the economic policy of the medieval city was born is the same everywhere; hence, the measures of this policy are also the same in their main features everywhere; even in *England*, for which one has recently argued a divergence, see Georg Brodnitz (1914, 1 ff.). Obviously differences exist between the municipal legislation in Germany and England, just as between that in Germany and France or

Chapter 11: The Economic Policy of the City

Italy. In particular, the position of the cities towards the state, as is universally known, is differently nuanced in England and France than in Germany and Italy. In both the latter countries, thanks to the stronger autonomy of the cities, the idea of civic economic policy is hence expressed perhaps somewhat more purely, especially in the egotistic enforcement of civic interests against the countryside. Thus, for example, the English cities, as Brodnitz claims, had no road law. Their grain supply policy was born though from the same spirit as that of the German cities. We recognise that from the provisions over collection, buying, and fixed prices, which literally read in the English statutes just like they do in the German or Italian. The differences between the individual lands are thus only differences of degree, not of nature — just that is now shown again by the work of Brodnitz.

In substance, the English cities were also just the same rigid and independently vital structures as they were everywhere in the Middle Ages, "a free self-governing community, a state within the state", as it is called by one of its best connoisseurs, J. R. Green (1894, 1:1 ff.), where a summary listing of the civil rights and liberties of the cities is found which holds its own next to the prerogatives of any German or Italian city.

We do not have to pursue here the thousandfold radiations of this leading idea. It is only needed to follow up here their effects in a specific direction, to where they condense into the system of an *economic policy*. Even in this, we again find in fact the same idea of community which dominates all civic life. It first of all defines formally the behaviour of the political powers — that is, the organ of community — for the separate economic processes. And indeed in the sense that it does not perhaps concede to the discretion of the individual how he will obtain his livelihood, any more than the head of a family leaves this to the discretion of his under-age children. That, on the contrary, the community and its representatives keeps watch over all the processes of economic life, and regulates them all according to a unitary plan, that it prescribes the individual's behaviour, and looks after the welfare of the individual. Just as, of its own accord, that powerful system of regulating norms and pioneering measures, which we see all the economic processes subjected to in the cities of the Middle Ages, ensues from the leading idea of community.

That same idea of community, however, also defines the material rationale upon which all economic policy of the medieval cities is based; the rationale which is none other than that which had regulated the economic constitution of the tribe, the village, and the manor — the principle of economic self-sufficiency, economic autarchy, the *principle of satisfaction of basic needs*. The residents of the city shall be amply provided with the good things which they require for their bodies' nourishment and needs[295]. But, since the life of the city rests on such a completely different basis to all earlier communities, since in accordance with the nature of the city men shall live for the first time without soil, it is understood by itself that thus the same fundamental idea, the satisfaction of these people's needs for economic goods, leads to measures which are very different from those which had regulated the economy of villagers or the people on the manor. From the same fundamental idea of satisfaction of basic needs thus grew an entirely new system of economic policy, which we must now make clear in its main features.

When one holds clearly before one's eyes this aim of civic economic policy — the care of obtaining a quantity of goods that are satisfying in amount and variety — then one will very easily understand the thousands of individual measures in which the activity of the civic authorities expressed itself, and will be able to fit them together into an internally coherent system.

It corresponds to the nature of the city, as we know, that it must obtain a large part of its livelihood through supplies from the outside. The same considerations thus which, in the framework of the closed economy of self-sufficiency, lead to measures which are dedicated to bringing every individual area of production to full efficiency — one thinks of the rules of the so-called *Capitulare de villis* — must induce the civic economic policymaker to protective measures by means of which he ensures that the necessary quantity of goods, which the city though does not produce itself anymore, are fed to it from the outside. The place of a pure production policy must be taken by a *supply policy*, which must then also in reality constitute the most important component of the overall civic economic policy.

We subsume a first part of the measures mentioned here under the description of the roads, trading [*Meilenrecht*], and staples law which the city sought to strive for. That is, of the law which leads through the city every goods train (it is especially the foodstuffs always, in particular the grain for bread,

Chapter 11: The Economic Policy of the City

for whose fetching the city authorities are plotting) which moves in a defined area surrounding the city, and holds the quantity of goods drawn in this way for at least a few days in the city and makes it available to the citizens for the satisfaction of any demand that is perhaps present. That is, thus, one forces the grain dealers, etc., who had bought the grain somewhere, to transport this — and even if by detours — through the city, and to "stockpile" it there before it can be led on to its destination.

Or one even impedes the farmers in the area surrounding the city — the further out the better — from selling their production anywhere but in the city. The "right" to compel this is called the market right by virtue of which the city residents thus secure a buyer monopoly.

When the countrymen now came with their products to the city, one also wanted to prevent a speculative mind from perhaps buying up the wares along the way, before they reached the market. You hence either forbade the purchase before the arrival at the market, or absolutely forbade every purchase of foodstuffs with the aim of resale, or forbade at least every supply agreement over foodstuffs. The obligation to bring the wares to markets was also established so that you could only thus satisfy yourself of their goodness and "legality".

One sought to protect the interests of the consumers against the dealers also by bestowing on them the so-called "right of acquisition", that is, the right to buy for himself as much as he needed (even against the dealer's will) of some lot which a dealer had brought in[296]. Or you first allowed the dealer the purchase after the consumer had supplied themselves: "donec burgenses ad suum opus emerint" [until the citizen has obtained his own need]; and more of the same rules.

That one worried about the good condition of the wares arriving for sale emerges already from the rule alluded to, which consistently recurred in almost all cities, that the foodstuffs brought into the city shall only be offered for sale at the public marketplaces designated for that purpose. But then one also sought to prevent spoilt articles from being offered for sale, too high a price being demanded, perhaps being weighed falsely, measured falsely, etc. — an extended system of rules for "policing the markets" regulated the trade at the market in the interests of the buyer. On the other hand, nothing stood in the way of one saddling his dear fellow Christians in the neighbourhood with sick cattle or rotten flesh: "thus they may drive and sell all the afflicted sheep and wethers actively into the countryside," Strasbourg ruled in the 15th century; just as Nuremberg in the year 1497 ruled: "drive from there all such unready and blemished cattle"*.

But institutions even were also created which ensured a good supply to the city, particularly of grain — warehouses were constructed at the cost of the city and stored grain and the like there.

The administration of the city did not need to be quite so anxious about the supply of manufactured products. First of all, because their lack did not call forth any real hardship, secondly, because in the rule enough of them were produced in the city itself. Nevertheless, it also devoted its attention to them. It ensured that foreign craftsmen and traders offered their wares at the annual fair, that the crafts were constantly well staffed, that the production in the city itself was carried out reputably and conscientiously (that no surrogate came into usage, different materials were not mixed, old and new material was not worked up together, that one did not work with subtle things at night — that is, after the onset of darkness), etc.

Measures of the last mentioned sort, however, pursue a different goal. They are meant to secure for the manufactured products of the civic producers sales out in the countryside or in distant parts. For one must say that, in a trading economy, the satisfaction of basic needs is half a sales problem — that only those craftsmen who have sold their own products beforehand acquire the means to provide themselves with the actual needed articles coming into the city (or even produced in the city). Hence, the special care for the wares destined for export (which one first put through an official examination). Certainly one reached the same goal (securing the sale of craftwork products) by a shorter path when one again com-

---

* [Tr.: not footnoted by Sombart.]

pelled the countryside in as wide a surrounding area as possible to supply themselves in the city with manufactured products. One achieved that by the proscription of all manufacturing activity in the countryside — the content of the so-called right of prohibition [*Bannrecht*].

With this concern for the sale of craftwork products, the civic policy now touched, however, on a different problem — that of the preservation of a specific organisation of civic production, the craftwork. And with that, the very problem whose solution had the same significance for the configuration of the city as the provision of the civic market. For the particular nature of the civic economy is contained precisely in that it brings this system of craftwork-based economy to its full development. At the end of the Middle Ages, it was really the craftwork interests which plainly formed the interests of the city. We must now thus seek next to create a clear idea of that "craftwork".

Chapter 12: The Economic System of Craftwork

I. The Concept of Craftwork

In accordance with our working plan, we must now form a clear notion of the "idea of craftwork". That is, we must seek to discern with conceptual clarity the essence of that economic system which we describe as craftwork or as a craftwork-based organisation of the economy and which we know dominated economic life during the European Middle Ages.

Craftwork as an economic system is that form of exchange-based organisation of caring for livelihoods by which the economic subjects are properly and economically independent, technical workers dominated by the idea of sustenance, acting traditionally, and standing in the service of a comprehensive organisation. The following parts are devoted to the analysis of this concept[297].

We call craftsmen all the economic subjects in an economy which is organised on a craftwork basis, may they be agricultural or manufactured goods producers, or those who transform or transport goods. In the narrow sense, craftsmen mean only the manufacturing producers in a craftwork-based economy. These are just as representative for the economic system of craftwork as the agricultural producers are for the economy of self-sufficiency, and the trader for the capitalist trading economy. I will hence treat them here as representatives of all other economic subjects of an economy organised on a craftwork basis, and demonstrate in them the essence of this economic system.

We will, however, it seems to me, be able to express with the greatest confidence what "a craftsman" is according to his inner nature, if we first summarise our proposition negatively in that we call a "craftsman" that manufacturing worker for whom none of the necessary conditions for the production and sale of goods are missing, be they of personal nature, or be they of objective nature, and in whose personality as a consequence all the characteristics of a manufacturing producer, or, as we can say in summary, the qualifications for production, are embedded without any differentiation. Since, for production, a fusion of tangible property and personal abilities must constantly take place, it thus arises from what has been said that the craftsman possesses, in addition to their personal qualities, the power of disposal over all the tangible goods necessary for production, that is, over *the means of production*[298] — no differentiation of personal and tangible property has taken place yet in the craftsman, or to put it in other words, the tangible property of the craftsman has not yet assumed the character of capital.

But the craftsman possesses not only the tangible property necessary for the practice of his trade, he also possesses all the *personal characteristics* required for it — he is a sort of manufacturing "Mr Microcosm". What later grew in numerous individuals into special aptitudes, all of that was united by the craftsman in his "crest of honour". Obviously, all was proportioned in miniature. His averageness corresponds by necessity to his universality.

The core of craftsmanship is its suitability for the *manufacturing worker*, in the sense that he possesses the technical abilities for realising the actions to carry out the manufacture of an object of use from raw materials. But with this, let us say, technical aptitude, he unites:

1. the *artistic* gaze perhaps required, the artistic feeling;
2. the *knowledge* required for production, especially also the knowledge of the tradition of proficiency, so as not to use the misleading expression of scientific aptitude. He unites in his personality all the wisdom of our "Doctors of Engineering" and all the results of research from our chemical laboratories.

Besides that, he functions:

3. as an *organiser* as well as the *manager* of production. He is managing director, foreman, and handyman in *one* person.

But he is:

4. also a *merchant*. All purchasing and sales activity, all organisation of distribution, in short everything which was later provided as speculative services by a few outstanding personalities is encompassed within his personal faculties.

II. The Overall Organisation of the Economy

If you want to discern the basic idea which defines all craftwork-based thinking and wanting, then you must, as I have already indicated in Chapter 4, become conscious of the guiding principle by which the old structure of farm holdings was sustained. For the system of craftwork-based activity is none other than *the transfer of the structure of holdings* onto manufacturing (and commercial, etc.) conditions. The analogy which exists between a rural community of holding owners and a corporation of craftsmen bound in a guild can be traced into the details. Both want to order in cooperative harmony the economic activity of the individual participants. Both take as their starting point a given quantity of work to be performed and of demand to be satisfied. That is, they are directed by the idea that each member receives a specific quantity of benefits and income — they are oriented from the viewpoint of 'sustenance'. Both share the total output among the individuals and leave a part which is to be performed by the cooperative as such — the communal pasture of the commons in the village corresponds to the collective use of the facilities erected by the guild (or city). Both regulate in detail the economic behaviour of each member, etc.

The ever-recurring, fundamental idea of every genuine craftsman or craftsman's friend is that the craft should 'maintain' its man. He wants to work as much that he obtains his livelihood, and he has, like the craftsmen in Jena (about whom Goethe tells us), "mostly the sensible idea of not working any more than they at all events need to for a lusty life"[*].

And anyone who is especially familiar with the testimonies from the Middle Ages knows that this fundamental idea speaks a thousandfold from every guild statute:

---

* [Tr.: in a letter written in Jena to Johann Heinrich Meyer on 24 April 1817.]

Do you want to hear what imperial law commands? — our forefathers were not fools — craftwork was invented so that every man obtains his daily bread with it and nobody shall seize another in his craftwork. With that the world provides your needs and may sustain every man.

So it says in the so-called Reformation of Emperor Sigismund[299].

But from the variety now of persons, and from the variety of sources of income which existed between farmers and non-agricultural workers, a different conception must also arise of the nature of "sustenance". The farmer wants to sit as his own master on his clod of earth and draw his livelihood from it in the framework of the economy of self-sufficiency. The craftsman is reliant on the sale of his products — he constantly stands in the framework of a trade-based form of economic organisation. He wants to be (and must be according to his essence) a manufacturing producer, and he wants to be a free, independent producer.

What the adequate size of his property is for the farmer, the sufficient extent of his sales is for the craftsmen. What the possession of land is for the former in particular, the character of the free and independent tradesman is for the latter.

One may assume that only by the disentangling of the worker from the clod of earth, thus into the city, did this strong emphasis on independence occur as we come across it in all craft-like dispositions. The civic craftsman thereby positions himself in a conscious contrast to the externally similar natures even of manufacturing workers, and thereby cultivates an essential feature of genuinely craft-based organisation more than ever[300].

III. The Task of the Craftsmen's Cooperative

The structure of holdings rested on the collaboration of the villagers in the village community. The craftsmen's cooperative, the *guild* or *fraternity*, suggests itself as corresponding to the organ which would have to take on the functions of the village community for the manufacturing 'farmers'.

Chapter 12: The Economic System of Craftwork

We have surely been rightly taught to contemplate the medieval *guild* in particular as a continuation of the old communities of blood and place — the guilds shall substitute in the cities for what the natural community in the countryside offered by itself, and shall complete what the larger city community is unable to accomplish for the individual[301].

Quite certainly, however, the guild of the individual craftsman helped with the performance of his economic goals in a similar way to how the village community had helped the farmer. It is firstly the one to ensure that a sufficiently large area of activity (and sales) was secured for the craft as a whole (like the village community defined the extent of the village fields in conformity with the interests of its members). It sought to achieve that by, wherever possible, monopolising the sales for the craftwork of a specified city, be it in this city itself, be it in foreign places, and furthermore, where the monopoly could not be executed fully, seeking at any rate to make difficult the intrusion of foreigners into its own sales area. Hence the numerous, ever recurring sharp regulations of the visitors' rights, the market and fair rules, etc. whereby fundamentally unfavourable or at least only equally favourable conditions of sale should be permitted for the non-indigenous[302].

And a striving after a monopoly of the supply of raw materials corresponded to the striving after a monopoly of use. Hence the numerous regulations which sought to hinder the export of the raw materials or even of semi-finished products from the "natural" area of supply of a craft.

The guild, however, applied itself also to all activities which would surpass the power of the individual, like the procurement of the necessary raw materials in bulk or from afar, or the organisation of the sale of products over a larger area.

It applied itself, insofar as the city itself did not advocate for them, to the erection of facilities which required a large outlay and hence could not be erected by individual craftsmen. They were then used jointly by the guild members (like the commons and the forest in the village community!)

Well-known examples for it are: the wool scouring facilities (in which the raw wool was cleaned); carding facilities in which it was carded; oil presses; fulling mills; cloth rollers;

dyeing facilities; sawmills; places where the cloth frames were erected for drying; gardens where bleaching was done; materials facilities for the building trade (brick yards, etc.); cloth halls in which the cloth was sold. In summary, everywhere a general work output or arrangement of production materials in bulk was necessary, the guild manifested, as we would say today, as a work cooperative.

IV. The Particular Nature of the Work of Craftsmen

The particular economic activity of the individual craftsman exists essentially in the technical manipulation and processing of the raw materials and semi-finished products into objects of use, which he carries out in his own person, as we have seen. But with that the particular nature of this activity is itself defined. What the skilfulness of his hands is able to achieve, what the spread of his arms is able to encompass, that is the sphere of his actions, which appears thus as an immediate discharge of his personality. In this sense, one has described the "craftwork" very succinctly as the "expression of an individual's specific activity distinctive to a life profession, which so to say *extends as far as the power of the individual hand is able to govern and create*"[303].

And as, at the same time, it cannot be any other way than that the work itself, thus the result of a craftsman's activity, is the faithful expression of the personality of its creator. The ware of a craftsman is, with all the tradition of the technique, always still an individual work. It bears a piece of soul out into the world, because it remains the creation of a man who, even if still so limited, is yet a living man. It can tell of the sorrows and joys of its creator. If each pair of shoes does not also turn out the way Sachs smashes them up on the night of John the Baptist's feast day — "I hold court with the hammer on the last"* — influences of various types are always recognisable, "every bother over the child, every quarrel with the wife"†; the thousands of perils of domestic life do not go by

---

* [Tr.: Richard Wagner, Die Meistersänger von Nürnburg, Act 2, Scene 6.]
† [Tr.: not footnoted by Sombart.]

without trace in the work of the craftsman. It remains within the scope of his abilities — but it is different from master to master, different from day to day.

V. The Professional Structure of Craftwork

The professional structure that is particular to craftwork also corresponds now to the idea of craftsman-like work as an operation of the entire personality, and takes account of the thought that the individuality of a man can and should stretch his powers over a specific circle of activities which is held together by an intellectual band, by the idea of a whole; that an expansion of this circle must shatter his powers whereas, on the other hand, if these powers are applied in too narrow a circle or even only in one direction, the worker sinks into the stupor of purely mechanical operation. Which as it were characterises the qualitative demarcation of individual crafts, whereas the quantitative assignment of the circle of activity is most distinct under the influence of the guiding principle of "sustenance". In both directions — we want to hold that tight — factors that are subjective and grounded in the personality of the craftsman are authoritative for the demarcation of the individual crafts.

The size of the circle of action within which the craftsman exercises his activities finds its expression, however, in the size of his operation. That this, in the rule, will not overstep the bounds of the individual operation just corresponds to the essence of craftwork.

VI. The Order of Craftwork

The orders of craftwork are focused on the attainment of these aims: that a specific scale of operation is now constantly secured for the craftsman (that is, thus a specific circle of consumers), that the one does not enlarge and get rich at the cost of the other, and that in contrast everyone retains as equal as possible a share in the overall sales area. Which is why we commonly label this part of their regulations simply as the *guild order*.

Serving the achievement of this aim are:

1. rules which shall configure the conditions of *raw materials supply* for all craftsmen equally; be it that they define that no master may buy anywhere but on the market days, at the advertised and appointed place and nowhere else; be it that the price of raw material must be officially set and stuck to by everyone; be it that the size of the amount being purchased by a person is limited; be it that quite generally all sorts of sale are forbidden; be it that each craftsman is allotted the right to participate in the purchase of another (so-called right of acquisition).

2. regulations to which the *expansion of operations* or *limits to the scale of production* were exposed. Here belongs the determination of the highest number of journeymen and apprentices which *one* master was permitted to employ. Where such a limit seemed infeasible or otherwise unworkable by the nature of the trade, other means were utilised to not allow the amount of production of an individual to become too great, and to prevent the development into large concerns.

Or the allowable amount of production which an individual was permitted to produce in a specified time was set directly. That is particularly the case where the products were essentially of the same type, thus especially in weaving, but then also in the furriery, tanning trade, and others.

3. regulations which aimed at evoking as *simultaneous and as similar an offering* as possible. Here belong the multifarious rules over the type, the place, and the time of sale, the *prohibition* against enticing away customers or buyers from a fellow guild member or taking a piece of work from him; here also belongs the prohibition against continuing work begun by a fellow guild member, and many others.

VII. The Inner Structure of Craftwork

Craftwork is represented by the masters (those who *understand* the craft, just as the village community was represented by the holding owners — those who *possessed* the soil). But the master must look after the junior staff so that the craft does not die out. The master needs in many cases the help of other persons in his operations. Thus it occurs that others also work next to him in the craft so that the individual craftwork operations frequently are not sole concerns in

Chapter 12: The Economic System of Craftwork

which only the master would be active, but rather (and it may even be seen as the typical case) operations with assistants.

Here again now, a feature specific to craftwork is the manner in which the persons collected together in it for an integrated activity are brought into a legal and economic relationship with each other — that relationship which one can call the *inner structure of craftwork*. For its particular nature follows from the topmost principle of craftwork-based organisation as it attains expression in the goal setting of its bearers.

The relationship of the manager of craftwork-based production — the "master" — to his assistants — the journeymen, menials, attendants, boys, servants, helpers, assistants, and however else the descriptions may otherwise read, as well as the apprentices — and these to him, will only then be correctly understood when one visualises the family-like character which all craftwork originally bore — *the family concern is the oldest bearer of this economic form*, and it still remains one when persons are drawn into the working relationship from without. Journeyman and apprentice enter into the family's union with their whole personality, and are encircled by it temporarily in the overall activity of their existence. The family together with journeymen and apprentices is both a production and a domestic unit. All its members are protected dependents of the master. They form with him an organic whole, just as children do with their parents.

But as the idea can now never arise at all that the parents are there because of the children or the children because of the parents, just as it would be foolish to think that the heart is there for the sake of the head or the latter for the sake of the former, so it follows also for the relationship of master to journeymen and apprentices that none of the participants may be thought of as acting for the other's sake, but rather that the complete group of people, thus also the assistants — journeymen and apprentices — appears as an end in itself, or what amounts to the same, as organs in the service of a common whole.

Corresponding to the nature of craftwork, the apprenticeship and the journeyman status constantly appear only as *preliminary stages to mastership*. That, I would like to say, is almost the most important feature of a genuinely craftwork-based organisation. As the student is only the future law clerk, and the latter only the future judge, so the apprentice is the journeyman-to-be, and the journeyman the master-to-be. It is often stressed that the prerequisite therefore is also a corresponding numerical relationship of aspirants for the master positions to the latter themselves, and with reason — one may assume that where the number of journeymen amounts to more than half the number of masters, an engagement as a master is already no longer guaranteed to every journeyman[304].

But where perhaps from technical operating or other reasons a larger number of helpers is required, one works it out by manner of obliterating materially and non-materially the difference between master and journeyman almost completely and seeing the master as a *primus inter pares* [first among equals]. That was the fundamental idea for example in construction work, in particular with the stonemasons in the Middle Ages, with whom the master was indeed indispensable as an organiser and manager, but the journeymen stood almost completely equal with him both in compensation and in respect and eminence.

With every episodic insurrection against the regime of the masters, the journeyman would remain mindful though that the same thing which he was undertaking against the master could some day befall him. The following jingle brings that consideration to a tangible expression:

> Each journeyman or lad
> He will want his proper state.
> It is with work or wandering
> That then his mastery has to do.
> In that he shall want already
> As he wants what one in pay does.
> Then as one serves on earth,
> So will he also be served.
> Think if I come to honour,
> One will serve me thus in turn.[305]

Chapter 13: The Conditions of Existence of Craftwork

Since we are limiting our investigation to the circle of western European cultures, we can leave out of consideration the conditionality of our form of economy in the particular nature of the land and the people. We shall instead let the possibility of craftwork-based organisation be dealt with by deducing it in substance from a specific (quantitative) configuration of the population conditions and the technology.

I. The Population

The population is in three ways a determining influence for the viability of a craftwork-based organisation[306]:
1. through the constitution of its tendency for reproduction. There it is to be noticed that the tinier the general growth rate of a population is, that is thus, the slower its absolute increase progresses, then the better it is for craftwork;
2. the growth rate of the agricultural, surplus population — thus that part of the population for whom there is no scope in the sphere of agricultural activity — is of decisive significance for the viability of an economic form of manufacturing production. Craftwork in trade and manufacturing is tied to the prerequisite that the agricultural, surplus population is small, or — which amounts to the same thing — that the possibility exists for the rural growth in population to utilise their manpower through intensity of cultivation or settlement of new land;
3. the degree of population density and agglomeration of population comes materially into consideration for the possibilities of existence of a manufacturing form of economy — craftwork requires a low degree for both.

II. The Technology

Technology is significant for craftwork in the sense of the type of procedure as well as through the quantitative efficiency. The *type of procedure* which corresponds to the idea of craftwork-based organisation is the empirical-organic.

We will call the technology empirical when it rests on an artificial procedure. The technical ability is constructed then on the practical personal knowledge of those who have learnt the "art", and indeed have learnt through instruction of another artist, another master of the art. The operation of the technique is empirical and experiential because it rests on none other than the tried and tested, because it has no other guiding principle than rules adjudged subjectively to be true, rules which the "master" has deduced from the actual process of his own work and has transferred like a personal possession to the "apprentice" as the rules of his art. He who understands the art knows though only the *how?* and the *what for?* of the overall procedure and all the details, not the *why?* The farmer spreads manure on his soil because he has personally learnt and was instructed by his father (as the latter learnt from the grandfather) that the seed on fertilised soil grows better than on unfertilised; the tanner prepares a tanning mixture from oak bark and specific amounts of water, and places the oxhide in it for a year because his master showed him it that way and because inspection confirms that this procedure is expedient for transforming hides into leather.

I call organic that technology whose procedures are defined by the extent and type of a vital being, and whose processes essentially come about through the active and passive participation of human or vegetable organisms. Organic in the passive sense is thus that technology by which men, animals, and plants are specifically used as assistants and materials; in the active sense, it is that technology by which the work itself is individual human work, that is, the immediate discharge of a living man who stands at the centre of the work of creation, and on whose natural organic activity the undisturbed course of the work process is dependent. The worker creates himself a system of aids — the tools — to be able to better complete his work. The tool, which only supports the

Chapter 13: The Conditions of Existence of Craftwork

worker in his work, is the means of labour corresponding to the organic process.

It surely now hardly demands a special rationale for why the empirical-organic technology and the craftwork-based organisation of the economy (just as, of course, the forms of individual operations) belong together in accordance with their being — the craftsman just wants to be active as a whole, vital personality in his work, wants to create work with his head and labour with his hands, wants to acquaint his essence with a part of external nature which he shall form — what a wonder it is that a technology is in accordance with him, which arranges all work around the vital personality of a worker — by which the countryman strides behind the plough, the cobbler under his shoemaker's globe sews soles with awl and thread; the carter sits with his dog in the driving seat; and the bargeman gives the direction downstream to his vessel one-handedly, and imparts the motion upstream himself.

But how else shall technical ability take root in that existence in which we get to know the craftsman, that existence which is experientially and traditionally disposed by its innermost nature, than by the personal instruction which he receives from the master? How else shall he be able to take hold of his art than as he learnt it, as it was handed down to his forefathers — he for whom a scientific grasp of the work process must naturally lie completely distant from the many-sided nature of his talents and his activity?

Just as an internally craftwork-based existence and an empirical-organic technology grew together next to each other, we detect an entire series of genuine traits of craftwork-based organisation which have their cause immediately in the use of that technology.

Thus the characteristically hierarchical structure of all craftwork — the "master" and "apprentice" system — is rooted ultimately in the particular nature of the empirical technology. The technical abilities adhered in it to a specific person — the "master". With him, it lives; with him, it dies. And for that reason, it required the personal instruction of an "apprentice" by the master so that the art remained preserved and reproduced itself. As long as all the business is contained in the house, the family tradition and the natural parent-child relationship ensures that the inventory of technical knowledge and abilities is not lost with the death of the one generation, but is transferred to the next generation. If this natural form of transmission ceases, then artificial artifices must be used which assure the continuity of possession of the technology to the future members of the house. This goal is served by the corporate associations (guilds, fraternities) which we find repeatedly with all craftwork.

The formation of the professional spheres in craftwork is explained furthermore from the particular nature of the organic procedures. They follow in an actual "organic" development, that is, in a connection with and under exclusive consideration of the personal capability of the producer; that is, without any regard thus for the objective requirements of the production process.

But also the professional pride, the particular "professional honour" of craftwork is unthinkable without the empirical procedure. It required the craftsmanship, handed down over centuries and purely personal, to let its bearers experience the feeling of a specific professional affiliation as a special stimulus. The miner, the stonemason, and the swordsmith were respectively the office holders of their particular arts, whose common possession, acquired through personal exchange, they obviously had to lock up against all the uninitiated. That a fertiliser factory, or a facility for the production of the best hair tonic or the most durable tires is incapable of producing similar core dispositions either in the entrepreneur or in the workers is obvious.

From the nature of the empirical procedure, however, can be effortlessly derived all the phenomena by which a timid awe arises before the "mysteries" of a manufacturing art or the striving of its followers to surround just their abilities with a mysterious veil and to guard against profanation.

It may be recalled how this basic conception of manufacturing activity as something supernatural because inexplicable leads us back to the myths of the divine origin of the arts and skills which are common to all European peoples. In the beginnings of culture, it is in particular the preparation of iron and the working of iron around which mystical ideas are weaved. "Like the astonishment of humanity over the won-

Chapter 13: The Conditions of Existence of Craftwork

derful art which involved the melting of hard metal in the fire and the forging of precious things from it, which led to ascribing the invention of the same to supernatural beings, thus one cannot also imagine the exercise of the same through earthly creatures without the aid of mysterious and magical means. This view applies [...] throughout Europe."[307]

But, even in the period of craftwork-based production, that conception meets us at every turn. The mystery-mongers in so many crafts, particularly in the construction trades, and particularly during the Middle Ages, are related most closely to it. Architecture was kept secret and hence kept veiled in a symbolic language and in symbolic forms. Any disclosure to strangers was forbidden. Likewise the written composition of the secret learning.[308] Here also belongs the custom of the oath of continuity which we meet so frequently in craftwork.

In *quantitative* respects, the technology must likewise fulfill specific demands in order for craftwork to be possible.

The productivity of agricultural work must as a result of a correspondingly developed technology have reached such a degree that *one person* was capable of producing enough means of sustenance and raw materials for two. Obviously only then can the processing and finishing of the latter into manufactured products be so well refined that now *one person* applies himself exclusively to this activity. Only then thus is the professional independence of commercial, manufacturing, and transportation activity upon which all craftwork-based organisation bases itself made possible.

If consequently a minimum state for the development of agricultural technology is to be assumed as the obvious precondition for every professionally practised, manufacturing activity, then on the other hand the well-being of the craftwork, as will then need to be demonstrated, is tied to a maximum productivity of the manufacturing and transportation work, and thus has for a prerequisite a correspondingly low state of manufacturing as well as transport technology.

The *sales conditions* are defined essentially through the degree of productivity of the technology, particularly in conjunction with the characteristic population circumstances suiting craftwork which were described above on page 225. But these may be identified as the decisive conditions for any economic system. It is valid thus to investigate what sort of sales conditions there must be for craftwork to be possible, and how they must be procured for craftwork to blossom — thus their optimal configuration for the craftwork-based organisation.

III. The Configuration of Selling Conditions[309]

I understand selling conditions in the wider sense as being a duality:
1. the conditions under which the producer places in his possession the necessary means of production; and
2. the conditions under which he disposes of his products.

We can in the first case speak of supply conditions, in the other of selling conditions in the narrow sense or conditions of utilisation.

1. The *supply conditions*, in order that they are suited to a craftwork-based organisation, must best be configured so clearly and simply that an average craftsman with his average mind is able without special knowledge and skills, besides those of his activity as a manufacturing worker, to oversee and command them as it were as a sideline. That applies everywhere where raw materials or semi-finished products are supplied in a traditional way by neighbouring farmers from the surrounding area or by neighbouring craftsmen from the next street, as is commonly the case in primitive economic situations. Wood, skins, horns, grain, flour, leather, flax, wool, dye stuffs, and ordinary pelts originate at the beginnings of the exchange economy mostly from the neighbouring region of the city or from the city itself. Under the prerequisite of the yet to be discussed stability and the very low capability for expansion of the manufacturing production of the old craftwork, it must be a simple thing for the craftsman under such conditions to obtain the necessary materials for his production without going too far out of his way.

Or, where the circle was already beginning to be drawn wider, with the products being required from a larger area (for example, the wool from an entire countryside), and raw materials being bought in larger quantities, then the agency of the guild or nominated buyers could still suffice so long as it involved regularly recurring, overseeable, undisturbed pro-

Chapter 13: The Conditions of Existence of Craftwork

cesses. And if it is only taken care of that the required raw materials are not perhaps taken away from the "natural" supply area. It is already an alarming shock to the foundations on which craftwork rests when that self-evident nature of raw materials procurement is put into question.

But one must not perhaps fancy that craftwork is necessarily and always reliant on a processing of raw materials from the neighbouring area. A superficial reflection suffices to realise that even just a moderately developed manufacturing existence cannot dispense with the products of specialised habitats and places of production for its materials — iron and bronze, precious metals, precious furs, useful stone for building, and precious stones, and diverse dyeing materials like alum have at all times had to be fetched from a wider region. And, for centuries, a genuinely craftwork-based production resigned itself to that quite well.

The prerequisite, however, is also here that the *selling conditions* are *certain* and *stable*, and dispense with every speculative element. The craftsman or his guild representative might now undertake himself the distant journey[310] or he might await the trader who is attending to bringing him the needed materials in the traditional manner.

Even faced with the trader, the craftsman did not need to be frightened, so long as the former is himself integrated into the steady structure of the quasi-stereotyped economic life, that is, the same wares delivered for the same conditions in regular contacts as a craftsman of selling[311].

But what was also of use to the craftsman with the configuration of the selling conditions, apart from its structure as it were, was a *low price* for raw materials and semi-finished goods. For such a thing extended the circle of those persons who were able to produce with their own assets, thus keeping themselves self-employed. But now the price of raw materials in relation to the total value which the work of the craftsman adds to the materials through processing is then lower when close supply takes place, thus only production expenses and not also transport costs need to be compensated for, and/or the share of the ground rent in driving the price of agricultural products up so enormously does not make itself as yet noticeable.

231

2. But of what sort must the *selling conditions* in the narrow sense be, that is, in what manner must the products be brought to the man in order to conform to the demands of craftwork? The answer even to this question at first reads quite generally — *the sales must be assured and stable* according to quality and quantity, or in other words, they must not become a problem yet. The sale may then be practised by the craftsman himself as a sideline, or they may practised by a professional class of traders, it remains the same. Even in the latter case, all the conditions can be fulfilled which make a craftwork-based organisation of the production possible or even perhaps necessary.

Whereon it is only important that the producer does not require any other qualities than those of a technical worker. That then applies, however, when the manufacturing worker never runs a danger in the calm continuance of his work of not being able to realise his product at all, or not realising it for a rewarding price.

But when is this the case, when are the sales of such sort assured and stable?

The ruling theory answers that it is when and for as long as the relationship between producers and consumers is a *customer relationship*, that is, as long as the sales take place without intermediaries or even only to familiar persons by order. The element of a regular trade between producers and a closed circle of consumers placing orders is undoubtedly a very essential one for assuring and stabilising the *selling conditions*, and a large part of all craftwork-based production was quite certainly marked by this customer relationship. But just as undoubtedly, it has already been pointed out, in no way did craftwork-based production and customer production always entirely coincide. Customer production in no way always created such sales conditions as would make possible the existence of craftwork-based producers. The tailors' craft, for example, perished despite nothing having changed to a large extent in the customer relationship with the consumers. The tailoring for consumers belongs among the earliest of capitalistically practised trades, which as craftwork had already been dislodged in London at the beginning of the 18th century[312]. And the cases are not so rare in which the craft-

Chapter 13: The Conditions of Existence of Craftwork

work-based organisation of a trade is destroyed first where it does not perhaps involve export outward, but sales in the same place, thus occurs in the framework of a more or less closed clientele. Conversely, there are enough cases in which a doubtlessly craftwork-based organisation of production did not prosper at all with a clientele-like consumer base, but rather prospered excellently despite that through exports and intermediary trade.

Sales are assured and stable rather everywhere and only where a constant equilibrium exists between demand and supply, or a disproportion exists in such a way that the demand rushes ahead of supply; but also exist where, for the individual producers, production conditions and selling conditions are approximately naturally equal.

That these signs of assured and stable sales are not only found with the pure customer relationship may with precise examination be beyond doubt. Even the market-visiting or peddling craftsman is in the same situation as the one delivering to customers on order, if he can calculate definitely on nobody else taking his place at the market before he arrives and nobody else trawling the street before he comes along with his pack or cart. And no less the craftsman selling to the traders, before whose door the respective merchant appears at the respective times to take away from him the respective quantity of products for the respective prices as always. Thus the causes which configure the sales assuredly and in a stable way must be sought for more deeply. And here arises perhaps the following:

1. Causes on the Demand Side

Demand must be qualitatively and quantitatively stable and assured. That is, a quantity of similar things must be in demand constantly.

Now the demand will be *qualitatively* more immutable, the less the categories of people who appear as buyers changes, and the less the tastes of these people is subjected to mutations. The less the stratification of societal relationships changes, that is, the more stable the structure of society is, then the more the types of buyers will remain always the same. Centuries long structuring of a people into the traditional "classes" of clergy, nobility, farmers, and bourgeoisie signifies thus stereotypical demand which is qualitatively the more stable, the less the habits and customs within these groups change — in modern terminology, the more seldom the style switches. A yeomanry, which over several centuries develops and preserves a uniform garb, and a modern big city population, which in ten years hounds ten clothing styles and five furniture styles to death, are perhaps the extremes in this respect.

The most essential guarantee of a qualitatively stable demand is offered, however, by the difficulty in altering production processes in the way they correspond to the empirical procedure. With this, the increase in technical knowledge and abilities (and with it the possibility of a change) remains either entirely left up to chance, so that no intention of change or making better, but rather only the intention of making just so again is present, and what by chance, in the course of activity as it were, falls into the worker's lap from without as a new experience merely accrues as innovation. Or, however, where improvement is absolutely being striven for, it is an awkward groping about and trying out in the dark without clear awareness of a task specifically to be solved.

Demand will be *quantitatively* stable and assured then, however, if the quantity of wares produced does not grow at a faster rate than the purchasing power of the buyers.

2. Causes on the Supply Side

What from the supply side troubles the easy comfort of confidently assured sales is the danger of being undercut by the neighbour in quality of products or cheapness of price. What thus assures the sales is the ceasing of the possibility of undercutting, at least as a regular phenomenon of economic life with which one must reckon. For it requires no further substantiation that occasional preemption is never entirely excluded. Which we can now also express thus with a modern catchphrase: *if craftwork shall be capable of existing, then competition must be made impossible.*

But when is competition of producers among each other not or only weakly present?

Chapter 13: The Conditions of Existence of Craftwork

To begin with then, obviously when on the whole, in proportion to demand, *little is produced*. For then the competing becomes a matter of the consumers; the producers can behave circumspectly, in the way that has appeared to every genuine craftsman in all periods to be the natural order of things[313]. But the extent of production will be constantly defined by two factors: the size of the workforce and the level of their productivity.

The fewer the producers, then the tinier the danger of "overproduction", thus of an obstruction to sales. There will, however, be few producers when the population grows slowly, or when the junior staff are trained with great difficulty (empirical procedure!). There will in particular be few producers in non-agricultural areas, however, when the agricultural population is tiny.

But when the number of producers is fixed, obviously their total supply will be dependent on the extent of their productivity. The less developed this is, then the lower the danger of sales difficulty.

But everything which was previously mentioned in the way of causes which make the existence of craftwork possible on the side of supply applies only for the configuration of selling conditions defined by total production. It remains to verify which conditions also guarantee a comparatively assured existence to the individual participants in the total production, to the individual craftsmen each for himself — that is thus, *also excluding competition amongst the members of the same trade*.

What the essence of competition amongst sellers of wares amounts to is the ability of individual producers to be able to bring wares to the market better or more cheaply than his neighbour. It is in short that already mentioned possibility of undercutting. Where this is lacking, competition is lacking[314]. It is, however, constantly present only in limited dimensions where:

1. the *empirical procedure* dominates. For the reason that this makes the cheapening or improvement possible certainly only by a long process of reshaping. We know how much rapid advances of technology are foreign to the essence of experiential knowledge. We know that it is only accidents as it

235

were which replace a traditional procedure with a more expedient one. But we also know that all empirical abilities adhere to the person, and can only be transferred through and with the person. Even if it is thus assumed, that some craftsman brings into use a substantive improvement by which a product could be delivered better or cheaper, this procedure would at first be restricted to the sphere of his personal efficiency. It is as it were a natural patent which the inventor then exploits. And only to the extent that he confers his higher abilities through personal instruction can it be universalised. At first it remains only an exclusive possession and affects the configuration of sales conditions only in the modest range in which the output of the possessor moves. Which appears to us today as a perquisite of artistic configuration — the restriction of the extent of production to the sphere of activity of a personality. We must, for the period of purely empirical technology, comprehend that of most improvements in procedures by which an increase in qualitative attractions or a diminishment of production costs for a product could be brought about.

2. However, this stagnation of technical advancement, grounded in the nature of empirical procedure, and the consequent hindering of successful competition in the market for wares is now felt in its effect more than ever where the means are absent which are first able to properly cause or introduce into practice underlying improvements in procedures. This is, as will be yet shown in detail, the utilisation of larger and more powerful forces of nature, but in particular, as we already know, the bringing together of numerous workers into a (large) corporate concern. If the former is dependent on the advances in technical knowledge, then the latter is dependent on two *social conditions*: firstly, the presence of masses of men willing to work, and secondly, the accumulation of assets which can serve for the provisional upkeep of workers who are active in large numbers, as well as serve for the procurement of the means of production that is required for their activity — generally speaking, a corresponding "accumulation of capital".

Where one of these conditions or even both are unfulfilled, it is with the best of wills impossible, even if a producer were

Chapter 13: The Conditions of Existence of Craftwork

in possession of a more perfect procedure, for him to sweep his neighbour from the field through triumphant competition. But with that our investigation already reaches over to an area which shall be considered first later. What was being expressed in the preceding sentences was the fundamentally self-evident idea that *craftwork has as a prerequisite of its prospering the nonfulfillment of those conditions to which the existence of capitalism is tied*. What these are, however, should be established more precisely first.

I would like just to express the thought here that, even apart from all the previously mentioned elements, a circumstance still exists which would, with the state of technology assumed by us, as good as exclude competition in the modern sense, at least between producers in different places. I mean the difficulty of dispatching over a larger area the products produced through an advantaged procedure or under somehow more favourable conditions. For *transport technology* shares not a little in the imperfection of the technology of a time period.

Chapter 14: The Configuration of Goods Demand

Preliminary Remarks — Sources and Literature

(for Chapters 14–16)

What we contemplated in the previous chapters were ideals. An investigation is now required into how *the economic life of a medieval city was configured in reality*; that is — spoken precisely — an answer to the questions of whether and when, and to what extent, and in what deviation from the ideal was craftwork spread in the cities. Whereby then, at the same time, the question will be answered as to the extent to which the objective conditions of existence of craftwork were fulfilled in the Middle Ages.

As rich as our knowledge of the manufacturing order of the Middle Ages is, we know so little of the trades themselves. Most sources always just reveal again how it was meant to have been, and their editors have almost sufficed throughout with bringing before our eyes in systematic detail this state which one wanted to bring about.

We possess only quite, quite few depictions of economic life itself, and insofar as I am able to survey the source material published up to now, it will also be difficult to spread more light at least over the manufacturing life in the narrower sense. It stands much better with the history of trade. That *could* at least be written, for a greater quantity of human documents as well as more statistical material exists for it. (In recent years, it has also begun to be written.)

For the reconstruction of manufacturing life in comparison, we are reliant on the few fruitful listings of citizens and tax rolls as our main sources, and must attempt to use the guild statutes and other legal sources as well as we can for an indirect line of reasoning. Besides that, occasional descriptions and particularly also pictorial depictions come into consideration.

In any case, all the attention of the writer of the history of the Middle Ages should be directed at increasing the source material for a manufacturing history. We have enough now really for guild history.

The following depiction shall again not be anything more than a programme.

We will do well to visualise as clearly as possible the real economic life of a medieval city, to contemplate this in sequence from the standpoint of the consumer and then from that of the producer. I will begin with the establishment of goods demand.

Of what sort and of what extent was the demand which needed to be satisfied *in the city*? To that, it will first be answered that it kept itself with respect to extent always in relatively (ie. for our concepts) narrow bounds. For consumers of manufactured products (and we want to steer our attention to these in particular), the following come into consideration:
1. the residents of the city itself;
2. the surrounding inhabitants, especially as visitors to the weekly markets; and
3. the foreigners who visited the annual fairs.

The residents of the city itself never represented a large multitude during the Middle Ages, for the number of inhabitants of the city kept itself always, as we now can reveal with certainty, within narrow bounds during the Middle Ages. The regular visitors to the (weekly) markets from the neighbouring surrounds could likewise not have been very numerous:
A. because the countrysides were very thinly settled;
B. because there were relatively many "cities" strewn across the entire countryside; and
C. because the rural economy of self-sufficiency still occurred at all events to a large extent.

The following numbers inform us about the *density of population* and the *agglomeration of population* during the Middle Ages.

England had from the 14th up to the 16th century, according to the calculations of the very scrupulous T. Rogers, perhaps 2½ million inhabitants[315]; according to the estimate of P. Fabre 2,880,000 at the time of Henry II[316].

In *France*, 40 people were supposed to have lived to the square kilometre in the 14th century, then the population count sank, and only at the end of the 16th century did it again reach the state it had held 200 years earlier[317].

The largest city of the European Middle Ages (that is, apart from Byzantium) will surely have been Paris. But I do not believe that it had, as is mostly suggested, already reached in

Chapter 14: The Configuration of Goods Demand

the 13th century the number of 100,000 residents, as I do not consider Géraud's calculation on the basis of the *Registre de la Taille*, which comes to more than 200,000, to be free from error[318].

London had 35,000 residents in 1377[319].

Cities with approximately equal or somewhat larger numbers of inhabitants (40–50,000) were, in the 14th century in any case, surely only to be found in Italy and in Flanders-Brabant: Milan, Venice, Genoa, Bologna, Florence, Naples, Palermo, Ypres, Bruges, and Ghent[320]. In Germany, no city will have reached these figures. Lübeck had in that period between 17 and 24,000 residents[321], Hamburg (1419) 22,000, Augsburg (1475!) 18,300, Nuremberg (1449) 20–25,000, Strasbourg (1473–77) 20–30,000, Ulm (1427) ca. 20,000, and Breslau (1348) 21,866[322]. The great majority of medieval cities, however, will have comprised small to medium-sized cities of less than 10,000 residents — counting all the same though no less important trading cities as Frankfurt am Main and Rostock, the former (1440) with perhaps 9,000, and the latter (1387) with 10,785. Dresden had around that time 3–5,000 residents, Freiburg in Silesia 5,000, Leipzig 4,000, etc.

In England, there were in the 14th century only two cities apart from London with more than approximately 10,000 residents: York with 11,000, and Bristol with 9,500[323]. The average even of the larger cities lay under 5,000[324].

A considerable number of buyers will have gathered at the annual markets, the more so at the famous fairs. How many naturally eludes every speculation. It remains, however, to be considered that (as I will yet show) the number of sellers was likewise very considerable and that these originated from numerous cities. Thus only ever a modest portion of that total number of all visitors fell to the producers of *one* city.

The small number, certainly even with inclusion of the fair clientele, of consumers for whom the civic commerce could in general produce was now also considerably reduced though by the fact that by far the greatest part effectively came not at all into consideration as buyers of manufactured products. The reasons for this:
- the still strongly developed self-sufficient production in the countryside;

- the tiny degree of affluence; and
- the unequal distribution of wealth.

For the first assertion, no evidence can be provided in the way of figures. For the evaluation of the degree of affluence, we possess valuable material with numbers, likewise for the distribution of wealth.

When Rogers rates the (soil) productivity in the Middle Ages for England at a quarter of today's[325], that does not yet imply very much. In comparison, the wealth and income statistics, which we at least possess for some cities of the Middle Ages, spread more light when we place them in contrast with the prices for manufactured products.

According to the investigations of Eulenburg[326], in the Rhineland-Palatinate (in the 14th century), wealth amounted to:
- for up to 20 guilders[327], 29.5% of all wealth;
- for up to 60 guilders, 61% of all wealth; and
- for up to 300 guilders, 93% of all wealth.

So that only 7% of the population possessed more than 300 guilders (thus 2,100 marks in present-day (1916) currency) in wealth. Quite similar results are delivered by the investigations for Meissen, Dresden, Mülhausen in Thuringia[328], and other places.

In Paris (1292), of 1,324 craftsmen, 821 had less than 250 francs in present-day (1916) currency, that is 62.2%, 1,196 had less than 1,000 francs, that is 90.6% of the total. (According to the calculations of Martin St Léons.)

In Basel[329] (1429), of 969 craftsmen:
- 488 (50%) had less than 50 fl. in wealth; and
- 904 (91%) had less than 300 fl. in wealth.

To be held opposite that is that the prices of manufactured products in the Middle Ages were in no way lower than today, but rather higher, as every comparison of numbers — so far as they are at all comparable — shows.

If we nevertheless want to compare the "purchasing power" of money vis-à-vis the manufactured products in the Middle Ages with that of today, what then is meant by incomes like those corresponding to the levels of wealth stated above? And, into the bargain, with a more heavily developed

Chapter 14: The Configuration of Goods Demand

home-based production for one's own use. And there was one such buyer in the Middle Ages where there is now 10 or 100.

Except for perhaps the city administration, only the few dependents of the uppermost layer of wealth thus come into serious consideration as consumers of the manufactured products of civic producers. In substance, the lords again, to whom a handful of prosperous moneymen (Lombards in Paris!) were joined in the course of the Middle Ages[330]. Of the overall wealth of the land, the lion's share was already allotted to them as a group. In the Rhineland-Palatinate, according to the already cited calculations of Eulenburg (1895, 450), the top 3% of the "rich" people (over 600 fl.) had almost a third of the property and the city's wealth in their hands — 42 of them possessed 55,292 fl., 435 of the poor in the last class of wealth together had only 8,554. So that thus (which is the important thing) a considerable income (wealth) was allotted to specific households.

From the *Registre de la Taille* (Géraud 1837), I calculate that 161 persons paid more then 10 livres — together 3,134 livres or 27% of the incoming total taxes (12,243 livres and 8 sous) — whereas their share in the number liable for tax amounted to only a little over 1%. The average amount of tax which each of these "upper 161" paid amounted to 20 livres or around 550 marks in present-day (1916) currency. Since the taxes levied *le cinquantième* [the fiftieth] of income, these 161 would have paid tax on an income of 27,500 marks on average — there already some would fall off more easily for the products of craftwork. *Free* of the *taille* [impost], however, were — the nobility and clergy!

What we thus know of the level and distribution of income in the Middle Ages impels us to the conclusion that craftwork (perhaps — but also only partly — leaving aside the foodstuffs industry) worked predominantly for a small minority of prosperous people. That would doubtlessly also be confirmed by an investigation that set itself the task of deriving from the nature of craftwork the type of clientele for which the craftwork was producing. I believe it could be established that the overwhelming majority of all metal industries, most of the clothing trade (all who produce and process somehow better materials), and almost the entire building trade, to say nothing of the actual luxury industry, sold only to the rich, by which I naturally also mean the entire clergy, as well as the lower nobility, etc. I do not of course deny that, in addition, the "folk" were also consumers of manufactured products. I mean only that their demand did not give the characteristic note to the total demand (as it does in part today)[331].

When we ask what sort of *demand* there was for manufactured products in the Middle Ages, we can ascertain a few traits which distinguish it, as it appears to me, with reasonable certainty.

It was firstly surely more diverse than one has from time to time assumed. At least in the larger cities of France and Italy, even perhaps in Paris, we encounter a wealth of manufactured objects which amazes us. Master Johannes de Garlandia lists in his *Dictionarius*[332], which he wrote in the first half of the 13th century, what an abundance of articles of demand there were (of which obviously a great part was already produced by craftwork).

In addition, we may assume that the sense of the time was directed not only to the glittering and the magnificent, but also to the lasting, the precious, the solid. The predisposition for mere show, for tinsel, for kitsch, for trash, in short for everything which one today subsumes under the designation "high modern", was surely not possessed by the Middle Ages. I do not want to determine why it did not possess this — perhaps because there was as yet no modern industry whose life nerve is formed by the production of trash; perhaps because the masses had not emerged yet as consumers. It is enough that the taste of the time was on this point of a different nature than it is today.

Finally, the demand was relatively more stable. Those times lacked still almost completely that which we today are accustomed to designate with the word "changes of fashion". "The sense of the Middle Ages was in itself directed to the conventional, the traditional. A rapid change in fashions is not to be observed in Germany before the middle of the 14th century, and took hold from then on more in the cut of clothes than the types of fabric. One believed in the Middle Ages unreservedly in a plain should-be in all areas, even in the area of economic needs and of technology."[333]

Chapter 14: The Configuration of Goods Demand

Those who deny that and want to award to the Middle Ages just as much change in fashions as in our time are to be reminded that the change in customs of use in the Middle Ages involved incomparably much longer periods. I refer the reader for the time being to my discussion of this problem in the second volume of this work.

All in all, the clientele for manufactured products was in the Middle Ages as mannered as a craftsman could not wish better for. The conditions of craftwork-based production were, as far as the configuration of sales conditions come into consideration, fulfilled in the optimal sense.

But we will now see in what manner the demand for manufactured products was satisfied in the Middle Ages.

Chapter 15: The Manner of Satisfaction of Demand

I. The Final Consumers

How does the civic population satisfy their demand for manufactured products? (That is thus almost their demand for economic goods in general, since down to the oddments of foodstuffs (eggs, milk, fruit, vegetables) all human demand is a demand for already processed "ennobled" raw materials, thus for manufactured products. Even the most important foodstuffs that we enjoy already have a series of ennobling processes behind them, i.e. bread, meat, salt, drinks, etc.)

Now, for the most part it is still by *production in the self-sufficient economy*. Here raw materials were still extracted — i.e. the grain as long as agriculture was still practised by the townsmen, although that surely formed the exception in the larger cities during the High Middle Ages[334]. But they certainly still produced to a large extent a part of the livestock — the pigs; yes, in the end even the cattle[335]; poultry, etc. — then, in the gardens which almost every larger house had, they produced fruit, vegetables, and where the situation permitted, vines.

We will also recall that an especially important group of civic residents were the rich estate owners of a secular or religious nature. And these obviously continued their self-sufficient economy for a long while even in the cities. They obtained thus a large part of the raw materials, especially the foodstuffs, through their own operations (of their estates far from the city), and also had things manufactured in part in their civic households, as will be shown shortly. Thus the Duc de Berry or the chapter of Notre Dame in Paris still consumed the grain of their own estates at the end of the 14th century[336].

One naturally had to buy a quite considerable portion of the raw materials or semi-finished products: the grains or the flour, the malt, the prepared flax, fabrics, leather, etc. And this especially — and this case shall be treated here first of all — when the manufacturing production still took place to a substantial extent in one's own house.

It may be beyond all doubt that in all cities, even in the largest, the *home-based manufacturing activity* during the Middle Ages played a large role.

At home, of course, there was not only cooking[337], but also baking[338], the preparation of wine and beer[339], butchering[340], and, of course, also smoking, salting, etc. At home, candles were made[341]. At home, there was spinning[342], in part also weaving[343]; there was tailoring[344] and shoemaking[345]. For many of these tasks, one brought in a learned craftsman, whom we call in German a *Störer* [disturber] (the craftsman in the house works "for the disturbance[*] [*auf dem Stör*]") — a baker, a cobbler, a tailor, a butcher, a cloth cutter, a goldsmith, a cooper, etc. Even for mending utensils, craftsmen[346] occasionally came into the house or took the utensils onto the street[347]. How diffused the *Stör* work must have been in the German cities up until the later centuries is demonstrated by the prohibition of this way of working outside the guilds, as these began a more exclusive policy — thus the tailors in Helmstädt were prohibited from it in 1301, the cobblers in Frankfurt in 1355, the goldsmiths in Lübeck in 1371, and others[348].

The remaining part of manufacturing work was then now exclusively craftsmen's work, and was as a result practised by specialists for payment.

This was commonly in the form of what we designate as *fee or wage work* — that is, by which the consumer (customer) delivers the material for production to the craftsman.

Milling was certainly to a considerable extent milling for a fee. We may infer that from the heavy stocks of grain which the individual townsfolk kept (and in part had to keep)[349]. But we also possess enough evidence in addition for this[350].

---

[*]   [Tr.: i.e. disturbance of the guild order.]

Chapter 15: The Manner of Satisfaction of Demand

Likewise, *baking* was in many cases baking for a fee.

Anyone who did not have their own oven sent the bread or pastry dough to the baker[351].

The bakers were generally divided into market and home bakers [*Feil- und Hausbäcker*].

We may assume that the large majority of all *building* was executed for wages — the building owner provided the raw materials at his cost and had them processed by bricklayers, stonemasons, and carpenters for daily wages. This is spoken for by the peculiar organisation of the building trade during the Middle Ages[352], by the fact that we only ever hear of the daily wages of the building craftsmen[353], by so many descriptions that we possess of the purchases of the building owners, particularly religious building owners[354], by the contracts themselves between building owners and building craftsmen, of which originals have been handed down to us[355], and by many regulations of the guild orders[356]. Perhaps the building owners even bought raw materials (limestone and clay), and had lime, bricks, and building stone made by lime-burners and brick makers for a fee[357].

The owner not only delivered the building materials, but also the scaffolding (which he then first had to have produced beforehand by wage workers, if possible from wood of his own provenance), and the buckets and tubs for preparing the mortar[358], and also undertook with long-lasting work to renew the craftsmen's equipment[359]. Occasionally they were provided with food and housed by the building owner[360], and received a part of their wages paid out in clothing material[361].

In addition to that, the individual components of building were contracted out so that the craftsman became a "craftsman for hire" [*Kaufhandwerker*]. And thus the architect and the building contractor also emerged in an embryonic state, at first probably in the large buildings in Italy and with the royal construction in Paris[362] which — as we will yet see — was exemplary in more than one respect for the organisation of the building trade.

Wage work will have been very common in the *textile industry* and the apparel manufacturing appertaining to it. The self-spun yarn was given to the weaver for weaving[363], the raw fabric was then probably given for further processing to the cloth cutter, the dyer, the calendrers[364]. Then the finished material was given to the tailor.

Or one bought finished cloth from the cloth dealer to then hand over to the *tailor*. We see the wealthy customers in Paris, in Bologna, and in Venice buying the cloth in the company of the tailor who stood by the side of the customer with his advice. As we experience today when we buy carpets in Constantinople with the dragoman [interpreter], it obviously happened commonly enough that the cloth dealer "greased" the tailor so that the latter led his customers to him and not to the "competition". That should be denied him[365].

Hats were finished from self-delivered material by milliners[366].

Among the *Parisian* tailors, we encounter in the 13th century[367] the *tailleur le Roy* [the King's tailor], *tailleur madame la Royne* [tailor to the King's consort], *tailleur aux enfans le Roy* [tailor to the King's child], *tailleur Monseigneur Challes* [tailor to Mr Challes], *tailleur la Comtesse de Valois* [tailor to the Countess of Valois], *tailleur l'Evesque* [tailor to l'Evesque], *tailleur des Marmousetz* [tailor to Marmousetz], *tailleur du Temple* [tailor of the temple]. The Duc de Normandie and the Duc de Berry also had their own tailors. A certain Gauteron was in the 14th century "couturier du vicomte d'Aunay" [couturier to Viscount d'Aunay][368].

The same custom existed in *England*, as we may infer from the regulations of English guild orders that it was forbidden to the members of a guild to wear the livery of their lords. In France, these court tailors wore the badges of the house in which they worked, but were nonetheless listed at the top of the guild members. They were employed for fixed salary and free board. When they went on journeys, perhaps to buy material, they received reimbursement for the journey. Likewise there were women tailors in the castles of the great[369].

The same custom in *Vienna*: "sartor, serviens domini abbatis Scotorum; sartor ducis" [a tailor, servant of the lord abbot of the Scots; tailor of the ruler].[370]

We have here the progeny of old courtly craftsmen before us, of whom there were some also in other branches of manufacturing — as, for example, in the building trade — during the entire Middle Ages, and who on the other hand — obvi-

Chapter 15: The Manner of Satisfaction of Demand

ously — became the progenitors of the "courtly suppliers" of the more recent period. It would be worthwhile to write their history.

But even in other trades, we encounter wage work.

The precious metals were taken to the *goldsmith* to have them processed into jewellery or receptacles[371]; iron to the *shield maker*[372], for him to make the armour out of, and to the *farrier*, for him to make horseshoes out of — if a squire came with his little steed to the *fabbro-ferraio* [blacksmith] and brought with him the iron in an unprocessed state, then he would pay six *bon.*[*] for a horseshoe with eight nails, but if he brought all the iron already finished, then the mere attaching would cost only four *bon*. Obviously it was only the wealthy who provided the material; the rate is only listed for the shoeing of horses. When a farmer or water seller came, or even a small man with his little ass, then our smith provided all the iron; he transformed himself into a "seller of a product!" [*Preiswerker*][373]

Anyone who still slaughtered in their own house had the hide of the animal processed by the *tanner* into leather[374] so that the *Störer*[†] could transform it into boots.

And whatever other possibilities of the sort.

One will, however, have satisfied a very large part of the demand for manufactured products with *craftsmen who offered products for sale [Kauf- oder Preishandwerker]*. That is, with the same bakers, butchers, joiners, smiths, locksmiths, furriers, bag makers, and cartwrights who provided the raw materials for themselves.

Certainly the production *"to order"* played the same important role in the medieval city as it has up into our time. And indeed, one ordered — one may assume — from the craftsmen present in the city itself; not, as it later became common, from the producers in the larger city. I mean that the lesser noble who resided in the small provincial city ordered his house chair not from the joiner in Florence or Paris (like the cottage and estate owners today who must live in a "coal district" or an outlying region), but had it made "in

---

*   [Tr: bolognino?]
†   [Tr.: see page 248 above.]

his home town". If he was not able to find the master he needed there, then he will have insisted rather on calling in the absent workers. But we can only suppose all these things.

On the other hand, we know that a certainly considerable part of the consumer goods were not ordered first, but were *bought finished "in the store" or at market*, even when the producer was themselves resident in the city. With some articles this was understood of its own accord, like baked goods, meat, etc. "In the store" is something we now have to imagine as primitively as possible. In most cases, it will have been the room next to the workshop, if a special space was even designated for sales.

On the pretty woodcuts which depict scenes from the lives of craftsmen — unfortunately only of the 16th century — in Nuremberg[375], it is the rule that the wife of the master sells in the one room whilst the master works in the workshop adjoining. It was thus in bag making, in the furriers' trade, in butchery (a beast was slaughtered next door!), in rope making, and in joinery; whereas shoes were sold in a sort of open hall which was attached to the workshop. In the sales room lay, hung, or stood a small "collection" of finished goods.

The belt maker had 18 handbags [*Gretchentaschen*] "in store", the cobbler perhaps a dozen pairs of boots and shoes, the furrier a half dozen fur coats, the rope maker a dozen finished cords, ropes, etc. The buyers at the rope maker's, the butcher's, and the cobbler's are country people, at the other's they are rich patricians or nobles' wives.

Perhaps such objects were already a late result of development; perhaps we must imagine the times of the Middle Ages to be still more primitive, perhaps like in the woodcuts in J. Amman's description of all the stalls where the workshop and "sales room" are one and the same small space, and only very few pieces (perhaps ordered?) lie or hang around.

But there were certainly small sales stalls, "stores" or, if one wants, windows, in which finished products were arranged for sale, even in the earlier period. The Parisian bakers in the 13th century had their bread laid out in the "shop windows"[376], the goldsmiths in Stettin displayed silver utensils on their window sills for sale[377]. Likewise we know enough about bread stalls [*Brotbänken*], meat stalls [*Fleischbänken*],

Chapter 15: The Manner of Satisfaction of Demand

etc., which are preserved for us in their medieval shape even today in some cities (for example, Breslau!).

In general, certainly, the purchases of finished wares will in the rule surely have been carried out at the public sales outlets designated for them, the *markets*. Even the craftsmen resident in the place moved on designated days with their wares into the sales stalls in the marketplace of the city, where the crowd desiring to purchase then gathered. These (weekly) markets were then visited alike by the rural sellers of vegetables, fruit, etc., and here surely the famed "exchange" between craftsmen and farmers took place which one erroneously wanted to make the focal point of civic economic life.

Thus we know that the Parisian craftsmen offered their wares for sale in their stores in the city from Monday to Thursday every week, whereas they moved with them on Friday and Saturday "aux halles" [to the hall] (they were obligated to move, so that it was seen as a privilege when one did not need to carry out this weekly move)[378].

For the market held on every Wednesday and Saturday in Oxford, the market regulations were established by the university in the year 1319. The articles for sale were comprised, in addition to agricultural products (hay, straw, wood, pigs, grain, dairy products, etc.), of beer, coal, varnish, gloves, furs, and linen. Here too the craftsmen stood behind sales stalls in the high street and at the grain market.

Constant markets, so to speak, were held in the *sales houses* [*Kaufhäuser*] or sales halls which we encounter frequently, especially in German cities. They served for the sale of an individual good which might, so we may assume, have been produced in the place itself or come from outside. There were cloth halls almost everywhere, which either took up an entire house (garment house) or were housed in other buildings. In addition we find shoe houses[379], linen houses, bread houses, grain houses, slaughter houses, and fur houses[380]; but special sales houses were also erected for the specialties of a place — for example, for the woad in Görlitz. The salt houses also belong here. Most sales houses in the German cities were built in the 14th and 15th centuries; they are already detectable, however, in the 13th century[381].

In the larger cities there were then, however, everywhere a larger number of *professional, resident retailers* as well, from whom the demand for foodstuffs and manufactured products, probably mostly of outside origin, was satisfied. In any case, we have information from the 13th century about their existence and also of the nature of their business activity[382].

We know in detail what wares a Parisian "mercier" [mercer] had for sale in the 14th century[383] and how the "stores" looked in the cities of the Middle Ages. For, obviously, all the beginnings of retail trade involve a still undifferentiated storehouse, a so-called *Kram*, in which everything in general distributed by a specific retailer stood all in a jumble for sale.

Lübeck's roll of citizens from 1353 allows the merchants to sell imported foodstuffs [*Kolonialwaren*], raw materials, manufactured goods, and haberdashery. Wehrmann (1864, 272 ff.). Similar conditions in *Breslau* (Borgius 1899, 44); in *Leipzig* (Moltke 1901, 73 ff.); in *southern German* cities (Eckert 1910, 32 ff.). — In the *French* statutes of the 15th century the three main groups of wares (*mercerie, quincaillerie* [hardware], and *epicerie* [spices]) overflow into each other; the superintendent of the *merciers* (*roy de merciers*) had oversight over all the dealers who traded in torches, candles, spices [*Pfundwaren*] such as pepper, saffron, etc. ... "et toutes *aultres merceries et espiceries*" [and all *other haberdashery and spices*] ... over all "portants merceriepour vendre ou chose qui touche mercerie ou poids, balances, aulnes ou mesures, *soyent quinqualleries ou aultres choses subjectes audict roy des merciers*" [carrying haberdashery for sale or things that touch on haberdashery or weights, scales, alders or measures, *hardware or other things shall be subject to examination by the superintendent of the merciers*] ... "generalement toutes choses qui se vendent ou puissent vendre en faict de marchandise, les quelles ne se peuvent priser ne estimer que trop ou peu, est chose subjecte a mercerie" [generally of all things that sell or merchandise that in fact sells, those which cannot be sniffed nor esteemed too much or too little are the things subject to haberdashery]. From the "Ordonnance et reiglements concernents les marchands merciers" (15th century) (Fagniez 1898, 2:301 § 166). The apothecaries blended with the *epiciers* [grocers] — there existed up to the 15th century the "Corps des marchands grossiers, espiciers et apothicaires" [body of wholesale dealers, spice traders and apothecaries]. Cf. A. Philippe (1858, 89 ff.).

I will speak in Chapter 17 over the inner structure of medieval trade, in particular its craftwork-based character. Here it interests us only as one of the forms by which manufactured products are offered.

For the purchase of everything else, there remained finally the annual markets [*Jahrmärkte*][384], which were probably

Chapter 15: The Manner of Satisfaction of Demand

held regularly in every larger city, and which grew in some places into imposing fairs at which were sold finished goods in large quantities to traders, and raw and processed materials, tools, etc. to producers or traders, but also to a considerable extent wares to final consumers. Certainly a quite respectable part of the demand for manufactured products apart from the townsmen's was satisfied from these market wares which thus had not been created at the place of consumption, but converged here at the marketplace from outside, often probably from far away. The following information can be given with regard to the inter-locale sales of manufactured products, which refers both to the cases in which the craftsmen offered their wares for sale in their own person, be it in the way of peddling, or be it at markets or fairs, and those in which professional traders undertook the distribution. These will surely in the rule (but not always — resident retailers! — dressmakers in the cloth halls!) have sold their wares at the annual markets.

The distant sale of goods during the Middle Ages[385]

We encounter in all lands during the Middle Ages the craftsman or the craftsman's wife moving, in the same way as they still do today, with their self-produced wares on their backs or in wheelbarrows from place to place to seek out their customers.

The most well-known peddled craft of the German Middle Ages, which were partly also wandering crafts, were the kettle menders [*Keßler*] and the brass workers [*Kaltschmiede*]. They and their organisation are treated by von Maurer (1870, 2:490 ff.) and R. Eberstadt (1899, 259 ff.). They were primarily at home in France in Normandy, in Germany in the southwest, and in Belgium in the city of Dinant. Incidentally, these peddling craftsmen, who certainly dabbled also with wage work, surely also preferred to visit the fairs and markets with their goods. In our time, the south Slavic mousetrap makers stick out. But also the potters, and later the watchmakers belong here. Over the pedlar-like distribution of glass wares by glass cooperatives, see E. Gothein (1892, 846). Also the products of weaving were commonly sold by craftsmen through peddling. Over peddling cloth makers in the district of Hagen before French control, see Jacobi (1857, 104). Historical material is also found in volume 77 onwards of the *Schriften des Vereins für Socialpolitik* (Verein für Socialpolitik 1898).

Still more common, however, naturally is the evidence for the market visits of distant craftsmen as well as the spread of the trade in manufactured products.

Even if the *bakers*[386] from outside may not have come from all too far away to the civic markets which the sources of the 12th century already tell us about, we do not need to assume offhand such a spatial limitation for the *shoemakers*[387] mentioned at the same time. We find outside craftsmen (from Winchester) in the Early Middle Ages at the fairs of neighbouring cities in England[388].

We have numerous documentary confirmations for the distant market visits of *weavers*[389].

We may consider as a given that the 12th century already had an extensive *trade* in cloth produced by craftwork[390].

For the 13th century, the verifiable cases of inter-locale cloth trade pile up. We may assume that the sale of cloth was partly managed, as already mentioned, by the craftsmen themselves, partly by the clothing makers, the *drapiers* or drapers, that is, by professional cloth dealers who were also specialised just like the craftsmen. What amounted to the characteristic feature of the development in the 14th century was, however, a tremendous boom of the cloth industry in all lands of production[391].

The inter-locale *linen production* was of just as great a significance during the Middle Ages[392].

The linen was partly also put into trade in a *manufactured* state. In the trader rolls of the city Anklam from the year 1330, we find the following mentioned as objects of craftwork: tablecloths, hand towels, rolls of linen, bed blankets, and pillow slips. All these articles were traded wholesale and retail[393].

From the beginning of their existence, we may thus assume, the *silk industry* as well as *cotton* and *fustian weaving* were reliant on the sale of their products in an inter-urban or international framework.

Since the extraction of *minerals* and *metals* only took place at discrete places of discovery strewn across the earth, their consumption could never take place in larger quantities without them becoming objects of inter-locale and international trade. They were then traded thus during the entire

Chapter 15: The Manner of Satisfaction of Demand

Middle Ages. *Tin* had always been an object of international trade[394], *pit coal* was from the 13th century in England described as sea-coal, since it was exported overseas[395]. *Bricks* in England were imported from Flanders (14th century)[396].

Iron and *bronze* were already imported into northern Italy in the 10th century[397]. We find iron as an imported article from Europe in Egypt in the 12th and 13th centuries[398], in England at the beginning of the 14th century[399], and as the object of German-Italian[400] and Hanseatic[401] trade during the entire Middle Ages.

We encounter German *silver* in the 13th century at the fairs of Champagne[402] and on the way to England[403]. It was traded in the 14th and 15th centuries by the great merchants of Danzig[404] as well as by the traders of Lübeck[405]; and it enjoyed an increasing vogue in German-Italian trade[406].

Likewise, *copper*, *brass*, and *lead* are already often named as objects of international goods exchange in the Early Middle Ages. We hear of them in the 10th century in German-Italian trade[407], in the 11th century in the trade with England[408], in the 12th century on the Rhine[409], in the 13th century in Eisenach[410], in Hamburg[411], in Flanders[412]. In the 14th century, the named metals formed a popular object of trade in England[413], in Lübeck[414], in Danzig[415], in German-Italian trade[416], and were traded wholesale and retail in cities like Anklam and Goslar[417].

Not only raw materials and semi-finished products, but also the finished *products of the metal industries* came into trade early on. Ahead of everything were *defensive arms and weaponry*. Already in the 10th century, the Venetians were bringing weapons from the smiths of Lombardy, Styria, and Carinthia to overseas peoples[418]. We find swords, lances, and armour as objects of trade on the thoroughfares of the Alps during the 10th century[419]. We receive mention of the "Cologne swords", however, on the Upper Rhine already in the 12th century[420], and in trade with England at the end of the 13th and beginning of the 14th century[421]. We encounter a weapons trade then commonly during the 13th century, thus in Pirna, in Eisenach[422], and still more often in the following centuries, thus in Osnabrück[423], in Danzig[424], and in Lübeck[425]. From this arbitrarily selected documentary evidence, we may infer offhand a prosperous, extensive international weapons trade[426] during the entire Middle Ages, even if the assumption of such a trade would not be already self-evident from general considerations alone.

Vying with weapons as objects of inter-locale goods exchange, and occupying in many cases the place of swords, suits of armour, helmets, etc. when these began to lose their circle of consumers through the development of the technology of modern warfare, were *other products of the metal industries*, especially *iron wares*: tools, knives, locks, pins, sewing needles, hooks, eyelets, and whatever else tends to be subsumed under the description of "small steel implements" [*eiserne Kurzwaren*][427]. That they in were traded in larger quantities is something we may extract from the customs duty regulations of the 13th or 14th centuries, in which it was stated that they shall have duty applied by the piece, *dozen*, or *three score*[428]. Nuremberg, as is generally known, was famous during the Middle Ages as a place of production for small steel implements. Hence for such things as well as for so-called *gallantry wares*, the expression "Nuremberg ware" tended to be used for a long time — up into our own time[429].

Of the other manufactured products which we find, in addition to those named above, as objects of inter-locale trade during the Middle Ages, a few of the more important may be recorded here briefly with indications of sources.

Wooden wares

10th century: bowls, wooden porringers on the German-Italian thoroughfares[430].

11th century: tubs, bowls[431], barrels (*dolia*), and *vasa lignea* [wooden vessels][432] are traded articles.

12th century: wooden wares offered at the fairs for Enns[433].

13th century: wooden wares are one of the articles imported to England[434].

14th century: staves, hoops, sticks, and bowls traded in the Mosel country[435]; troughs, scoops, and bowls traded in Danzig[436].

15th century: Hamburg vats were permitted to be offered for sale in Sneek (Friesia)[437] also outside of the annual markets.

Chapter 15: The Manner of Satisfaction of Demand

Skins and Leather

Skins and leather were traded early on — steer, goat, cow, and sheep skins were mentioned in the Trier customs duties of 1248[438]. Tanning was one of the most common export crafts — in the 15th century Basel had 59 rich tanning masters with a work maximum of 360 skins annually (in total 21,240 skins, thus very much craftwork dimensions of production) alongside ca. 10,000 residents with 133 shoemakers[439]. We learn of a leather trade in England during the 13th century[440], and in Sweden during the 14th century[441]. Leather is an object of trade in the Middle Ages for Dortmund[442], Breslau[443], Erfurt[444], and Nuremberg[445]. And leather is mentioned as a wholesale and retail article of trade in the trader regulations of Goslar (14th century)[446]. Numerous types of leather are listed in the customs duty roll of Margaret of Flanders (1252)[447]. There was also a lively leather trade in Poitou during the 13th and 14th centuries[448].

The path which the leather took from producers to consumers was more often longer in the Middle Ages than it is today. Now the large shoe factory buys from the leather factory, which itself perhaps has its wholesale buyers in India. In contrast, we learn from medieval England that the guild members had the privilege of buying untanned skins (*corea recencia emere*) which they deposited with the tanner, whose product, the tanned leather, was then delivered to the cobblers[449].

Leather Wares

German saddlework was prized in foreign countries in the 10th century[450]; German reins and Saxon saddles were used by Lombard bishops during the entire Early Middle Ages[451]; and harnesses were objects of Dortmund's trade in the Middle Ages[452]. Pouches, belts, bags, etc. from "foreign places with permission" [*vremdim steten von gesten*] were put on sale in Schweidnitz (1336)[453].

Various Small Items

Ivory *combs* were objects of international trade in the earliest Middle Ages[454]. Horn combs are found (14th century) in the customs duty registers of Basel and Strasbourg[455], in the stores of Anklam[456], and all sorts of "small things" in those of Schweidnitz[457]. *Paternosters* of various materials formed an important article of trade during the entire Middle Ages for obvious reasons — wax, dried fish, and paternosters symbolise as it were the deeply religious character of those times. Wooden and lead paternosters have already been spoken of. But those of amber come into consideration particularly as sought-after articles of trade. The place where they were mostly produced was Lübeck. Here the paternoster-making formed during the entire Middle Ages a strong, prosperous, amply staffed craftwork that saw to the purchase of amber co-operatively[458].

Clothing and Finery

12th century: clothes are mentioned as an article of trade in the Freiburg municipal law[459].

13th century: merchants from Lille trade trousers from Bruges to Italy[460];
- trousers (1252) are mentioned in the guild rolls of Margaret of Flanders[461], and (1262) in the Hamburg customs duty rolls "in packs"[462];
- we find shoes traded at the fair below the the castle of Lags, the seat of the Counts for Upper Rhaetia[463];
- gloves, belts, purses, violin strings with the Parisian "merciers"[464];
- fur goods were objects of Pisa's trade (1218)[465].

14th century: trousers, caps, felt hats, ribbons, lace, buckles, etc. were sold in the traders' stores of Lübeck[466], Danzig[467], Anklam[468], Goslar[469], and Schweidnitz[470];

14th century: cobblers and tailors in Bergen sold their products over the sea[471];
- Strasbourg berets and trousers are traded to Italy[472], and Lübeck's to Venice[473];
- in Neustadt Brandenburg, "delremundsche Kleder" [? clothes] are encountered in a regulation[474]; extensive trade in clothes and finery is conducted by the brothers Bonis in Montauban[475], also Vicko von Geldersen traded in them[476];
- German hats were imported to Milan[477], and were imported in quantity into Basel[478].

Chapter 15: The Manner of Satisfaction of Demand

How that all now came together into a colourful and lively whole at a great fair is shown to us by a description of the events at the famous fair at Winchester in England, in the 14th century, which I will reproduce here (in the rendering of Ashley) in its main features[479].

William II permitted the Bishop of Winchester to hold a three-day fair on the eastern hill outside the city. The immediate successors to the King granted it a longer duration until it finally was extended by a charter of Henry II to 16 days, from 31 August to 15 September. On the morning of 31 August, the *iusticiare* [judges] of the Bishop's tent proclaimed the fair open from the top of the hill; after that, they rode through the city, received the keys to the gates, covered the scales at the civic wool market so that they would not be used during the fair; and rode, with the mayor and the bailiffs in their retinue, back to the great tent or pavilion on the hill. Here they nominated a special mayor, a bailiff, and an official of the court to rule over the city in the Bishop's name during the time of the fair. The hill was soon covered with rows of wooden stalls; in one stood the merchants of Flanders, in a second those of Caen or another Norman city, in a third the traders of Bristol. Here there was a goldsmith, there a row of cloth makers. Around the whole was drawn a fence with guarded entry — precautionary measures which did not always prevent enterprising adventurers from escaping the payment of duty, as they channeled a way into the interior of the market by digging under the fence. Also appearing on horse and in full armour before the Bishop's *iusticiaries* on the first day were all those dependents of the Bishop who were obliged by their fief to come, among whom three or four had to keep watch that the judgments of the fair's court and the orders of the Bishop's marshal were carried out in a law-abiding way, both at the fair and in Winchester and Southampton.

All trading in Winchester and within a circle of seven miles was forcibly proscribed for the time of the fair. At outlying posts, on bridges and other thoroughfares, guards were posted who had to see to it that there was no breach of the Bishop's rights. In Southampton, which lay outside the ban, only foodstuffs were permitted to be sold during the fair, and even the merchants from Winchester had to move to the hill and practise their trade there. There was a hierarchy of duties and fees: all merchants coming in the first week from London, Winchester, or Wallingford were free of entry duties; those coming after this period paid duty, excluding the members of the merchants' guild of Winchester. For the weighing of a bale of wool, four pence was paid as "Bishop's weighing fee", in addition to one penny each from buyer and seller to the master of the scales; it was conducted similarly with the fees for other wares. At every fair, there was a court of pieponder (so called from the dusty feet of those seeking justice), a special court of the fair at which the representative of the lord decided over all disputes occurring, according to mercantile law, as he at the same time abrogated the usual jurisdiction of the city temporarily; in Winchester, this court was called the "pavilion-bourt" (tent court). Here the Bishop's servants brought all the weights and measures for testing; here the judge established a valuation or a specific weight for bread, wine, beer, and other foodstuffs, and every baker whose bread did not prove full in weight was condemned to the pillory; here, finally, debt disputes between the merchants were arbitrated daily under presentation and comparison of notched tallies by the jurors.

A parallel to this description is formed by the poem which was sung to the "Lendit", that is, the fair in St Denis, in the 14th century, "La plus roial foire du monde".

The poet describes first how the procession draws past from Notre Dame, which blesses the entire body of merchants. Then he begins the enumeration of stalls with the various craftsmen and traders who offer their services (*barbiers, tavenciers*, etc.) or wares for sale. It is just as colourful a series as we have encountered in Winchester — there is no point in naming them individually. The poem offers special interest to the economic geographer through its long list of places from which the wares offered for sale there originated. The poem is in the collection printed by Barbazan and Méon (1808, 2:301 ff.), and forms No. 79 in Fagniez (1898, 2:173 ff.).

II. The Producers

The manner in which the producers satisfied their demand for the means of production has already been dealt with in the preceding pages; for it is in substance the same as that which served the final consumers for procuring the consumption goods they desired. It is hence unnecessary to give a ref-

Chapter 15: The Manner of Satisfaction of Demand

erenced depiction of the business practice followed here. For the sake of coherence and a better overview, I want just to specify in brief for the most important crafts the delivery possibilities that are worth considering.

The *baker* either received the flour delivered by the customer or he had the miller grind the grain which he bought himself or had delivered to him by the customer. He had his baking oven built by the bricklayer next door, though he may or may not have provided the materials for it. He ordered his equipment from the neighbouring smith or cartwright, or the cooper or brush maker, or he bought them finished at the annual market.

The *butcher* bought the cattle at the civic cattle market from producers or from licensed cattle dealers (as in Paris), or he went and bought in the villages or the neighbouring markets, or he raised cattle himself[480].

The candlemaker bought the tallow from the butcher; the spinner bought the sheepskin.

The *iron, lead, and copper-working trade* satisfied their demand for raw materials from traders at the markets.

The *wood-working trade* bought the wood in the neighbouring forests or from the rafters in the city if it lay by a river. There will surely also though have been wood dealers.

The *leather-working trade* found their raw material at the leather market, when they did not purchase skins which they had tanned by the tanner for a fee.

In the *building trade*, there were lime, brick, and stone traders from whom the bricklayers or stonemasons (in the case where the building owner did not provide the materials) could buy. They had the raw materials worked into intermediate goods by lime-burners and brick makers (we are familiar with such cases from above). The building glaziers surely found glass at the stalls of the annual markets or bought it from wandering glassmakers, if they did not seek out their huts themselves.

In the *textile industry*, all sorts of delivery ran together in all directions. Wool, flax, and hemp were offered for sale by producers or traders at the markets. Silk was bought from *merciers*. The specific intermediate steps of manufacturing production were frequently carried out in mutual wage work

— the weaver had the raw material spun by the spinner, the dyer worked for the weaver for a fee, or the weaver for the dyer, the fuller for the weaver, the dyer for the tailor, and so forth in motley confusion. The seller of the finished fabric (the dressmaker, *drapier*, draper) frequently had a few or all of the intermediate processes carried out as wage work. Equipment, hand tools, and processing materials were also procured for the textile industry in part from the neighbouring craftsmen by order (I have never founded anything in the sources over who manufactured looms — the cartwright?, the joiner?), in part from specialty markets (madder! woad!), and in part at the annual markets (foreign dyes!).

In summary, let us say that the procurement of the means of production played out in the same manner as today with the following differences from today's procedure. The purchase of finished objects always took place in the form of immediate purchase [*Lokokauf*] and indeed almost uniformly in the public purchase places (sales houses, halls, and market stalls) designated for it. In almost all cities, selling directly from traders (or producers) to the buyer with avoidance of the public purchase places was forbidden. And the prohibition was enforced, as numerous court proceedings testify. The sale for trial is as good as completely absent, thus the consignment delivery which played out essentially in writing.

Chapter 16: The Organisation of Manufacturing Work

I. The Linking of the Producers with the Market

If we now want to look at the manufacturing life of the medieval city from the viewpoint of the selling producers, we will — in immediate connection to the insight obtained up to now — first of all classify the various manufacturing workers with respect to the manner in which they bring their products or their services to the man (or to the woman). We have already become acquainted with all these types and need only define expressly once more that there were in the medieval cities:
1. manufacturing producers who worked in the houses of consumers;
2. manufacturing producers who did wage work for final consumers, and then on a large scale those who did wage work for other producers (dyers, fullers, etc.);
3. manufacturing producers who produced goods for the local market, be it again on order or be it for store; and
4. manufacturing producers who produced for a large (interlocale) market — "export manufacturing".

In summary, all of the ways in which the producer can in general be linked with the market occurred in the cities of the Middle Ages.

II. The Location of Manufacturing

From the preceding list of the types of manufacturing producers it can be deduced without further ado that there was in the Middle Ages not merely trade limited to the local market[481], but that in contrast the one city produced for the other.

The question to be asked is: according to what laws was the location of those manufacturers who produced for a large market determined in those times. An investigation of this has never been undertaken to my knowledge and a task deserving of thanks arises here again for the economic historian (who has some spirit).

What can already be said with some certainty is this:

1. The *local specialisation* was for several important trades in the Middle Ages *very great*, probably greater than today. That is, specific products were only produced in this city, and others in that city.

In the well-known handbook of an English jurist from the middle of the 13th century[482], we find recorded as cities specialising in cloth manufacture the following: Lincoln for scarlet cloth, Bligh for woollen blankets, Beverley for brown cloth (burnet), Colchester for coarse cloth (russet) — in the Acts of Parliament from the year 1301, eight weavers from this city are listed. Linen production was recorded in Shaftesbury, Lewes, and Aylesham; cord in Warwick and Bridport, the latter was also famed for its hemp fabrics. Fine bread was provided by Wycombe, Hungerford, and St Albans; knives by Maastead; needles by Wilton; and razors by Leicester. Banbury was well-known for its drinks, Hitchin for its mead, and Ely for its ale. Gloucester is the main place for iron, Bristol for leather, Coventry for soap, Doncaster for saddle girths, Chester and Shrewsbury for skins and pelts, Corfe for marble, and Cornwall for tin. Grimsby provided dried cod, Rye whitings, Yarmouth herrings, and Berwick salmon; Ripon was a horse market even in the 16th century; one bought gloves in Haverhill, oxen in Nottingham, and saddlery in Northampton.

The local specialisation was especially great in the *textile industry*, but also in other export trades, like, for example, the weapons industry.

There was no talk of a consistent dominance of all branches of the textile industry. The opposite applied: here blue was coloured better, there red better; here one understood better the preparation of loden cloth, there that of linen[483].

Chapter 16: The Organisation of Manufacturing Work

Already early on, *schürlitz** weaving, for example, had specialised: red was coloured in Ulm, black in Augsburg; Cologne was famed, alongside green and black in particular, for the blue and white checked "Cölsch"; the Basel *vogelschürlitz*† was blue, or blue and white[484], etc.

The silk industry remained limited to individual cities much longer even than the wool or linen industry. It took centuries before it spread itself in Italy from Lucca to Genoa, Milan, and other cities.

The great extent to which the second great export trade of the Middle Ages, the metal industry, in particular the *weapons branch*, developed specialisation is well known. The blades of Toledo, Brescia, and Passau; and the armour of Milan, Innsbruck, and Nuremberg had a monopoly everywhere[485].

To get a proper idea of the local nature of medieval manufacturing, we must compare it perhaps with the production of *modern agricultural* specialities. Even today agriculture has, thanks to its dependency on the natural conditions of the place of production, particularly for delicacies, preserved a widely wrought localisation of its products. There are special maps for gourmets on which the most famous places of production for the ingredients of a good kitchen are recorded[486]. A map of the geography of manufacturing in the Middle Ages would look similar.

Well-known is the partiality of the Middle Ages for conferring a specific epithet on the various cities, or for otherwise characterising them by a specific quirk which would separate them from one another. Here we commonly find the production of manufactured specialties brought into use as a distinguishing feature.

It must, however, be called to attention that the regional distribution of manufacturing in the Middle Ages, even where it was specialised, differs in one point essentially from today's arrangement of the individual branches of manufacturing: the production of a specialised article took place only in a city, and, in addition, it also took place entirely, from beginning to

---

*   [Tr.: a fabric with linen warp and cotton weft.]
†   [Tr.: Schürlitz woven with a bird pattern.]

end, in that city. Whereas today the sub-processes of production are commonly placed in different localities, they played out in the Middle Ages more frequently in one and the same place. For example, if a city was famous for its blades, then it did not usually obtain the prepared steel bars and the grips from two other cities, but instead produced them itself. Whereas today a weaver draws his yarn from various places, in the Middle Ages all the necessary acts for producing the material, from the raw materials to the finished fabric, were carried out in one and the same city — one thinks of the weaving cities like Florence! Sometimes the guild statutes prescribe this unification of all the process steps in the same place, like that of the linen weavers in Paris. No joiner will buy their boards today on-the-spot, they obtain them from the sawmills by the distant border, etc.

Though, here it is not perhaps about a different specialisation of the work process itself. This can, on the contrary, be shaped in the same way as today. That is, the occupations can be separated also in the horizontal direction: the beating, stretching, spinning, and weaving of the wool, and the cutting, dyeing, and dressing of the cloth can form the matter of special professions just like today (or more like today); what alone makes the difference between then and now is the (frequently, not always!) different spatial arrangement of the various occupations.

2. The *reasons* for this strong and idiosyncratic specialisation of manufacturing production are in part the same as those which define the location of manufacturing still today. For a very considerable part, there were in the Middle Ages idiosyncratic reasons which turned out to be operative here. In a time in which the empirical procedure alone dominated, a specific craftsmanship (for weaving, for dyeing, for smelting, for chasing, etc.) in particular had to remain limited far longer, even permanently in some circumstances, to a small circle of inducted producers, because the exercise of this competence remained the "secret" of this circle, and could in any case only be learnt with great difficulty by others who did not ply the craft on-the-spot. Only through the migration of masters could the art be transferred from one place to another. (Whereas today the technological science is ubiquitous.)

Chapter 16: The Organisation of Manufacturing Work

In what quantitative relationship the manufacturing production for the local market stood to that for an inter-urban market is something we will be able to ascertain exactly and numerically for the Middle Ages probably just as little as for the present-day. That the local goods production had a relatively greater significance than today may, according to all that we know about the economic conditions of the Middle Ages, not be questioned. Some trades which these days are only found in particular places were in the Middle Ages in almost every city, like for example (and especially!) weaving. If one wants to indicate with the expression "closed city economy" this preponderance of a spatially bounded satisfaction of demand, then I have nothing to object against this usage. But use it with caution!

III. *The Number of Manufacturing Producers and their Productivity*

We know very little about the numerical share of the manufacturing workers in the total population or even just the civic population. It has been claimed that manufacturing in the narrow sense would more likely have taken up a broader space in the cities than today. But we are unable to say whether the few investigations which we possess are typical, and considerations of a general nature hardly justify the employment in favour of a definite assumption. Bücher assumes, for the end of the 14th century, 50–60% as the share of the craftsmen's professions in the (civic!) population[487]. For the craft groupings II–IX (thus manufacturing in the narrow sense), he calculates 51.4% for Frankfurt in the year 1387 against 36.7% in the year 1875. In comparison, Eulenburg[488] comes to fundamentally different results: the manufacturing population of Heidelberg made up only 46.6% of the total population in the year 1588 against 47.7% in the year 1882.

The manufacturing producers, however, surely formed a still much smaller share of the total population in the large cities of the Middle Ages. In Paris, the number of "craftsmen" (*artisans*; but amongst whom all retailers are counted) amounted (according to the tax registers) to 4,159 in the year 1292, and 5,844 in the year 1300[489]. To these numbers are also appended, however, in part the assistants. We will thus at most be permitted to multiply by four to obtain the manufacturing population; this would thus have numbered in the respective years around 17,000 and 23,000 heads; that would be, by my estimate of the number of inhabitants of Paris, perhaps 25–30%. If one takes as a basis the usual estimates of the number of inhabitants (100,000–200,000), then only 10–20% would be the result.

Two things are certain in comparison on the other hand:
1. The share in the total population of those engaged in manufacturing in the narrow sense was in the Middle Ages quite considerably lower than perhaps today, since the great majority of manufacturing producers sat in the cities and these comprised in the highest case 10% of the land's population (estimate of Rogers);
2. The number of manufacturing producers was during the entire Middle Ages proportionately scarce, that is, in relation to the demand for their services. Yes — at specific times, a shortage of craftsmen even dominated. In the 14th and in the first half of the 15th century, we see (in Germany) frequently entire cities endeavouring to obtain one or more dyers, like Brietzen in 1355, Esslingen in 1401, and Leipzig in 1469[490]. In Vienna in the 14th century, there was a lack "of craftsmen everywhere"[491].

The best evidence for the scarcity of craftsmen are the preferential treatments through privileges of every sort, innate to all the earlier period, whereby princes and cities attempted to shackle foreign craftsmen to their territory.

Also the price ceilings, which were enacted around that time in many places for craftwork[492], confirm this scantiness of manufacturing labour.

If we now ask what conjunction of conditions was necessary to cause such a state, we may perhaps mention the following as the primary determining ones.

First of all, the difficulty of training the staff technically is to be considered. As long as it required a long step-wise process, a regular apprenticeship, and the personal, conscientious instruction by the master (as the empirical procedure requires), the growth of the progeny of manufacturing producers was kept in narrow bounds by nature. That the empirical

Chapter 16: The Organisation of Manufacturing Work

technology likewise made difficult the transfer of a skilled procedure to another group has been ascertained in another connection already.

But then — and above all — we will, in order to explain this, have to call on the idiosyncrasy of the conditions of population in the Middle Ages. This consisted:
1. in a slow increase of population in general; and
2. in a relatively low rate of agricultural population surplus.

For which in the following, as far as the sparseness of the material allows it, a few indications can be made.

As sparse as even the demographic sources for the Middle Ages run[493], the following can be ascertained with some confidence.

In *Germany*, we must assume a slow increase in population up until the 13th century. The annual growth rate in the regions investigated by Lamprecht amounted to 0.5% for 1100–1150, 0.4% for 1150–1200, and 0.35% for 1200–1237[494]. In comparison, the judgment of Schmoller is in agreement "that there can be no talk of a general increase in population from 1250 to 1450"[495].

The same picture is provided by other lands:
- in *England*, increase between Domesday Book and Hundred Rolls, then standstill until 1500[496];
- in *France*, growth up to the 14th century, then stagnation or decrease up to the 16th century[497]; and
- in *Belgium*, strong population increase in the 12th and 13th centuries[498], which apparently subsided in the 14th century[499].

With respect to the conditions of existence of the medieval population, these statements will not amaze us. For the positive "checks to population" were, as we know, so powerful that even the highest numbers for births were incapable of plugging the rising gaps. We need to remind ourselves of some well-known things:
1. the deficiency in all hygiene in the city and countryside[500];
2. the frequency and bloodiness of wars; but above all,
3. both the scourges of the Middle Ages: famines and epidemics, which liked to appear together[501].

All lands were regularly beset by them[502] and everywhere they worked in the same devastating manner. The 14th century suffered most of all: it is the century of the plague κατ' ἐξοχήν [par excellence].

One may argue over to what degree the information of contemporaries regarding the magnitude of the numbers of those who died deserves to be believed — whether, for example, in England a third or half of the population or even more fell victim to the plague[503] — but no doubt can prevail about the ravages being sufficient to constrain the increase in population for a long time.

Keeping the agricultural population surplus within narrow bounds then helped a series of other circumstances, particularly the possibility, which did not decrease during the entire Middle Ages, of settling down on one's own clod of earth, even if only as a dependent of a lord.

In *Germany*, the reconquest of the east by Germans signified in itself an enormous expansion of the existing area of settlement. But even in other lands, the *terra libera* [free land] only dwindled in the later course of the Middle Ages. It only applies to *France* for the period of 1200–1350: "chaque jour signale de nouvelles appropriations du sol, de nouvelles conquêtes du laboureur" [every day heralds new appropriations of the soil, new conquests of the ploughman][504]. The area of settlement in the *England* of the 14th century was, like in Germany, artificially enlarged by the dissolution of the landed estates[505]. A relatively densely settled area like *Belgium* sent a surplus of population into the neighbouring, thinly settled lands of Germany[506] and England[507]. And then the crusades and what was associated with them!

A last reason for the low supply of manufactured products lies in that the already sparse producers were also incapable of producing more because the *level of productivity of the manufacturing technology* during those centuries must be assumed to have been unusually low.

Since we unfortunately possess no indicator for measuring the level of productivity of labour, we are reliant on inferences from the symptoms. Such symptoms of a low level of productivity are the following.

1. The *level of prices* of numerous manufactured products.

As undoubtedly correct as this claim is, it is difficult to prove numerically because we can almost never ascertain the complete uniformity of quality of the manufactured products whose prices we want to compare.

Chapter 16: The Organisation of Manufacturing Work

It is possible with approximate certainty, for example, with iron: a ton of iron cost £9 in England in the 14th century, that is £27 in present-day (1916) currency, whereas a ton of best German foundry pig iron straight from the factory in Düsseldorf in 1913 costs 77.5 marks (J. E. T. Rogers 1898, 10). In comparison, the descriptions "a hat", "a pair of boots", and "a coat" are quite vague; even with fabrics, the difference in quality can be very large. But we can ascertain with confidence that manufactured products — like, for example, fabrics — were dearer, the more labour and less material was embodied in them, and that the difference between the highest and lowest prices was much greater than today. Evidence for the lower productivity and lower technical efficiency of the manufacturing labour! Cibrario* shares prices for material from the period 1261–1400 which diverge in a ratio of 1:140; Uzzano† (15th century) specified for the most expensive cloth a price 35–40 times higher than for the cheapest. Cf. in addition, Roscher (1854, 1:264ff. § 134), and the numerous prices quoted for manufactured products in D'Avenel (1894, 3:339 ff.; 4:).

2. The *multitude of employed workers*: in Wesel in the year 1428, 5,140 pieces of cloth were produced by 342 master weavers[508]. If one calculates for one master weaver (or weaver in general according to Schmoller) only two other persons also occupied with the preparation of cloth (which is certainly much to low), then the production of those 5,140 pieces (which is the monthly production of a large factory of the present-day) would require 1,000 persons, easily twenty times the current number. These figures seem to have been typical for the Middle Ages: in Beauvais, the master weavers reported that they were 400 head strong and had made "up to 100 pieces of cloth" a week[509].

3. The *duration of the production process*: to manufacture a good lock still occupied 14 days at the end of the 15th century[510]. Where it involved artistic efforts, one reckoned in years. The entire secret of architectural and artisanal achievements of the Middle Ages, which often amaze us, lies in the enormous length of the production periods. Well-known are the centuries long building times of the town halls and churches. But even the production of furnishings often occupied years — one just reads through the lists of the names of makers of choir stools, inlays, cabinets, etc., which we possess in great number, to see how generations took turns with the

---

* [Tr.: work not detailed by Sombart, but probably Cibrario (1839).]
† [Tr.: a town in Tuscany.]

production of some outstanding objects[511]. The first goldsmiths were occupied on the St Jacob altar in Pistoia and in the baptistery in Florence for more than 150 years; Ghiberti worked for 40 years on the great gates which were worthy of closing the entrance to Paradise[512].

IV. The Form of Economy

Was the organisation of manufacturing work in the cities of the Middle Ages now craftwork-based? Was the idea of craftwork realised? Had the guild spirit embodied itself in the fabric of life?

An entirely definitive answer to that will probably never be given. We will always be reliant in substance on an inference from certain indications, and a judgment will be formed variously according to the material known to the individual, and according to the higher or lower assessment which he bestows on this or that symptom. We must be attentive to what sorts of evidence are at our disposal and what we may infer from them.

In particular, no doubt shall prevail that reality distanced itself in quite essential points and often quite far from the ideal of a perfect craftsman-like nature of manufacturing life that lay at the basis of the guild regulations.

One thing is meanwhile quite certain: the guilds' paramount goal of transforming the entire field of manufacturing life was surely never achieved by them during the Middle Ages. What we know of the sphere of domination of the guilds in the various cities confirms the correctness of what Bücher asserted about the circumstances in Frankfurt am Main:

> A part of the industrial production was always performed on the basis of free operations. Thus the civic authorities, often also the affected parties themselves, took great pains even in later centuries to extend to these circles of work as well the organisation that had been proven elsewhere. It was usually those producers for whose products an extensive demand was never present; often, however, they were those who later attained great prominence and maintain this still today (for example, the joiners, beer brewers, saddlers, and

Chapter 16: The Organisation of Manufacturing Work

goldsmiths), whereas others (in Frankfurt, for example, the adornment makers [*Posamentierer*], calico smoothers, fustian weavers, and button makers) vanished into thin air after prospering for shorter or longer periods. For the period of the 14th century, in which the town council was sparing with the granting of rights to form guilds and keep drinking rooms, a quite significant part of the manufacturing population of the city still stood outside the publicly recognised "crafts", even if not outside any organisation.[513]

We frequently observe how contrary tendencies from other circles cross the direction of the guilds' interests. For example, those tendencies of sovereign origin, as there were in early times already in Vienna and similar places. Hence on the face of it the guild ideal — the enforcement of the guild [*Zunftzwang*] — was never fully realised anywhere.

But what I think is much more important is that we also materially observe substantial deviations from the idea of the craftwork-based organisation. In particular, there can be no talk of the "sustenance" which was allotted to the individual craftsman, or which accrued to him in the course of time, as having consisted perhaps in an entirely equally sized sphere of production or in an entirely equally high income.

The thought of a mass of economically equally situated tradesmen can, as far as can be ascertained, make no claim to correctness for any time in which craftwork had already in general arrived at a higher level of development. There were for all periods crafts which totally surpassed others many times over in affluence, and within the individual crafts there were masters who towered high over their colleagues in riches, if the word is appropriate here[514]. A few figures will be sufficient as evidence of this fact, because they result for quite various times and quite various places in a quite consistent picture of a strong differentiation of wealth among the craftsmen.

We are fell informed about the earning conditions for *Parisian craftsmen* in the 13th century through the *Registre de la taille* (of 1292) (Géraud 1837). According to it, there was one felt hat maker with an income of 19,000 francs, a cloth maker with 9,000 francs, a few other craftsmen with an income of more than 5,000 francs, and over 100 with an income of more than 1,000 francs, whereas the great majority of craftsmen drew fewer than 250 francs of income. In particular, the following figures arose:

Incomes of:	Craftsmen:
more than 10,000 francs	1
5,000–10,000 francs	6
1,000–5,000 francs	121
250–1,000 francs	375
50–250 francs	821

The picture which the 15th century craftsmen of *Basel* impart to us is quite similar[515]. Here the distribution of wealth (1429) for the various crafts was:

	less than 50 fl.	from 50 300 fl.	300 to 1,000 fl.	over 1,000 fl.
Wool weavers [*Grautücher*]	159	51	2	1
Smiths	42	86	36	8
Butchers	34	35	18	10
Bakers	19	31	14	6
Tailors and furriers	65	47	9	2
Carpenters and masons	86	100	28	5
Shearers (?), painters and saddlers	24	34	16	2
Linen and other weavers	53	32	3	–
	488	416	131	34

The following wealth differences were displayed by the craftsmen of *Heidelberg* in the 15th century. The shares of wealth in guilders per head of the various guilds was[516]:

Butchers' guild 199
Bakers' guild 167
Tailors' guild 119
Shoemakers' guild 113

Chapter 16: The Organisation of Manufacturing Work

Smiths' guild 100

Weavers' guild 62

And "even within the individual guilds, no equality of property reigned, but rather quite large variation. On the other hand, the middling incomes did not constitute the rule throughout, but rather only a few rose above the average. [...] Among the 91 smiths of Heidelberg in the 15th century, nine pertained to the 'large' wealth and 58 to the 'small'," etc.[517]

What glaring differences of wealth existed between the individual masters of the same craft in the Middle Ages is also shown by the following comparison. Of the wool weavers in Frankfurt am Main in the 14th century, 11 had the right of supply to the fair for 36 pieces of cloth, 22 for 24 pieces, 10 for 18 pieces, 8 for 12 pieces, 20 for 10 pieces, 13 for 8 pieces, and 49 for only 4 pieces[518]. There were thus also differences in the extent of production like 1:9.

The disparities in the *English* cloth making seem to have been almost greater still[519].

For *Cologne*, the individual guilds differentiated the independent members, that is, those members working on their own account, into brothers and masters. Mone[520] assumes, as the reason for this difference, that the middle step of so-called brothers was erected between masters and journeymen so that they could still ply a craft independently as small tradesmen; hence they only had to pay half the entry money. Once they had acquired the necessary assets, they entered the class of the masters.

Incidentally, as one knows, the documents of the Middle Ages themselves frequently mention poor and rich members of the guilds, and many regulations are encountered in them for preserving the poor members independently from the rich despite the material difference, and for enforcing the fundamental equality of both[521].

What a lively image of the strong differentiation in the Parisian butchers' trade is given to us by the complaint of the poor, pitiful beings who have their 10 pieces of meat and perhaps a few slices of ham for sale on their table, and whose handiwork should be placed by the right pretentious big butchers[522].

And as the figures just advised already indicate and other signs confirm, there were certainly in the Middle Ages forms of manufacturing businesses which hardly deserve the name of craftwork; be it that masters fell into strong dependence on merchants, or be it that they themselves grew to be small entrepreneurs. We indeed do not know, for example, whether the cloth maker who had an income in the year 1292 of 9,000 francs obtained all this from making cloth. It is improbable. But that amongst the Parisian cloth makers, of whom quite a number appear in the statistics with quite high incomes, there were certainly already many a one who exceeded the scope of craftwork-based organisation can even be inferred from a few regulations of the guild statutes. These namely prescribe the maximum number of looms which someone may employ in his house (N.B. that is the requirement!) to be two broad and one narrow loom for each of the master, every unmarried son, one nephew and one brother. Thus, if that was fully exploited by someone, 15–20 looms could easily be found together underneath one roof. According to the figures provided by Salzmann[523], a cloth maker in the year 1395 in the west of England would have presented 1,080 (short) pieces (12 yards in length) of narrow cloth to the cloth measurer, another 1,005, nine others 1,600 together. If that was really a year's production, then we may infer a workforce of up to 30 with the largest cloth makers.

And that, with such a state of affairs, the craftwork-based structure was split apart and a class of lifelong assistants began to form may be seen as the self-evident consequence of the enlargement of the operations. (Although one should not think with every association of journeymen of modern trade associations)[524].

It is itself not to be disputed that in some cities an entire branch of industry during the Middle Ages had already stopped being craftwork and had begun the development into capitalism. The impression which we receive on the strength of the in-depth and meticulous description by Doren of the state of the Florentine cloth industry in the second half of the 14th century is that this trade at the time was already imbued strongly with capitalist elements. And there were certainly also similar industries in other cities of the Middle Ages.

Chapter 16: The Organisation of Manufacturing Work

And yet! Despite all that, our judgment will have to be that the form of organisation of the manufacturing work during the Middle Ages was also in reality that of craftwork. Craftwork lent its particular stamp to the overall structure of manufacturing life. Craftwork was not only the predominant, but also the almost exclusively dominant form of economy.

And to prove the correctness of this conception — I have said it already — we possess no authentic material. We must attempt to arrive there by detours — at least in order to make probable that the postulated claim is correct. These detours are of two sorts: indicative (symptomatic) evidence, and theoretic (deductive) evidence. I will attempt to lead the reader on both paths.

Let us look around first at what symptoms for the existence of craftwork we know about.

To begin with — and recognisable with complete clarity — there are these certain signs of craftwork-based organisation:

1. The (as one could say) *organic specialisation of occupation*. It recurred everywhere that we find manufacturing work in the cities in the Middle Ages and with almost entirely consistent features. It was based everywhere on the same fundamental ideas: that the individual manufacturing occupations should be demarcated from each other insomuch as they befit a living "craftsman"; and that they bestow a meaningful content on his highly personalised operations.

I said this emblem of genuinely craftwork-based organisation would be clearly recognisable. In fact, it is thus virtually the only thing which the research into the structure of manufacturing life in the Middle Ages has laid bare with reasonably faultless evidence. We possess from various types of medieval cities the lists of persons employed in manufacturing, so that we are able with some certainty to apprehend the main regular features of the configuration. We can even reveal with certainty that in the professional structure of the medieval cities the extent of manufacturing specialisation was defined by the degree of industrial development. I want to say that the progressive refinement of manufacturing production expressed itself in an increasing segregation of individually specialised activities condensed into independent professions; thus that the number of named professions offers an approximately safe yardstick for the knowledge of the degree of development which the manufacturing life of a city has attained. A "law"!

Of course, it must be assumed thereby that the reports which we possess about individual cities display the same measure of accuracy (and the editors the same measure of mathematical aptitude!). If, for example, Hirsch ascertains for Danzig in the Late Middle Ages only 60 different crafts, then we can (according to what we know of Danzig's economic life in comparison to the other cities) say without any further ado that here the lists are incomplete. Also that Riga in the 13th and 14th centuries shall have only had 75 professions in the wider sense appears doubtful to me. In contrast, the figures which Eulenburg has ascertained for Heidelberg, Bücher for Frankfurt, and Schönberg for Basel seem faultless to me. We can, I think, calmly compare them with one another.

Independent professions shown:

> Heidelberg 103
>
> Basel 120
>
> Frankfurt (1440) 191

In these figures, the various high degrees of development of the three cities can be revealed, although the number for Basel is overly low. Perhaps this has its cause in that it only relates to two parishes. If we want to be entirely certain, then we discard it also and compare only Heidelberg and Frankfurt. With which it is still to be noted straightaway that the number of professions in Frankfurt from 1387–1440 increased by around 43, which is new evidence for the validity of our "law".

These figures obtain their full significance, however, only when we now again compare them with the figures which we possess from actual "big cities" of the Middle Ages. As is well-known, the sources flow most amply in the greatest city of the Middle Ages: Paris. And anyone who wants to learn what medieval manufacturing existence was in it fullest development will have to turn his gaze away from Heidelberg and Frankfurt and will always have Paris in view.

Chapter 16: The Organisation of Manufacturing Work

There a life welled up though, which was entirely different from that in the former cities, and, in particular, the degree of specialisation is exceptionally higher than in them. When Bücher (1886, 227) suggests: "the wealth of the structure of labour which opens up here before us — namely in Frankfurt — surpasses everything which has become similarly known about any medieval city since that time," that is, with respect to the figures which the *Registre de la Taille* (published 1837) offers us, unable to be upheld. For in this the number of listed professions amounts to more than double as many as in Frankfurt — I number them, with omission of the persons described as *chambrière* [chamberlains] and *valet* [servants], as being 448. And of those, perhaps two thirds are manufacturing professions in the narrow sense — according to the determinations of Fagniez, 350 various craftsmen were distinguished — that would thus be the climax of the medieval state of manufacturing with regard to the structure of professions.

(Unfortunately, I must forsake showing a closer interest in the *Registre de la Taille*; here again rest buried treasures — despite the commendable works which Géraud, Fagniez, and others have published over it. Again, a tempting task for an economic historian (with some spirit) would be the processing of the *Registre de la Taille* under the viewpoints established in this work!)

2. Another important symptom for the predominance of craftwork-based organisation is the *smallness of operations*. Unfortunately, we do not know much about it, by no means as much as over the specialisation of professions. For the sources from which we discern the latter are not fruitful where it concerns the shape of the operations. In the best case, we know the number of assistants (journeymen) who lived in a city, but not the distribution for the individual craftwork operations (with one — to my knowledge — isolated exception). Nevertheless, the overall number of assistants provides some foothold because, where it has become known to us, it was always considerably lower than the number of independent tradesmen, so that we may infer with some probability very small operations as the rule. Thus Bücher assumes for Frankfurt 660–700 journeymen with in total

1,498 independent craftsmen (an estimate!). H. Paasche ascertains for Rostock (1584), next to 2,350 independent, 1,036 male servants and 1,423 maids. In London (around 1528), 220 foreign shoemakers shall have had employed "over" 400 helpers. The information is, however, extracted from a grievance of native cobblers, in which they complained about the prevalence of foreigners, so will have been presumably exaggerated[525]. And that was already in the 16th century! In the *Livre des métiers* are listed only 47 *sergents* [servants], 113 *valets*, 119 *chambrière*, and altogether 359 assistants. That is naturally by far not everyone. Where are the rest hiding, since every adult person was taxed? Amongst those who bore no professional description? Or (which is yet more probable) in the households of the masters? That suggests as well a generally tiny size of operations. Against that, I would not like to infer the structure of reality offhand from the regulations of the guild statutes over the maximum size of operations. In contrast, I would like to conclude thus, that where a maximum of production or a minimum number of allowable helpers is prescribed, a tendency already exists for the enlargement of operations. It is precisely in these operations that we may expect therefore operations of somewhat more than the average size. On the other hand (may we infer?), where — naturally in places and at times where in general such regulations were already enacted — the limits are missing in the statutes, the small operation still formed the rule. In the *Livre des métiers*, there are in fact only a few trades (cloth making!) in which maximum numbers of allowable helpers are given. Thus (?) in Parisian craftwork at the end of the 13th century, the small operation was the rule.

The statistical exception, of which the talk was above, concerns the craftsmen in Heidelberg about whose operational circumstances Eulenburg (1896, 132) cheerfully provides us precise information. According to him, for the manufacturing operations:

One man operations: 240 = 53.3%

Operations with 1 male journeyman: 123 = 27.5%

Operations with 2 male journeymen: 55 = 12.4%

Chapter 16: The Organisation of Manufacturing Work

Operations with 3 male journeymen: 24 = 5.3%
Operations with 4 male journeymen: 6 = 1.3%
Operations with 5 male journeymen: 1 = 0.2%

This largest operation belonged to the stonemasons' trade. Otherwise, as stated, we are reliant on inferences or at least on calculations. Thus one could in any case, for example, use the numbers given above for the production maximums in the Frankfurt cloth making trade to form the following statistics on the sizes of operations — we assume that the annual production minimum of a master by himself is 2×4 pieces of cloth. (This quantity, however, is potentially also the annual production of a non-permanent worker or a worker in part weaving for wages, but we can put aside this eventuality for the time being — if it applies then the level of the sizes of operations correspondingly falls.) Under this assumption, the following sizes of operations would thus have existed in the Frankfurt cloth making trade:

One man operations: 49 = 37.5%
Operations with 1–2 male journeymen: 41 = 30.7%
Operations with 3–5 male journeymen: 32 = 24.0%
Operations with 6–8 male journeymen: 11 = 7.3%

When one considers that the figures apply to Frankfurt's largest export trade, and one takes into consideration the various levels of economic development in both cities, then these figures agree with those established from the sources for Heidelberg quite well and can perhaps be considered an image of reality.

Also for the *English* cloth industry in the 14th century, we obtain the same impression from the above mentioned figures of cloth measurement calculations — that the great mass of producers were small operations. In Suffolk, 733 pieces of broad cloth were made by 120 persons, just seven or eight produced 20 pieces each. 9,200 short pieces of narrow cloth (of which I reckon 30 as the annual production of *one* weaver) were produced by 300 cloth makers; 15 of them delivered 120–160 pieces. In Essex, 1,200 narrow pieces originated from nine cloth makers, in Braintree 2,400 from eight. Thereunder lies annual production of 200 to 600 pieces. They are thus (if it is true!) those large operations of which I spoke above. In Devonshire, 65 masters produced 3,565 pieces. In Cornwall, 13 cloth makers delivered 90 pieces of (surely broad) cloth. In Salisbury, 158 masters produced 6,600 pieces; only one produced more than 150. In Winchester, 3,000 pieces were produced; only three cloth makers produced more than 100 pieces each. In Yorkshire, average production was 10 pieces of (broad) cloth. In Kent, there was only one cloth maker who finished more than 50 pieces, and three others who finished more than 25 pieces.*

That the manufacturing operations of the Middle Ages were individual operations, and that the operation of a master working alone surely predominated amongst them in most branches of production, seems to me to also be confirmed by *the images* which we possess of the scenes of manufacturing life from the Middle Ages (or even from a somewhat later time). I am thinking of the images of craftsmen on the woodcuts in the Germanisches Nationalmuseum as well as in J. Ammans descriptions of all the professions which have already been spoken of above. In particular, the stand-alone woodcuts are instructive for us. They originate first of all from a much later time (16th century), and secondly had doubtlessly the aim of showing Nuremberg manufacturing in its splendour. There we see now:

- in the leather worker's workplace: the master cutting the leather, next to him two journeymen finishing the bags;
- in the shoemaker's workplace: the master again cutting the leather, and three journeymen making the boots;
- in the furrier's workplace: the master and two journeymen, all three equally occupied in sewing fur things; a third carrying a fur piece to the master's wife (who is selling in the adjoining room); and on the street, three young people (apprentices?) are beating a pelt;
- in the butcher's workplace: two journeymen felling a steer; whilst in the shop, the master is chopping up meat for sale;
- in the tannery: the master with three journeymen;

---

* [Tr.: these figures not referenced or footnoted by Sombart.]

Chapter 16: The Organisation of Manufacturing Work

- in the rope maker's workplace: the rope maker spinning, with an apprentice carrying hemp;
- in the joiner's workplace: the master planing, with a journeyman sawing a board.

I am suggesting that such stereotypical depictions have a certain conclusiveness, particularly when they agree conspicuously with results obtained in other ways. That again some masters who produced Nuremberg ware will have employed, just like many artisans (Veit Stoss!*), more than two to three journeymen need not be drawn into doubt[526]. But we see on our nice woodcuts before us surely the rule, the typical, the predominant, the normal, the accustomed state.

3. A conclusion to the smallness of operations and with it the craftwork-based organisation can be made from the *number of craftsmen resident in one place*, if we place them in comparison with the number of residents of the city, assuming that it concerns local craftsmen. One must some day carry out such calculations for a series of important crafts on a broader scale — they would all lead to the same result. Just to show in an example what I mean, Paris had in the 13th century alone 68 mills on the Seine, mills also demonstrably lay on the Bièvre, and there were also windmills. Milling was almost universally milling for a fee. All mills worked thus for the local consumer. Thus, there were not even 1,000 people per mill. Thus, these could only be small operations. Certainly under the assumption that perhaps a few would not have dealt with the greatest part of the production. We can exclude this possibility if we take into consideration the site of the mills about whose topography we are precisely informed[527].

I will name in brief a few other symptoms from whose appearance (which is beyond question and hence needs not be substantiated in detail) the dominance of craftwork-based organisation may be inferred.

4. *The master remains*, as far as we know, everywhere during the Middle Ages (with exception perhaps of a few textile operations in Italy, Flanders, and Brabant) as *a manufacturing worker*, that is, he works alongside in the workplace — the function of bare management has still not been separated out.

---

* [Tr.: Veit Stoss was a German wood sculptor of the 15th/16th century.]

5. *The structure of society* remains in general that of the guild, during the last centuries it arrived at its full expression more than ever in the political organisation. What we know (always aside from the social movements in a few Italian and Belgian big cities) of the journeymen's associations and their policy, of the discontent and uprisings of journeymen, does not entitle us to the assumption that the vertical structure of society was already being driven out by the horizontal. That would also have been rare. Do we not see still in 1789 and even 1848 the structure of craftwork so intact that the journeymen for the greater part are fighting the battles *for* the masters. Certainly in these times, next to craftwork, a new form of organisation, the capitalist, had already come into development, and with it the elements of a horizontal structure of society. But there can be no talk of that in the Middle Ages.

With these last remarks, I lead the reader to the second type of evidence of which I spoke: the *theoretical*, which I can attend to in a few words.

I understand thereunder the following: when one examines precisely (as has happened in the course of this depiction at various times) the conditions under which manufacturing production took place in the Middle Ages, then one arrives at the result that they approach in optimal degree those ideal conditions which we were able to determine to be theoretically favourable for craftwork (see Chapter 12). Above all, empirical technology and a slow increase in population ensured, in combination with the constantly present, well funded demand for manufactured products, a highly stable turnover, and excluded the competition of craftsmen amongst each other to a high degree. How this came about does not need to be presented here once more. Craftwork *was able* thus to exist. But that craftwork *should have* existed, for that speaks the spirit of the time, which we became familiar with when we attempted to explain the idea of craftwork.

I could yet add now that just as all the conditions for craftwork-based organisation were fulfilled in the Middle Ages, so did almost all the conditions for another economic form remain unfulfilled, a form which alone was destined to oust the craftwork-based production: the capitalist — but the following volumes will deal with that.

Chapter 16: The Organisation of Manufacturing Work

Here I only want still to note of this that our result, to which the investigation on the last pages has led us (that the economic form of manufacturing production during the Middle Ages was craftwork), applies equally for every form of craftwork, thus even for that craftwork which laboured for an inter-locale market. With it the evidence is supplied for the correctness of the statement that the craftwork-based organisation is in no way bound to the customer relationship. In other words, that production for a local market does not necessarily belong to the conditions whose fulfillment make craftwork possible. On the contrary, craftwork can exist very well also as an export trade which produces for the "world market", only if the conditions for its existence are otherwise fulfilled. Since this fact is so often ignored or the correctness of this finding outright denied, I want in the following chapter to produce some more evidence that even those trades which we know also produced for the "world market" in the Middle Ages preserved their craftwork-based organisation. When I refer the reader at the same time in part to the depictions of credible informants, it happens so as to not fill the space of these pages all too much with a body of facts. The interested reader can of course easily verify the source evidence in the works indicated.

Chapter 17: The Organisation of Export Manufacturing

Were then the *cloth makers* supplying the tailors in the 14th century really still "craftsmen" and not perhaps already home entrepreneurs [*Hausindustrielle*]? This question was also posed by Schmoller: "it would be of great interest to determine whether perhaps somewhere — ie. except in Cologne where the weavers preserved the right of cutting clothes — the tailors were the underwriters [*Verleger*] and employers of cloth makers"[528].

Schmoller himself avoids giving a smooth and neat answer to his own question. In fact, documentary evidence will be difficult to obtain. We are thus reliant on conclusions from other circumstances. Schmoller lists among these, justifiably in the first rank, the fact that in the guild struggles of the 14th century almost everywhere the cloth makers were the leading guild and that the struggle against the councils and the merchants even degenerated in many places to a struggle with the tailors over the cutting of clothes. But it seems to me now that this political role, which the cloth makers and weavers played universally in the 14th century, their striving to assist their guild and the other craftsmen to a seat and voice on the councils, and the altogether guild-like spirit, which their regulations breathed still in the 15th century[529], by all means speaks for their still purely craftwork-based character. Home entrepreneurs would have possessed neither the resilience, nor the specifically guild-like interest for that protagonist's position which the cloth makers of that time took up. But no evidence is furnished in my view even for the economically squeezed situation of the weaving craft at that time. The inferences which lead Schmoller to the claim that the relationship of cloth makers to tailors, where every retail sale was forbidden to them, must have been "a pinched, absolutely unfavourable one", are in my view not sound. The same applies for the combative *Flemish* weaving guilds in the 14th century[530]. The newly accessible source material[531] strengthens the impression that the Flemish textile industry in the 14th century had a substantively craftwork-based organisation.

The *Florentine* cloth making was ,especially early on, as we know, organised capitalistically, but even for Florence we may assume that up to the turn of the 13th century the elements of mercantilistic large industry had not yet obtained preeminence over the small masters[532].

The inter-locale linen weaving also preserved itself for a long time across the Middle Ages as craftwork. Even in the 18th century, the *Silesian* linen dealers were by no means always underwriters, but often only recipients of the linen produced by independent producers[533].

That the *silk industry*, which surely became an export trade very early on, was also organised on a craftwork basis is attested by evidence we possess for Genoa, from where silk products were already exported in the 13th and 14th centuries, whereas the home entrepreneurs' capitalist organisation only had its beginning in the 15th century and needed the entire century, as has been shown by expert analysis[534], to prevail against the craftwork-based organisation. For a long time even after the underwriting system had taken root, we find, for example, the silk weavers working also on their own account in addition to for underwriters.

Quite similar to the circumstances in Genoa were those in *Venice* and in the mother-city of the European silk industry, *Lucca*. There was undoubtedly also craftwork-based organisation of the silk industry in Venice and Lucca. Those silk weavers who migrated at the beginning of the 14th century from Lucca to Venice — a count of 31 is named — were certainly neither wage workers (they themselves rather employed journeymen), nor even home entrepreneurs (how could they then have migrated?), but rather certainly mostly craftsmen[535].

Only in 1432 were the Venetian silk weavers allowed to weave at a loom on their own account[536]. Likewise the silk

Chapter 17: The Organisation of Export Manufacturing

weavers in Lucca obtained only in 1531 through the uprising of the *straccioni* the right to weave at a loom on their own account[537].

The silk industry in the *Swiss* cities was also one of craftwork up into the 16th century[538].

But often to start with we even find the *fustian* and *cotton weaving*, which had a tendency to export from the outset, still in an entirely craftwork-based framework. This emerges especially clearly with the Basel *schürlitz* weaving of the 15th and 16th centuries, which, even though it worked for the inter-locale market, was purely craftwork[539].

A mistake to which many historians of the medieval textile industry have fallen victim is that they already emphasise a capitalist organisation where, for example, a cloth dealer "has woven" for himself; the more so when they find prohibitions of the trucking system in the sources. One must, however, clarify that this "others having worked for them for wages" quite surely is compatible with craftwork-based organisation — it is then just "wage workers" who are though just as much craftsmen as the craftsmen producing the works for sale.

The wage work manufacturing [*Lohngewerbe*] was very common in the Middle Ages, commoner than today (it plays incidentally a large role also in the framework of capitalist organisation), but obviously in and of itself demonstrates nothing against a strictly craftwork-based organisation of manufacturing. The trucking prohibition also does not prove that capitalism had now moved into manufacturing. We learn from the sources rather that even from craftsman to craftsman the habit or bad habit existed of paying in wares instead of cash — the fullers of the city of Paris, to whom it was forbidden (!) in the year 1293 and later to let themselves be paid in other than money, were genuine guild master craftsmen who themselves employed journeymen.

But were metals then the *products of craftsmen*? This question is also to be answered in the affirmative. We are informed sufficiently by a series of new investigations[540] over the beginnings of *mining* and metal extraction about how the earliest organisation even of this branch of manufacturing was entirely craftwork-based. Admittedly in a specific nuance, there were almost always from the beginning, in any case from very early on, craftsmen cooperatives which managed according to a joint plan the yield of the pits and in part also the smelting of the ore. Since the path of our investigation will lead us once more to the peculiar form of craftwork-based organisation in mining, a closer investigation into it shall remain undone until then. Here it may just be mentioned that the extraction of salt was originally organised quite analogously to mining.

Undoubtedly, the *extraction of iron* moved in a craftwork-based context throughout the entire Middle Ages, right up to the 16th and 17th century — quite certainly as long as the bloomery [*Rennwerksbetrieb*] predominated (and it did for a long time over the Middle Ages, even when the blast furnace had long since been "invented"), but partly also still when one was already smelting iron in blast furnaces[541].

But that the weapons maker's production was also craftwork is something we know from numerous investigations, amongst which the work of Thun over the Solingen sword works still takes a prominent place[542].

An almost always certain sign for the intactness of craftwork-based organisation of a trade is the strictly realised separation between the guild of manufacturing producers and those traders of the same branch, or the prohibition of the traders producing themselves the wares they trade. We encounter such a prohibition in the *Florentine* weapons industry. There the guild of *armaiuoli* (weapons dealers) strictly forbade the practising of the armour and spear making crafts — they absolutely only dealt with purchased wares.

Who were the *producers of Nuremberg wares*, especially the products of its metal industry? We know that already early on an extensive specialisation was carried out amongst the individual production areas. There were in the 13th century cutting blade makers, scythe smiths, fork smiths, compass smiths, and chain smiths. Then amongst the weapon smiths: armour makers, armoured shirt makers, helmet makers, blade makers, sword polishers, etc. That alone would infer that, even if we otherwise had no evidence at all which spoke on its behalf, we are at least outwardly dealing with an absolutely craftwork-based organisation of the metal trade — the area of production is bounded in complete purity by the

Chapter 17: The Organisation of Export Manufacturing

technical capability of the master according to quantity and quality. But were these master craftsmen as such perhaps only virtual existences, were they fundamentally wholesale piece masters? That the wholesale system [*Verlagssystem*] seized ground early on in Nuremberg is not subject to doubt. The investigations of Schoenlank have proven its incidence already at the beginning of the 14th century[543]. If we, however, look over the documentary material which refers to the prohibition or the regulation of home industry, and of which Schoenlank utilised a large part, we must come to the conclusion that it only ever concerns exceptions up until into the 16th century, and that only in this epoch did a general tendency for capitalist organisation take place.

What we can take from Hans Sachsen's description of all the classes (1568) also suggests an essentially craftwork-based organisation for all Nuremberg export manufacturing even in the 16th century.

That the producers of these "Nuremberg wares" in the Middle Ages were craftsmen[544], or in any case could have been, is spoken for by the fact that the frequently similar products produced for the large market by the so-called *Rhenish* small iron industry — the Solingen knife works, the Remscheid industry — and the *Schmalkalden* industry preserved their pure craftwork-based character until deep into the modern period. Craftwork was fully intact in Solingen up into the 16th century, the struggle began in the 17th century, but even in 1687 the complete restoration of the guild constitution formally took place. The Remscheid industry, in contrast, is found by Thun in the 1870s still in an essentially craftwork-based organisation. The *Schmalkalden* small iron industry was during its prime in the 16th century strongly guild-based[545] and preserved its craftwork character up into the 18th century[546].

I refer the reader in addition once more to my depiction of the circumstance of manufacturing production in the age of early capitalism (in a later volume), where I always take up the erstwhile craftwork-based organisation of a branch of manufacturing when it is reshaped in a capitalist way, and highlight its persistence in a craftwork-based structure when that reshaping does not take place until the end of the early capitalist age.

***

But my claim now goes even further. Not only did all the professional manufacturing production carry a craftwork-based imprint during the Middle Ages, but so too the professionally practised *trade*, which I want to talk about in-depth in a following chapter. A thorough discussion over medieval trade is so much more necessary when trade and craftwork are far too commonly brought into contrast with one another because one likes to think of any trade as a manifestation of capitalism[547]. On the other hand, it is to be shown that just like manufacturing production, trade also existed for a long time as an equal and compatible brother of craftwork-based manufacturing. The following chapter is dedicated to the depiction of this pre-capitalist trade.

Chapter 18: Trade as Craftwork

Preliminary Remarks

I will preface the depiction with the following remarks:
1. With regards to terminology, the difference between retail and wholesale trade must now be determined. The latter is the sale of wares (as a profession) to producers and traders; the former to final consumers. The difference is the same as that between retailers and wholesalers, but has nothing to do with the difference between small and large trade. A small scrounger can be a "wholesaler" [*Großhändler*], the Bon Marché in Paris with annual sales of 200 million francs practises "retail trade". That even Eulenburg (1893, 278) does not keep this particular distinction sharply apart is astounding.
2. There was in the Middle Ages *not only* craftwork-based trade, but also (and to a considerable extent alongside) an *opportunistic trade* which has already been spoken of* and over which I also note the following.

It formed in the European Middle Ages no less than in classical antiquity a common occurrence that quite significant trading operations were carried out by non-merchants. Those categories which come especially into consideration as opportunistic traders were (and indeed in the south just as in the north):

    a) the councillors and mayors of the cities — the Doge of Venice no less than the councillor of Hamburg or Lübeck (Vicko von Geldersen! the Wittenborgs!);

    b) the noble houses, especially the rich estate-owning families;

    c) the chapters, monasteries, orders, and clergymen of all grades.

In short, whoever was wealthy in the Middle Ages.

With numerous of these wealthy powers of the Middle Ages, in the course of time, as we shall see, a sort of excess of money established itself, and the thought of applying the surplus money profitably in another way than through the expansion of the estate suggested itself. Now came the time when occasional amounts were assigned as a loan perhaps first gratuitously to the demanding town borough, but soon also for a consideration to distinguished gentlemen. The time came

---

* [Tr.: see pages 146–148 above.]

when one entrusted sums to a factor, with which he should practise outwardly trading activities — thus the period of the opportunistic trade. It always concerned at first occasional trade ventures, or trading companies for a short time. The affluent townsfolk remained themselves in the beginning mostly in their home town, where they devoted themselves to the public interests and the governance of their estates lying there. (Cf. Bücher (1886, 246–47).) Only as such opportunistic traders is one to rightly understand a Venetian noble or a Wittenborg or Geldersen. If one takes the trouble for once of counting the number of items which are recorded in the "trade book" of such a councilman, one comes to astounding results: in one year, no more than 20–30 entries are made; thus one every fourteen days. What would the man have initiated with his time, if he had really, as one surely occasionally assumes, been a professional merchant? The difference between the craftwork-based professional traders and the old houses undertaking (opportunistic) trade is especially clear in Vienna. See Voltelini (1913, 67 ff.). Then in the course of time with specific families, this sporadic, intermittent activity as banker or trader grew naturally into a profession. The talk here now is not of these opportunistic traders, only trade as craftwork shall be brought into the depiction here.

I. The Extent of Business

The exact knowledge of its scale would be of decisive importance for a proper understanding of pre-capitalist trade, particularly knowledge of the scale of quantities or values of goods dealt by one trader. Unfortunately we are thus far reliant for this on occasional information from the sources and we will surely remain so essentially for all time. For all that, what we know today about the business extent of medieval trade is enough to obtain an approximate idea of its quantitative significance. Figures of the most various sorts, authenticated by the sources, and combined also with a gradual development of the statistical sense for the numbers of the trading operations, are beginning gradually — certainly much slower than in the area of population statistics! — to clear up the fanciful ideas of scale, like those which perhaps the numerical details of Moncenigo and Marino Sanuto for Venice, and Villani for Florence have produced in the heads of many historians, and like those, for example, playing a role in the well-known treatise of the Postmaster-General Stephan[548]. We must accustom ourselves to look with suspicion also, and just with reference to the trade and intercourse, at the numbers from the past whose manner of origin we cannot precisely

Chapter 18: Trade as Craftwork

verify. It is conspicuous that the historians of the subject, whose meticulousness with reference to the literary and documentary tradition has experienced the highest schooling, make use of everything they find in the way of statistical figures in the sources frequently enough uncritically and with a naive dilettantism. Someone who writes, for example, not indiscriminately but in compliance with his predecessors, that the turnover of wares in Fondaco dei Tedeschi* in Venice amounted annually to 1,000,000 ducats. And yet it is not known to me that some factual foothold exists which could make us inclined to find believable that fanciful figure of a gas-bagging mayor.

An equally suspicious figure is the famed 100,000 pieces of cloth of Villani, which were supposed to have been manufactured in Florence in 1308, and which Doren even describes as "unobjectionable"[549]. But one needs, in order to prove their incredibility, only to make the following calculation. At the end of the 13th century, the total exports of wool from England to Italy amounted to perhaps 4,000 sacks[550]. Now one calculated at that time on three pieces of cloth to one sack of wool[551]. The total amount of wool reaching Italy would have thus resulted in a yield of 12,000 pieces. Although Florence may have also obtained its wool elsewhere, its main source was England. And that export figure refers not only to the wool reaching Florence, but to the wool reaching all of Italy!

This only *exempli gratia* [as an example][552].

In order to arrive at correct ideas of the business extent of a trader in the earlier period, two paths stand open to us: the division of total turnovers of a place by the number of merchants involved in it, and the direct business evidence of the individual trader or the establishing of the quantities of goods traded by the individual.

Figures for the total turnover of a place or the quantity of goods moved over a thoroughfare are naturally for the earlier period especially rare. Nonetheless, a few very instructive and quite reliable statistics stand at our command, of which the following may be provided here as specimens.

---

* [Tr.: a building containing the headquarters and some living quarters for the city's German merchants.]

Firstly the volumes for the export trade of the most important Hanseatic cities in the 14th century. They amounted to, in the last years for which our informant discloses figures[553]:

	Lübeck marks	marks in present-day (1887) currency
Tallinn (1384)	131,085	1,245,305
Hamburg (1400)	336,000	3,192,000
Lübeck (1384)	293,760	2,790,720
Rostock (1384)	76,640	728,080
Stralsund (1378)	330,240	3,137,280

According to the calculations of Schulte, the annual trade moving over St Gotthard in the Late Middle Ages is estimated at a total weight of 1250 t. — that is, as is well-known, the content of one or two goods trains.

We are informed quite exactly about the extent of the civic *grain trade* in the Middle Ages and for the beginning of the modern period. The amount of grain which in the 16th and 17th centuries was traded in the important grain trading places of Stettin and Hamburg amounted in Stettin to 2–3,000 t., in Hamburg to double that. The total annual turnover of Stettin in grain in its prime comprised thus one of our present-day shiploads, and that of Hamburg two[554].

We know even more precisely the quantities of wool exported by foreigners from England during the Middle Ages[555]. They amounted, for example, in the years 1277/78 to 14,301 sacks, the sacks calculated at around 2 cwt., thus all up not quite 30,000 cwt. or 3,000 t. The wool exported by the Hanseatic merchants in this year amounted in comparison to 1,655 sacks, around 3,300 cwt. or 330 t.[556], whereas in recent years about 200,000 t. of wool was imported into Germany annually.

Nothing changes in this picture either when we insert the money value for the quantity of goods. The price for the sack of wool amounted in England during the 14th century to around 90–100 shillings, which would be in present-day (1916) currency around 300 marks (the English penny at the

Chapter 18: Trade as Craftwork

time was calculated at 20,625 troy grains* of sterling silver). The total exports of English wool would thus have corresponded to a value of 4–5 million marks in present-day (1916) currency, that of the Hanseatics' to a value of around 500,000 marks in present-day (1916) currency. In the year 1913, however, raw sheep's wool was imported for 412.7 million marks in present-day (1916) currency.

Now all these figures, however, only become interesting for us when we know at the same time the *number of traders* who effected that turnover. The number of grain dealers in Hamburg during the 16th century is given to us as being 6–12, admittedly by an informant whose interests make an underestimate of the figure probable. Nevertheless, other information also allows us the conclusion that a "large" grain dealer of that already relatively late period turned over no more than at most 400 lasts† of grain557.

There were, however, involved in the wool exports from England in the specified years no less than 252 traders, so that for every trader there arose an average of 56 sacks or around 110 cwt. of wool, and a turnover of around 15,000 marks in present-day (1916) currency, whereas the number of German traders amounted to 37, their average share thus to 45 sacks or 90 cwt., and their average turnover to 13–14,000 marks in present-day (1916) currency.

In general, we may assume that as small as the quantity of the overall turnover of wares in the Middle Ages was, the number of traders involved in it was just as small.

One has ridiculed those historians who "peopled the numerous cities from Cologne and Augsburg to Medebach and Radolfzell with merchants in the modern sense, thus with a professionally developed class of traders"558. Certainly with reason, as far as it concerns the attribution of modern large merchants to the medieval cities. With injustice, however, in my view, as long as only the number of (admittedly absolutely craftsmen-like) traders comes into question. This was certainly very high. In fact, the medieval cities, at least as far as

---

* [Tr.: one troy ounce = 480 troy grains = 1.09714 imperial ounces = ~31 grams.]
† [Tr.: a last was a measure of weight approximating 2,000 kg.]

they practised trade, seemingly swarmed with traders and traders' assistants. If one immerses oneself in the conditions of Genoa or Venice in the 12th or 13th century, or in that of a Hanseatic city even at the end of the Middle Ages, one always hits upon the same heap of small and middling traders. One understands though what that means: 252 wool traders are involved in the export of 30,000 cwt. of wool! One ponders how it required 48 chartered grain measurers and 132 chartered grain porters for the accomplishment of the grain trade in Hamburg characterised above. Or one visualises the swarm in Fondaco dei Tedeschi in Venice, which up to 1505 contained for living purposes alone 56 small rooms, later 72 then 80, which were always occupied, and in which 30 brokers, 38 bale binders, 40 auctioneers, and a vast number of administrative personnel plied their existence[559]. Or one thinks of the army of specialised officials which existed under the *prevôst* [provost] and the *échevins* [commissioner] in Paris for the procurement of the sharply demarcated transactions assisting trade. Or one leafs through the *chartae* in the *Historiae patriae Monumenta* to be astounded that almost every day a *commenda* [company] agreement was concluded in the Genoa of the 12th century over some commercial undertaking of the smallest size.

But it will recommend itself more for our purposes if, instead of engaging ourselves in these considerations of a general nature[560], we look for concrete figures for the business extent or turnover of individual traders. Fortunately, it is not lacking. Even the last mentioned source gives us in its notaries' agreements over temporary "commercial undertakings", because the amounts of inflowing operating funds are specified therein, an excellent clue to the correct assessment of the scale of medieval trade. In the second volume of the *chartae* published in 1853 are found from No. 293 on, that is, from 16 April 1156, a large number of *commenda* and *societas* [partnership] agreements with details of the inflowing assets. I have assembled the first 50 such agreements and obtained the average of the "company assets" given therein. There is, from a total amount of 7,470 Genoan pounds which the 50 agreements contain, an average of around 150 lb, that is, with a relationship of the lira to the florin of 5:4, of 120½

Chapter 18: Trade as Craftwork

fl., that is thus around 1,000–1,100 marks in present-day (1916) currency.

The highest amongst the agreements is over 900 lb, two further of more than 400 lb, two over 300 lb, and the rest remaining below this sum. At the same time, it involves in many cases business with distant lands:
- No. 431 is an agreement over 297 lb trading to Alexandria;
- No. 434, 224 lb to Tunis;
- No. 441, 150 lb to Alexandria;
- No. 457, 300 lb to Sicily; etc.

Commonly one of the shares was rendered in wares (*in pannis* [in garments]) — it associated a craftsman who made cloth with another who would take the cloth over land or sea.

We find quite similar figures to the Genoa of the 12th century in the company agreements of Lübeck in the 14th and 15th century. In the partnership agreements published by P. Rehme, which are recorded in the Lübeck *Niederstadtbuch* [lower town register] (where incidentally only the material business specifically with distant persons was entered), the greatest part of the agreements (72) remain under 100 Lübeck marks (around 1,000 marks in present-day (1916) currency), the agreements going down as low as 4 marks. A small portion revolve around 200 marks. Five agreements are found between 460 and 1,000 marks, further agreements at 1,350, 1,400, 3,200, and 4,600. Both the last two, the only ones thus which step out of the frame of a craftwork-based extent of business, are paid by the same two persons (Abraham Bere and Johann de Alen)[561].

If one had made the small effort earlier to calculate the sums which underlay the *commenda* and *societas* agreements, much wasteful talk over the "economic nature" of these forms of association, in which one from the start has wanted to hear the rustling of the wingbeats of capitalism, would have been avoided[562].

Just as the company agreements permit an idea of the dimensions of the turnover of medieval trading businesses, so to do the figures which the *wealth* of the merchants express.

We may assume confidently with the length of the turnover periods at that time that no trader turned over more wares annually than the value of his wealth, which was still for the most part placed in real estate. Now we hear, however, for example, that in 1429 in the rich trading city of *Basel* only five merchants possessed more than 4,000 fl., of which four possessed between 4,000 and 6,500 fl., 30 called their own a wealth of between 1,000 and 4,000 fl., 14 between 500 and 1,000 fl., 22 between 100 and 500 fl., and six under 100 fl.[563] Even in *Augsburg* we find at the end of the 15th century only 70 people who possess a *wealth* of more than 6,000 fl., 15 who possess one of over 15,000 fl., and four of over 30,000 fl.[564] And of the 70 people only a small part belonged to the caste of professional traders.

A further symptom for the smallness also of sea trade in the pre-capitalist period is *the tiny scale of the ships* which moreover, despite their tiny size, were mostly owned by several people — it is known that part ownership was until well into the modern period the characteristic form of the shipping company[565].

The ships which in the 13th century ran out from Newcastle with pit coal as ballast carried less than 40 t.[566]

"In the year 1470, seven Spanish ships loaded with iron, wine, fruits, and wool were seized on the way to Flanders by English vessels and brought into English seaports. The owners turned to King Henry IV for their release and made an oath over the value of the ships and the cargo. The following were the declarations of value:"[567]

   One ship of 100 t. = £107 10 sh. value
   One ship of 70 t. = £70 value
   One ship of 120 t. = £110 value
   One ship of 40 t. = £70 value
   One ship of 110 t. = £140 value
   One ship of 110 t. = £150 value
   One ship of 120 t. = £180 value

In the years 1368–1384, sea going vessels which frequented the harbours of Tallinn, Riga, or Pernau were rewarded with 475–3,421 marks in present-day (1916) currency[568]. During the 14th century, sea going vessels with cargo space of

Chapter 18: Trade as Craftwork

more than 100 t. were not yet common in the northern German cities, and those of 150 t. were extraordinarily rare[569].

Even the sea going vessels of the Venetian trade fleet, which were probably the largest of their time, were tiny measured against the dimensions of the smaller Spree barges of our day. According to the *Venetae reipublicae Statuta navium*[570], which applies to the 13th century, the load carrying capacity of the Venetian sea going vessels amounted to between 200,000 and one million pounds. That would be, if we assume net pounds, $66\frac{2}{3}$–$333\frac{1}{3}$ t., with gross pounds, 96–480 t. Moreover the statutes do not indicate whether the larger types were built — only in the case that they were built were they subjected to specific rules. In comparison, there were (1912) amongst the German *inland-going* vessels 9,100 ships with tonnage of more than 250 t., within that 2,317 with 400–600 t., 1,423 with 600–800 t., and 1,650 with 1,800 t. or more. The Rhine barge already has an *average* tonnage of more than 500 t.

If now into the bargain a whole crowd of merchants were involved in the generally small cargo of such a ship, as was the rule, then a certain conclusion can be drawn from that as to the tiny size of individual businesses. Stieda has provided us with extraordinarily instructive details for the year 1369 over the values of the cargoes of 12 ships out-bound from Tallinn, as well as over the number of merchants involved. According to that, the number of merchants who conveyed wares on these 12 ships were 178; the total value of the 12 ships' cargos, however, amounted to 29,304½ Lübeck marks. Every single merchant had thus on average freighted wares of a value of 164 Lübeck marks or about 1,600 marks[571]. That the scale, however, was in no way abnormal is something we are taught by numerous other cases which impart a quite similar picture. The wool traders in England have already been considered in general. Let us turn back to them for a moment to look at them somewhat more precisely. Let us put ourselves in England's main export port for wool in the 13th and 14th centuries: Boston. Thus we encounter there[572], for example, in the year 1303 no less than 47 Hanseatic wool traders who together exported 749 sacks of wool. Of them, the most significant was a Walter from Tallinn, who exported 91 sacks and 1½ stone* (for perhaps 30,000 marks in present-day (1916) currency); the next largest shipped 68 sacks and 15½ stones; then followed three who exported more than 40 sacks, and seven who exported more than 10 sacks; for the rest — 35 traders — it amounted to 305 sacks and 17½ stone altogether, every single one of them had thus travelled to England to bring home less than 20 cwt. of wool for less than 300 marks in present-day (1916) currency.

What quotas amounted to with a Hanseatic ship's cargo for the individual shippers is shown by Document No. 352 in Ehmck and von Bippen (1873, 4:462 No. 352)[573]. Including Captain Kolingh, who also had wares on board, there were 15 shippers who together loaded wares of 384 nobles (⅓ of a £). Ten of them had wares in value up to 30 nobles; thereunder two with six, and one with three nobles. One loaded 42, one 44 nobles, three with 60 each, one with 80, one with 100, one with 225 (six lasts of wheat and two lasts of beer).

Entirely the same picture occurs even in Venice — the value of a ship's cargo was (in the 12th century), for example, specified as 632 perpers (around 6,000 marks), of which one of the participants had loaded 158 perpers. Another gave 70 perpers as well[574]; all thus sums with which the grocers today trade in Bentschen†. The turnovers of the Florentine trading houses, though they were so significant as money lending businesses, were themselves tiny even in the 14th century. In 1312, the Bardi received for two scarlet cloths from Ypres 270 fl., for 13 pieces of French cloth £389, 17 sh., 2 d. In the year 1322, they exported 74 pieces of cloth and five bales of silk material to Pisa — thus a wholesaler's turnover in Leitomischel‡. In October 1330, several ships were embargoed by them in the harbour, whose cargo *together* (!) constituted a value of 11,000 fl.[575] Thereunder were 360,000 pounds of cheese. That looks to be something, but is nothing — it is 180 t. (Imports to

---

* [Tr.: a *stone* was 350 lbs or about 153 kg, and there were 28 stones to a wool *sack*, with 12 sacks forming a *last*.]

† [Tr.: Bentschen was a small German town with population less than 10,000. It is now part of Poland and called Zbąszyń.]

‡ [Tr.: Leitomischel is the former German name of the Bohemian town of Litomyšl, now in the Czech Republic, known for its cloth in the Middle Ages.]

Chapter 18: Trade as Craftwork

Germany in the year 1913 were 26,264 t.) The turnovers with which the Medici in Florence occupied themselves in the 15th century were almost unbelievably small[576].

That the *trade with the countryside* still unwound in smaller quantities is a priori probable and is confirmed by our comprehensive source material. That it was worth one's while in the 13th century to conclude a *commenda* agreement over "3 pecias telarum de Basle" [3 pieces of weaving from Basel][577] will not surprise us when we see even in the 16th century Joseph Kramer, one of the richest men of Augsburg, send his factor to Venice to purchase 16 sacks of cotton, four ducats and 17 gross per hundredweight[578]. Two merchants from Lille, who were robbed in 1222 at Como, were carrying 13½ pieces of cloth and 12 pairs of trousers with them[579]. The value of a caravan of Basel merchants travelling to the Frankfurt fair and plundered by knights in the year 1391 was estimated at 9,544 fl. or 12,430 lb. Involved in that, however, were no less than 61 (!) merchants, who each had set off on the onerous journey with wares worth on average 156 fl. The annual turnover of the richest merchants in Basel amounted at the time to 1,200–1,400 fl., but most did not attain anything approaching this amount with their turnover. Among those 61 traders visiting the Frankfurt fair were 27 who had reported a loss of less than 100 fl., and individuals down to 13, 10, 9, 8, and 7¼ fl.[580] The amounts of the bills of exchange at the Flemish trading places in their prime agree with these figures. Of 102 Ypre ships' charters from the period 1251–1291, only 17 display a larger amount than £100. The highest amount is £239, 6 sh.[581]

The figures over the turnovers of the Cologne colonial goods[*] market [*Krautwage*] in the years 1491–1495 are also interesting[582]. They are unbelievably tiny.

It on the other hand gains in credibility when we hear that the common German merchant in Novgorod in the 14th century turned over at a maximum 1,000 marks, thus not even 10,000 marks in present-day (1916) currency.

---

*   [Tr.: e.g. sugar, rice, silk, wool, coffee, tea, cocoa and tobacco.]

Everywhere the same picture is offered to us — there was, apart from a few larger, often perhaps even not professional merchants, a teeming crowd of small and tiny traders.

II. The Traders

Those responsible for professional trade during the pre-capitalist period were, as it may be supposed by the extent of their business activity, none other than craftwork-based entities. Their entire thought and feeling, their social position, their type of activity, everything has them appear related to the small and middling manufacturers of their time. There is in fact nothing more foolish than to populate the Middle Ages with capitalistically-feeling and economically-schooled merchants. The craftwork-based essence of the trader of the old bent cropped up above all in the particular nature of his goal setting. Also, nothing lay further from the bottom of his heart than a striving for profit in the sense of modern entrepreneurship; he also wanted nothing other, no less, but also no more, than to earn by the work of his hands for better or worse the livelihood appropriate to his status; his entire activity was also dominated by the *idea of sustenance*.

We will see how this idea was expressed above all in the peculiar configuration of the legal order and customs of the old commerce.

Here it may be recalled how the craftwork-based spirit of this natural trade found its confirmation as the self-evident core disposition of the many centuries of the Middle Ages as it were in all the numerous writings of penance and reform which sprouted from the ground at the beginning of the modern period. The same reformation of Emperor Sigismund, which we could already call on for the characterisation of the craftwork-based manufacturers, had only permitted the merchants compensation for the travel and transport costs and wanted to prohibit all entrepreneurial profit. But the way the reformers, in particular Martin Luther, had with an accurate instinct correctly depicted the old trade as vouching for the "sustenance" is expressed mostly clearly in the following passage:

Chapter 18: Trade as Craftwork

For that reason, you must resolve then to search for your fair sustenance in such trade by which cost, effort, work, and danger is calculated and set aside, and the prices of the wares themselves thus fixed, lowered, or raised so that you thereby have reward for your work and trouble.[583]

The line of thought of the famous writing of Christian Kuppener's over usury (1508) moves in entirely the same direction. The same comparison here too: the new men who strive for the boundless profit, and the *petit commerce solide* [small solid trader] who had preserved for the honest craftwork trader complete with his family a living appropriate to his status[584]. In the centre of the considerations of all these critics is the thought that the trader should also see in his income only a compensation for work expended — here is the root of the idea of the "fair" price, which dominated the entire Middle Ages. For the trader is also in their eyes — or at least he should be because it had been custom and practice since time immemorial — nothing more than a *technical worker*[585]. And with that they strike again at the essence of the matter. If we want to create a proper picture of the merchant of the old bent, then we must first of all forget everything that we know about modern trade and those responsible for it.

These are in particular, and today almost exclusively, the organisers of sales. Their art, which they practise and which they have studied further into a science — from causes which are presented more precisely in another connection — exists, as we call it, in the "control of the market". That is, they make it their task — and the particular nature of modern economic life entails that the fulfillment of this task is seen as the practice of a highly remunerative function — to bring the wares to the man. The actual sphere of activity of the modern mercantilist existence is everywhere where the market is construed, where two producers run after *one* buyer. Then the merchant becomes lord of the situation, then he begins to bring the producers into dependency on himself. Then he is, however, also a good merchant only if he understands how to plan ahead astutely, calculate, and speculate. Of all that, however, the earlier time now knew, and especially the centuries which we call the Middle Ages knew, thanks to their undeveloped production technology, as good as nothing. Sales hardship is foreign to them. Two buyers run as a rule after *one* producer. Sales move in an accustomed framework, on fixed rails. The quantity of wares turned over are tiny. *Where* thus in all the world would the trader find something to plan ahead for, to calculate, or to speculate? But these same conditions which hold back his development into a capitalist entrepreneur enforce on him a number of work procedures of a technical nature of which the merchant of the present day is relieved. If no opportunity was found for him to plan ahead, to calculate, and to speculate, then he had all the more to package up, to measure up, to transport, to particularise, even occasionally still to manufacture. One knows[586] what arduous and mostly dangerous work every business of trade was which had a requirement for a change of place of the wares (and it almost always involved that), and knows that the trader himself had to set off on his journey girded with the sword, and played wagon driver and hosteler in his own person for weeks or months at a time, in order to bring his few goods safely to their destination. Much more than today, the merchant was on the road; we find the numerous small traders of the Middle Ages constantly strewn across quite wide lands, some emerging in this city, some in that[587].

A document from 1271 describes fittingly the medieval trader: "Mercatores, qui de loco ad locum merces et necessaria deferre consueverunt." [Merchants who had been accustomed to carry merchandise and necessities from place to place.][588]

Andreas Ryff visited 30 or more markets a year. He said of himself: "I had a little rest so that the saddle did not burn my backside."[589]

But when he returned to his home town, it meant, just as before at the fairs and markets in foreign places, standing behind the counter and diligently working measures and scales[590]. The dealer prepared the various spices [*Spieswurz, Gutwurz, Kintpetterwurz oder gefärbten Wurz*] from the obtained saffron, pepper, and ginger[591]. How great a value was placed in the technical skills of the spice dealer is shown by an edict of Charles VIII of France from the year 1484, which ordered an exact revision of weights and scales of all those who sold sugar and spices, and prescribing: "that because of the importance of the work with sugar and confectionary, the adherence to a four year apprenticeship and to the production of a successful masterpiece was to be strictly observed"[592]. Thus an analogy to the apothecaries! Technical work procedures wherever we look form the principal activity of the precapitalist trader. Self-evidently then besides that, the special mercantilist function of turning over goods, thus buying and selling, also applied to him. And more than his colleagues behind the vise or the carpenter's bench, his profession instructed him in the mysterious world of numbers. But even as much as he was a trader in the narrower and fundamental understanding, we must comprehend his activity as still being uncorrupted by any economic rationalism. His "business management", his process, is, like that of his manufacturing colleagues, absolutely empirical and traditional.

The *art of reading and writing* was, in Italy up into the 13th century, in the rest of Europe throughout the Middle Ages, certainly only entrusted to a fraction of the professional traders. We know just from the Venice of the 10th century that only a few merchants could even sign their name[593] — presumably this relationship of those unacquainted with reading and writing to those who were literate was also in later centuries of the Middle Ages only gradually altered. Certainly we know on the other hand that the *arithmetic*, which was almost even more important for the professional merchant, remained at the lowest level during many centuries and had to be accomplished almost throughout the entire Middle Ages without the aid of writing. Here we must also assume an interval of 200 years between Italy and the rest of Europe. Italy was during the entire Late Middle Ages teacher of the North in the *ars computandi* [art of computation]. Lukas Rem went at the beginning of the 16th century to Venice to learn to calculate[594]. And the sort of computation it involved! Hardly more than the learning of the four species of computation with whole numbers, the solution of simple geometry problems, and an elementary "business reckoning". It was already a sign of higher merchant's training when someone could even divide correctly. Even at the end of the 16th century, Hieronymus

Froben and Andreas Ryff benefited somewhat from being able to correctly work out the quotients in division[595].

Computation itself was done in the cumbersome form of the abacus, or of counting tokens, and had to be accomplished still (in Italy up to the 13th century, in the North up to the 15th century) without figures with place values, and without zero.

Over arithmetic in the Middle Ages, I have put together the following:

At the start of the 15th century, the penmen [*Modisten*] appeared in Germany. "In all these schools [...] the teaching of computation cannot be thought of as elementary enough. Hardly anywhere did it exceed calculating with whole numbers." (Unger 1888b, 17–19). A clear picture of the state of arithmetic is given to us by the earliest books of computation or compendiums of mathematics of the European Middle Ages. What Leonardo Pisano, who incidentally like Jordanus had hurried ahead of his time, achieved for Italy at the beginning of the 13th century, the books of computation from the end of the 15th century barely achieved for Germany. How low even the level of the monastic schools was, is shown us, for example, by Bernard's book of computation from the year 1445, which tried to teach nothing more than the old learned computation which we trace back in Europe to Jordanus. And even at the universities, we find "the computation [...] at no higher level than at the preparatory schools" (Cantor 1880, 2:159-160). "From Grammateus we learn that the *Algorithmus* of M. Georgii Peurbachii, which perhaps contains the same extent of arithmetical knowledge which ten year old children currently possess, 'was made for the students of the high school in Vienna'." (Unger 1888b, 25).

The first printed German book of computation, the Bamberger of 1483, contains likewise only the first elements of algebra. And yet the publication of such a textbook intended for merchants already signified an enormous progress compared with earlier. It was the Arab spirit in Italy, the Italian in the North, which induced this flowering. Over the various types of books of computation, cf. Unger (1888b, 37 ff.); Cantor (1880, 2:202 ff.).

For the 16th century, Unger (1888b, 112) remarks in summary: "To be able to competently calculate did not rate as a simple thing, but as an art in the fullest sense of the word."

In Italy, the *Arab numerals with place value and zero* became naturalised in the course of the 13th century, but obviously only slowly. Even in 1299, their use was forbidden to the members of the Calimala guild in Florence! In Germany, they did not become common property earlier than around the year 1500, in England around the same time; cf.

Chapter 18: Trade as Craftwork

apart from the works of Unger and Cantor, Hankel (1874, 340 ff.). The oldest known German *Algorismus* (a Basel manuscript) dates back to the year 1445. It is edited and translated by Unger (1888a, 125 ff.).

How slowly arithmetic progressed even in Italy is shown by the manuscript "Introductorius liber qui et pulveris dicitur in mathematicam disciplinam" [Introductory book that is about dust and called mathematics instruction] from the second half of the 14th century, whose author uses a mishmash of Arab numerals with place values, Roman numerals, finger and joint numbers (Cantor 1880, 2:142 f.).

Computation with the abacus was just as common north of the Alps even during the entire Late Middle Ages as the use of counting tokens (*jetons*, counters), which remained in use up into the 18th century.

In Italy, it's was broken with earlier; at the end of the 15th century, Ermolao Barbaro († 1495) spoke of the computation with *jetons* as of a custom, "qui [...] hodie apud barbaros fere omnes servatur" [which [...] today is preserved amongst nearly all foreigners], thus quelled in Italy. Cf. again Cantor (1880, 2:100; 2:112; 2:197 ff.). How cumbersome calculating on the line, however, was compared with numeric computation had already been recognised by the computation master Simon Jacob of Coburg when he wrote, "as much advantage as a pedestrian who is light-footed and laden with no burden has against one who is stuck under a heavy load, an arithmetician also has with the numbers against one with the lines." (Unger 1888b, 70).

That with this state of arithmetic, there can be no talk of a precise computation is obvious. Even if one had placed more worth on it than at that time. In reality, one did not, however, want even to be "exact" at all. It is a thoroughly modern idea that computations must necessarily "agree". All earlier times only ever proceeded in the modern numerical-like parlance to a quite approximate circumscription of the proportions. Anyone who has dealt with the computations of the Middle Ages knows that reviews of the sums marked down by them quite often result in deviating figures. Errors of cursoriness and computation are par for the course[596]. The transposing of numbers in the formation of an example computation forms, one would almost like to say, the rule. We must just think that the difficulties for those men of keeping figures in their heads for even a short time were enormously large. Like as occurs today with children.

All this deficiency in exact computational will and ability is expressed now, however, most clearly in the *bookkeeping* of the Middle Ages. Anyone who leafs through the records of a Tölner, a Vicko von Geldersen, a Wittenborg, or an Otto Ruland has trouble imagining that the writers had been significant merchants of their time. For their entire bookkeeping consists of nothing but a disordered noting of amounts of their purchases and sales, like those which any grocer today in a small provincial town tends to make. They are in the true sense only "journals", "memorandums", that is, notebooks which take the place of the knots in the handkerchiefs of the farmers who go to the market in the city. And peppered with inaccuracies into the bargain. Also lax and liberal in the capture of debt or claim amounts. "And also a package with gloves, I don't know how many there is;" "and also there is one more, bought it with the above; exactly 19 guilders remain to me too and a mix of paternosters [...] I have forgotten the name." Also the name of a customer occasionally "escaped" the Soranzos (in the Venice of the 15th century!)[597]. But what stamps these collections of notes by the medieval merchants with quite especially clear signs of a thoroughly craft-work-based operation is their personal nature. They are not to be separated from their organiser at all. No other person can or should be able to find their way in this confusion of individual records. They thus carry an exceedingly empirical imprint[598]. There can be no talk at all of a somehow systematic objectification of asset valuation. But if the larger traders kept accounts in such a way, then we may conclude that the great majority of the merchants of that time found their way without the existence of any accounts.

And this complete lack of a calculating and systematically objectifying mind corresponds to the state of existence of *weights and measures*, which, as is well-known, were likewise still ordered in a thoroughly empirical manner, in an even stronger dependance on the organic methods of weighing and measuring.

III. The Regulation of Pre-Capitalist Trade

It is not my intention to discuss the many layered problem which is suggested by this heading, any more than in its main features. It has been undertaken not without application of spirit and with much knowledge in recent times by numerous scholars whose investigations have been taken as the basis for the following short remarks. These have no other goal than to confirm that the non-capitalistic character of trade in the

Chapter 18: Trade as Craftwork

Middle Ages can also be inferred from the configuration of the laws and customs of merchants.

At the same time, I am not thinking so much of that component of the legal order which finds its explanation in the original equating of trade and robbery — in which I count the law of salvage [*Grundruhr*], the law of flotsam [*Strandrecht*], the law relating to foreigners, and many others — but rather of the regulation of craftwork-based trade itself. It is shown in individual examples how the craftwork nature of pre-capitalist trade is distinctly evident from the norms regulating it.

1. The *corporate law* [*Gesellschaftsrecht*] and its development in particular allows us deep insights into the character of trade *quo ante*.

It is well-known how arduously the concept developed of a quota-like sharing by individual associates in the costs and profits. The originally mostly family-like associations knew only a joint fund from which the individual participants covered their upkeep according to their personal needs[599]. Can the *principle of satisfaction of basic needs* as the goal of economic activity be more brusquely imagined or represented than in this old point of view of joint use and joint upkeep? I think not. But how much then the entire activity of traders stands under the idea of craftwork, and how the trader was seen as nothing else but a technical worker are things I would like to extract from the manner in which the relationships between the individual associates on the trading journeys undertaken by several of them were tied and legally formulated, and especially those relationships between the wandering craftsmen-traders and the investors staying at home. I am thinking here in particular of the much contested institution of the *commenda* and related forms of association. It is well-known that one likes to see in all *commenda* relationships forms of capitalist trade organisation. But nothing seems to me to be more inverted than this. The *commenda* is actually the agency for the thoroughly craftwork-based character of that period. Lastig's investigations have also proven that in my view, so much as Lastig's terminology and also his own conception seem to lean towards the contrary significance of the *commenda* (as a form of capitalist trade). According to Lastig[600], the *commenda* is "a work contract; the capitalist, *accommendant*, draws another person (worker), *accommendatarius*, into his service so that the latter pursues with a consigned capital (!) [...] a trading business for his (the capitalist's) account but in his own (the worker's) name for a share of the profit". The *commenda* is, in his conception, a "one-sided work association". "The *commendatarius* or general partner stands simply in the service of the *comandor* or *accomandans*, or rather of the *societas accommendantium* [...] he has the obligation of plying business with the capital consigned to him, and within the bounds foisted on him, for the account of his master but in his own name, and receives for it — commonly in addition to a fixed salary — a quota of the business's net profit [...] Only the *commendatarius* or general partner is entitled and obligated to a third." This construction has at the first glance something directly repellent to it for the economist. It seems to have tipped on its head the real facts of the case. At a closer look, it is on the other hand absolutely valid, if it also makes provision for the economic relationships. It confirms particularly exactly the plain craftwork-based character of trade of that time in that it clearly expresses the complete separation between investor and trader. The investor still stands *outside of every nexus* with the trading activity itself, which on the contrary is the exclusive concern of a technical worker. The money consigned to be utilised has not yet assumed the character of capital, but is rather none other than the operational funds[601]. I evoke also the size of the sums which underlay most of the *commenda* agreements — amounts of a few hundred marks in our money, which would already be incapable because of their minuteness of assuming the attributes of capital in respect of the sophistication of the workforce in the earlier period. That then, in the further course of development from those partnerships between investors and craftsmen, relationships of dependency and in the end capitalist enterprises grew shall of course not be denied. But that does not preclude that originally those forms of business owed their origin directly to the purely craftwork-based organisation of economic life.

Finally, however, I would like to sweep out one last viewpoint which to me never properly finds the attention it is due in the literature over the pre-capitalist mercantile law (which

Chapter 18: Trade as Craftwork

was certainly written almost exclusively by legal experts!) — that namely evidence for its craftwork-based nature also exists in *the mere fact of the predominance of corporately practised trade undertakings*. It was in general mostly only possible through the accumulation of tiny tangible assets, which were amassed in the hands of individual persons, to practise a trade over distance even only within modest bounds[602]. Just like a ship, even by the small measurements of the sea-going vessels of the time, could only ever be fitted out by several people together. Hence, the shipping companies[603], more properly shipping cooperatives, just like the trading companies, more properly trader cooperatives, are characteristic legal forms throughout medieval trade and transportation.

2. No less significant for the understanding of the craftwork-based character of medieval trade are the legal norms and customs which rule the *forms of the trading businesses*, as well as these themselves of course. I can recall that the oldest known bill of exchange which was made by German merchants dates from the year 1323[604], but that even in France the beginnings of bills of exchange does not date back past the 13th century[605]; I can recall that we encounter in France still in the 13th century[606], and in Germany still during the 15th century, a prohibition on consignment business, indeed surely of all credit business[607]; that even in the Florence of the 14th century, the forms of money trading, compared with the modern forms, were still by all means stuck at the beginnings of their development[608].

But what I deem still worthy of mention here is the conclusive force of the *canonical prohibition of interest* for the craftwork-based nature of medieval trade[609]. More attention should, I think, be given in the argument over the question of the practical scope of that prohibition to the thought that a profit without technically performed labour, that is, without the visible exercising of external nature on objects, could for all times which were caught up in craftwork-based ideas be seen in fact only as dishonest, as not allowed[610]. Nothing more is expressed surely in that law prohibiting interest than the recognition of the economic principle, suited to economic life organised on the basis of craftwork, of satisfaction of basic

315

needs through creative work. Which was why the prohibition already extended to the mere striving for profit[611]. The outlawing or despising of taking interest objectively found its justification in the circumstance that, by the rule, even in the predominant majority of all cases, money did not actually possess the power of breeding from itself, so long namely as it had assumed none of the qualities of capital, that is, its use was still unable to cause an increase in the productivity of labour. Originally therefore money lending was also none other than a *nobile officium* [prominent office], a service which the associate rendered to the associate, the townsmen to his city, and the benefactor to the poor and oppressed, obviously without aiming at any profit thereby, *nihil inde sperans* [hoping for nothing from it], just as one today helps out the friend in need and only at their urging allows interest to be paid on the outstretched sums.

> "Item si ascun homme ou femme de la dite fraternite [...] sanz sa defaute propre chiete en pouert, la dite fraternite luy apprestera une somme dargent pur merchander et profiter pur un an ou deux a lour auys sanz rien prendre de gayn."
> [In the same way if any man or woman of the said fraternity [...] without their own fault falls into poverty, the said fraternity will apprehend them a sum of money for merchandise and to take advantage of for a year or two at their expense without taking any gain]
> Statute of the "Gilda Mercatoria de Couentre" (from the 14th century) (Gross 1890, 2:50).

Likewise the German journeymen's associations lent to their members without interest; cf. Schanz (1877, 72). Numerous *examples of lending without interest*, particularly to cities which find themselves in need, even in the 15th century, are in Neumann (1865, 507 ff.), who incidentally in my view does not sufficiently acknowledge the originally self-evident nature of lending without interest. It is though in substance only the conception corresponding to the natural sense, when it, for example, in a Venetian document of 1187 states:

> "cum nos — dum videremus nostro comuni necessarium esse pro guerra — pecuniam invenire ad eos precibus duximus recurrendum, qui possunt nostre patrie hoc necessitatis temporis subvenire. Rogovimus igitur omnes viros, quorum nomina inferius continentur, ut pro sua liberalitate comuni nostro in tali necessitate hoc tempore constituto de praefata pecunia subvenirit, qui quoniam terre nostre veri sunt amatores promiserunt nostro communi dictam pecuniam se daturos"

Chapter 18: Trade as Craftwork

[when we — as we see it as our common need for war — to find the money we have thought fit to have recourse to prayers to those who can assist our country in this time of need. I beg, therefore, of all the men whose names are given below, as an act of their own liberality to our community in its time of need, to make available the aforesaid sum of money, for those who are lovers of our land promised they would give money to our community] (Lenel 1897, 43).

A quite similar rationale occurs in the Winchester ordinances (E. Smirke 1852, 73). — One of the most popular forms in which the monasteries during the early period of the Middle Ages came to the help of their dependents and faithful with material services was the lending of money or goods, with which though there was again no talk of paying interest, even if one saw strictly to the return of what was lent. Cf. Sackur (1893, 163 ff.). Cunningham (1890, 1:239) reports of a private individual (12th century) who "vicinis suis indigentibus nummos non tamen ad usuras accomodabat" [he provided to his needy neighbours no money however at interest]. In Tyrol, lending without interest was common up until the end of the 13th century (Voltelini 1904, 25). Fedor Schneider mentions this finding in his discussion of Voltelini (1906, 392) with the comment: "a new fact, which the reviewer commends to the attention of researchers, which explains interest as self-evident for the earliest money economy, even for the barter economy".

Only in traffic with strangers (Jews! Lombards!) could the idea, ugly to the unsophisticated nature, of an interest bearing loan occur. Anyone, however, who engaged in this loathsome activity of taking interest from the money seeker placed in hardship must obviously have appeared to be ostracised, and would have been by custom whether a religious prohibition on interest had existed or not, as such a thing was only the expression of the voice of the people in this case. It would otherwise certainly not have been comprehended that even in the Italian cities up into the 15th and 16th centuries the "usurarii" remained excluded from the merchants' guilds and chambers of commerce.

According to the statutes of the cloth dealers in *Florence* (14th century), the usurer was either entirely excluded from the guild or, if the usurious dealings were already far in the past, had to atone for the stigma with double the registration fee. Usury is also sufficient motive for the same guild to eject a member who is judged guilty by a vote of the associates. From 1429, the silk weavers' guild also excluded the recidivist usurer. In the statute of the money changers guild from 1367, it was expressly forbidden "to lend on interest, be it against pawn or promissory note, or to practise other usury, on penalty of 100 lire". At the end of the 14th century, the prohibition on interest in the curtest form then found entry into the statutes of all the Florentine guilds

(Pöhlmann 1878, 53, 84). Similar regulations are in the statutes of Milan (1396), Bergamo (1497), and Pesaro (1532). Cf. Lattes (1899, 32–33, 147 f.) and Zdekauer (1896, 63 ff.).

Only the transformation of money into capital, and the self-evidence of interest thereby created, freed the usurer (for whom each loan is for the goals of consumption) within certain limits from his infamy. From that, however, we are obviously authorised to draw the conclusion that centuries in which the interest-bearing loan was frowned on by legislation and the feelings of the people could have felt no breath yet of the capitalist economic manner.

3. Especially transparent is, however, finally the *corporate law* in medieval commerce. Here the genuinely craftwork-based structure of trade at the time shimmers through in distinct contours.

It is well-known indeed that commonly enough no strict division at all existed between craftsmen's guilds and traders' guilds, and that the guilds of wholesalers had the closest relations with those of the retailers. But we must accustom ourselves to the idea that the professional traders of the Middle Ages surely occasionally thought themselves to be more prestigious than some craftsmen, but no differently than the members of an arbitrary "higher" guild of manufacturers. What distinguished the merchant from the craftsman were only ever differences of degree, not of essence. He was often a "better" craftsman, like the goldsmith or the baker elsewhere, but he belonged with his thinking and feeling to the circle of craftsmen.

Anyone who should still doubt it need only leaf through the statutes of the merchant guilds, the regulations of the "courts" and "branches" in foreign cities[612]. There he will find on every page a confirmation of the correctness of my view. The ideology of the craftsmen's guilds is transferred almost without alteration into them.

In particular, we encounter in the statutes of the traders' guilds everywhere the paramount principles of craftwork-based organisation — that to every associate who performs his work in the manner of his fathers, a living shall be assured, and his sustenance guaranteed[613]. Struggling for as large as possible an area of sales, secured against the inroads of neighbours; and uniformly regulated distribution of the in-

Chapter 18: Trade as Craftwork

dividual shares among the associates, thus precluding any competition outwardly as well as inwardly[614] — that is the foundation on which all pre-capitalist trade also rests. And all the prohibitions and commands of the guild statutes are then dedicated in particular to the achievement of that goal, to the guaranteeing of an unrivalled, calm labour-in-place kept far apart from any change resulting from individual speculation and intrigue. What we find with the craftsmen's guilds returns here in stereotypical modifications — the limitation of the extent of business[615]; the prohibition of preemption[616]; the obligation of letting the associates enter into the sales contract[617]; the prohibition on carrying off customers; the prohibition on price fixing, and many similar regulations.

"nullus de societate vocet aliquem comparatorem donec est ad bancam alterius ad emendum nec sibi faciat cignum vel insignam aliquam" [nobody of the society may make any sale as long as he is at the stall of another to buy nor may he produce himself a cignus* or some insignia]. From the statute of Pizzicagnoli (for *Bologna* around 1242) (Gaudenzi 1896, 2:175). The statute of the *Florentine Societas campsorum* [society of bankers] of the year 1299 forbade the members of the guild from walking around in the city to look for money changing business. The "bankers" were meant to wait calmly by their stalls until the customers came to them, so that the opportunity of earning was as equal as possible for all members of the guild (Sieveking 1898, 2:44). A Strasbourg law over the rights of fellow lodgers from the 1380s implies the same (in § 35): "Es sol ouch nieman in deheins würtes husz gon wehsseln, der würt sende dann mit namen nach ime oder der gaste, der do wehsseln wil" [Nobody shall also change money in the landlord's house, the landlord will then send by name (?) always or the guest who wants to change money there]; (in § 37): "Die an dem fritage uff dem bloche sitzent und wechsselnt, die sollent nieman ruffen über den graben noch winken" [Those sitting on Friday at the bench and changing money, they shall call nobody across the street nor wave] (Eheberg 1879, 188–89). The dating, deviating from Eheberg's, is from Cahn (1895, 31).

For prohibitions of price fixing in the Italian cities, see Kohler (1897). In addition, cf. Lizier (1900, 510).

Thus from all sides comes the confirmation of the statement that the professional trade of the Middle Ages, more precisely stated the trade of Italy until deep into the 14th century, and that of the rest of Europe until into the 16th century, bore the unmistakable stamp of craftwork. A depiction of the

---

*   [Tr.: third of an ounce.]

real conditions of existence of pre-capitalist trade can be dispensed with — they are the same as are made possible by the continued existence of craftwork.

Postscript to the Second Edition

The preceding depiction has in substance been adopted unaltered, only supplemented by new material, from the first edition. Hardly any other chapter have I been able to exploit again as a whole in such a manner as this one, although against no other (with exception of that which contains my so-called "Theory of Ground Rents" [*Grundrententheorie*]) have as many critical objections been raised as against this one. I have repeated my depiction after careful consideration in substantially the same framework. For the criticism which referred to this part of my work has not refuted me in any single essential point.

It is in particular the following writings which contend with my views:

Adolf Nuglisch (1904).
Gustav Beckmann (1904).
Friedrich Keutgen (1906).
Wilhelm Silberschmidt (1905, 129 ff., esp. 148; 1910).
Reinhard Heynen (1905). Heynen mocks himself and does not know it when he tries to substantiate "the size" of medieval trade by having his hero Mairano, a man renowned through his wealth (πλουτω διαφερων [excessively wealthy]), undertake the construction of an enormous (!) ship fitted out with three (!) huge (!) sails, which later causes a general sensation in Constantinople. The same Mairano who, when his business had reached its zenith, engaged a partner (Heynen 1905, 104) and borrowed from his father-in-law 150, and from his cousin 50 marks (!).

An in-depth, valuable review of Heynen's book has been published by Silberschmidt (1906).

Adolf Schaube (1908). Schaube in fact pointed out an error to me. I put the amount of wool exported from England in the year 1273 by foreigners on a level with the wool exported overall — it is about ⅔. Apart from that, the essay, written in a spiteful tone, contains a welcome confirmation of the correctness of my own depiction. But where have we come to, when we criticise an author in every respect because the posited error slipped in on him, so that no dog takes a piece of bread from him anymore! That is an intolerable, spiritless pedantry in the worst sense.

Robert Davidsohn (1896a, 4:268 ff.).

What the critics have said against my conception of medieval trade is the following in particular:

1. The trader is always — even in the Middle Ages — intent on profit, and not only seeking to satisfy his need for a living — the idea of 'sustenance' does not thus dominate him. I have already commented on this objection, and I refer the reader to what I have noted on pages 63 ff.

Chapter 18: Trade as Craftwork

I stand by the conclusion that the *regulating idea* also remained for trade during the Middle Ages for a long time the same as the regulating idea for (manufacturing) craftwork. The trader's world of ideas was in substance the same as that of his brother, the manufacturing producer. It is to be confessed that the new ideas made themselves rather more noticeable in the sphere of trade than in other economic spheres. I also always ask for the *totality of capitalistic spirit* (striving for profit *in connection with* economic rationalism and the dissolution of all qualities in the one quantity of money — which will be first covered by a later volume!) to be seen as the antithesis of the spirit of the medieval trader. Of course, the pack bearer in Naples will also have preferred having three lira to having one. But anyone who perceives no difference in the direction of the spirit between him and Pierpont Morgan is simply psychologically colour-blind and eliminates himself as a critic (or even a writer of history).

2. That trade in the Middle Ages was *not "as small"* at all as I have depicted it. Now, *actually*, not a single one of my numeric details (up to the figure corrected by Schaube) has been proven to be wrong[618].

I am then reproached for not having correctly *appreciated* the smallness of medieval trade. *One* (Nuglisch) refers me to the buying power of money being drawn into consideration when one wants to determine the significance of a sum of money at a period. That was also previously not entirely unfamiliar to me. But anyone who even knows only a tiny bit about the difficulty of the problem which we indicate with the words "purchasing power of money" will be wary of expressing a sum of money in any other way than by its metal value, as I have done. How the "purchasing power" of money in the Middle Ages (I only want to reveal this in passing to the named gentleman) relates to that in our time is not to be expressed at all in a ratio. What shall such determinations as these mean: "for a few pfennigs, one could eat oneself full, for a few guilders house oneself" (Adolf Nuglisch 1904, 241). They do not mean anything, absolutely anything at all. What is meant by "eat oneself full", with what? Quality of food! What is meant by "house oneself"? Where? Even today, one does not live in the countryside much dearer than in the Middle Ages. And the prices for other important things? For example, for all the manufactured products which cost many times over what they do today? For all the transport? For all the so-called amusements? For the "spiritual sustenance"? For all the drinks and tobacco? For the use of manpower? And whatever else can be brought for money? See, in addition, what I say about that in a later volume.

Others consider to be mistaken my method of *comparing* the figures of medieval trade statistics with the present. Latterly Rudolf Häpke, whose judgment in matters of trade history deserves to be heard, has expressed himself with this in mind (Häpke 1908). The actual results which he obtains confirm in a gratifying manner the correctness of my conception. His summarises his opinion as follows (Häpke 1908, 268): "On the whole, trade rested on a broadly democratic basis, and trade magnates were rarely only involved in the goods trade. All the less to be expected with these large merchants were quantities of wares which impress the modern eye to some degree." But then he adds: "Medieval and present-day turnover admit no comparison at all", and in another place, he says, "he will seek large dimensions in vain, even if he is accustomed to seeing with medieval eyes."

With respect to this, I have the following to remark:

a) we must directly compare figures of the past with present-day figures — it is the *only* possibility of making them clear to us in their size;

b) we must directly look at the Middle Ages with "modern", not with "medieval" eyes, in order to learn to understand it in its particular nature and in its deviation from the present. We should extricate ourselves directly from the views of contemporaries, for which of course the respective height reached by commercial trade, for example, was the peak. Häpke himself warns of phrases like "enormous turnover of wares" and the like which do not mean anything. All fertile historical research rests on seeing with *one's own* eyes and thereby recognising the *distinctiveness* of earlier conditions. I evoke the felicitous results of population research, and in particular research into the statistics of cities — only now do we comprehend the essence of the medieval city when we know that it had not 200,000, but 20,000 inhabitants.

But obviously, my critics have something else on their mind — I could not explain otherwise the hostile tone into which they lapse when they come to speak of my conception of the "smallness" of medieval trade. They presume that I wanted thereby to belittle the *worth, the significance of the Middle Ages*. As if the greatness of a period could be measured by the amount of wares traded! I mean, nothing makes the "greatness" of the Middle Ages so clear as my demonstration that the extent of trade in the Middle Ages was quite negligible when we compare it with the present. The period was great because it brought forth the minstrels and the Strasbourg cathedral, Dante and Giotto, Emperor Rothbart and Thomas Aquinas, despite perhaps only a hundredth or thousandth as much cheese being "moved" by trade as is today.

3. I would have liked most of all to have improved the section over *the law*, especially the *corporate law* in medieval trade, in some points, and to have deepened some pages. I will make up for some things later when I bring up in a later volume the development of the trading companies during the age of early capitalism. But in the basic conception, I have not been swayed here either, as qualified as some objections of my legal critics, particularly in the distinguished works of Silberschmidt, appear to be. Rather the efforts of this astute and well informed researcher have directly contributed to strengthening my views in the crucial points, as I believe that our opinions do not diverge further than corresponds to the more legal and more sociological view of the matters.

I want to reproduce the wording of the criticisms here in their main points.

Chapter 18: Trade as Craftwork

In his essay in the *Archiv für bürgerliches Recht*, Silberschmidt says:

> Most recently, Werner Sombart, investigating the contrast between craftwork-based and capitalist operations in the history of trade, has found directly therein the plainly craftwork-based character of the trade of that time (ie. that in all ownership structures the activity of the non-locals for the absentees, the *work*, was the decisive thing in that time). Even if one wants to admit to that, the further proposition, that the "investor still stands outside of every nexus with the trading activity itself, which on the contrary is the exclusive concern of a technical worker"*, is not substantiated by the sources. In a later period, the *commenda* was used by non-merchants as a capital investment, but even for the earlier period, the principal was always (?) a merchant. That the money provided — at first wares were in general given — never had the character of capital, even in the Sombartian sense, must be just as doubtful as the proposition that the predominance of corporately practised undertakings forms the best proof for the craftwork-based nature of the operations. On the contrary, the proposition may be justified from the above correspondence in connection with the earlier sources — the urge grounded in the nature of trade to sell and exchange the available wares above the satisfaction of need, above the man's sustenance and as advantageously as possible often and rapidly (!) was the reason for sending such wares also to foreign lands, and for ordering so that they also were turned over in a place in which the merchant could not personally be; one enlisted these foreigners so that they had a higher interest in the matter, and thus arose contractual and corporate relationships. (1905, 148)

To that, I respond as follows. Silberschmidt is technically doubtlessly correct when he claims that the investors [*Kommendanten*] frequently (certainly not always) would have themselves been professional traders. Objectively, my claim is not thereby rebutted — through the dedication of a sum of money (or wares for sale) to a craftsman-trader, even if the giver is a professional trader, the craftwork-based character of trade is in no way abrogated. I meant that with the separation of the investors and the traders accepting the money that the management of the business did not yet thereby migrate to the investor. Neither the latter, if he was a craftsman, nor the trader moving to the foreign parts were capitalist entrepreneurs merely through the fact that they united. Silberschmidt himself has described these *commenda* relationships to us in a graphic way. He shows (already in his work *Die Commenda in ihrer frühesten Entwicklung bis zum 13. Jahrhundert* (Silberschmidt 1884); then in the *Archiv für bürgerliches Recht* (Silberschmidt 1904; 1905)) how in the *commenda* one at first commanded one's own wares

---

* [Tr.: see page 314 above.]

only occasionally and for individual journeys, later more and more generally for a relative or friend who himself made the journey, that is, "entrusted in the own interest of the giver", whereby the trader [*Kommendatar*] fulfilled the contract quite gratuitously or was involved in an honest way in the profit of the undertaking. Thus arose the *sendeve* business and beside it the *colleganza* (association of friends) — the union of several sums of money for joint business. Silberschmidt compares with complete justice the primitive *commenda* of the *socida*, the cattle driving agreement (Silberschmidt 1904, 7) and remarks once (Silberschmidt 1905, 147) fittingly, "how today still in simple rural circumstances the farmer travelling to the nearest city deals with buying and selling for his fellow citizens, so we find also here cases of pure goodwill. This activity in foreign places for others, however, frequently turns into a perpetual, professional one", etc.

Thus, in any case, the form of various business contracts is also *conceivable* in the framework of a craftwork-based economy. Its occurrence in itself proves thus nothing *against* this. And here I recall now all the signs which otherwise speak for the craftwork-based character of medieval trade, recall the minutely small *commenda* amounts, the tiny turnover, the guild-like regulation, etc., and I come to the conclusion that just this corporate trade, be it in the form of *commenda*, be it in the form of *societas*, was in its typical appearance, that is, as a mass phenomenon, still for many centuries craftwork. I will myself attempt to show in a later volume how it gradually developed into capitalist forms.

***

Here I would like only to make two remarks of a more general sort which will perhaps contribute to reducing the tension between the *legal* critics and myself.

I have already pointed out the dissimilar approach of the legal experts and the sociological economists — the former are interested in the form, we in the content of economic life. Belonging to content first and foremost are the living spirit in the economic subjects and the dimensions of their processes and objects. One and the same legal relationship (as in this case the *commenda*) can now take as its basis economic acts which are quite various as to quality and quantity. Whether I lend 100 marks or 100,000 marks to a producer so that he uses it in his business makes no difference legally if the legal form of the business is the same; economically, it *establishes* the essential difference between the two businesses.

But then the legal experts must also keep themselves informed in the area of economic and sociological research and must be conversant with the concepts which this research has nurtured in the course of recent generations, particularly also for historical research. It befalls us quite peculiarly — the historians reproach us for having too many concepts and too many "theories", the legal experts complain about the inadequacy of our concept formation. This reproach of a marked backwardness of economic concepts has been frequently raised by, for example, Lastig in his historical works on trade law. Thus he says, for

Chapter 18: Trade as Craftwork

example, in the *Zeitschrift für das gesamte Handelsrecht* (Lastig 1879, 408): "Economics operates with the concepts of capital and labour, jurisprudence on the other hand with infinitely finer terms." At the time that he published his seminal research (1879), Lastig was right to a certain degree with such a reproach. But, since then, there has now also been work by us, and many legal historians seem to have disregarded that. When they come to speak of economic relationships, they often still today use such simplistic concepts as "money economy", "capital" (in the sense of money or means of production), and speak of "trade" as a uniform phenomenon, etc.

Just to mention one example from recent years, I want to point out a few sentences from an otherwise admirable work of legal history by Hacman (1910, 467). It reads:

> With that [the beginning of the exchange economy from the 8th century], however, the entire life was also steered onto new rails, onto those *in which it still moves almost exclusively today*, namely in the paths (!) of trade (!). That this could soon arrive at such a rampant unfolding is attributed to the circumstance that it turned out to be an excellent means for increasing wealth (!), on which it depended in the main (!). Now where the powers of the individual did not suffice to arrive at the fervently desired goal (!), at great wealth, then he sought the connection to other like-minded people, and they found themselves very soon (!), [...] in the period in which, in the area of the general (!) national economy, that fundamental revolution was accomplished which has led to the acceptance of a special stage of development in the history of the national economy, under the dominance of money and credit (!) [...]

If we tried to write with such general, meaningless expressions over legal matters, the legal historians would certainly receive a shock. But then they should also accustom themselves to treating *our* problems in the strict system of concepts which we have now gradually evolved. I do not doubt that it will contribute to the understanding of one another substantially.

Bibliography

Achtnich, Karl. 1910. *Der Bürgerstand in Strassburg bis zur Mitte des XIII. Jahrhunderts.* Strasbourg: Quelle & Meyer.

Albers, Bruno. 1900. *Consuetudines farfenses ex archetypo vaticano.* Consuetudines monasticae 1. Stuttgart & Vienna: J. Roth.

Alberti, Leon Battista. 1908. *I libri della famiglia.* Edited by Giralamo Mancini. Florence: G. Carnesecchi e Figli.

Ammianus Marcellinus. 1935. *Ammianus Marcellinus, with an English Translation.* Translated by John C. Rolfe. London: W. Heinemann.

Anderson, Adam. 1764. *An Historical and Chronological Deduction of the Origin of Commerce: From the Earliest Accounts to the Present Time. Containing, an History of the Great Commercial Interests of the British Empire. To Which Is Prefixed, an Introduction, Exhibiting a View of the Ancient and Modern State of Europe; of the Importance of Our Colonies, and of the Commerce, Shipping, Manufactures, Fisheries, Etc. of Great Britain and Ireland; and Their Influence on the Landed Interest. With an Appendix, Containing the Modern Politico-Commercial Geography of the Several Countries of Europe.* 2 vols. London: A. Millar, J. and R. Tonson et al.

Andree, Karl. 1867. *Geographie des Welthandels.* 3 vols. Stuttgart: J. Engelhorn.

Andrews, Charles M. 1894. "Die Stadt in Neu-England, ihr Ursprung und ihre agrarische Grundlage." *Zeitschrift für Social- und Wirtschaftsgeschichte* 2 (1): 103–31.

Anton, Karl Gottlob. 1799. *Geschichte Der Teutschen Landwirtschaft von Den Ältesten Zeiten Bis Zu Ende Des 15. Jahrhunderts.* 3 vols. Görlitz: Anton.

Aquinas, St Thomas. 1895. *Opera Omnia.* 16 vols. Rome: Typographia Polyglotta.

Arco, Giovanni Battista Gherardo: d'. 1782. *Dell'armonia politico-economica fra la città ed il suo territorio.* Cremona: Lorenzo Manini.

Aristotle. 1872. *Aristoteles' Politik: Erstes, zweites und drittes Buch mit erklärenden Zusätzen ins deutsche Übertragen.* Edited by Jakob Bernays. Berlin: Wilhelm Hertz.

Arnold, Wilhelm. 1854. *Verfassungsgeschichte der deutschen Freistädte im Anschluss an die Verfassungsgeschichte der Stadt Worms.* 2 vols. Gotha: F. A. Perthes.

Aronius, Julius, Albert Dresdner, and Ludwig Lewinski. 1902. *Regesten zur Geschichte der Juden im fränkischen und deutschen Reiche bis zum Jahre 1273.* Berlin: L. Simion.

Ashley, William James. 1896. *Englische Wirtschaftsgeschichte.* 2 vols. Sammlung älterer und neuerer staatswissenschaftlicher Schriften des In- und Auslandes 7. Duncker & Humblot.

Barbazan, Etienne, and Dominique Martin Méon, eds. 1808. *Fabliaux et contes des poètes françois des XI, XII, XIII, XIVe et XVe siècles, tirés des meilleurs auteurs.* 3 vols. Paris: Imprimerie de Crapelet.

Baudi di Vesme, Carlo, Cornelio Desimoni, and Vittorio Poggi, eds. 1873. *Codex Diplomaticus Langobardiae.* Historiae patriae Monumenta 13. Turin: E. regio typographeo.

Baudrillart, Henri. 1880. *Histoire du luxe privé et public depuis l'antiquité jusqu'à nos jours.* 2nd ed. 4 vols. Paris: Hachette et cie.

Beck, Ludwig. 1884. *Die Geschichte des Eisens in technischer und kulturgeschichtlicher Beziehung.* 5 vols. Brunswick: F. Vieweg.

Beckmann, Gustav. 1904. "Die Bedeutung des Handwerks im Wirtschaftsleben nach den Darstellungen Sombarts und Lamprechts." *Beilage zur Allgemeinen Zeitung* 1904 (106–108): 241–44, 249–52, 257–59.

Beckmann, Johann. 1777. *Beyträge zur Oekonomie, Technologie, Polizey- und Cameralwissenschaft.* 12 vols. Göttingen: Vandenhoeck & Ruprecht.

Bede, the Venerable. 1838. *Venerabilis Bedae Historia Ecclesiastica gentis Anglorum.* London: Sumptibus Societatis.

Behrends, Peter Wilhelm. 1834. "Liber bonorum monasterii sancti Ludgeri Helmonstadensis, mit historisch-topgraphischen Bemerkungen." *Neue Mitteilungen des thüringisch-sächsischen Vereins* I (4): 21–50.

Beissel, Stephan. 1885. *Geldwerth und Arbeitslohn im Mittelalter, eine culturgeschichtliche Studie.* Freiburg im Breisgau: Herder.

Beloch, Julius. 1895. "Die Entwicklung der Grossstädte in Europa." In *Huitième Congrès International D'hygiène Et de Démographie Tenu À Budapest Du 1 Au 9 Septembre 1894, Comptes-rendus Et Mémoires,* edited by Zsigmond Gerlóczy. Vol. 7. Budapest: Pesti könyvnyomda-részvénytársaság.

Below, Georg von. 1889. *Entstehung der deutschen Stadtgemeinde.* Düsseldorf: L. Voss.

———. 1892. *Der Ursprung der deutschen Stadtverfassung.* Düsseldorf: L. Voss & Cie.

———. 1897. "Die Entstehung des Handwerks in Deutschland." *Zeitschrift für Social- und Wirtschaftsgeschichte* 5: 124–64, 225–47.

———. 1900a. "Grosshändler und Kleinhändler im deutschen Mittelalter." *Jahrbücher für Nationalökonomie und Statistik* 20: 1–51.

———. 1900b. *Territorium und Stadt: Aufsätze zur deutschen Verfassungs-, Verwaltungs- und Wirtschaftsgeschichte.* Historische Bibliothek 11. Munich & Leipzig: R. Oldenbourg.

———. 1905. *Das ältere deutsche Städtewesen und Bürgertum*. Edited by Wilhelm Heyd. Monographien zur Weltgeschichte, VI. Bielefeld & Leipzig: Velhagen & Klasing.

———. 1912. "Die Motive der Zunftbildung im deutschen Mittelalter." *Historische Zeitschrift* 109: 23–48.

———. 1914a. *Der deutsche Staat des Mittelalters. Ein Grundriß der deutschen Verfassungsgeschichte: Die allgemeinen Fragen*. 2 vols. Leipzig: Quelle & Mayer.

———. 1914b. "Handwerk und Hofrecht. Eine Entgegnung." *Vierteljahrschrift für Social- und Wirtschaftsgeschichte* 12: 1–21.

Benedict, St. 1895. *Benedicti Regula monachorum*. Edited by Eduard Wölfflin. Leipzig: Teubner.

Bernard of Clairvaux, St. 1839. *Opera omnia Sancti Bernardi abbatis Claræ-Vallensis: post horstium denuo recognita, repurgata, et in meliorem digesta ordinem*. Edited by Jean Mabillon and Jakob Merlo-Horstius. Vol. 2.2. Paris: Gaume.

Bertagnolli, Carlo. 1881. *Delle vicende dell'agricoltura in Italia;* Florence: G. Barbèra.

Bethmann-Hollweg, Moritz August. 1846. *Ursprung der lombardischen Städtefreiheit: eine geschichtliche Untersuchung*. Bonn: A. Marcus.

Beyer, Heinrich, ed. 1860. *Urkundenbuch zur Geschichte der, jetzt die preussischen Regierungsbezirke Coblenz und Trier bildenden mittelrheinischen Territorien*. 3 vols. Coblenz: J. Hölscher.

Bianchi, Giulio. 1891. *La proprietà fondiaria e le classi rurali nel medio evo e nella età moderna: studio economico-sociale*. Pisa: Galileiana.

Binterim, Anton Joseph, and Joseph Hubert Mooren. 1828. *Die alte und neue erzdiözese Köln in Dekanate eingetheilt oder Das Erzbisthum Köln mit den Stiften, Dekanaten, Pfarreien und Vikarien sammt deren Einkommen und Collatoren wie es war*. 2 vols. Mainz: S. Müller.

Bitterauf, Theodor, ed. 1905. *Die Traditionen des Hochstifts Freising*. Vol. 1. Quellen und Erörterungen zur bayerischen und deutschen Geschichte, New Series, Vol. 4. Aalen: Scientia.

Blümcke, O. 1884. "Die Handwerkszünfte im mittelalterlichen Stettin." *Baltische Studien* XXXIV: 81–247.

Boeheim, Wendelin. 1897. *Meister der Waffenschmiedekunst vom XIV. bis ins XVIII. Jahrhundert*. Berlin: W. Moeser.

———. 1898. "Die Waffe und ihre einstige Bedeutung im Welthandel." *Zeitschrift für historische Waffenkunde* 1 (7): 171–84.

Boehm, Willy. 1876. *Friedrich Reiser's Reformation des K. Sigmund. Mit Benutzung der ältesten Handschriften nebst einer kritischen Einleitung und einem erklärenden Commentar*. Leipzig: Veit & Comp.

Boileau, Étienne. 1837. *Réglemens sur les arts et métiers de Paris, rédigés au 13 siècle, et connus sous le nom du Livre des métiers d'Étienne Boileau*. Paris: Crapelet.

———. 1879. *Les métiers et corporations de la ville de Paris : XIIIe siècle. Le livre des métiers d'Étienne Boileau*. Edited by René de Lespinasse and François Bonnardot. Paris: Imprimerie Nationale.

Boissonnade, Prosper. 1900. *Essai sur l'organisation du travail au Poitou: Depuis le XIe siècle jusqu'à la Révolution*. 2 vols. Paris: H. Champion.

Bonifacio, Giovanni. 1744. *Istoria di Trivigi*. Venice: Gianbatista Albrizzi Q. Gir.

Borchgrave, Émile de. 1865. *Histoire des colonies Belges qui s'etablirent en Allemagne*. Brussels: C. Muquardt.

Borgius, Walther. 1899. "Wandlungen im modernen Detailhandel." *Archiv für soziale Gesetzgebung und Statistik* 13: 41–84.

Botero, Giovanni. 1588. *Delle cause della grandezza delle citta*. 3 vols. Rome: Appresso Giouanni Martinelli.

———. 1665. *Libri tres de origine urbium, earum excellentia et augendi ratione quibus accesserunt Hippoliti a Collibus Incrementa urbium sive de causis magnitudinis urbium*. 3 vols. Helmstedt: Johannis Heitmulleri.

Bouquet, Martin, ed. 1840. *Rerum gallicarum et francicarum scriptores*. 24 vols. Victor Palmé. http://gallica.bnf.fr/ark:/12148/bpt6k50123x.

———, ed. 1869. "Ex Panegyrico Eumenii: In Constantium." In *Recueil des Historiens des Gaules et de la France [Rerum gallicarum et francicarum scriptores.]*. Vol. 1. Paris: Victor Palmé.

Bourgeois, René. 1904. *Du mouvement communal dans le comté de Champagne aux XIIe et XIIIe siècles*. Paris: H. Jouve.

Boutié, Louis. 1911. *Paris au temps de saint Louis : d'après les documents contemporains et les travaux les plus récents*. Paris: Librairie Académique.

Brackmann, Albert. 1899. "Urkundliche Geschichte des Halberstädter Domkapitels im Mittelalter: Ein Beitrag zur Verfassungs- und Verwaltungsgeschichte der deutschen Domkapitel." *Zeitschrift des Harz-Vereins für Geschichte und Altertumskunde* 32: 1–147.

Bransford, V. 1906. "Science and Citizenship." *American Journal of Sociology* 11 (6): 722–62.

Bibliography

Brants, Victor. 1880. *Essai historique sur la condition des classes rurales en Belgique jusqu'a la fin du XVIIIe siècle*. Louvain: C. Peeters.
Bresslau, Harry. 1884. *Jahrbücher des Deutschen Reichs unter Konrad II*. Vol. 2. Jahrbücher der Deutschen Geschichte. Duncker & Humblot.
Breton, Guillaume le. 1841. *Philippide; extraits concernant les guerres de Flandre*. Bruges: Vandecasteele-Werbrouck.
Brodnitz, Georg. 1914. "Die Stadtwirtschaft in England." *Jahrbücher für Nationalökonomie und Statistik* 47 (1): 1–39.
Broglio d'Ajano, Romolo. 1893. *Die Venetianische Seidenindustrie und ihre Organisation bis zum Ausgang des Mittelalters*. Munchener Volkswirtschaftliche Studien 2. Stuttgart: Cotta.
Bücher, Karl. 1886. *Die Bevölkerung von Frankfurt am Main in 14. und 15. Jahrhundert*. Tübingen: Laupp.
———. 1892. "Gewerbe." In *Handwörterbuch der Staatswissenschaften*, edited by Johann Conrad, 1st ed., 3:922–50. Jena: G. Fischer.
———. 1893. *Entstehung der Volkswirtschaft. Sechs Vorträge*. Tübingen: Laupp.
Bückmann, Rudolf. 1912. *Das Domkapitel zu Verden im Mittelalter*. Hildesheim: A. Lax.
Bugge, Alexander. 1906. "Die nordeuropäischen Verkehrswege im frühen Mittelalter und die Bedeutung für die Entwicklung des europäischen Handels und der europäischen Schiffahrt." *Vierteljahrsschrift für Sozial- und Wirtschaftsgeschichte* IV: 227–77.
———. 1914. "Der Untergang der norwegischen Schiffahrt in Mittelalter." *Vierteljahrsschrift für Sozial- und Wirtschaftsgeschichte* XII: 92–151.
Bungers, Hans. 1896. *Beiträge zur mittelalterlichen Topographie, Rechtsgeschichte und Socialstatistik der Stadt Köln, insbesonderer der Immunität Unterlan*. Leipzig: Duncker & Humblot.
Cahn, Julius. 1895. *Münz- und Geldgeschichte der Stadt Straßburg im Mittelalter*. Strasbourg: Karl J. Trübner.
Cantillon, Richard. 1755. *Essai sur la Nature du Commerce*. London: Fletcher Gyles.
Cantor, Moritz Benedikt. 1880. *Vorlesungen über Geschichte der Mathematik*. 4 vols. Leipzig: B.G. Teubner.
Cardauns, Hermann. 1880. *Konrad von Hostaden, Erzbischof von Köln (1238-61)*. Köln: J.P. Bachern.
Caro, Georg. 1908. *Sozial- und Wirtschaftsgeschichte der Juden im Mittelalter und der Neuzeit*. Grundriss der Gesamtwissenschaft des Judentums. Leipzig: Gustav Fock.

Cenni, Gaietano. 1760. *Monumenta Dominationis Pontificiae, sive Codex Carolinus iuxta autographum Vindobonense, Epistula Leonis III Carolo Augusto, Diplomata Ludovici, Otthonis et Henrici, Chartula Comitissae Mathildae, et Codex Rudolphinus ineditus.* 2 vols. Rome: Typographia Palladis.

Chatillon-Plessis. 1894. *La vie à table à la fin du XIXe siècle: théorie, pratique et historique de gastronomie moderne.* Paris: Firmin-Didot & Co.

Cibrario, Luigi. 1839. *Economia politica del medio evo.* Turin: Eredi Botta.

Conrad, Johann, Ludwig Elster, Wilhelm Lexis, and Edgar Loening, eds. 1898. *Handwörterbuch der Staatswissenschaften.* 2nd ed. 7 vols. Jena: G. Fischer.

Conze, Friedrich. 1889. "Kauf nach hanseatischen Quellen." Bonn: University of Bonn.

Corradi, Alfonso. 1865. *Annali delle epidemie occorse in Italia dalle prime memorie fino al 1850.* Bologna: Gamberini e Parmeggiani.

Crapelet, Georges Adrien, and Guillaume de la Villeneuve. 1831. *Proverbes et dictons populaires, avec les dits du Mercier et des Marchands, et les Crieries de Paris, aux XIIIe et XIVe siècles.* Paris: Crapelet.

Creighton, Charles. 1891. *A History of Epidemics in Britain from A.D. 664 to the Extinction of Plague.* Cambridge: Cambridge University Press.

Cunningham, William. 1890. *The Growth of English Industry and Commerce during the Early and Middle Ages.* 2 vols. Cambridge: Cambridge University Press.

———. 1895. "Die Einwanderung von Ausländern nach England im XII. Jahrhundert." *Zeitschrift für Social- und Wirtschaftsgeschichte* 3 (2): 177–203.

Curschmann, Fritz. 1900. *Hungersnöte im Mittelalter: ein Beitrag zur deutschen Wirtschaftsgeschichte des 8. bis 13. Jahrhunderts.* Leipziger Studien aus dem Gebiet der Geschichte 6. Leipzig: B.G. Teubner.

Custodi, Pietro, ed. 1804. *Scrittori classici italiani di Economia politica: Parte Moderna.* Milan: G.G. Destefanis.

Dahn, Felix. 1879. *Bausteine. Gesammelte kleine schriften.* Berlin: O. Janke.

———. 1897. *Die Könige der Germanen: Das Wesen des ältesten Königthums der germanischen Stämme und seine Geschichte bis zur Auflösung des karolingischen Reiches: Die Franken unter den Karolingen.* Vol. VIII.4. Leipzig: Breitkopf und Härtel.

———. 1900. *Die Könige der Germanen: Das Wesen des ältesten Königthums der germanischen Stämme und seine Geschichte bis zur Auflösung des karolingischen Reiches: Die Franken unter den Karolingen.* Vol. VIII.6. Leipzig: Breitkopf und Härtel.

———. 1902. *Die Könige Der Germanen: Das Wesen Des Ältesten Königthums Der Germanischen Stämme Und Seine Geschichte Bis Zur Auflösung Des Karolingischen Reiches: Die Alamannen.* Vol. IX.1. Leipzig: Breitkopf und Härtel.

———. 1905. *Die Könige Der Germanen: Das Wesen Des Ältesten Königthums Der Germanischen Stämme Und Seine Geschichte Bis Zur Auflösung Des Karolingischen Reiches: Die Baiern.* Vol. IX.2. Leipzig: Breitkopf und Härtel.

Damas, Paul. 1879. "Beiträge zur Geschichte der deutschen Städte zur Zeit der fränkischen Kaiser." Breslau: Breslau.

D'Arbois de Jubainville, H. 1858. *Études sur l'état intérieur des abbayes cisterciennes et principalement de Clairvaux, au XIIe et au XIIIe siècle.* Paris: A. Durand.

Das königliche Staatsarchiv in Stuttgart, ed. 1849. *Wirtembergisches Urkundenbuch.* Vol. 1. Stuttgart: F. H. Köhler.

D'Avenel, Georges. 1894. *Histoire économique de la propriété, des salaires, des denrées et de tous les prix en général, depuis l'an 1200 jusqu'en l'an 1800.* 7 vols. Paris: Imprimerie Nationale.

Davidsohn, Robert. 1896a. *Forschungen zur alteren Geschichte von Florenz.* 4 vols. Berlin: Mittler & Sohn.

———. 1896b. *Geschichte von Florenz.* 4 vols. Berlin: Mittler & Sohn.

De la Court, Pieter. 1911. *Het welvaren van Leiden: handschrift uit het jaar 1659.* Translated by Felix Driessen. Gravenhage: Nijhoff.

De la Tour, Imbart. 1896. "Des immunitiés commerciales accordés aux églises du VIIe au IXe siècle." In *Etudes d'Histoire du moyen âge dédiées à Gabriel Monod*, 77–87. Paris: Leopold Cerf and Felix Alcan.

Delbrück, Hans. 1907. *Geschichte der Kriegskunst im Rahmen der politischen Geschichte.* 4 vols. Berlin: G. Stilke.

Demolins, Edmond. 1900. *La Réforme sociale.* Paris: Secretariat de la Société D'Économie Sociale.

Denton, William. 1888. *England in the Fifteenth Century.* London: George Bell and Sons.

Der historischen Kommission bei der Königlichen Akademie der Wissenschaften, ed. 1884. *Die Chronikon der niedersächsischen Städte: Lübeck.* Der Chroniken der deutschen Städte von 14. bis ins 16. Jahrhundert 28. Leipzig: S. Hirzel.

Des Marez, Guillaume. 1901. *La lettre de foire a Ypres au XIIIe siècle, contribution à l'étude des papiers de crédit.*. Brussels: H. Lamertin.

Dillen, J.G. van. 1914. *Het economisch Karakter der middelleuwschen Stad*. Amsterdam: Kruyt.

Diodorus. 1831. *Historische Bibliothek*. Translated by Julius Friedrich Wurm. 4 vols. Stuttgart: J. B. Metzler.

Dopsch, Alfons. 1904. *Die landesfürstlichen Urbare Nieder- und Oberösterreichs aus dem 13. und 14. Jahrhundert*. Österreichische Urbare 1. Vienna and Leipzig: Wilhelm Braumüller.

———. 1912a. *Die Wirtschaftsentwicklung der Karolingerzeit vornehmlich in Deutschland*. 2 vols. Weimar: Bohlau.

———. 1912b. *Die Wirtschaftsentwicklung der Karolingerzeit vornehmlich in Deutschland*. Vol. 1. 2 vols. Weimar: Bohlau.

———. 1913. *Die Wirtschaftsentwicklung der Karolingerzeit vornehmlich in Deutschland*. Vol. 2. 2 vols. Weimar: Bohlau.

———. 1914. "Berichtigung." *Jahrbuch für Gesetzgebung, Verwaltung und Volkswirtschaft im Deutschen Reiche* 38 (2): 1070–72.

Doren, Alfred. 1893. *Untersuchungen zur Geschichte der Kaufmannsgilden des Mittelalters. Ein Beitrag zur Wirtschafts-, Social- und Verfassungsgeschichte der mittelalterlichen Städte*. Staats- und socialwissenschaftliche Forschungen, 12.2. Leipzig: Duncker & Humblot.

———. 1901. *Studien aus der Florentiner Wirtschaftsgeschichte*. 2 vols. Stuttgart: Cotta.

Du Bourg, Antoine. 1882. *Étude sur les coutumes communales du sud-ouest de la France*. Mémoires de la Société archéologique du Midi de la France 12. Paris: Librairie de la Société bibliographique.

Du Maroussem, Pierre-Robert Planteau. 1891. *La question ouvrière*. 4 vols. Paris: Arthur Rousseau.

Dunn, Matthias. 1844. *An Historical, Geological, and Descriptive View of the Coal Trade of the North of England; Comprehending Its Rise, Progress, Present State, and Future Prospects. To Which Are Appended a Concise Notice of the Peculiarities of Certain Coal Fields in Great Britain and Ireland; and Also a General Description of the Coal Mines of Belgium, Drawn up from Actual Inspection*. Newcastle upon Tyne: Pattison and Ross.

Duyse, Hermann van. 1897. "Ueber den Handel mit Hiebwaffen in verschiedenen Epochen." *Zeitschrift für historische Waffenkunde* 1 (3): 65–66.

Bibliography

Eberstadt, Rudolph. 1899. *Das französische Gewerberecht und die Schaffung staatlicher Gesetzgebung und Verwaltung in Frankreich vom dreizehnten Jahrhundert bis 1581.* Staats- und socialwissenschaftliche Forschungen 17. Leipzig: Duncker & Humblot.

———. 1916. *Der Ursprung des Zunftwesens und die älteren Handwerkerverbände des Mittelalters.* 2nd ed. Leipzig: Duncker & Humblot.

Eckert, Heinrich. 1910. *Die Krämer in süddeutschen Städten bis zum Ausgang des Mittelalters.* Abhandlungen zur mittleren und neueren Geschichte 16. Berlin: Rothschild.

Edwards, Edward, ed. 1866. *Liber Monasterii de Hyda.* Rerum Brittanicarum Medii Ævi Scriptores or Chronicles and Memorials of Great Britain and Ireland during the Middle Ages. London: Longmans, Green, Reader, and Dyer.

Eheberg, Karl Theodor von. 1879. *Über das ältere deutsche Münzwesen und die Hausgenossenschaften besonders in volkswirthschaftlicher Beziehung. Mit einigen bisher ungedruckten Urkunden über die Strassburger Hausgenossen.* Staats- und socialwissenschaftliche Forschungen, 2.5. Leipzig: Duncker & Humblot.

Ehmck, Dietrich Rudolf, and Wilhelm von Bippen, eds. 1873. *Bremisches Urkundenbuch.* 5 vols. Bremen: C. Ed. Müller.

Ehrenberg, Richard. 1901. "Entstehung und Bedeutung groser Vermögen. IV: Die Brüder Siemens." *Die Deutschen Rundschau,* April 15, 1901.

Ennen, Leonard. 1863. *Geschichte Der Stadt Köln, Meist Aus Den Quellen Des Kölner Stadt-Archivs.* Vol. 1. Cologne & Neuß: L. Schwann.

Ennen, Leonard, and Gottfried Eckertz, eds. 1860. *Quellen zur Geschichte der Stadt Köln.* 6 vols. Köln: M. DuMont-Schauberg.

Ermisch, Hubert. 1890. "Zur Statistik der sächsischen Städte im Jahre 1474." *Neues Archiv für Sächsische Geschichte und Altertumskunde* 11: 145–53.

———. 1891. "Wanderungen durch die Stadt Freiberg im Mittelalter." *Neues Archiv für Sächsische Geschichte und Altertumskunde* 12: 86–162.

Ersch, J. S., J. G. Gruber, G. Hassel, and A. G. Hoffmann, eds. 1828. *Allgemeine Encyclopädie der Wissenschaften und Künste, in alphabet. Folge von genannten Schriftstellern.* Vol. 2.3 Harrich-Hebung. Leipzig: J. F. Sieditsch.

Espinas, Georges, and Henri Pirenne, eds. 1906. *Recueil de documents relatifs à l'histoire de l'industrie drapière en Flandre.* 4 vols. Brussels: Kiessling et Cie.

Eulenburg, Franz. 1892. *Über Innungen der Stadt Breslau vom 13. bis 15. Jahrhundert.* Berlin: Mayer & Müller.

———. 1893. "Das Wiener Zunftwesen. I." *Zeitschrift für Social- und Wirtschaftsgeschichte* 1 (2/3): 264–317.
———. 1895. "Zur Bevölkerungs- und Vermögensstatistik des 15. Jahrhunderts." *Zeitschrift für Social- und Wirtschaftsgeschichte* 3: 424–67.
———. 1896. "Städtische Berufs- und Gewerbestatistik (Heidelbergs) im 16. Jahrhundert." *Zeitschrift für Geschichte des Oberrheins* 11: 81–141.
———. 1904. *Die Frequenz der deutschen Universitäten von ihrer Gründung bis zur Gegenwart*. Leipzig: B.G. Teubner.
Fabre, Paul. 1893. "Eine Nachricht über die Bevölkerungsziffer Englands zu Zeiten Heinrichs II." *Zeitschrift für Social- und Wirtschaftsgeschichte* 1: 149–53.
Fagniez, Gustave. 1877. *Études sur l'industrie et la classe industrielle à Paris au XIIIe et au XIVe siècles*. Paris: F. Vieweg.
———, ed. 1898. *Documents relatifs à l'histoire de l'industrie et du commerce en France*. 2 vols. Paris: A. Picard et fils.
Falke, Johannes. 1859. *Die Geschichte des deutschen Handels*. 2 vols. Deutsches Leben 3. Leipzig: Gustav Maher.
———. 1869. *Die Geschichte des deutschen Zollwesens von seiner Entstehung bis zum Abschluss des deutschen Zollvereins*. Leipzig: Veit & Comp.
Fecht, Ottmar. 1909. *Die Gewerbe der Stadt Zürich im Mittelalter*. Lahr: Schauenburg.
Fengler, Otto. 1907. "Quentowic, seine maritime Bedeutung unter Merowingern und Karolingern." *Hansische Geschichtsblätter* 13 (34): 91–108.
Feudrix de Bréquigny, Louis George Oudard, and F. J. G. La Porte du Theil, eds. 1791. *Diplomata, chartae, epistolae et alia documenta, ad res Francicas spectantia*. Vol. 1.1. Paris: Nyon.
Flach, Jacques. 1893. *Les Origines de l'ancienne France*. 2 vols. Paris: L. Larose et Forcel.
Forestié, Édouard, ed. 1890. *Les livres de comptes des Frères Bonis, marchands montalbanais du XIVe siècle*. 2 vols. Archives historiques de la Gascogne 20, 23. Paris: H. Champion.
Förster, Ernst. 1869. *Geschichte der Italienischen Kunst*. 5 vols. Leipzig: Weigel.
France, ed. 1763. *Statuts et ordonnances des marchands maîtres, tailleurs d'habits, pourpointiers, chaussetiers de la ville, fauxbourgs & banlieue de Paris*. Paris: Knapen.

Bibliography

Frankenstein, Kuno. 1887. *Bevölkerung und Hausindustrie in Kreise Schmalkalden seit Anfang dieses Jahrhunderts. Ein Beitrag zur Socialstatistik und zur Wirtschaftsgeschichte Thüringens.* Beiträge zur Geschichte der Bevölkerung in Deutschland seit dem Anfang dieses Jahrhunderts 2. Tübingen: H. Laupp.

Franklin, Alfred. 1894. *Les magasins de nouveautés. La vie privée d'autrefois. Arts et métiers modes, moeurs, usages des Parisiens du XIIe au XVIIIe siècle 15.* Paris: E. Plon, Nourrit et Cie.

Frensdorff, Ferdinand. 1882. *Dortmunder Statuten und Urtheile.* Hansische Geschichtsquellen, III. Halle: Buchhandlung des Waisenhauses.

Frensdorff, Ferdinand, Matthias von Lexer, and Friedrich Roth. 1865. *Die Chroniken der schwäbischen Städte.* Vol. 2. 2 vols. Die Chroniken der deutschen Städte vom 14. ins 16. Jahrhundert 5. Leipzig: S. Hirzel.

Freytag, Gustav. 1867. *Bilder aus der deutschen Vergangenheit.* 2 vols. Leipzig: S. Hirzel.

Friedländer, Ludwig Heinrich. 1901. *Darstellungen aus der Sittengeschichte Roms in der Zeit von August bis zum Ausgang der Antonine.* 7th ed. 3 vols. Leipzig: S. Hirzel.

Fritz, Johann. 1894. *Deutsche Stadtanlagen.* Strasbourg: Heitz.

Garnier, Russell Montague. 1892. *History of the English Landed Interest, Its Customs, Laws and Agriculture.* 2 vols. London: Swan Sonnenschein & Co.

Gaudenzi, Augusto. 1896. *Statuti della Società del Popolo di Bologna.* Fonti per la Storia d'Italia 4. Rome: Istituto Storico Italiano.

Geering, Traugott. 1886. *Handel und Industrie der Stadt Basel. Zunftwesen und Wirtschaftsgeschichte bis zum Ende des XVII. Jahrhunderts.* Basel: Felix Schneider.

–––. 1887. "Kölns Colonialwaarenhandel vor 400 Jahren." Edited by Konstantin Höhlbaum. *Mitteilungen aus dem Stadtarchiv von Köln*, no. 11: 41–65.

Gengler, Heinrich. 1882. *Deutsche Stadtrechtsaltertümer.* Erlangen: Andreas Deichert.

Géraud, Hercule, ed. 1837. *Paris sous Philippe - le - Bel: d'après des documents originaux et notamment d'après un manuscript contenant Le Rôle de la taille imposée sur les habitants de Paris en 1292.* Collection des documents inédits sur l'histoire de France, I. Paris: Imprimerie de Crapelet.

Gerken, G. W. 1775. *Codex Diplomaticus Brandenburgensis.* Stendal: Franzen.

Gerson, Johannes. 1483. *Opera.* 4 vols. Cologne: Johann Koelhoff.

Gibbins, H. de B. 1897. *Industry In England: Historical Outlines*. London: Methuen And Company Limited.

Giles, John Allen, ed. 1845. *Vita s. Thomæ Cantuariensis archiepiscopi et martyris, ab auctoribus contemporaneis*. 2 vols. Oxford: J. H. Parker.

Goethe, Johann Wolfgang von. 1839. *Goethe's Faust: Part II*. Translated by L. J. Bernays. London: S. Low.

———. 1888. *Faust*. Edited by Ludwig Wilhelm Hasper. Klassische deutsche Dichtungen 10. Gotha: F. A. Perthes.

———. 1907. *Goethe Maximen und Reflexionen*. Edited by Max Hecker. Vol. 21. Schriften der Goethe-Gesellschaft. Weimar: Verlag der Goethe Gesellschaft.

Goldschmidt, Levin. 1891. *Universalgeschichte des Handelsrechts*. Stuttgart: Ferdinand Enke.

Gothein, Eberhard. 1892. *Wirtschaftsgeschichte des Schwarzwaldes und der angrenzenden Landschaften*. Strasbourg: Karl J. Trübner.

Gouw, J. ter. 1879. *Geschiedenis van Amsterdam*. 8 vols. Amsterdam: Scheltema & Holkema.

Grandidier, Philippe Andre. 1897. "Etat écclesiastique de la diocèse de Strassbourg en 1454." *Bulletin de la Société pour la conservation des monuments historiques d'Alsace*, 2, 18.

Green, J. R. 1894. *Town Life in the Fifteenth Century*. London: Macmillan & Company.

Gregorovius, Ferdinand. 1859. *Geschichte der Stadt Rom im Mittelalter: Vom fünften Jahrhundert bis zum sechzehnten Jahrhundert*. 8 vols. Stuttgart: Cotta.

Greving, Joseph. 1904. "Wohnungs- Und Besitzverhältnisse Im Kölner Kirchspiel St. Kolumba." *Die Annalen Des Historischen Vereins Für Den Niederrhein* 78.

Gross, Charles. 1890. *The Gild Merchant: A Contribution to British Municipal History*. 2 vols. Oxford: Clarendon Press.

Grünhagen, Colmar. 1884. "Schlesien am Ausgange des Mittelalters. Eine kultur-historische Übersicht." *Zeitschrift für Geschichte und Alterthum Schlesiens* XVIII: 26–67.

Guérard, M. B., ed. 1840. *Cartulaire de L'Abbaye de Saint-Bertin*. Collection des Cartulaires de France 3. Paris: Chapelet.

———. 1844. *Polyptyque de l'abbé Irminon de Saint-Germain-des-Prés, ou dénombrement des manses, des serfs et des revenus de l'abbaye de Saint-Germain-des-Prés sous le règne de Charlemagne*. 2 vols. Paris: L'Imprimerie Royale.

Bibliography

———. 1853. *Polyptyque de l'abbé de Saint-Remi de Reims, ou dénombrement des manses, des serfs et des revenus de cette abbaye, vers le milieu du neuvième siècle de notre ère.* Paris: L'Imprimerie Royale.

Hacman, M. 1910. "Beitrag zur Entwickelung der offenen Handelsgesellschaft." *Zeitschrift für das gesamte Handelsrecht und Konkursrecht* 68: 439–82.

Hale, William Hale, ed. 1865. *Registrum sive liber irrotularius et consuetudinarius prioratus Beatae Mariae Wigorniensis.* London: Camden Society.

Hamilton, N.E.S.A., ed. 1870. *Willelmi Malmesbiriensis Monachi De Gestis Pontificum Anglorum Libri Quinque.* London: Longman & Co.

Hanauer, Auguste. 1876. *Études économiques sur l'Alsace ancienne et moderne.* 2 vols. Strasbourg: Simon.

Handloike, Max. 1883. *Die lombardischen Städte unter der Herrschaft der Bischöfe und die Entstehung der Communen.* Berlin: W. Weber.

Hankel, Hermann. 1874. *Zur Geschichte der Mathematik in Alterthum und Mittelalter.* Leipzig: Teubner.

Hansen, Johannes. 1912. *Beiträge zur Geschichte des Getreidehandels und der Getreidepolitik Lübecks.* Veröffentlichungen zur Geschichte der Freien und Hansestadt Lübeck 1. Lübeck: Max Schmidt.

Hanssen, Georg. 1880. *Agrarhistorische Abhandlungen.* 2 vols. Osnabrück: Zeller.

Häpke, Rudolf. 1905. "Die Entstehung der grossen bürgerlichen Vermögen im Mittelalter." *Jahrbuch für Gesetzgebung, Verwaltung und Volkswirtschaft im Deutschen Reiche* 29: 1052–87.

———. 1906. "Die Herkunft der friesischen Gewebe." *Hansische Geschichtsblätter* 12: 309–25.

———. 1908. *Brügges Entwicklung zum mittelalterlichen Weltmarkt.* Abhandlungen zur Verkehrs- und Seegeschichte 1. Berlin: Karl Curtius.

Hart, William Henry, and Ponsonby Annesley Lyons, eds. 1884. *Cartularium Monasterii de Rameseia.* Vol. 1. London: Master of the Rolls.

Hartmann, Ludo Moritz. 1890. "Bemerkungen zum Codex Bavarus." *Mitteilungen des Instituts für österreichische Geschichtsforschung* XI (3): 361–71.

———. 1892. *Urkunde einer römischen Gärtnergenossenschaft vom Jahre 1030, mit Einleitung und Erläuterungen.* Freiburg im Breisgau: J. C. B. Mohr.

———. 1895. "Zur Geschichte der Zünfte im frühen Mittelalter." *Zeitschrift für Social- und Wirtschaftsgeschichte* 3: 109–29.

———. 1900. *Geschichte Italiens im Mittelalter*. 2 vols. 32. Gotha: F. A. Perthes.

———. 1904a. "Die wirtschaftlichen Anfänge Venedigs." *Vierteljahrsschrift für Sozial- und Wirtschaftsgeschichte* 2: 432–42.

———. 1904b. *Zur Wirtschaftsgeschichte Italiens im frühen Mittelalter: Analekten*. Gotha: F. A. Perthes.

Hartung, Johannes. 1895a. "Die Augsburger Zuschlagsteuer von 1475. Ein Beitrag zur Geschichte des städtischen Steuerwesens, sowie der socialen und Einkommensverhältnisse am Ausgange des Mittelalters." *Jahrbuch für Gesetzgebung, Verwaltung und Volkswirtschaft im Deutschen Reiche* 19: 95–136.

———. 1895b. "Die augsburgische Vermögenssteuer und die Entwickelung der Besitzverhältnisse im 16. Jahrhundert." *Jahrbuch für Gesetzgebung, Verwaltung und Volkswirtschaft im Deutschen Reiche* 19: 867–83.

Hartwig, Otto. 1875. *Quellen und Forschungen zur ältesten Geschichte der Stadt Florenz*. 2 vols. Marburg: Elwert.

Hauck, Albert. 1904. *Kirchengeschichte Deutschlands*. 5 vols. Leipzig: J.C. Hinrichs'sche.

Haupt, Moriz. 1859. "Hermanni contracti conflictus ovis et lini." *Zeitschrift für deutsches Alterthum*, 1, 11: 216–38.

Heck, Philipp. 1900. *Die Gemeinfreien der Karolingischen Volksrechte. Beiträge zur Rechtsgeschichte der deutschen Stände im Mittelalter*, I. Halle: Max Niemeyer.

———. 1906. "Die kleinen Grundbesitzer der brevium exempla." *Vierteljahrsschrift für Sozial- und Wirtschaftsgeschichte* 4: 349–55.

Hecker, Justus Friedrich Carl, and August Hirsch. 1865. *Die grossen Volkskrankheiten des Mittelalters. Historisch-pathologische Untersuchungen*. Th. Chr. Fr. Enslin: Berlin.

Hegel, Karl. 1891. *Städte und Gilden der germanischen Völker im Mittelalter*. 2 vols. Leipzig: Duncker & Humblot.

Hegel, Karl von. 1847. *Geschichte der Städteverfassung von Italien: seit der Zeit der römischen Herrschaft bis zum Ausgang des zwölften Jahrhunderts*. 2 vols. Leipzig: Weidmannsche Buchhandlung.

Heideloff, Carl Alexander von. 1844. *Die Bauhütte des Mittelalters in Deutschland*. Nuremberg: Johann Adam Stein.

Heineken, Hermann. 1908. *Der Salzhandel Lüneburgs mit Lübeck bis zum Anfang des 15. Jahrhunderts*. Historische Studien 63. Berlin: E. Ebering.

Hellpach, Willy. 1912. "Die Arbeitsteilung im geistigen Leben." *Archiv für Sozialwissenschaft und Sozialpolitik* 35: 665–700.

Helmolt, Hans F., ed. 1899. *Weltgeschichte*. 9 vols. Leipzig & Vienna: Bibliographisches Institut Leipzig.
Henaux, Ferdinand. 1851. *Histoire du pays de liège*. Liège: J. Desoer.
Hénaux, Ferdinand. 1872. *Histoire du pays de Liège*. 3rd ed. Liège: J. Desoer.
Herrmann, Ferdinand. 1900. *Schilderung und Beurteilung der gesellschaftlichen Verhältnisse Frankreichs in der Fabliauxdichtung des 12. und 13. Jahrhunderts*. Coburg: Rossteutscher.
Hertzberg, Gustav Friedrich. 1889. *Geschichte der Stadt Halle an der Saale von den Anfängen bis zur Neuzeit*. 3 vols. Halle: Buchhandlung des Waisenhauses.
Herzog, Anton. 1909. *Die Lebensmittelpolitik der Stadt Strassburg im Mittelalter*. Berlin & Leipzig: Rothschild.
Heyd, Wilhelm. 1879. *Geschichte des Levantehandels im Mittelalter*. 2 vols. Stuttgart: J.G. Cotta.
Heynen, Reinhard. 1905. *Zur Entstehung des Kapitalismus in Venedig*. Stuttgart & Berlin: Cotta.
Hieronymus, Sophronius Eusebius. 1766. *Sancti Eusebii Hieronymi Stridonensis Presbyteri Operum*. Edited by Domenico Vallarsi and Scipione Maffei. Vol. 2.1. Venice: Zerletti.
Hildebrand, Bruno. 1866. "Zur Geschichte der deutschen Wollenindustrie." *Jahrbücher für Nationalökonomie und Statistik* 6: 186–254.
Hirsch, Theodor. 1858. *Danzigs Handels- und Gewerbsgeschichte unter der Herrschaft des Deutschen Ordens*. Leipzig: S. Hirzel.
Hodgkin, Thomas. 1895. *Italy and Her Invaders: The Lombard Kingdom, 600-744*. Oxford: Clarendon Press.
Hoeniger, Robert. 1882. *Der schwarze Tod in Deutschland. Ein Beitrag zur Geschichte des vierzehnten Jahrhunderts*. Berlin: Grosser.
Hoffmann, Johann Gottfried. 1839. *Die Bevölkerung des Preußischen Staats 1837*. Berlin: Nicolaischen Buchhandlung.
Hoffmann, Max. 1889. *Geschichte der freien und Hansestadt Lübeck*. 2 vols. Lübeck: E. Schmersahl.
Höhlbaum, Konstantin, ed. 1876. *Hansisches Urkundenbuch*. 11 vols. Halle: Buchhandlung des Waisenhauses.
Hone, Nathaniel J. 1906. *The Manor and Manorial Records*. 1st ed. London: Methuen & Co. Ltd.
Hontheim, Johann Nikolaus von. 1750. *Historia Trevirensis diplomatica et pragmatica*. 3 vols. Augsburg.
Hume, David. 1793. *Essays and Treatises on Several Subjects*. 2 vols. Basel: Tourneisen.
Hunter, William Wilson. 1886. *The Indian Empire: Its Peoples, History, and Products*. 2nd ed. London: Trübner & Co.

Huvelin, Paul-Louis. 1897. *Essai historique sur le droit des marchés & des foires*. Paris: Arthur Rousseau.
Ilgen, Thomas. 1902. "Die Entstehung Der Städte Des Erzstifts Köln Am Niederrhein." *Die Annalen Des Historischen Vereins Für Den Niederrhein* 74: 1–26.
Inama-Sternegg, Karl Theodor. 1879. *Deutsche Wirtschaftsgeschichte*. 3 vols. Leipzig: Duncker & Humblot.
———. 1889. *Sallandstudien: Sonderabdruck aus der Festgabe für Georg Hanssen zum 31. Mai 1889*. Tübingen: Laupp.
———. 1899. "Bevölkerung des Mittelalters und der neueren Zeit bis Ende des 18. Jahrhunderts in Europa." In *Handwörterbuch der Staatswissenschaften*, edited by Johann Conrad, Wilhelm Lexis, Ludwig Elster, and Edgar Loening, 2nd ed., 2:660–74. Jena: G. Fischer.
Jacob, Georg. 1887. *Der nordisch-baltische Handel der Araber im Mittelalter*. Leipzig: G. Böhme.
———. 1896. *Ein Arabischer Berichterstatter Aus Dem 10. Jahrhundert Über Fulda, Schleswig, Soest, Paderborn Und Andere Städte Des Abendlandes: Artikel Aus Quazwînîs Āthâr al-Bilâd Aus Dem Arabischen Übertragen, Mit Commentar Und Einer Einleitung Versehen*. 3rd ed. Berlin: Mayer & Müller.
Jacob, William. 1838. *Ueber Production und Consumtion der edlen Metalle: eine geschichtliche Untersuchung*. Translated by Carl Theodor von Kleinschrod. 2 vols. Rein'sche Buchhandlung.
Jacobi, Ludwig Hermann Wilhelm. 1857. *Das Berg-, Hütten und Gewerbewesen des Regierungs-Bezirks Arnsberg in statistischer Darstellung*. Gewerbe-Statistik von Preußen 1. Iserlohn: J. Bädeker.
Jaffé, Philipp. 1869. *Monumenta Bambergensia*. Bibliotheca rerum Germanicarum 5. Weidmann.
Janicke, Karl, ed. 1873. *Urkundenbuch der Stadt Quedlinburg*. 2 vols. Geschichtsquellen der Provinz Sachsen und angrenzender Gebiete. Halle: Buchhandlung des Waisenhauses.
Janner, Ferdinand. 1876. *Die Bauhütten des Mittelalters*. Leipzig: Seemann.
Janssen, Johannes. 1874. *Geschichte des deutschen Volkes seit dem Ausgang des Mittelalters*. 8 vols. Freiburg im Breisgau: Herder.
Jastrow, J. 1886. *Die Volkszahl deutscher Städte zu Ende des Mittelalters und zu Beginn der Neuzeit. Ein Überblick über Stand und Mittel der Forschung*. Historische Untersuchungen 1. Berlin: R. Gaertner.

Bibliography

Jowitt Whitwell, Robert. 1904. "English Monasteries and the Wool Trade in the 13th Century." *Vierteljahrsschrift Für Sozial- Und Wirtschaftsgeschichte* 2: 1–33.

Justi, Johann Heinrich Gottlobs von. 1758. *Staatswirtschaft oder systematische Abhandlung aller Oekonomischen un Cameralwissenschaften, die zur Regierung eines Landes erfordert werden*. 2nd ed. 2 vols. Leipzig: Bernhard Christoph Breitkopf.

Kallen, Gerhard. 1907. *Die oberschwäbischen Pfründen des Bistums Konstanz und ihre Besetzung (1275-1508): Ein Beitrag zur Pfründengeschichte vor der Reformation*. Kirchenrechtliche Abhandlungen, 45/46. Stuttgart: Enke.

Kallsen, Otto. 1891. *Die deutschen Städte im Mittelalter*. Halle: Buchhandlung des Waisenhauses.

Kemble, John Mitchell, ed. 1839. *Codex diplomaticus aevi saxonici*. 6 vols. London: Sumptibus Societatis.

Keutgen, Friedrich. 1903. *Ämter und Zünfte: Zur Entstehung des Zunftwesens*. Jena: Gustav Fischer.

———. 1906. "Hansische Handelsgesellschaften, vornehmlich des 14. Jahrhunderts." *Vierteljahrschrift für Sozial- und Wirtschaftsgeschichte* 4 (2–4): 278–324, 461–514, 567–632.

Kiesselbach, Wilhelm. 1860. *Der Gang des Welthandels und die Entwicklung des europäischen Völkerlebens im Mittelalter*. Stuttgart: J.G. Cotta.

Kindlinger, Nikolaus. 1787. *Münsterische Beiträge zur Geschichte Deutschlandes hauptsächlich Westfalens*. 3 vols. Münster: Theißing.

Kisky, Wilhelm. 1906. *Die Domkapitel der geistlichen Kurfürsten in ihrer persönlichen Zusammensetzung im vierzehnten und fünfzehnten Jahrhundert*. Weimar: Hof-Buchdruckerei.

Kissel, Clemens. 1907. *Die Garnisonbewegungen in Mainz von der Römerzeit an*. Mainz: Lehrlingshaus.

Kitchin, George William, ed. 1886. *A Charter of Edward the Third Confirming and Enlarging the Privileges of St. Giles Fair, Winchester: A.D. 1349*. Winchester Cathedral Records 2. Winchester: Warren & Son.

Klöden, Karl Friedrich. 1841. *Ueber die Stellung des Kaufmanns während des Mittelalters, besonders im nordöstlichen Deutschlande*. 4 vols. Berlin: Rauck.

Klöden, Karl Friedrich von. 1845. *Beiträge zur Geschichte des Oderhandels*. 7 vols. Berlin: A.W. Hayn.

Klumker, Christian Jasper. 1899. "Der friesische Tuchhandel zur Zeit Karls des Grossen und sein Verhältnis zur Weberei jener Zeit." *Jahrbuch der Gesellschaft für bildende Kunst und vaterländische Altertümer zu Emden* 13 (1): 29–69.

Knieke, August. 1893. *Die Einwanderung in den westfälischen Städten bis 1400: ein Beitrag zur Geschichte der deutschen Städte*. Münster: Regensberg.

Kober, Erich. 1908. *Die Anfänge des deutschen Wollgewerbes*. Abhandlungen zur Mittleren und Neueren Geschichte 8. Berlin & Leipzig: Walther Rothschild.

Koehne, Carl. 1904. *Das Recht der Mühlen bis zum Ende der Karolingerzeit*. Breslau: Marcus.

———. 1906a. "Der 'faber publice probatus' der Lex Alam. LXXIV 5." *Vierteljahrschrift für Social- und Wirtschaftsgeschichte* 4: 186–89.

———. 1906b. "Zur sogenannten Reformation K. Sigmunds." *Neuen Archiv der Gesellschaft für ältere deutsche Geschichtskunde* 31 (1): 214–37.

Köhler, Gustav. 1893. *Geschichte der Festungen Danzig und Weichselmünde bis zum Jahre 1814*. 3 vols. Breslau: Koebner.

Kohler, Josef. 1897. *Das Strafrecht der italienischen Statuten vom 12.–16. Jahrhundert*. Studien aus dem Strafrecht 2–6. Mannheim: J. Bensheimer.

Kothe, Wilhelm. 1903. *Kirchliche Zustände Strassburgs im vierzehnten Jahrhundert: ein Beitrag zur Stadt- und Kulturgeschichte des Mittelalters*. Strasbourg: Herder.

Kötzschke, Rudolf. 1901. *Studien zur Verwaltungsgeschichte der Großgrundherrschaft Werden an der Ruhr*. Leipzig: Anton Doll.

———. 1911. *Grundzüge der deutschen Wirtschaftsgeschichte bis zum 17. Jahrhundert*. 2nd ed. Grundriss der Geschichtswissenschaft zur Einführung in das Studium der Deutschen Geschichte des Mittelalters und der Neuzeit, II.1. Leipzig: Teubner.

Kowalewsky, Maxime. 1895. "Die wirthschaftlichen Folgen des schwarzen Todes in Italien." *Zeitschrift für Social- und Wirtschaftsgeschichte* 3: 406–23.

———. 1901. *Die ökonomische Entwicklung Europas bis zum Beginn der kapitalistischen Wirtschaftsform*. Translated by Leo Motzkin. 7 vols. Bibliothek der Volkswirtschaftslehre und Gesellschaftswissenschaft, XI. Berlin: R. L. Prager.

Kulischer, Josef. 1899. "Zur Entwicklungsgeschichte des Kapitalzinses." *Jahrbücher für Nationalökonomie und Statistik*, III, XVIII: 305–71.

Bibliography

Kunze, Karl. 1891. *Hanseakten aus England, 1275-1412.* Hansische Geschichtsquellen, VI. Halle: Buchhandlung des Waisenhauses.

Laband, Paul. 1864. "Das Seerecht von Amalfi (La Tabula de Amalfi)." *Zeitschrift für das gesamte Handelsrecht* 7: 296–337.

Labarte, Jules. 1864. *Histoire des arts industriels au moyen âge et à l'époque de la renaissance.* 4 vols. Paris: A. Morel et cie.

Lacomblet, Theodor Joseph. 1840. *Urkundenbuch für die Geschichte des Niederrheins oder des Erzstifts Cöln, der Fürstenthümer Jülich und Berg, Geldern, Meurs, Kleve und Mark, und der Reichsstifte Elten, Essen und Werden: aus den Quellen in dem Königlichen Provinzial-Archiv zu Düsseldorf und in den Kirchen- und Stadt-Archiven der Provinz, vollständig und erläutert.* 4 vols. Düsseldorf: Wolff.

Lamey, Andreas, ed. 1768. *Codex principis olim Laureshamensis Abbatiae diplomaticus ex aevo Maxime Carolingico diu multumque desideratus.* 3 vols. Mannheim: Typis Academicis.

———, ed. 1770. *Codex principis olim Laureshamensis Abbatiae diplomaticus ex aevo Maxime Carolingico diu multumque desideratus.* Vol. 3. 3 vols. Mannheim: Typis Academicis.

Lamprecht, Karl. 1885. *Deutsches Wirtschaftsleben im Mittelalter. Untersuchungen über die Entwicklung der materiellen Kultur des Platten Landes auf Grund der Quellen zunächst des Mosellandes.* 4 vols. Leipzig: Alphons Dürr.

Landau, Georg. 1862. *Das Salgut: Ein Beitrag zur deutschen Rechts- und Verfassungsgeschichte.* Kassel: Theodor Fischer.

Lastig, Gustav. 1879. "Beiträge zur Geschichte des Handelsrechts." *Zeitschrift für das gesamte Handelsrecht* 24: 387–449.

Lattes, Alessandro. 1899. *Il diritto consuetudinario delle città lombarde.* Milan: Ulrico Hoepli.

Lechner, Karl. 1884. *Das grosse Sterben in Deutschland in den Jahren 1348 bis 1351 und der folgenden Pestepidemien bis zum Schlusse des 14. Jahrhunderts.* Innsbruck: Wagner.

Lenel, Walter. 1897. *Die Entstehung der Vorherrschaft Venedigs an der Adria mit Beiträgen zur Verfassungsgeschichte.* Strasbourg: Trübner.

Leo, Heinrich, ed. 1842. *Rectitudines Singularum Personarum: Nebst Einer Einleitenden Abhandlung Über Landansiedlung, Landbau, Gutsherrliche Und Bäuerliche Verhältnisse Der Angelsachsen.* Halle: E. Anton.

Leroux de Lincy, Antoine Jean Victor, and Lazare Maurice Tisserand. 1867. *Paris et ses historiens aux 14e et 15e siècles; documents et écrits originaux recueillis et commentés par Le Roux de Lincy et L.M. Tisserand*. Histoire Générale de Paris. Paris Impr. impériale.

Lesser, Friedrich. 1888. *Erzbischof Poppo von Trier (1016-1047): ein Beitrag zur Geschichte des deutschen Episkopates vor Ausbruch des Investiturstreites*. Leipzig: Duncker & Humblot.

Lethmate, Franz. 1912. *Die Bevölkerung Münsters i. W. in der zweiten Hälfte des 16. Jahrhunderts*. Münsterische Beiträge zur Geschichtsforschung 41. Münster in Westfalen: Coppenrath.

Letourneau, Charles Jean Marie. 1897. *L'évolution du commerce dans les diverses races humaines*. Bibliothèque anthropologique 18. Paris: Vigot.

Leuthold, Karl Edwin. 1889. "Untersuchungen zur ältesten Geschichte Freibergs." *Neues Archiv für Sächsische Geschichte und Alterthumskunde* 10: 304–29.

Levasseur, Emile. 1889. *La population française*. 2 vols. Paris: Arthur Rousseau.

———. 1900. *Histoire des classes ouvrières et de l'industrie en France avant 1789*. 2 vols. Paris: Arthur Rousseau.

———. 1903. *Histoire des classes ouvrières et de l'industrie en France de 1789 à 1870*. 2 vols. Paris: Arthur Rousseau.

Levison, Wilhelm. 1902. "Kleine Beiträge zu Quellen der fränkischen Geschichte." *Neues Archiv der Gesellschaft für Ältere Deutsche Geschichtskunde zur Beförderung einer Gesammtausgabe der Quellenschriften Deutscher Geschichten des Mittelalters* 27: 331–408.

Lewis, George Randall. 1908. *The Stannaries. A Study of the English Tin Miner*. Boston & New York: Houghton, Mifflin and Company.

Liesegang, Erich. 1897. *Niederrheinisches Städtewesen vornehmlich im Mittelalter. Untersuchungen zur Verfassungsgeschichte der klevischen Städte*. Untersuchungen zur deutschen Staats- und Rechtsgeschichte 52. Breslau: Wilhelm Koebner.

Lindenschmit, Ludwig. 1880. *Die Alterthümer der Merovingischen Zeit*. 3 vols. Handbuch der deutschen Alterthumskunde: Übersicht der Denkmale und Gräberfunde frühgeschichtlicher und vorgeschichtlicher Zeit in drei Theilen 1. Brunswick: Verlag Vieweg und Sohn.

Lippert, Julius. 1896. *Social-Geschichte Böhmens in vorhussitischer zeit: Ausschliesslich aus quellen*. 2 vols. Vienna: F. Tempsky.

Lizier, Augusto. 1900. "La vita sociale del secolo XII.–XVI. nella legislazione penale degli Statuti italiani di quel tempo." *Rivista Internazionale di Scienze Sociali e Discipline Ausiliarie* 22 (88): 505–33.
Löffler, Emil von. 1881. *Geschichte der Festung Ulm*. Ulm: Wohler.
Lüntzel, Hermann Adolf. 1858. *Geschichte der Diözese und Stadt Hildesheim*. 2 vols. Hildesheim: Gerstenberg.
Luther, Martin. 1899. *D. Martin Luthers Werke. Kritische Gesamtausgabe*. Edited by O. Albrecht, Arnold E. Berger, G. Buchwald, and P. Pietsch. Vol. 15. Weimar: Hermann Böhlaus Nachfolger.
Mabillon, Jean. 1681. *De re diplomatica libri VI*. Paris: Charles Robustel.
Maitland, Frederic William. 1907. *Domesday Book and Beyond: Three Essays in the Early History of England*. Cambridge: Cambridge University Press.
Marx, Karl. 1903. *Das Kapital: Kritik Der Politischen Ökonomie*. 5th ed. 4 vols. Hamburg: Otto Meissner.
———. 1906. *Capital. A Critique of Political Economy*. Edited by Frederick Engels. Translated by Samuel Moore and Edward Aveling. New York: The Modern Library.
Matthaei, Georg. 1877. *Die Klosterpolitik Kaiser Heinrichs II.: ein Beitrag zur Geschichte der Reichsabteien*. Grünberg in Schlesien: Levysohn.
Maunier, René. 1910. *L'origine et la fonction économique des villes: Etude de morphologie sociale*. Paris: V. Giard & E. Briere.
Maurer, Georg Ludwig von. 1862. *Geschichte der Fronhöfe, der Bauernhöfe und der Hofverfassung in Deutschland*. 4 vols. Erlangen: Ferdinand Enke.
———. 1870. *Geschichte der Städteverfassung in Deutschland*. Erlangen: Ferdinand Enke.
Mayer, Anton. 1897. "Das kirchliche Leben und die christliche Caritas (Wohlthätigkeitsanstalten)." In *Geschichte der Stadt Wien*, I:445–80. Vienna: Adolf Holzhausen.
Meitzen, August. 1895. *Siedelung Und Agrarwesen Der Westgermanen Und Ostgermanen, Der Kelten, Römer, Finnen Und Slawen*. 3 vols. Wanderungen, Anbau Und Agrarrecht Der Völker Europas Nördlich Der Alpen 1. Berlin: Wilhelm Hertz.
Merlet, Lucien, ed. 1883. *Cartulaire de l'Abbaye de la Sainte Trinité de Tiron*. 2 vols. Chartres: Garnier.
Michael, Emil. 1897. *Geschichte des deutschen Volkes seit dem dreizehnten Jahrhundert bis zum Ausgang des Mittelalters*. 6 vols. Freiburg im Breisgau: Herder.

Michel, Francisque. 1852. *Recherches sur le commerce, la fabrication et l'usage des étoffes de soie, d'or et d'argent et autres tissus précieux en Occident, principalement en France, pendant le Moyen Age*. Vol. 1. Paris: Crapelet.

Moltke, Siegfried. 1901. *Die Leipziger Kramer-Innung im 15. und 16. Jahrhundert*. Leipzig: Verlag der Handelskammer.

Mommsen, Theodor. 1893. "Die Bewirtschaftung der Kirchengüter unter Papst Gregor I." *Zeitschrift für Social- und Wirtschaftsgeschichte* 1: 43–60.

Mone, Franz Josef, ed. 1848. *Quellensammlung zur badischen Landesgeschichte*. 4 vols. Karlsruhe: Macklot.

———, ed. 1853. *Zeitschrift für die Geschichte des Oberrheins*. Vol. 4. Karlsruhe: G. Braun.

Mone, Franz Joseph. 1865. "Zunftorganisation vom 13.-16. Jahrhundert in der Schweiz, Baden, Elsaß, Bayern und Hessen." *Zeitschrift für die Geschichte des Oberrheins* 18: 12–32.

Montaiglon, Anatole de, and Gaston Raynaud. 1872. *Recueil général et complet des fabliaux des 13e et 14e siecles*. 6 vols. Paris: Librairie des bibliophiles.

Montalembert, Charles Forbes. 1863. *Die Mönche des Abendlandes vom H. Benedikt bis zum H. Bernhard*. Edited by Karl Brandes. 7 vols. Regensburg: G. J. Manz.

Montesquieu, Charles Louis. 1834. *De l'esprit des Lois*. 6 vols. De l'esprit des lois.Francés. París: Lebigre Frères.

Monticolo, Giovanni. 1896. *I Capitolari delle Arti Veneziane*. Fonti per la Storia d'Italia 26. Rome: Istituto Storico Italiano.

Much, Matthäus. 1902. "Prähistorischer Bergbau in Den Alpen." *Die Zeitschrift Des Deutschen Und Österreichischen Alpenvereins* 33: 1–31.

Muffat, Karl August, ed. 1856. "Schenkungsbuch der ehemaligen Probstei Berchtesgaden." *Quellen und Erörterungen zur bayerischen und deutschen Geschichte* 1: 225–364.

Müller, Richard. 1900. "Wiens räumliche Entwicklung und topographische Benennung 1522–1740." In *Geschichte der Stadt Wien*. Vol. II.1. Vienna: Adolf Holzhausen.

Müller, Walther. 1910. *Zur Frage des Ursprungs der mittelalterlichen Zünfte. Eine wirtschafts- und verfassungsgeschichtliche Untersuchung*. Leipziger historische Abhandlungen 22. Leipzig: Quelle & Mayer.

Müllner, Alfons. 1909. *Geschichte Des Eisens in Inner-Österreich von Der Urzeit Bis Zum Anfange Des XIX. Jahrhunderts*. Vol. 1. Vienna and Leipzig: Helm und Goldmann.

Bibliography

Mummenhoff, Ernst. 1901. *Der Handwerker in der deutschen Vergangenheit. Mit 151 Abbildungen und Beilagen nach den Originalen aus dem fünfzehnten bis achtzehnten Jahrhundert.* Leipzig: E. Diederichs.

Muratori, Lodovico Antonio. 1739. *Antiquitates Italicæ Medii Ævi, Sive Dissertationes.* Bologna: Arnaldo Forni Editore.

Naudé, Wilhelm. 1889. *Deutsche städtische Getreidehandelspolitik vom 15. bis 17. Jahrhundert, mit besonderer Berücksichtigung Stettins und Hamburgs.* Staats- und socialwissenschaftliche Forschungen 8. Leipzig: Duncker & Humblot.

Neilson, Nellie. 1898. "Economic Conditions on the Manors of Ramsey Abbey." Lower Merion Township: Bryn Mawr College.

Neuberg, C. 1892. *Goslars Bergbau Bis 1552.Ein Beitrag Zur Wirthschafts- Und Verfassungsgeschichte Des Mittelalters.* Hanover.

Neumann, Max. 1865. *Geschichte des Wuchers in Deutschland bis zur Begründung der heutigen Zinsengesetze (1654).* Halle: Buchhandlung des Waisenhauses.

Nirrnheim, Hans, ed. 1895. *Das Handlungsbuch Vickos von Geldersen.* Hamburg & Leipzig: L. Voss.

Nitzsch, Friedrich Wilhelm. 1872. "Die oberrheinische Tiefebene und das Deutsche Reich im Mittelalter." *Preussische Jahrbücher* 30.

Nuglisch, Adolf. 1904. "Zur Frage nach der Entstehung des modernen Kapitalismus." *Jahrbücher für Nationalökonomie und Statistik*, 3, 28 (2): 238–50.

Otto, Eduard. 1893. "Die Bevölkerung der Stadt Butzbach während des Mittelalters." Gießen.

Pabst, H. 1862. "Geschichte des langobardischen Herzogtums." *Die Forschungen zur deutschen Geschichte* 2: 405–518.

Pantaleoni, Maffeo. 1899. "L'origine del baratto: A proposito di un nuovo studio del Cognetti." *Giornale pegli Economisti*, IIa, XVIII, XIX, XX.

Pardessus, Jean Marie, ed. 1843. *Diplomata chartae, epistolae, leges aliaque instrumenta ad res Gallo- Francicas spectantia.* 2 vols. Paris: Ex Typographio Regio.

Paris, Julien, ed. 1670. *Nomasticon Cisterciense: Seu antiquiores Ordinis Cisterciensis constitutiones.* Paris: Sebastian Mabre-Cramoisy.

Pauen, Heinrich. 1913. *Die Klostergrundherrschaft Heisterbach: Studien zur Geschichte ihrer Wirtschaft, Verwaltung und Verfassung.* Beiträge zur Geschichte des alten Mönchtums und des Benediktinerordens 4. Münster: Aschendorff.

Pauli, Carl Wilhelm. 1847. *Lübeckische Zustände Zu Anfang Des Vierzehnten Jahrhunderts.* Lübeck: F. Aschenfelde.

Peetz, Hartwig. 1883. *Volkswissenschaftliche Studien*. Augsburg: Lampart & Co.

Petz, Hans, Hermann von Grauert, and Johann Mayerhofer, eds. 1880. *Drei bayerische Traditionsbücher aus dem 12. Jahrhundert: Festschrift zum 700 jährigen Jubiläum der Wittelsbacher Thronbesteigung*. Munich: Kellerer.

Philippi, Friedrich. 1894. *Zur Verfassungsgeschichte der westfälischen Bischofsstädte*. Osnabrück: Rackhorst.

———. 1909. *Die erste Industrialisierung Deutschlands (im Mittelalter): EIn Vortrag*. Münster: F. Coppenrath.

Phillippe, Adrien. 1858. *Geschichte der Apotheker bei den wichtigsten Völkern der Erde seit dem ältesten Zeiten bis auf unsere Tage*. Translated by Hermann Ludwig. 2nd ed. Jena: Mauke.

Pigeonneau, Henri. 1887. *Histoire du commerce de la France*. 2 vols. Paris: Leopold Cerf.

Pirenne, Henri. 1895. "L'origine des constitutions urbaines au Moyen Âge." *Revue historique* 57.

———. 1898. "Villes, marchés et marchands au Moyen Âge." *Revue historique* 67: 59–70.

———. 1899. *Geschichte Belgiens*. 4 vols. Geschichte der europäischen Staaten 30. Gotha: F. A. Perthes.

———. 1905. "Les villes flamandes avant le XIIe siècle." *Annales de l'Est et du Nord* 1: 9–32.

———. 1910. *Les anciennes démocraties des Pays-Bas*. Paris: E. Flammarion.

Pivano, Silvio. 1904. *I contratti agrari in Italia nell'alto Medio-Evo: precaria e livello, enfiteusi, pastinato e parzionaria, masseria e colonia, usufrutto vitalizio, contratto a tempo e parziaria*. Turin: Unione tipografico-editrice.

———. 1909. "Sistema curtense." *Bullettino dell'istituto storico italiano* 30: 91–145.

Poggi, Enrico. 1845. *Cenni storici delle leggi sull' agricoltura dai tempi romani fino ai nostri*. 2 vols. Florence: F. Le Monnier.

Pöhlmann, Robert. 1878. *Die Wirthschaftspolitik der Florentiner Renaissance und das Princip der Verkehrsfreiheit*. Leipzig: S. Hirzel.

———. 1884. *Die Überbevölkerung der antiken Grossstädte im Zusammenhange mit der Gesammtentwicklung städtischer Civilisation Gekrönte Preisschrift*. Leipzig: S. Hirzel.

Polain, Mathieu Lambert. 1847. *Histoire de l'ancien pays de Liége*. 2 vols. Liège: J. Ledoux.

Bibliography

Próspero de Bofarull y Mascaró. 1851. *Colección de documentos inéditos del archivo general de la Corona de Aragón.* 8 vols. Barcelona: José Eusebio Monfort.

Provisorischen Komitee des Zentralereins zur Reorganisierung des Handwerkerstandes in Breslau. 1848. "Denkschrift Des Zentralvereins Zur Reorganisierung Des Handwerkerstandes in Breslau Als Entwurf Der Generalversammlung Der Handwerksgenossen Schlesiens Am 19. Juni 1848 Zur Prüfung Und Beratung Vorgelegt Vom Provisorischen Komitee Des Vereins." Zentralverein zur Reorganisierung des Handwerkerstandes in Breslau.

Püschel, Alfred. 1910. *Das Anwachsen der deutschen Städte in der Zeit der mittelalterlichen Kolonialbewegung.* Abhandlung zur Verkehrs- und Seegeschichte, IV. Berlin: Karl Curtius.

Rathgen, Karl. 1881. "Die Entstehung der Märkte in Deutschland." Strasbourg: Strasbourg.

Ratzel, Friedrich. 1891. *Anthropogeographie.* 2 vols. Stuttgart: J. Engelhorn.

Rehme, Paul. 1894. "Die Lübecker Handelsgesellschaften in der ersten Hälfte des 14. Jahrhunderts." *Zeitschrift für das gesamte Handelsrecht* 42: 367–410.

Reisner, Wilhelm. 1903. *Die Einwohnerzahl deutscher Städte in früheren Jahrhunderten mit besonderer Berücksichtigung Lübecks.* Sammlung nationalökonomischer und statistischer Abhandlungen des staatswissenschaftlichen Seminars zu Halle 36. Jena: G. Fischer.

Rem, Lucas. 1861. *Tagebuch des Lucas Rem aus den Jahren 1494-1541: Ein Beitrag zur Handelsgeschichte der Stadt Augsburg. Mitgetheilt, mit erläuternden Bemerkungen und einem Anhange von noch ungedruckten Briefen und Berichten über die Entdeckungen des neuen Seeweges nach Amerika und Ostindien versehen.* Edited by B. Greiff. Augsburg: J.N. Hartmann.

Reuter, Fritz. 1905. *Ut mine Stromtid: olle Kamellen.* Bibliothek der Gesamtliteratur des In- und Auslandes, Nr. 1840/1848. Berlin: Hendel.

Réville, André. 1898. *Le soulèvement des travailleurs d'Angleterre en 1381.* Mémoires et documents publiès par la Société de l'École des chartes, II. Paris: A. Picard et fils.

Richter, Emil Ludwig, and Emil Friedberg, eds. 1879. *Corpus Iuris Canonici.* 2 vols. Leipzig: Tauchnitz.

Rietschel, Siegfried. 1894. *Die Civitas auf deutschem Boden bis zum Ausgang der Karolingerzeit: Ein Beitrag zur Geschichte der deutschen Stadt.* Leipzig: Veit.

———. 1897. *Markt und Stadt in ihrem rechtlichen Verhältnis. Ein Beitrag zur Geschichte der deutschen Stadtverfassung.* Leipzig: Veit.

———. 1905. *Das Burggrafenamt und die hohe Gerichtsbarkeit in den deutschen Bischofsstädten während des früheren Mittelalters. Untersuchungen zur Geschichte der deutschen Stadtverfassung 1.* Leipzig: Veit.

Riley, Henry Thomas, ed. 1868. *Memorials of London and London Life, in the XIIIth, XIVth, and XVth Centuries. Being a Series of Extracts, Local, Social, and Political, from the Early Archives of the City of London, A.D. 1276-1419.* London: Longmans, Green and Co.

Rivet, Auguste. 1891. *Le régime des biens de l'église avant Justinien, spécialement sous les empereurs chrétiens.* Lyons: E. Vitte.

Rogers, James Edwin Thorold. 1866. *A History of Agriculture and Prices in England: From the Year after the Oxford Parliament (1259) to the Commencement of the Continental War (1793).* 7 vols. Oxford: Clarendon Press.

———. 1884. *Six Centuries of Work and Wages; the History of English Labour.* London: Putnam.

———. 1898. *The Industrial and Commercial History of England (Lectures Delivered to the University of Oxford) by the Late James E. Thorold Rogers ..* Edited by Arthur George Liddon Rogers. London: T. Fisher Unwin.

Roscher, Wilhelm Georg Friedrich. 1854. *System der Volkswirthschaft.* 5 vols. Stuttgart: Cotta.

Roth, Johann Ferdinand. 1800. *Geschichte des Nürnbergischen Handels - Ein Versuch.* 4 vols. Leipzig: Böhme.

Rumohr, Carl Friedrich von. 1830. *Ursprung der Besitzlosigkeit des Colonen im neueren Toscana.* Hamburg: Perthes und Besser.

Rymer, Thomas. 1727. *Foedera, conventiones, literæ, et cujuscumque generis acta publica, inter reges Angliæ, et alios quosvis imperatores, reges, pontifices, principes, vel communitates, ab Ineunte sæculo duodecimo, viz. ab Anno 1101. Ad nostra usque tempora, habita aut tractata: Ex Autographis, infra Secretiores archivorum regiorum thesaurarius per multa Sæcula reconditis, fidelitur exscripta, in lucem missa de mandato nuperæ reginæ.* 2nd ed. 20 vols. London: J. Tonson.

Sackur, Ernst. 1893. "Beiträge zur Wirtschaftsgeschichte französischer und lothringischer Klöster im 10. und 11. Jahrhundert." *Zeitschrift für Social- und Wirtschaftsgeschichte* 1: 154–90.

Saitschik, Robert. 1891. *Beiträge zur Geschichte der rechtlichen Stellung der Juden, namentlich im Gebiete des heutigen Österreich-Ungarn vom 10. bis 16. Jahrhundert.* Frankfurt: Kauffmann.

Salzmann, Louis Francis. 1913. *English Industries of the Middle Ages: Being an Introduction to the Industrial History of Medieval England*. London: Constable & Co.
Sander, Paul. 1906. *Feudalstaat und bürgerliche Verfassung: Ein Versuch über das Grundproblem der deutschen Verfassungsgeschichte*. Berlin: A. Bath.
―――. 1913a. "Für und wider den hofrechtlichen Ursprung der Zünfte." *Historische Vierteljahrschrift* 16: 366–74.
―――. 1913b. "Über die Wirtschaftsentwicklung der Karolingerzeit." *Jahrbuch für Gesetzgebung, Verwaltung und Volkswirtschaft im Deutschen Reiche* 37: 383-408,2113-2116.
―――. 1914. "Antwort." *Jahrbuch für Gesetzgebung, Verwaltung und Volkswirtschaft im Deutschen Reiche* 38 (2): 1073–87.
Sandi, Vettor. 1755. *Principi di storia civile della Repubblica di Venezia dalla sua fondazione sino all'anno di N. S. 1700*. 6 vols. Venice: Sebastian Coleti.
Santini, Pietro. 1887. *Società delle Torri in Firenze*. Archivio Storico Italiano, 4/20. Florence: G.P. Vieusseux.
―――. 1895. *Documenti dell'antica costituzione del comune di Firenze*. Documenti di storia Italiana, X. Firenze: G.P. Vieusseux.
Sattler, Carl, ed. 1887. *Handelsrechnungen des Deutschen Ordens*. Leipzig: Duncker & Humblot.
Schaefer, Heinrich. 1903. *Pfarrkirche und Stift im deutschen Mittelalter*. Stuttgart: F. Enke.
Schäfer, Dietrich. 1905. "Die agrarii milites des Widukind." In *Sitzungsberichte der königlich preussischen Akademie der Wissenschaften*, XXVII:569–77. Berlin: Verlag der Akademie der Wissenschaften.
Schäfer, Karl Heinrich. 1907. *Die Kanonissenstifter im deutschen Mittelalter: Ihre Entwicklung und innere Einrichtung im Zusammenhang mit dem altchristlichen Sanktimonialentum*. Kirchenrechtliche Abhandlungen, 43/44. Stuttgart: Ferdinand Enke.
Schannat, Johann Friedrich. 1729. *Historia Fuldensis*. 2 vols. Frankfurt am Main: Andreae & Hort.
Schanz, Georg von. 1877. *Zur Geschichte der deutschen Gesellen-Verbände*. Leipzig: Duncker & Humblot.
―――. 1881. *Englische Handelspolitik gegen Ende des Mittelalters, mit besonderer Berücksichtigung des Zeitalters der beiden ersten Tudors Heinrich VII. und Heinrich VIII*. 2 vols. Leipzig: Duncker & Humblot.

Schaube, Adolf. 1897. "Ein Italienischer Coursbericht von Der Messe von Troyes Aus Dem 13. Jahrhundert." *Zeitschrift Für Social- Und Wirtschaftsgeschichte* 5 (2): 248–308.

———. 1906. *Handelsgeschichte der romanischen Völker des Mittelmeergebiets bis zum Ende der Kreuzzüge*. Handbuch der mittelalterlichen und neueren Geschichte, III. Munich: R. Oldenbourg.

———. 1908. "Die Wollausfuhr Englands vom Jahre 1273." *Vierteljahrschrift für Sozial- und Wirtschaftsgeschichte* 6: 39–72.

Scheffer-Boichorst, Paul. 1885. "Zur Geschichte der Syrer im Abendlande." *Mitteilungen des Instituts für Österreichische Geschichtsforschung*, no. 6: 521.

Scheler, Auguste. 1867. *Lexicographie latine du XIIe et du XIIIe siècle: trois traités de Jean de Garlande, Alexandre Neckam et Adam du Petit-Pont: publiés avec les gloses françaises*. Leipzig: F. A. Brockhaus.

Schipper, Ignacy. 1907. *Anfänge Des Kapitalismus Bei Den Abendländischen Juden Im Früheren Mittelalter(Bis Zum Ausgang Des XII. Jahrhunderts)*. Vienna & Leipzig: Wilhelm Branmüller.

Schlosser, Julius von. 1889. *Die abendländische Klosteranlage des früheren Mittelalters*. Vienna: Carl Gerold's Son.

Schmidt, Anton. 1772. *Thesaurus Juris Ecclesiastici, potissimum Germanici sive Dissertationes selectae in jus ecclesiasticum*. 7 vols. Heidelberg: Goebhardt.

Schmidt, Gustav, ed. 1883. *Urkundenbuch des Hochstifts Halberstadt und seiner Bischöfe*. 4 vols. Publikationen aus den königlich-preußischen Staatsarchiven 17, 21, 27, 40. Leipzig: S. Hirzel.

Schmidt, Theodor. 1859. *Zur Geschichte Der Früheren Stettiner Handels-Compagnien, Der Draker-, Der Falster-, Der Elboger-Compagnie. Ein Vortrag, Gehalten in Der Gesellschaft Für Pommersche Geschichte Und Alterthumskunde*. Stettin.

Schmoller, Gustav. 1871. "Die historische Entwicklung des Fleischconsums, sowie der Vieh- und Fleischpreise in Deutschland." *Zeitschrift für die gesammte Staatswissenschaft* 27 (2): 284–362.

Schmoller, Gustav von. 1870. *Zur Geschichte der deutschen Kleingewerbe im 19. Jahrhundert. Statistische und nationalökonomische Untersuchungen*. Halle: Buchhandlung des Waisenhauses.

———. 1895. *Untersuchungen des Vereins für Sozialpolitik über die Lage des Handwerks*. 9 vols. Schriften des Vereins für Sozialpolitik. Leipzig: Duncker & Humblot.

———. 1897. *Die Strassburger Tucher und Weberzunft. Urkunden und Darstellung nebst Regesten und Glossar. Ein Beitrag zur Geschichte der deutschen Weberei und des deutschen Gewerberechts, vom XIII-XVII Jahrhundert*. Strasbourg: Karl J. Trübner.

———. 1899. "Die Tatsachen der Arbeitsteilung." *Jahrbuch für Gesetzgebung, Verwaltung und Volkswirtschaft im Deutschen Reiche* 13: 1003–74.

———. 1900. *Grundriß der allgemeinen Volkswirtschaftslehre. Erster größerer Teil. Begriff. Psychologische und sittliche Grundlage. Litteratur und Methode. Land, Leute und Technik. Die gesellschaftliche Verfassung der Volkswirtschaft*. Vol. 1. 2 vols. Leipzig: Duncker & Humblot.

———. 1911. "Die Bevölkerungsbewegung der deutschen Städte von ihrem Ursprung bis ins 19. Jahrhundert." In *Festschrift für Otto Gierke zum siebzigsten Geburtstag, dargebracht von Schülern, Freunden und Verehrern*, by Otto von Gierke, 167–222. Weimar: Böhlau.

Schneider, Fedor. 1906. "Voltelini, Hans von, Die ältesten Pfandleihenbanken und Lombardenprivilegien Tirols." *Vierteljahrschrift für Social- und Wirtschaftsgeschichte* 4: 391–92.

Schneider, Philipp. 1885. *Die bischöflichen Domkapitel, ihre Entwicklung und rechtliche Stellung im Organismus der Kirche*. Mainz: Kirchheim.

Schneller, Christian. 1898. *Tridentinische Urbare aus dem 13. Jahrhundert: Mit einer Urkunde aus Judicarien von 1244-1247*. Quellen und Forschungen zur Geschichte, Literatur und Sprache Österreichs und seiner Kronländer 4. Innsbruck: Wagner.

Schönberg, Gustav. 1879. *Finanzverhältnisse der Stadt Basel im 14. und 15. Jahrhundert*. Tübingen: Laupp.

Schönlank, Bruno. 1894. *Sociale Kämpfe vor dreihundert Jahren*. Leipzig: Duncker & Humblot.

Schöpflin, Johann Daniel. 1772. *Alsatia aevi Merovingici, Carolingici, Saxonici, Salici, Suevici diplomatica*. 2 vols. Mannheim: Ex Typographia Academica.

Schrader, Otto. 1886. *Linguistisch-Historische Forschungen Zur Handelsgeschichte Und Warenkunde*. Jena: H. Costenoble.

———. 1890. *Sprachvergleichung und Urgeschichte. Linguitisch-historische Beiträge zur Erforschung des indogermanischen Altertums*. 2nd ed. Jena: Hermann Costenoble.

Schreckenstein, Karl Heinrich Roth von. 1856. *Das Patriziat in den deutschen Städten, besonders Reichsstädten*. Tübingen: Laupp.

Schreiber, Heinrich, ed. 1828. *Urkundenbuch der Stadt Freiburg im Breisgau*. 2 vols. Freiburg im Breisgau: Herder.
Schulte, Aloys. 1900. *Geschichte des mittelalterlichen Handels und Verkehrs zwischen Westdeutschland und Italien mit Ausschluss von Venedig*. 2 vols. Leipzig: Duncker & Humblot.
———. 1910. *Der Adel und die deutsche Kirche im Mittelalter: Studien zur Sozial-, Rechts- und Kirchengeschichte*. Kirchenrechtliche Abhandlungen, 63/64. Stuttgart: Ferdinand Enke.
Schulten, Adolf. 1896. *Die römischen Grundherrschaften. Eine agrarhistorische Untersuchung*. Weimar: E. Felber.
Schwarz, Sebald. 1892. *Anfänge des Städtewesens in den Elb- und Saale-Gegenden*. Kiel: H. Fiencke.
Secousse, Denis-François. 1734. *Collection des ordonnances des roys de France de la troisieme race, recueillies par ordre chronologique*. Vol. 4. 21 vols. Paris: Imprimerie Royale.
Seebohm, Frederic. 1883. *The English Village Community, Examined in Its Relations to the Manorial and Tribal Systems and to the Common or Open Field System of Husbandry; an Essay in Economic History*. London and New York: Longmans, Green and Co.
Seeliger, Gerhard. 1903. *Die soziale und politische Bedeutung der Grundherrschaften im früheren Mittelalter*. Leipzig: B.G. Teubner.
———. 1913. "Handwerk und Hofrecht." *Historische Vierteljahrschrift* 16: 472–519.
Sello, Georg. 1884. "Brandenburgische Stadtrechtsquellen." *Märkische Forschungen* 18: 1–108.
Semper, Gottfried. 1878. *Der Stil in den technischen und tektonischen Künsten oder Praktische Ästhetik*. 2nd ed. 2 vols. Munich: Bruckmann.
Sharpe, Reginald Robinson. 1894. *London and the Kingdom*. 3 vols. London: Longmans, Green and Co.
Siebeck, Oskar. 1904. *Das Arbeitssystem der Grundherrschaft des deutschen Mittelalters: Seine Entstehung und seine sociale Bedeutung*. Tübingen: Laupp.
Sieveking, Heinrich. 1897. "Die Genueser Seidenindustrie im 15. und 16. Jahrhundert." *Jahrbuch für Gesetzgebung, Verwaltung und Volkswirtschaft im Deutschen Reiche* 21: 101–34.
———. 1898. *Genueser Finanzwesen*. 2 vols. Volkswirtschaftliche Abhandlungen der Badischen Hochschulen. Freiburg im Breisgau: J. C. B. Mohr.

———. 1902. "Aus venetianischen Handelsbüchern. Ein Beitrag zur Geschichte des Großhandels im 15. Jahrhundert. II." *Jahrbuch für Gesetzgebung, Verwaltung und Volkswirtschaft im Deutschen Reiche* 26: 189–225.

———. 1906. *Die Handlungsbücher Der Medici*. Sitzungsberichte Der Akademie Der Wissenschaft Wien, Philosophisch-Historische Klasse 151. Vienna: Hölder.

Siewert, Franz, ed. 1897. *Geschichte und Urkunden der Rigafahrer in Lübeck im 16. und 17. Jahrhundert.* Hansische Geschichtsquellen, I. Berlin: Pass & Garleb.

Silberschmidt, Wilhelm. 1884. *Die Commenda in ihrer frühesten Entwicklung bis zum 13. Jahrhundert: ein Beitrag zur Geschichte der Commandit- und der stillen Gesellschaft.* Würzburg: Adalbert Stuber.

———. 1904. "Kumpanie und Sendeve. Ein Beitrag zur Geschichte der Handelsgesellschaften in Deutschland." *Archiv für bürgerliches Recht* 23: 1–68.

———. 1905. "Das Senden und Befehlen der Waren nach der kaufmännischen Korrespondenz des 15. Jahrhunderts." *Archiv für bürgerliches Recht* 25: 129–48.

———. 1906. "Reinhard Heynen. Zur Entstehung des Kapitalismus in Venedig." *Zeitschrift für das gesamte Handelsrecht* 58: 625–31.

———. 1910. "Das Sendegeschäft im Hansagebiet." *Zeitschrift für das gesamte Handelsrecht und Konkursrecht* 68: 405–38.

Simmel, Georg. 1900. *Philosophie des Geldes*. Leipzig: Duncker & Humblot.

Simonsfeld, Henry. 1887. *Der Fondaco dei Tedeschi in Venedig und die deutsch-venetianischen Handelsbeziehungen*. 2 vols. Stuttgart: J.G. Cotta.

Slaski, Witold von, ed. 1905. *Danziger Handel im XV. Jahrhundert auf Grund eines im Danziger Stadtarchiv befindlichen Handlungsbuches geschildert*. Heidelberg: C.F. Beisel Nachfolger.

Smirke, E. 1852. "Original Documents: Ancient Consuetudinary of the City of Winchester." *Archaeological Journal* 9 (1): 69–89.

Smirke, Edward. 1849. "Appendix to Notice of the Custumal of Bleadon, Somersetshire, and of the Agricultural Tenures of the 13th Century." *Proceedings of Archaeological Institue, Salisbury*, 182–210.

Smith, Adam. 1776. *An Inquiry Into the Nature and Causes of the Wealth of Nations*. 3 vols. London: A. Strahan and T. Cadell.

Soetbeer, Adolf. 1862. "Beiträge zur Geschichte des Geld- und Munzwesens in Deutchland." *Forschungen zur deutschen Geschichte* 1, 2, 4, 6.

Sohm, Rudolf. 1890. *Die Entstehung des deutschen Städtewesens.* Leipzig: Duncker & Humblot.

Sombart, Werner. 1890. "Naudé, Wilhelm: Deutsche städtische Getreidehandelspolitik vom 15. bis 17. Jahrhundert, mit besonderer Berücksichtigung Stettins und Hamburgs." *Jahrbuch für Gesetzgebung, Verwaltung und Volkswirtschaft im Deutschen Reiche* 14: 312–13.

———. 1902. *Der moderne Kapitalismus.* 1st ed. 2 vols. Leipzig: Duncker & Humblot.

———. 1908. *Kunstgewerbe und Kultur.* Berlin: Marquardt.

———. 1911. *Die Juden und das Wirtschaftsleben.* Leipzig: Leipzig Duncker & Humblot.

———. 1912. *Luxus und Kapitalismus.* Munich & Leipzig: Duncker & Humblot.

———. 1913a. *Der Bourgeois: Zur Geistesgeschichte Des Modernen Wirtschaftsmenschen.* Munich & Leipzig: Duncker & Humblot.

———. 1913b. "Die Elemente des Wirtschaftslebens." *Archiv für Sozialwissenschaft und Sozialpolitik* 37.

———. 1915. *The Quintessence of Capitalism: A Study of the History and Psychology of the Modern Business Man.* Translated by Mortimer Epstein. London: T. Fisher Unwin.

———. 1962. *The Jews and Modern Capitalism.* Translated by Mortimer Epstein. New York: Collier Books.

———. 1967. *Luxury and Capitalism.* Translated by W.R. Dittmar. Ann Arbor: University of Michigan Press.

Stanhope, Walter. 1887. *Monastic London: An Analytical Sketch of the Monks and Monasteries Within the Metropolitan Area During the Centuries 1200 to 1600.* London: Remington & Company.

Stapleton, Thomas, ed. 1849. *Chronicon Angliae Petriburgense.* London: Camden Society.

Steffen, Gustaf Fredrik. 1901. *Studien zur Geschichte der englischen Lohnarbeiter mit besonderer Berücksichtigung der Veränderungen ihrer Lebenshaltungen.* Translated by Margarete Langfeldt. 3 vols. Stuttgart: Hobbing & Büchle.

Stephan, Heinrich. 1869. "Das Verkehrsleben im Mittelalter." Edited by Freidrich von Raumer. *Historischem Taschenbuch* 4/10: 279–438.

Stieda, Wilhelm. 1884. "Schiffahrtsregister." *Hansische Geschichtsblätter* 13: 77–118.

———. 1887. *Revaler Zollbücher und -Quittungen des 14. Jahrhunderts.* Hansische Geschichtsquellen, V. Halle: Buchhandlung des Waisenhauses.

———. 1894. *Hansische Vereinbarungen über städtisches Gewerbe im 14. und 15. Jahrhundert. Festschrift der Landes-Universität Rostock zur zweiten Säcularfeier der Universität Halle a. S.* Leipzig: Jäh & Schunke.

Stubbs, William. 1874. *The Constitutional History of England in Its Origin and Development.* 5th ed. 3 vols. Oxford: Clarendon Press.

Stutz, Ulrich. 1892. *Die Verwaltung und Nutzung des kirchlichen Vermögens in den Gebieten des westeuropäischen Reichs von Konstantin der Große bis zum Eintritt der germanischen Stämme in die katholische Kirche.* Naumburg an der Saale: Pätz.

Sugenheim, Samuel. 1861. *Geschichte der Aufhebung der Leibeigenschaft und Hörigkeit in Europa bis um die Mitte des neunzehnten Jahrhunderts.* St. Petersburg: Eggers.

Tacitus, Publius Cornelius. 1903. *Germania.* Edited by Oskar Altenburg. Leipzig & Berlin: Teubner.

Tafel, Gottlieb Lukas Friedrich, and Georg Martin Thomas, eds. 1856. *Urkunden zur älteren Handels- und Staatsgeschichte der Republik Venedig, mit besonderer Beziehung auf Byzanz und die Levante. Vom neunten bis zum Ausgang des fünfzehnten Jahrhunderts.* 3 vols. Fontes Rerum Austriacarum 12–14. Vienna: Hof- und Staatsdruckerei.

Terrick Hamilton, trans. 1819. *Antar: A Bedoueen Romance.* 4 vols. John Murray.

Thévenin, Marcel. 1886. "Études Sur La Propriété Au Moyen Âge." *Revue Historique* 31 (May): 241.

Thorpe, Benjamin. 1834. *Analecta Anglo-Saxonica: A Selection in Prose and Verse from Anglo-Saxon Authors of Various Ages with a Glossary.* London: John and Arthur Arch.

———, ed. 1840. *Ancient Laws and Institutes of England, Comprising the Laws Enacted under the Anglo-Saxon Kings from Ethelbert to Canut, with an English Translation.* Translated by Benjamin Thorpe. Vol. 1. London: The Commissioners of the Public Records of the Kingdom.

Thun, Alphons. 1879. *Die Industrie am Niederrhein und ihre Arbeiter.* 2 vols. Staats- und socialwissenschaftliche Forschungen 2. Leipzig: Duncker & Humblot.

Tölner, Johann. 1885. *Johann Tölners Handlungsbuch von 1345-1350.* Edited by Karl Koppmann. Geschichtsquellen der Stadt Rostock 1. Rostock: Werther.

Tommasi, Girolamo. 1847. *Sommario della storia di Lucca dall'anno MIV all'anno MDCC.* Archivio Storico Italiano 10. Florence: G. P. Vieussaux.

Toniolo, Guiseppe. 1895. "L'economia di credito e le origini del capitalismo nella Repubblica Fiorentina." *Rivista internazionale di science sociali e discipline ausiliarie* 8: 560–76.

Tönnies, Ferdinand. 1887. *Gemeinschaft und Gesellschaft: Abhandlung des Communismus und des Socialismus als empirischer Culturformen*. Leipzig: Fues's Verlag.

Topham, J. 1785. "XXXVI. Subsidy Roll of 51 Edward III. Communicated by John Topham, Esq. F.R.S. F.S.A." *Archaeologia* 7: 337–47.

Torfs, Louis. 1839. *Fastes des calamités publiques survenues dans les Pays-Bas et particulièrement en Belgique depuis les temps les plus reculés jusqu'a nos jours*. Paris & Tournai: H. Casterman.

Uhlhorn, Gerhard. 1882. *Die christliche Liebestätigkeit in der alten Kirche*. 2 vols. Stuttgart: D. Gundert.

Uhlirz, Karl. 1886. "Review: [untitled]." *Mitteilungen des Instituts für österreichische Geschichtsforschung* VII: 166–73.

Unger, Friedrich. 1888a. "Das älteste deutsche Rechenbuch." *Zeitschrift für Mathematik und Physik* 33 (Historisch-literarische Abtheilung): 125–45.

———. 1888b. *Die Methodik der praktischen Arithmetik in historischer Entwickelung vom Ausgange des Mittelalters bis auf die Gegenwart*. Leipzig: B.G. Teubner.

Vandenpeereboom, Alphonse. 1878. *Ypriana: notices, études, notes et documents sur Ypres*. 7 vols. Bruges: A. de Zuttere.

Vanderkindere, Léon. 1879. *Le siècle des Artevelde: etudes sur la civilisation morale et politique de la Flandre et du Brabant*. Brussels: A-N. Lebègue.

Varges, Willi. 1893. "Zur Entstehung der deutschen Stadtverfassung." *Jahrbücher für Nationalökonomie und Statistik*, III, VI: 161–214.

———. 1903. *Der deutsche Handel von der Urzeit bis zur Entstehung des Frankenreichs*. Ruhrort: Brendow.

Verci, Giambatista. 1786. *Storia Della Marca Trivigiana e Veronese*. Vol. 1. Venice: Presso G. Storti.

Verein für Geschichte und Alterthum Schlesiens, ed. 1857. *Codex diplomaticus Silesiae*. 36 vols. Breslau: Josef Max & Co.

Verein für Socialpolitik. 1898. *Untersuchungen über die Lage des Hausiergewerbes in Deutschland*. 5 vols. Schriften des Vereins für Socialpolitik 77–81. Leipzig: Duncker & Humblot.

Vetter, Arno. 1910. *Bevölkerungsverhältnisse der ehemals Freien Reichsstadt Mühlhausen in Thüringen im 15. und 16. Jahrhundert*. Leipziger historische Abhandlungen 17. Leipzig: Quelle & Meyer.

Bibliography

Vierkandt, Alfred. 1908. *Die Stetigkeit im Kulturwandel: Eine soziologische Studie*. Munich & Leipzig: Duncker & Humblot.
Vinogradoff, Paul. 1905. *The Growth of the Manor*. London: Swan Sonnenschein & Co.
———. 1908. *English Society in the Eleventh Century: Essays in English Mediaeval History*. Oxford: Clarendon Press.
Vogel, Sabine. 2008. "Die Berliner Autorin Iris Hanika ist für den Deutschen Buchpreis nominiert: Was ziehe ich bloß an?" Berliner Zeitung. October 13, 2008. http://www.berliner-zeitung.de/archiv/die-berliner-autorin-iris-hanika-ist-fuer-den-deutschen-buchpreis-nominiert-was-ziehe-ich-bloss-an-,10810590,10592500.html.
Voltelini, Hans von. 1904. "Die ältesten Pfandleihbanken und Lombarden-Privilegien Tirols." In *Beiträge zur Rechtsgeschichte Tirols. Festschrift*, edited by Alfred Wretschko, 1–70. Innsbruck: Wagner.
———. 1913. *Die Anfänge der Stadt Wien*. Vienna: C. Fromme.
Wagner, Thomas. 1791. *Corpus Juris Metallici recentissimi et antiquioris*. Leipzig.
Waitz, Georg. 1844. *Deutsche Verfassungsgeschichte*. 8 vols. Kiel: Homann.
Waltershausen, A. Sartorius von. 1896. "Entstehung des Tauschhandels in Polynesien." *Zeitschrift für Social- und Wirtschaftsgeschichte* 4: 1–66.
Warncke, Johannes. 1912. *Handwerk und Zünfte in Lübeck*. Lübeck: Borchers.
Wauters, Alphonse. 1878. *Les libertés communales*. Brussels: A. N. Lebègue et cie.
Webb, Sidney, and Beatrice Potter Webb. 1894. *The History of Trade Unionism*. London and New York: Longmans, Green and Co.
Weber, Alfred. 1912. *Ueber den Standort der Industrien*. 2 vols. Tübingen: J.C.B. Mohr.
———. 1929. *Theory of the Location of Industries*. Translated by Carl J. Friedrich. Chicago: University of Chicago Press.
Weber, Max. 1889. *Zur Geschichte der Handelsgesellschaften im Mittelalter. Nach südeuropäischen Quellen*. Stuttgart: Ferdinand Enke.
———. 1891. *Die römische Agrargeschichte in ihrer Bedeutung für das Staats- und Privatrecht*. Stuttgart: Ferdinand Enke.
———. 1904. "Die protestantische Ethik und der 'Geist' des Kapitalismus." *Archiv für Sozialwissenschaft und Sozialpolitik* 20: 1–54.
———. 1905. "Die protestantische Ethik und der 'Geist' des Kapitalismus." *Archiv für Sozialwissenschaft und Sozialpolitik* 21: 1–110.

Wehrmann, Carl Friedrich, ed. 1864. *Die Älteren Lübeckischen Zunftrollen.* Lübeck: Aschenfeldt.

Wendt, Oscar. 1902. *Lübecks Schiffs- und Warenverkehr in den Jahren 1368 und 1369.* Marburg: H. Bauer.

Wiegand, Wilhelm, ed. 1886. *Urkundenbuch der Stadt Strassburg. Zweiter Band: Politische Urkunden von 1266 bis 1332.* Strasbourg: Karl J. Trübner.

Wittich, Werner. 1896. *Die Grundherrschaft in Nordwestdeutschland.* Leipzig: Duncker & Humblot.

———. 1901. "Die Frage der Freibauern: Untersuchungen über die soziale Gliederung des deutschen Volkes in altgermanischer und frühkarolingischer Zeit." *Zeitschrift der Savigny-Stiftung für Rechtsgeschichte: Die Germanistische Abteilung* 22: 245–353.

———. 1906. "Altfreiheit und Dienstbarkeit des Uradels in Niedersachsen." *Vierteljahrsschrift für Sozial- und Wirtschaftsgeschichte* 4: 1–127.

Woikowsky-Biedau, Victor von. 1891. "Das Armenwesen des mittelalterlichen Köln in seiner Beziehung zur wirtschaftlichen und politischen Geschichte der Stadt." Breslau: Breslau.

Xenophon. 1897. *Wirtschaftslehre.* Translated by Max Hodermann. Leipzig: Reclam.

Zdekauer, Lodovico. 1896. *L'interno d'un Banco di pegno nel 1417.* Archivio Storico Italiano, 5/17. Florence: G.P. Vieusseux.

Zechlin, Erich. 1907. *Lüneburgs Hospitäler im Mittelalter.* Forschungen zur Geschichte Niedersachsens 6. Hanover: Hahn.

Zeuss, Johann Caspar, ed. 1842. *Traditiones possessionesque Wizenburgenses. Codices duo cum supplementis; impensis societatis historicae Palatinae.* Speyer: Libraria Neidhardiana.

Ziehen, J. 1914. "?" *Zeitschrift für Kommunalwissenschaft* I (1).

Zillner, Franz Valentin. 1890. *Geschichte der Stadt Salzburg.* 2 vols. Salzburg: Gesellschaft für Salzburger Landeskunde.

Zimmermann, Heinrich, Anton Mayer, and Albert Starzer, eds. 1897. *Geschichte der Stadt Wien.* 6 vols. Vienna: Adolf Holzhausen.

End Notes

End Notes

1 Goethe (1907, 21:31, No. 176).
2 Marx (1903, 1:142; 1906, 200).
3 Marx (1903, 1:142; 1906, 200).
4 Hellpach (1912).
5 More precisely, look in the first edition of this work and in Sombart (1913b, 12 ff.).
6 Aquinas (1895, 10:129, quest. 141, art. 6).
7 I handled the problem of the forms of concerns in more detail in the first edition and in (1913b, 12 ff.). There I also grappled with the literature arising subsequent to my classification.
8 Only the scheme of possibilities is drawn up here, and they are sketched briefly. The various "possibilities" will be described in detail in the appropriate places.
9 Xenophon (1897, Ch. 6).
10 Goethe (1888, 82, Lines 1583–84).
11 The objections which were raised to this fundamental view of mine by countless critics of the first edition of this work have only confirmed in me the conviction that my approach alone provides a deepened insight into the nature of economic organisation. I have attempted to refute the arguments cited against me, and to prove the justification of my standpoint, in (1913a, 3 ff., 441 ff.; 1915, 342 ff.).
12 Schmoller (1900).
13 Bücher (1893).
14 Cunningham (1890).
15 Levasseur (1900; 1903).
16 Inama-Sternegg (1879).
17 Kötzschke (1911).
18 Kowalewsky (1901).
19 Weber (1904, 1–54; 1905, 1–110).
20 "Divitiae comparantur ad oeconomicam non sicut finis ultimus, sed sicut instrumenta quaedam, ut dicitur in I Polit. *Finis* autem ultimus oeconomicae est totum bene vivere secundum domesticam conversationem."
[Riches are acquired by an economic unit not as the final end, but as its instruments, as is related in Aristotle's Politics, Book I. But, on the other hand, the final aim of economy is to live quite contentedly in domestic familiarity.] (Aquinas 1895, 8:376, quest. 50, art. 3).
Compare with the following note.
21 The main position stated by Thomas Aquinas, in the version of the new edition of the complete works according to which I always cite, is entirely as follows:

> Bona autem exteriora habent rationem utilium ad finem, [...] Unde necesse est quod bonum hominis circa ea consistat in quadam mensura: dum scilicet homo secundum aliquam mensuram quaerit habere exteriores divitias, prout sunt *necessaria ad vitam eius secundum suam conditionem*. Et ideo in excessu huius mensurae consistit peccatum: dum scilicet aliquis supra debitum modum vult

> eas vel acquirere vel retinere. Quod pertinet ad rationem avaritiae, quae definitur esse immoderatus amor habendi.

> [Now external goods have the character of utility to an extent, [...] Hence it is necessary that the good of man consists in that measure by which a man seeks to have external riches to some extent, as they are *necessary for the way he lives his life*. And, therefore, sin consists of an excess of this kind of measurement, until of course someone above wants to acquire or keep the debt. Which is the notion of avarice; which is defined as the immoderate love of possession.] (1895, 9:455, quest. 118, art. 1)

These guiding principles are defended and explained by the glossator Cardinal Gaetanus [Thomas Cajetan] as follows:

> appellatione *vitae* intellige non solum cibum et potum, sed quaecunque opportuna commoda et delectabilia, salva honestate.

> [understand by the term mode of *life* not solely food and drink, but the advantageous, convenient and delightful in whatever way, honour well.] (Aquinas 1895, 9:456).

22 Cf. Sombart (1912, 102 ff.; 1967, 86 ff.).
23 Aquinas (1895, 9:452, quest. 117, art. 4).
24 "[I preti] vogliono tutti soprastare agli altri di pompa e ostentatione, vogliono molto numero di grassissime e ornatissime cavalcature, vogliono uscire in pubblico con molto exercitio di mangiatori, et insieme ànno di dì in dì voglie per troppo otio e per poca virtù lascivissime, temerarie, inconsulte. A'quali, perchè pur gli soppedita et sominstra la fortuna, sono incontentissimi, e senza risparmio o masserizia, solo curano satisfare a'suoi incitati appetiti [...] sempre *l'entrata manca e più sono le spese che l'ordinarie sue ricchezze*. Cosi loro conviene altronde essere rapaci e alle onestissime spese, ad aitare e suoi, a sovenire agli amici, a levare la famiglia sua in onorato stato e degno grado, sono inumani, tenacissimi, tardi, miserimi." (Alberti 1908, 265, Part 4, § 28).
25 Aristotle (1872, Book I).
26 Keutgen (1903, 84).
27 Peetz (1883, 186 ff).
28 Vierkandt (1908, 103 ff.), where many sensitive and subtle observations are made on the theme of "traditionalism". Understandably a quite far-reaching parallel exists between the psyche of the pre-capitalist European man and that of the "primitive peoples"; see ibid. 120 ff.
29 Tönnies (1887, 108 f.).
30 Vierkandt (1908, 105).
31 Bouquet (1869, 713).
32 "per quos tractus — from Mainz to Cologne — nec civitas ulla visitur nec castellum nisi quod apud Confluentes [...] Rigomagum oppidum est et una prope ipsam Coloniam turris"

[In all that region there is no city to be seen and no stronghold, except that at the Confluence (Coblenz) [...] there is the town of Rheinmagen (Remagen) — and a single tower near Cologne itself.]. (Ammianus Marcellinus 1935, 210–11, Bk. XVI, Ch. 3). [Tr.: Translation taken from that work, with modern place names added in brackets.]

33   Hieronymus (1766, 2.1:914, epist. 123, c. 16) cited by Rietschel (1894, 32).
34   Rietschel (1894, 33).
35   See the passages in Lamprecht (1885, I.1:78).
36   For example, for Cologne: Ennen (1863, 1:81); also for Vienna.
37   Rietschel (1894, 85). There examples can also be found for the availability of ground used agriculturally in the "cities" of that time. Cf. also Chapter 10.
38   Jacob (1896, 37).
39   Voltelini (1913, 8–9).
40   Flach (1893, 2:237 ff. and passim) gives his opinions over the fate of the French cities.
41   See Weber (1891, 267), where these processes are depicted best of all.
42   "Pauli historia Langobardorum" in MGH SS rer. Lang. (Liber IV, § 28, 125).
43   "Pauli historia Langobardorum" in MGH SS rer. Lang. (Liber IV, § 45, 135).
44   "Fredegarii et aliorum chronica: Vitae sanctorum" in MGH rer. Merov. (Vol. 2, § 71, 157).
45   Hartmann (1900, 2.2:100, 105).
46   For Aquitane see the reports of the annals of St Bertin for the year 846:

   Luporum incursio inferiorum Galliae partium homines audentisseme devorat, sed et in partibus Aquitaniae in modum exercitus usque ad trecentos ferme conglobati et per viam facto agmine gradientes, volentibusque resistere fortiter unanimiterque contrastare feruntur.

   [The invasion of wolves audaciously devoured the men in the lower part of Gaul, but also in parts of Aquitaine in the form of armies, always about three hundred in a mass, and in fact the packs advanced along the road like a column, boldly charging in mass all those who wish to resist them.]

   "Annales Bertiniani" in MGH SS rer. Germ. (§ 846, 33).

47   "Ex Gregorii Magni Dialogorum" in MGH SS rer. Lang. (Liber III, § 38, 539).
48   "Pauli historia Langobardorum" in MGH SS rer. Lang. (Liber V, § 29, 154).
49   Muratori (1739, 2:154, 164, 171, 180); Verci (1786, 1:Doc. No. IV).
50   Muratori (1739, 2:150, 164, 171, 180). Evidence for the "extremely wide forestation of the region of Florence-Fiesole", right up into the eleventh century, has been put together by Davidsohn (1896a, 1:36 f.).
51   See the examples in Kowalewsky (1901, 3:431).

52 Forests represent by far the greatest part of the area in all endowments of that time.
53 See the examples in Inama-Sternegg (1879, 1:215); Lamprecht (1885, I.1:94). For the 'solitudines' in Bavaria see Bitterauf (1905, 1:LXXXI).
54 These include the investigations in Lamprecht (1885). In addition, the very conscientious work of Maitland (1907, 20 f.).
55 An inexhaustibly rich source on all problems of settlement is the work by Meitzen (1895). – As far as the investigations of Meitzen reach, we are on certain ground; where they stop, our analysis must also stop. The latter applies – unfortunately! – to the area south of the Alps.
56 Compare the overview maps in the Map Volume of Meitzen (1895), where the geographic spread of the various settlement forms is portrayed graphically, at least for Europe north of the Alps.
57 Hanssen (1880, 1:497).
58 Hanssen (1880, 1:518).
59 Tönnies (1887).
60 Much new material in Müllner (1909, 1:111 ff.).
61 "Pactus legis Salicae" in MGH LL nat. Germ. (Vol. 4:1, § XXII, 87), cited in Lamprecht (1885, I.1:17). In the Domesday Book, "sometimes the ownership of a mill is divided into so many shares that we are tempted to think that this mill has been erected at the cost of the vill." (Maitland 1907, 144).
62 In a well-known place in the "Lex Baiwariorum" in MGH LL nat. Germ. (Vol. 5:2, § IX:2, 367), churches, ducal palaces, mills, and smithies are named as public buildings which enjoyed a privileged position. "Such buildings were like farming equipment left defenceless in the field, they weren't inhabited permanently but rather only called on for work purposes and often lay isolated by a river, shielded by their privileged position. They stood continually open, as did the smithies (just like the mills). *These public workplaces were communal property and all members of the community were permitted to use them on a rotating basis.*" Dahn (1905, IX.2:443). Koehne (1904, 74 ff.) examines whether the mills stood as "private property" or as property of the community (the people of the mark [*Markgenossenschaft*]). There was in my opinion:
1. "private mills" of farmers (a quite primitive sort);
2. community mills;
3. private mills of the lords of the manor which could, or (later) had to be used by the farmers.
Further to this debate cf. also Thévenin (1886).
63 The smith, *faber ferrarius* in the "Pactus legis Salicae" in MGH LL nat. Germ. (Vol. 4:1, § X:6, 53–54; § XXXV:9, 132); in the "Lex Baiwariorum" in MGH LL nat. Germ. (Vol. 5:2, § XI, 440); in the "Leges Alamannorum" in MGH LL nat. Germ. (Vol. 5:1, § LXXIX:7, 139, and passim); the *carpentarius* in the "Pactus legis Salicae" in MGH LL nat. Germ. (Vol. 4:1, § X:6, 53–54) (these passages might equally refer to workers employed on the manor or by the monastery).

64 See for example Dahn (1902, IX.1:443; 1905, IX.2:419). According to Meitzen (1895, 2:592 f.), the three field system is first mentioned in the region of Gaul and Raetia. One finds the agricultural "antiquities" still best collected in Anton (1799). — Misunderstandings are certainly no rarity with Anton.
65 "Ceteris servis non in nostrum morem, discriptis per familiam ministeriis, utuntur: suam quisque sedem, suos penates regit. frumenti modum dominus aut pecoris aut vestis ut colono iniungit, et servus hactenus paret: cetera domus officia uxor ac liberi exsequuntur."
[The other slaves are not used in our fashion, distributed about the domestic duties: each has his own place, he rules his own dwelling. The master takes a measure of the grain, or the cattle, or the clothing, like with the tenant farmer, and the slave submits as far as this: the other domestic duties are carried out by the wife and children.]
(Tacitus 1903, 12, § 25).
For similar circumstances with the Celts, see Meitzen (1895, 1:88).
66 Max Weber (1891, 243 ff.). Adolf Schulten (1896) Also cf. Oskar Siebeck (1904, 11 ff., 23).
67 Cf. Seebohm (1883, Ch. VIII), Kowalewsky (1901, 3: passim), Meitzen (1895, 1: passim), and Vinogradoff (1905, 37 ff.). A good survey across the state of the research is given by Silvio Pivano (1909, 107 ff.).
68 Auguste Rivet (1891), Ulrich Stutz (1892), Theodor Mommsen (1893, 43 ff.).
69 According to the English sources, the income of the smallest lord of the manor is estimated at £5–£20 (the same as £100–£400 in present-day (1916) currency). (1906, 14).
70 Dopsch (1912a, 1:271 ff.) draws up a list of bestowals and fiefdoms given to secular lords from the royal estate, with information for the Carolingian period on the sizes of possessions. Already in this list of individual bestowals, the size vary from one holding to 104 holdings with 300 dependents besides the demesne.
71 See, for example, the listing of the pieces of women's jewellery in the Carolingian period by the writer of the life story of the venerable Hathumod of Gandersheim in MGH SS (Vol. 4, § 2, 167). Of course, the venerable man will have filled his mouth richly. In view of such evidence, for God's sake, one must guard against the assumption that the time was already corrupted by luxury, an assumption which Dopsch himself now affects. If one wants to form a correct idea of a generation's life character then one must not, so my lay understanding tells me, base one's judgment on the listing of objects of jewellery by a zealous preacher of morals, but rather one must take a look, for example, at how an estate was structured and what was listed under furniture and equipment in the inventory of a medieval manor. One will then come to a completely different picture. See, for example, the description of an English manor of the early period by Nathan J. Hone (1906, 26 ff.).
72 End of the value-taxes which Charlemagne declared at the Frankfurt Synod in 794, in MGH LL (Vol. 1, § 4, 72).

73 Cf. also the statements of Lamprecht (1885, I.2:844) and the sources quoted there in note 3. In addition, see the letter of Wala for the monastery Bobbio in Hartmann (1904b, 63 ff.). "Only, the worry which is laid down in the various rules of the time, as in the earlier time, is not how the monastery's wealth can be increased somewhat through profits, but in what way consumption is to be regulated." (Hartmann 1904b, 67).

74 See Philipp Schneider (1885, 26 ff.).

75 "Statuta antiqua abbatiae S. Petri Corbeiensis" in the Appendices to Guérard (1844, 2:306 ff.).

76 Guérard (1844, 2:311–312).

77 See the "Liber niger" of the monastery of Peterborough in the Appendices to the *Chronicon Angliae Petriburgense* (Stapleton 1849, 167 ff.).

78 See the sources in Lamprecht (1885, I.2:845 f.) for the complement of the German monasteries. Cf. also with the delivery orders of the abbey of Reichenau (a document from 843) (Das königliche Staatsarchiv in Stuttgart 1849, 1:124–26).

79 In the Codex Bavarus (middle of the 10th century), which gives us information about the organisation of the Archbishop of Ravenna's land ownership. See Hartmann (1890).

80 Guérard (1844, 1:45).

81 For Italy, see the foundational work of Silvio Pivano (1904). There one also finds further literature. Cf. also Dopsch (1912b; 1913).

82 Cf. p. 137.

83 "Codex Falksteiniensis" in Petz, et al. (1880, XXII–XXIII).

84 Already in the common law; then in the *Capitulare de villis vel curtis imperii*; then in the *Rectitudines singularum personarum*, in which no less than 16 different professions of estate day labourers are listed.

85 "Qui […] non habent animalia, sive animal ad hoc utile, veniet quando ei precipitur a nostro ministro cum suo fossorio et cooperabitur aliis hominibus hoc quod ei iniunctum fuerit."
[Anyone who […] does not have animals, or an animal of use for this, will come, when ordered by our agent, with his own hoe (?) and be combined with other men, with respect to this it may be enjoined on him.]
Cesarius on the "Prümer Urbar" in (Beyer 1860, 1:145 note 3).

86 In *England* (also in other lands?), the supervisors were obligated farmers who were chosen in the estate courts by their comrades. Thus the reeve who oversaw the ploughing, the hayward who had the responsibility for the harvest work, the constable, etc. (Hone 1906, 67 ff.).

87 (Beyer 1860, 1:145 note 1).

88 The best overviews are contained in Guérard (1844) (9th century) and the *Cartularium Monasterii de Rameseia* (Hart and Lyons 1884, 1:CCIV f., 281 ff.) (13th century).

89 See the evidence in Georg Landau (1862, 35 ff.). Cf. also von Below (1889, 16).

90 Cf. also von Below (1897, 128 f.), and now especially the penetrating critique of the, "so-called" by him, *Capitulare de villis vel curtis*

imperii in Dopsch (1912a, 1:26 ff.).

91 In the "Beneficiorum fiscorumque regalium describendorum formulae" in MGH Capit. (Vol. 1, 179) it says of one villa:

> Ministeriales non invenimus, aurifices, neque argentarios, ferrarios, neque ad venandum, neque in reliquis obsequiis.

> [We do not discover liegemen, goldsmiths, nor silversmiths, blacksmiths, nor those who can come, nor in the remainder of the retinue.]

92 For those village inhabitants obliged to provide "manufacturing" services, we have up to now no designation. I have nothing against describing them as "craftsmen" and then as "country craftsmen" in contrast to the "manorial craftsmen" employed on the manor itself, as per the procedure of Friedrich Philippi (1909, 9). But, but, careful! Rather place "", and even better describe them somewhat long-windedly as inhabitants obligated to manufacture goods (farmers). In any case, do not forget: *they form the backbone of the manor — i.e. of a self-sufficient economy!*

93 That applies most of all for *England*: see Kemble (1839, 1:193, cf. 296, 299, 311; 2:46, 355); also the Ramsey Cartular (Hart and Lyons 1884), and cf. in addition the diligent work of Nellie Neilson (1898). In the sources of other countries, bread deliveries have seldom been encountered by me. For example, in the Prümer Urbar (Lamprecht 1885, I.2:787); also in the Urbar of the Abbey Werden (Kötzschke 1901, 17), where (again a somewhat different form!), from the 2 *modii* [tr.: a Roman dry measure] of rye which the estate delivered, 24 loaves were baked by the farmers; perhaps even in the estate 'Bachus' [bakehouse]?

94 The monastery St Germain received the payments (consisting of grain, flour, malt, and money) of 71 mills (Guérard 1844, 1:§ 342). 15 mills together contributed payments of 2,000 *modii* of flour to the abbey of Corbie; see the "Statuta antiqua abbatiae S. Petri Corbeiensis" from 828 (Guérard 1844, 2:312). In the "traditions book" of the abbey of Weißenburg, the following turn of phrase is frequent: "molendini [...] unde [...] veniunt modii" [mill-house [...] from which [...] *modii* come] (Zeuss 1842, passim).

95 Both buildings together are called 'Camba': "Cambam vulgariter appellamus 'bahchus' et 'bruhus'" [The 'bahchus' and 'bruhus' are usually called *Camba*], see the gloss of Cesarius in Prümer Urbar (Beyer 1860, 1:144 note 5). *Cambae* were very common, but probably not on every manor, as we may conclude from the fact that in the estate lists their presence was especially emphasised (Beyer 1860). We find the 'Camba' in *France* as well — see the plan of the abbey De la Sainte Trinité de Tiron (Merlet 1883); also the collected inventories published in Guérard (1844); in *England*, see the Ramsey Cartular (Hart and Lyons 1884), and the "Liber niger" in the appendices to the "Chronicon Angliae Petriburgense" (Stapleton 1849, 167 ff.).

96 Estate mills are already mentioned in the deeds of donation of Chlodwig, and are just as common in all later deeds. See, for example, the purchase contracts of the Church of St Bertin from the 8th century; in the following century, the monastery then erected the first undershot mills. From the "Folquini Chartularium" (Guérard 1840, 67, No. 48); cited by Kowalewsky (1901, 1:240–241). Cf. the previously mentioned *English* sources and, in addition, Hale (1865).

The estate mills then became "banalities" with time: "est ibi molendinum venterititum, ad quod omnes villani de Broughtone, Wardeboys, Caldecote, Wodehyrst et Waldhyrst debent sectam" [there is a windmill which all the tenants of Broughtone, Wardeboys, Caldecote, Wodehyrst and Waldhyrst are obliged to share] (Hart and Lyons 1884, 1:333). Over 'Bann' mills and related things in *German* law, see Waitz (1844, 8:275 ff.). In the descriptions of the *French* monastic institutions, the mills are not missing: Clairvaux (13th century), see the "Descriptio positionis seu situationis Mon. Clarae Vallensis" in the works of St Bernard of Clairvaux (1839, 2.2:2529–34); and for the abbey of De la Sainte Trinité de Tiron see Merlet (1883).

97 "unicuique molinario mansus et VI bonuaria de terra dentur: quia volumus ut habeat unde ea quae ei jubentur perficere valeat, et illam molturam salvam faciat: id est, ut boves et reliquam pecuniam habeat, cum quibus laborare possit, unde et ipse et omnis familia ejus possit vivere"

[to each miller a holding and 6 parcels of land is allocated: because we wish that he is able to complete what he is ordered to, and have that grain milled well: it is when he has the oxen and the rest of the expenses, with which he can work, and by which he and all his family can live off it]

From the "Statuta antiqua Abbatiae Sancti Petri Corbeiensis" in Guérard (1844, 2:313, Caput VII).

Then: The miller had, 1) to pay in flour (see note 94); and 2) instead of a work obligation, from which he was expressly freed, to mill the lord's grain. For *England*, see Kowalewsky (1901, 3:183). The grain was probably commonly ground up on the way straight from the contributing farm to the manor, as it is graphically described in the *Cartularium Monasterii de Rameseia* (Hart and Lyons 1884, 1:290):

> ducet unam ringam frumenti ad molendinum de Houchthone; quam unus cottarius de Sancto Ivone custodiet salvo, quosque illud frumentum redactum fuerit in farinam quam postmodum idem Ricardus ibidem recipiet et ducet apud Rameseyam.

> [he will take a hoop of grain to the mill of Houchthone (Houghton?); a crofter of St Ives will keep it safe, and when that grain has been reduced into flour, afterwards that same Richard will receive it and take it to Ramesey]

Incidentally, one is never able to know in this and similar cases whether it concerns an old village mill becoming obligated or an estate

End Notes

mill erected by the lord of the manor.

98 "Sunt ibi farinarii III, vnus molendinarius tenet de terra iornalem pro sua uestimenta"
[There are three millers, one of the millers takes a day's work on the land for his clothes] (Beyer 1860, 1:147, § 135).
"illi farinarii qui in circuitu sunt, unusquisque facit dies V inter messem, et pratum, et corvadas"
[those millers are in a circuit, each one does five days between the harvest, and the field, and the obligation to the lord] (Beyer 1860, 1:163, § 135).

Probably only the mills lying comfortably by the manor had the milling obligation (note 97), whereas one imposed the usual field obligations on those situated 'in circuitu'.

99 In the *Camba*:

> tenentur homines ibidem manentes panem fermentatum coquere, et cervisiam braxare.

> [the men remaining in the same place are bound to bake leavened bread, and brew beer.]

From those close in, a few regularly had the office of bread baking and beer brewing to practise. With that came extra benefits (for the farmers?), for example, when the abbot came into the area:

> tenentur frumentum de curia dominica ad molendinum deducere, et molere, et ad cambam dominicam reportare, et panem facere, et coquere, similiter et ceruisiam braxare.

> [they are bound to take the grain of the lord's house to the mill and grind it, and carry it back to the lord's bakery, and make bread, and cook, and similarly brew beer.]

Just as when the people in the fields (during the harvest?) were supplied with bread and beer:

> illum panem, ac ceruisiam, ipsa familia in suo ordine tenetur et coquere et brazare.

> [the family itself is bound to bake that bread and to brew the beer.]

From the commentary of the Abbot Cesarius in the "Reginonis Abbatis Prümiensis Chronicon" (Beyer 1860, 1:144 note 5, § 135).

> "bracium et panem per ordinem preparare" [to orderly supply malt and bread] (Zeuss 1842, 274, § III & IIII);

> "per ordinem panem et cervisiam parare" [to orderly supply bread and beer] (Zeuss 1842, 277, § XIIII);

> "et panem quando opus est parare" [and when it is useful to supply food] (Zeuss 1842, 277, § XV). Cf. also Kowalewsky (1901, 3:59).

In the monastery Peterborough, we find in the bakehouse: two bakers, 'qui victum militis habent' [who have the feeding of soldiers], one *van-*

nator (grain purifier), two bakers with two loaves and two 'bisos cum cervisia' [brown (loaves?) with beer] daily, two *caratores* [curators], two *servientes molantes* [serving milling]; in the brewhouse: one master brewer (*braccharius*), two *caratores ligni* [curators of firewood], and three *servientes aquarum* [serving water]. The board was provided either 'ad panes' or 'ad blada', that is, the concession is given in the form of bread or grain. Alongside, money wages are also paid (at the beginning of the 12th century) (Stapleton 1849, 187 ff.).

100 Lamprecht (1885), whose area of investigation is indeed a specific wine country.

101 An illustrative picture of the extraction of oil is given by the "Placitum Arpirandi Diaconi" (from 882), which is disclosed in Guérard (1844, 2:348). It refers to the northern Italian conditions: *servi homines* [servants and men] etc.

> querunt se subtrahere ad colligendum olivas ex olivetis illas qui sunt dominicates de ista curte de Lemunta, et eas premere, vel oleum que exinde exiit evegere nolunt, sicut suorum fecerunt parentes et consortes de ipsas locas, Cevenna, Cantoligo, Selvaniaco et Mandrenino a longo tempore

> [asked to take away themselves the harvest of olives from the oliveyards of the demesne of that farm of Lemunta, and squeeze them, or thereafter they do not wish to carry away the oil discharged, as their parents and the partners of their own localities, Cevenna, Cantoligo, Selvaniaco et Mandrenino, did for a long time].

We run across a 'pressoir banal' [common press] also at the abbey De la Sainte-Trinité de Tiron. See the plans for the monastery in Merlet (1883). About the extraction of oil at the abbey of the Blessed Julia in Brescia, see Baudi di Vesme, et al. (1873, 713, No. 419); for the abbey of Bobbio, see Hartmann (1904b, 52 f.).

102 In a document from 716 (Kemble 1839, 1:80, No. LXVII), King Aethelbald exchanged with the monastery at Worcester land to set up a saltworks: three sheds (*casuli*) and six ovens. In the 13th century, we find the monastery itself in possession of a saltworks in Wich (Droitwich), which delivered it annually 280 *mittae* (= 2800 bushels [Tr.: 1 (imperial) bushel = 36.4 litres]) — thus already essentially for sale (Hale 1865, XI). For other places see Leo (1842, 203). Bestowal of interests in saltworks to churches and monasteries was common in *Italy*. References in Adolf Schaube (1906, 46 note 3) (11th century). We also find numerous churches and monasteries in possession of saltworks (10th century). Cf. Schaube (1906, 72, 83). For *Germany*, see the in-depth depiction in Inama-Sternegg (1879, 2:238 ff.), and in Dahn (1905, IX.2:428 ff.) (for the region of the 'Baiern' [Bavarians]).

103 Over salt duties and payments in salt, see Schaube (1906, 83 f.).

104 Cf. from the abundance of places in the sources, for example:
- for *England*: the "Liber niger" of the monastery of Peterborough (Stapleton 1849, 159, 162, 163, 165) ("ulnas de panno" [cubits of

End Notes

cloth], "ulnas de lineo panno" [cubits of linen cloth]);
- for *France*: the urbarium of the abbey St Bertin in Guérard (1840, 99, No. XXI): "Ancillae XXII faciunt ladmones XII" [22 maids make 12 pieces of cloth] ("ladmo [est] pensum textile [...] mulieribus lidis vel obnoxiis impositum" [*ladmo* [is] the cloth woven [...] by the women subject to imposition or obligation] (Guérard 1844, 2:453)) "de illis ingenuis feminis XIII veniunt ladmones VI et dimidius" [from the 13 freeborn women comes six and a half pieces of cloth] (Guérard 1840, 99, No. XXI; similarly XXIV, XXV, and elsewhere);
- for *Germany*: the urbaria of Prüm, Fulda, Lorsch, Weißenburg, etc.; also Wittich (1896, 297 ff.) (12th century).
- Cf. also the references mentioned in notes 105 and 106.

105 "Ille femine, que camsilis faciunt, colligunt linum, et trahunt de aqua. et parant" [Those woman who make shirts, they gather flax, and draw water, and prepare it] (Beyer 1860, 1:150).
"Pannum ex proprio lino [debent]" [They [are obligated to provide] cloth from their own linen] (Lamey 1770, 3:219).
"Lidi LX quorum singuli pannum ex proprio lino [...] debent" [They must provide 60 items of cloth each from their own linen] (Schannat 1729, 1:31).
"de proprio lino camsile [...] facere debent" [they must make the shirts from their own linen] (Zeuss 1842, 275, § VIII).

106 "[Iste lidae ancillae] si datur eis linificium, faciunt camsilos. [...] Et illa ancilla facit de lana dominica sarcilum"
[[These obligated maids] if given that linen, they make shirts. [...] And that maid makes the master's bag out of wool]
(Guérard 1844, 2:150, 176; cf. 109, 212, 244, and elsewhere).
It is surely not right when von Below (1900b, 342) assumes that the tribute-obliged farmers would have only ever processed raw materials produced themselves. Incidentally, it is self-evident here that the talk is of neither "wage-work", nor "handwork". Cf. for the overall organisation of the wool production in the German manors, see Erich Kober (1908, 13 ff.).

107 The abbey of Farfa (10th century):

> in fronte ipsius sit alia domus longitudinis pedes XL et V, latitudines XXX. Nam ipsius longitudo pertingat usque as sacristiam et ibi sedeant omnes *sartores* atque *sutores* ad suendum, quod camerarius eis praecipit. Et ut praeparatam habeant ibi tabulam longitudinis XXX pedes et alia tabula afixa sit cum ea, quarum latitudo ambarum tabularum habeat VII pedes

> [at the front, the house would be a distinct length of 40 feet and five, and width 30. For the length of it extends all the way to the vestry and there are seated all the tailors and also the cobblers sewing away, because the chamberlain commands them to. And for preparation, they have there a table of length 30 feet and a separate table would be attached to it, and the width of both those tables

is seven feet] (Albers 1900, 138–39).

"In sartrino" of the monastery Peterborough sat two tailors, two *homines qui abluunt pannos* [men who wash cloth], one *homo qui affert ligna* [man who brings the wood], and one *corvesarius* (cobbler) (Albers 1900, 167 ff.). Cf., in addition, Julius von Schlosser (1889).

108 At the abbey of Corbie in the 9th century, as well as at the abbey of Clairvaux in the 13th century (see below on p.113), like at the monastery Subiaco in the 11th century. From the *Reg. Subiac.* 98 and 154, cited in Adolf Schaube (1906, 46).

109 *Vermiculum* (= vermeil = scarlet?) had to be delivered by the farmers to the monks of St Remi de Reims (Guérard 1844, 1:XXX); it is also found as a detail in the Prümer Urbar (Beyer 1860, 1:§ 135); cf. Lamprecht (1885, I.2:787).

110 Davidsohn (1896a, 3:211). Cf. note 111.

111 *battitor lane* [beater of wool] (Davidsohn 1896a, 3:211). In addition, a *tintor* [dyer] and a *tirator pannorum* [stretcher of cloth] are found (document from 1303).

112 The English abbey Meaux even had its own tannery in the year 1396. More precise details in L. F. Salzmann (1913, 173).

113 On a Superintendent's estate [*Schultenhof*] of the abbey of Werden, we encounter amongst the staff a stonemason whom the Superintendent had to send for a long time every year to Werden for the use of the lord (11th, 12th century) (Kötzschke 1901, 80).

114 "[mansionarii] horreum nostrum usque ad tectum construunt" [[residents] construct our barn all the way to the roof] (Lamprecht 1885, I.1:588).

"XV unusquisque ex hiis quando opus est edificare" [15 each from this is there because of the work to build] (Zeuss 1842, 277, § XVI); "quando opus est edificium quod infra dom. curtem est meliorare" [because the work is to make better a building which is incomplete below the manor] (Zeuss 1842, 278, § XVII); "[...] dom. edificium facere V" [five to construct the manor building] (i.e. 26½ manors in the dominion Greyzingen) (Zeuss 1842, 279, § XIX).

115 "sepes [...] facere" [to build [...] fences] (Zeuss 1842, 279); "murum facere" [to build the wall] (Hart and Lyons 1884, 1:335, 366). For Werden: see Kötzschke (1901, 17).

116 "Item habet [i.e. monasterium] in Boningaham mansa IIII per bunaria XII; nichil aliud faciunt per totum annum, nisi emendant tecta monasterii."
[Likewise [the monastery] has in Boningaham four waiting per 12 bunaria [Tr.: a land measure]; they do nothing else throughout the year, except repairing the rooves of the monastery.] From the "Fragmenta ampliora Polyptychi Sithiensis" (Guérard 1844, 2:403, § 21).

117 Every (?) farmhouse of the monastery Weißenburg each delivered "½ carratam lignorum" ([½ a cartload of] building or firewood?) (Zeuss 1842, 274).

118 According to the same source (as in note 117) each delivered "L tegulae" ([50] bricks or shingles?) (Zeuss 1842, 274).
119 This tribute is quite prevalent. Shingles are the *scintuli, scintulae, scindulae*, etc.; battens the *axiles, asiles, axiculi, (vulgariter appellati "esselingi"* according to Cesarius) of the sources. What Lamprecht (1885, I.2:787 note 3) is thinking of when he translates *axiculi* as pieces of wood, I do not know. According to Lamprecht's calculations, the abbey of Prüm received for example in total 14,232 *axiles* and 57,038 *scindulae* (1885, II:143). Abundant evidence for the existence of this tribute can be found in the collections of polyptyques in Guérard (1844).
120 Either "sine precio" [without price] or for a fixed price (then it was already the beginning of a trading relationship): abbeys of St Maixent and Montierneuf. Evidence in Boissonnade (1900, 1:117).
121 Bede (1838, 393, Liber V, Caput XXI), cited in Montalembert (1863, 5:6). According to the same source, Abbot Benedict had French glassmakers come in the year 674 to insert windows in the new building of the abbey of Weremouth (Anderson 1764, 1:26).
122 "De Conversione Bagoariorum et Carantanorum Libellus" in MGH SS (Vol. 11, 1–17) (for the year 872), cited in Dahn (1905, IX.2:444).
123 "[...] petimus, ut per comites vestros, qui in Italia sunt actores, ipsum jam dictum stannum dirigere jubeatis, per unumquemque comitem libras centum"
[we require that, by your Counts who are the agents in Italy, you should order them to send the tin already mentioned, a hundred pounds for each Count] (Cenni 1760, 1:472); cited by von Hegel (1847, 2:12 note 3).
124 At the abbey of Corbie, we find in 822 no less than six blacksmiths, two goldsmiths, two shield makers, and four carpenters.
We learn of the Anglo-Saxon lords of the manor that they went travelling with their "smith". Was that an armourer? A shield bearer? A sort of "gunsmith"? See the *Ines dômas* § 63 (Thorpe 1840, 1:63); the *Aðelbirthes dômas* § 7 (Thorpe 1840, 1:2), the conversations, and the *Leges Edwardi Confessoris* § 21 (Thorpe 1840, 1:194), to which Heinrich Leo alludes in the introduction to his edition of the *Rectitudines singularum personarum* (1842, 132). Noteworthy is that all "craftsmen" are called "smiðas" in Anglo-Saxon, like in Old-Norse even the cobbler is called "skô-smidr".
125 Gloss of Cesarius (Beyer 1860, 1:155 note 1). Cf. the places in Beyer (Beyer 1860, 1:144 ff.) with those in the "Fragmenta Polyptychi S. Remigii Remensis" in Guérard (1844, 2:288).
126 Someone gifted the monastery Lorsch "tertiam partem de sua mina ad faciendum ferrum" [the third part of their silver coin for the iron needing to be made] (Lamey 1768, 3:239 § MMMDCCI). Cf. also the places in Beyer (Beyer 1860, 2:) which refer to the Trier Archdiocese.
127 The collected polyptyques which Guérard edited and annotated (1844) contain iron delivery as a tribute obligation on farmers. Similarly in the Lorsch Codex (Lamey 1768, 3:182, § MMMDCLVII; 226, § MMMDCLXXXI), in the Fulda Codex (Schannat 1729), and in the Urbarium of

St Emmeran. Count Siboto von Falkenstein also received iron as tribute (Petz, Grauert, and Mayerhofer 1880, XXIV). The same tribute is in the inventory of St Julia's in Brescia (Baudi di Vesme, Desimoni, and Poggi 1873, No. 419, No. 712, No. 716). For the abbey of Bobbio, see Hartmann (1904b, 61, 86).

128 "N. [...] facit ferra carrucarum et Prior inveniet ei ferrum et carbonem [...]"
[N. [...] makes iron things for carriages and beforehand will find for it iron and charcoal] Hale (1865, 56a) cited in Ashley (1896, 1:62 note 111).
"Faber [...] carbones inveniet" [The smith [...] will get charcoal] (Seebohm 1883, 70).

129 Around 985, there existed in the abbey of St Florent de Saumur a 'factory' in which the monks wove "des tapisseries ornées de fleurs et de figures d'animaux"
[tapestries adorned with flowers and animal figures]; in 1025, one finds in Poitiers a similar establishment (Michel 1852, 1:71).

130 See the technical treatise found in the Cathedral of Lucca which Muratori has published (1739, 2:365–388), and published in part in Fagniez (1898, 1:53–54, Doc. 94). The art of goldsmithing still flourished in the 13th century in the English (St Alban!) and French monasteries — see the documents in Henri Baudrillart (1880, 3:188 f.).

131 "[scimus, eam] numerosas cubicularias ad varietatem textrilium rerum instructas habere, et in preciosis vestibus conficiendis pene omnes nostrarum regionum mulieres superare"
[[We know her] to have numerous chambermaids instructed in a variety of matters of weaving, and to surpass almost all the women of our lands in the making of precious clothes], Alpertus of Metz in MGH SS (Vol. 3, 702).

132 "nec vero nobiles illas palatio adhaerentes silentio praeteriri convenit officinas, ubi in fila variis distincta coloribus serum vellera tenuantur"
[nor however does he neglect to assemble workshops at his famous palaces, where fleeces are kept bound in distinct strands of various colours] See *Historia Hugonis Falcandis Siculi de rebus gestis in Siciliae regno*, cited in Michel (1852, 1:81–82).

I have attempted to fundamentally appraise these self-sufficiently organised arts and crafts in my work *Kunstgewerbe und Kultur* (1908, 19 ff.).

133 In the European Middle Ages, this distrust belonging to the new tribes entering the historical records was more quickly conquered when they were suddenly penetrated by higher cultures. It nevertheless finds its expression still in the ornate systems of *laws for foreigners*, which depict nothing else but a sum of protective laws for comrades against the feared encroachment of those alien to the tribe (town).

134 According to Arab sources. See Georg Jacob (1887, 124).

135 If we want to give credence to the tales of Diodorus (1831, 1:518, Book 5 § 22), then the tribes which resided in the so-called younger Stone Age (1500–1000 B.C.) in Great Britain and on the western coast of Ger-

many would already have conducted "trade" (with tin and amber) (Varges 1903, 7 ff.). Varges speaks about the "trading" of the Germanic tribes in the beginning of the historical period (1903, 24 ff.). Cf. in addition the general works about the primitive culture of the European tribes.

136 I think still the best general view of the economic culture of Roman Imperial Era is presented to us by Ludwig Friedländer (1901). The dispute between Karl Bücher and Eduard Meyer has not made public any new knowledge.

137 See Max Weber (1891, 262 ff.).

138 One can be doubtful as to whether the exchange-based organisation of the economy was pushed back the furthest after the columns of Longobard's and Saracens (thus perhaps in the 8th century), or only after the invasion and plundering of Hungary (thus in the second half of the 10th century). Schaube assumes this point occurred for the mediterranean peoples in the 10th century (1906). I see no essential changes in either century. The fact also deserves attention that the volume of money in Europe, particularly in Germany decreases constantly up to the close of the Carolingian period, and that only under Otto I does a rise in the production of precious metals set in. See the depiction on p. 141 ff.

139 "The manorial/monastic household was not completely self-contained, but also neither was the farming concern." (Below 1914a, 127).

140 The trade with these eastern regions will have fashioned itself strongly and actively in their favour. In particular — in my view — the great quantity of Arab coins found in bulk are suggestive of this. The sellers of pelts, etc. bought nothing from the Arab traders and were hence paid in cash. They buried the coins or used them as jewellery (G. Jacob 1887, 59 ff.).

141 See what I remarked about it on p. 88.

142 From a document of the year 1168, we learn, for example, how the officers of the lord had to ask around all the farmers in the month of August for whether anyone had saleable wine. In Schöpflin (1772, 1:197 ff., No. 249); cited by Kowalewsky (1901, 3:289).

143 Already in the 9th century, the export of dried fish from the coast of the North Sea had obtained considerable dimensions (Bugge 1906, 229 ff.).

144 Prime examples are Commachio and Venice. See "Commachio und der Pohandel" in Hartmann (1904b, 74 ff.), for the 8th century.

145 "Antiquitus tanta copia vini ac salis proveniebat ecclesie de curtibus nostris quod oportebat quasi de necessitate superflua (one notices the 'spirit'!) venundare"
[In ancient times the wine and such a great abundance of salt resulted from the church of our court that it was required as if out of necessity to sell the excess] (Beyer 1860, 1:148 note 1).

146 We are informed about the considerable number of meadows on the properties of St Paul's Church in London around the turn of the 12th century by the source shared in Kowalewsky (1901, 3:73). An abundance of material is contained in the article by Robert Jowitt Whitwell,

"English Monasteries and the Wool Trade in the 13th Century" (1904).
147 "Codex Falksteiniensis" in Petz, et al. (1880, XXVI).
148 C. Schneller (1898, 6).
149 At the end of the 12th century, the abbey St Pantaleon in Cologne collected 438 Mlr. "tritici" (rye?), of which 187 Mlr. were consumed; 577 Mlr. "siliginis" (wheat?), of which 313 Mlr. were able to be consumed; 891 Mlr. "avene" (oats), of which almost all remained to be sold [Tr.: an *Mlr.* is perhaps a *maldarium* (see the note on p. 135)]. From an unpublished document cited in Lamprecht (1885, I.2:839).
150 In the benefice book of the monastery St Petri in Soissons: "solvunt in anno friscingas duas [...] in villa Uscladinas coloni tres [...] solidos tres solvunt."
[they pay annually two young pigs [...] to the estate of Uscladinas, three farmers pay three gold coins] (Pardessus 1843, 1:39, No. 65).
151 For *England* depicted by Kowalewsky (1901, 3:139); also the analogous development with the Normans in *Sicily* (1901, 3:381 f.). See for *Germany*, for example, the Prümer Urbar (Beyer 1860, 1:147–149); for *France*, Flach (1893, 2:198 and passim).
152 W. Wittich (1896, 312 ff., 317 ff.).
153 Enrico Poggi (1845, 2:184 ff.); cf. von Rumohr (1830, 110 ff.) (a collection of documents for the period after 1250).
154 Lamprecht (1885, 1:148 f.).
155 Lamprecht (1885, 1, 529 ff., 557 ff.), citing Beyer (1860, 1:650; 3:504).
156 Carlo Bertagnolli (1881, 180).
157 See the evidence in Kowalewsky (1901, 3:169 ff.).
158 See, for example, the documents in Guérard (1844, 1:383).
159 G. Freytag (1867, 2:46). In addition to that source, the usual historical depictions of the countryside give the desired information.
160 P. Schneider (1885, 41 ff.).
161 These connections are depicted by A. Brackmann (1899, 2); and R. Bückmann (1912, 16 f.). Cf. Schulte (1910, 274 ff.).
162 Graphically described by K. H. Schäfer (1907, 191 ff.).
163 Kötzschke (1901, 114), where this transformation of the monastic form is described in an especially in-depth and lively way. Over the general development, see Georg Matthaei (1877, 14 ff.); and Anton Hauck (1904, 3:314, 443 ff.).
164 W. Arnold (1854, 2:162 f.); cf. Kötzschke (1901, 114).
165 Our knowledge of the early history of the mining of precious metals is extraordinarily scanty. What is present in source materials will be found collected in the following places: W. Jacob (1838, 1:151 ff.), the translator has made worthy additions; A. Soetbeer (1862); A. Hanauer (1876); Inama-Sternegg (1879, 2:330 f.); Dopsch (1912a, 2:173 f.).
I will also add:
- ad annum 963: from Widukind, "terra Saxonia venas argenti aperuerit" [the land of Saxony opened a vein of silver] in MGH SS (Vol. 3, Liber 3, § 63 462);
- ad 961: from the Thietmari chronicon, "Temporibus suis aureum illuxit seculum; apud nos inventa est primum vena argenti" [In

End Notes

- that time a golden age shone; a vein of silver was found by us for the first time] in MGH SS (Vol. 3, Liber II, § 8, 747); and
- we are informed about prehistoric times by M. Much (1902, 1 ff.).

166 See the illuminating instruction for monks visiting the market, which conveys:

> "periculosum quidem est minusque honestum Religiosis frequentare nundinas"

[it is risky for the less honest clergy to frequent the fair]

But which then permits them to go there, though to stay away for no more than three days (Paris 1670, 260).

167 A few "negotiatores" of the monasteries are mentioned for the first time in a document of the monastery St Denis from the year 775, after that more frequently (De la Tour 1896, 79). When von Below (1897, 140 f.) criticises as unsuccessful the attempt at a source-wise corroboration of the fact that even in Germany the monasteries, etc. possessed their own "negotiatores", then he may be right. But that the appointment of their own 'negotiatores' *existed* everywhere there were larger manorial/monastic estates, can surely not be placed in doubt by anybody who has delved into the affairs of a monastery which regularly sold large quantities of its own produce and therefore had to buy other things from afar.

168 From the comprehensive literature over this question, cf. von Maurer (1870, 1:332); Goldschmidt (1891, 127 ff.) (with abundant source evidence); W. Varges (1893, 172 ff., 201 ff.); S. Rietschel (1897, 42 ff, 140 ff. (summary), and elsewhere); von Below (1897, 138; 1900a, 20, 23); H. Pirenne (1898, 64 ff.); and K. Bücher (1893).

169 J. W. von Goethe (1839, 179).

170 "The Gothic merchants (from the island of Gotland), who visited Novgorod and England, all lived in the countryside and were farmers." (Bugge 1906, 267). Even the "negotiatores were settled and [...] demanded pasturage" (Hartmann 1904b, 112).

171 "[...] in Vico qui hodieque Traiectus [Maastricht in 882] vocatur, [...] estque *Habitantium et praecipue negotiatorum* multitudine frequentissimus"
[in the city still called Traiectus [Maastricht in 882], it is crowded with inhabitants and especially a multitude of merchants], in "Translatio et Miracula Sanctorum Marcellini et Petri Auctore Einhardo", MGH SS (Vol. 15.1, Liber XVIII, § 81, 261), cited in F. Henaux (1851, 136).
"Forum quoque, quod erat ante portam Mediam constitutum et frequentia comprovincialium satis celebre et famosum, orta *inter cives et negotiatores* gravi simultate, ex eo loco in Wagasatiam translatum est."
[At the market, which was at the gate of Trier, which made it quite famous and celebrated, there arose grave hostility between the citizens and merchants which was transferred from there to Wadgassen], in "Gesta Treverorum", MGH SS (Vol. 8, § 24, 162).

Does the following amendment also belong here (from MGH DD O II, No. 198, 225)?:

> "inhabitantibus *aut* in posterum habitaturis negotiatoribus sive (!) Iudeis"

> [the current *or* future resident merchants, or alternatively (!) Jews]

172 W. Kiesselbach (1860, 25). Cf. Scheffer-Boichorst (1885).
173 I. Schipper (1907, 14). G. Caro (1908, 1:53 ff., 128 ff). Cf. more especially the good work of R. Saitschik (1891, 2 ff.).
174 See, for example, "Capitulare de disciplina Palatii" from 809 in MGH LL (Vol. 1, 158 f.); "Capitula de Iudaeis" in MGH Capit. (Vol. 1, § 131, 258 f.); "Ansegisi abbatis capitularium collectio" in MGH Capit. (Vol. 1, § 131, 410); MGH DD O II (No. 29, 38; No. 198, 225; No. 300, 352 ff.). And cf. Heyd (1879, 1:87); Inama-Sternegg (1879, 1:448); Goldschmidt (1891, 107 ff.); Schulte (1910, 1:77 f.); Schaube (1906, see subject index); and Schipper (1907, 15 ff.).
175 Schaube (1906, 33) (Amalfi), admittedly in the 11th century.
176 Davidsohn (1896b, 1:39 f.).
177 F. Dahn (1879, 2:301 f.).
178 Schulte (1910); Jacob (1838); Heyd (1879). For France, there is much evidence in F. Dahn (1897, VIII.4:232 ff.).
179 Bede, cited in Anderson (1764, 1:).
180 "de omnes nationes quod ibidem ad ipso marcado adveniunt" [all the nations that arrive in the same place at that market], in a document from 769 in Mabillon (1681, 496), cited by von Maurer (1870, 1:284).
181 "Lex Visigothorum" in MGH LL nat. Germ. (Vol. 1, Liber XI, Titulus III, 404).
182 "Mag. Adami gesta Hammenburgensis ecclesiae pontificum" in MGH SS (Vol. 7, Liber 3, § 57, 359).
183 "Inquisitio de Theloneis Raffelstettensis" (from 903–906) in MGH Capit. (Vol. 2, § 5, 251).
184 Bugge (1906, 246).
185 One thinks of Hænsa-Thorir! [Tr.: Hænsa-Thorir is the subject of an Icelandic saga of that name, a poor man who acquires wealth as a merchant.] In the Laws of King Liutprand, in MGH LL (Vol. 4, § 18.IIII, 115), it states:

> "Si quis negotium peragendum [...] *intra provincia* vel extra provincia ambulaverit"

> [If any business must be carried out [...] one can travel *within the province* or outside it]

One can think of traders, certainly also of producers, who offered their own products for sale.
186 As they are thus called by Heyd (1879, 1:87), and Inama-Sternegg (1879, 1:448).
187 "Quicunque vero servum suum aurificem, argentarium, ferrarium, fabrum aerarium, sartorem vel sutorem, in publicum adtributum

artificium exercere permiserit"
[Anyone who is a servant and a goldsmith, silversmith, blacksmith, coppersmith, tailor, or cobbler is permitted to exercise the trade in public]
from "Leges Burgundionum" in MGH LL (Vol. 3, Titulus XXI § 2, 542).

188 Despite the already enormously hackneyed "puer Parisiacus cuius artis erat vestimenta componere" [The boy of the Parisians whose skill was in composing clothes], who was "ingenuus genere" [a class of freeman] ("Gregorii Episcopi Turonensis Liber II de Virtutibus S. Martini" in MGH SS rer. Merov. (Vol. 2, 178, § 58) cited in von Maurer (1862, 1:181 n.30), and everywhere else where the talk is of the "Beginnings of Craftwork"). For we know that a 'homo ingenuus' could very surely be under obligation. A case of mistaking personal freedom for freedom of production! See Sombart (1902, 1:88). Still much less for the existence of a "free" craftwork is proved of course by the "faber publice probatus" [officially tried craftsman] of the "Leges Alamannorum" in MGH LL nat. Germ. (Vol. 5.1, LXXIV, § 5, 139). "Publice probatus" does not mean perhaps "publicly tested" or something similar, but rather only "public" = generally tried and tested, and was expressed of the worker in the manorial/monastic economy, as was latterly claimed with good grounds by Carl Koehne in(1906a, 186 ff.). In passing, Koehne strays when he suggests that the *aurifex* occurred only in those laws "which were given to themselves by those Germanic ethnic groups, Burgundians, and Visigoths who were settled entirely in the areas of Roman culture". Even the Lex Salica (see MGH LL nat. Germ. (Vol. 4.1, X § 6, 54)) has the *aurifex*. It is entirely inadmissible, however, to infer from the concept of manufacturing workers (*faber, carpentarius*, etc.) some evidence in the primary sources for an independent craftwork. An overview over the state of the research is given by W. Müller (1910). Contention is again linked to this work which represents the views of Seeliger; see von Below (1912; 1914b); as well as Seeliger (1913) and Sander (1913a). New results have not been brought to light. Cf. also R. Eberstadt (1916).

189 L. M. Hartmann (1892, 10 ff.; 1895, 109 ff.; 1904b, 94 ff., plus 16 ff. reprints 1895 article). Cf. also Hegel (1847, 2:61 ff.).

190 K. H. Schreckenstein (1856, 28).

191 O. Kallsen (1891, 1:238).

192 S. Schwarz (1892, 10).

193 W. Varges (1893, 164).

194 G. von Below (1905, 4–5).

195 V. Bransford (1906, 733).

196 P. Sander (1906, 129).

197 René Maunier (1910, 44). There itself is also found on page 34 and following pages an anthology of yet further earlier definitions of the "city".

198 R. Maunier misjudges that now fundamentally again in the book mentioned in the preceding note, which otherwise contains some nice thinking. His unfortunate concept also proves itself to be a bad compass in the enormous sea of facts in which the little scientific ship of

the author roves about helplessly.
199 I have added the word 'larger' to my definition from the first edition (1902, 2:191); in the full consciousness of the gentle ambiguity which I thereby add to the definition. One will never be able to establish numerically when a group of people living in a "civic manner" is large enough to form a "city". A certain size must surely be present though — an individual man cannot form a "city". The quantity flips at a specific point into the quality (city). For my aims, as one will see, the small ambiguity does not matter.
200 Ilgen (1902, 14).
201 Schulten (1896, 45).
202 Rietschel (1897, 147 f.); Keutgen (1903, 75).
203 There was ,"enclosed by colossal fortifications, an entire complex of more or less loosely connected city districts containing territories" with fields and meadows to enable the feeding of the populace in the case of an encompassment. (Pöhlmann 1884, 3–4).
204 The older Indian cities are described to us as a group of villages which just had their common meadows 'amidst the town'. Like the old mark? (Hunter 1886, 46).
205 "The walled cities of the Central Asia enclose within their brick walls many spaces larger than necessary for the city alone. In Bukhara, China, etc. far more than half the ground area is taken up with fields and gardens, deserted places, ponds and marshes, groves of elms and poplars, vast cattle yards [...] One calculates by these enclosures on the necessity of independent inner preservation during sieges." (Ratzel 1891, 2:447).
206 "It is the surplus of the county only [...] that constitutes the subsistence of the town, which can therefore increase only with the increase of this surplus produce." (Smith 1776, Bk. III, Ch. 1). The topic is treated very in-depth, if also not always very calmly, by the older sources in the treatise of Count d'Arco (1782), reprinted in Custodi (1804, Vol. XXX).
207 G. Botero (1588, 1:12-14).
208 "On construit ordinairement les grandes villes sur le bord de la Mer ou des grandes Rivières, pour la commodité des transports; parce que le transport par eau des denrées et marchandises nécessaires pour la subsistance et commodité des habitants, est à bien meilleur marché, que les voitures et transport par terre."
[In general, large cities are built on the shores of the sea or the great rivers for convenience of transport, because the transport by water of the commodities and goods necessary for the subsistence and convenience of the inhabitants is much cheaper than by wagons and transport over land.] (Cantillon 1755, 22–23).
In the age of railroads, the correctness of this sentence will have to be strongly doubted. For the Middle Ages, see the study of F. W. Nitzsch (1872, 239 ff.).
209 It is remarkable how correctly the problem of city formation was recognised by the men of earlier times. Did that lie in the simpler circumstances which one could more easily see through? Where does one

meet in the literature of the 19th and 20th centuries a portrayal like this: "If one wants to maintain that the commerce which one usually conducts in guilds has increased significantly since that time, this has to be ruled out. For since this depends only on the local consumption and the number of inhabitants, nobody, as is generally known, who engage themselves thereby, can ever form a populous and flourishing city, but must *in contrast as a necessary consequence* be considered the advantageous inhabitants of a flourishing city." Pieter de la Court's manuscript "Het Welvaren van Leiden" from 1659, published (with German translation) by Felix Driessen (1911, chap. 11). Cf. also the author in the essentially correct "Theory of Cities" [*Städtetheorie*] in Chapter 1.
210 G. Freytag (1867, 2:119 f.).
211 Keutgen (1903, 110). The same thought traverses Rietschel (1897) like a red thread.
212 Pauli (1847, 59).
213 Rietschel (1897, 46).
214 J. Fritz (1894, 26).
215 The term "bishop's city" has a double meaning. It can have a meaning in constitutional law or (as here) a real meaning. The history of cities up to now has spoken of bishop's cities only in the first sense, and is of course correct for the history of the city's *constitution* when it does that. For the genesis of the *city*, it is quite incidental whether the bishop was lord of the city at the time or not. Florence is in terms of civic history eminently a "bishop's city", for it is the bishop obviously who brought Florence to power and eminence, size and wealth. And yet Florence was never ever an immunity; its constitution transformed directly from a lordship to a municipal one (Davidsohn 1896b, 1:336).
216 H. Pabst (1862, 437 f.); Bethmann-Hollweg (1846, 66 f., 74 ff.).
217 Rietschel (1894, 94).
218 "basilica eadem ex una parte habuit domum episcopi, ex alia praetorium ducis"
[in one part of the same building was the bishop's residence, in another the duke's headquarters]
From the "Mag. Adami gesta Hammenburgensis ecclesiae pontificum" in MGH SS (Vol. 7, Liber 2, § 68, 331), cited in Maurer (1862, 1:63).
219 According to the view of a stern connoisseur of early Florence, the city was enlarged during the 11th century as a result "very significantly", because it became at this time the centre of the anti-imperial, hierarchic party in Tuscany (Hartwig 1875, 1:93).
220 J. ter Gouw (1879, 1:43 ff.), regarding Gijsbrecht III:

"Hem komt regt de eertitel toe: Stichter van Amsterdam."

[He does justice to the title of honour: Founder of Amsterdam.]
221 A. Vandenpeereboom (1878, 3:94 ff.).
222 See, for example, Flach (1893, 2:329).
223 One place had made such a beautiful start in its development into a "great city". I do not doubt for a moment that, next to Byzantium,

Aachen was in the year 800 the greatest European "city". If we estimate quite lowly the number of moths whirring around Charlemagne's sun permanently or in passing, we will yet have to assume a few thousand "inhabitants" of the "Palatium" and its dependencies. One receives the most distinct impression of the size of Aachen in the Carolingian period from the depiction of F. Dahn (1900, VIII.6:102 ff.), where probably all the source material we possess has been utilised.

224 W. Stubbs (1874, 1:415).
225 Anton Dopsch (1904, 1:CCXXV). Cf. Hans von Voltelini (1913, 44 ff.).
226 W. Kothe (1903, 2).
227 J. Greving (1904, 24 f.).
228 According to the "Liber Valoris: Ecclesiarum Coloniensis Dioecesis" (Binterim and Mooren 1828, 1:51 ff.). The conditions in Hildesheim are reported (badly) by H. A. Lüntzel (1858, 1:288 ff.; 2:23 ff.).
229 General monastic schedules for Germany in A. Hauck (1904, 4:975 ff.), and M. Schulte (1910).
230 W. Arnold (1854, 2:178 ff.) (for Regensburg, Speyer, Cologne, Mainz, Strasbourg, Basel, Worms); K. Bücher (1893, 514) (for Frankfurt am Main).
231 Monastic schools and their spread in Europe are handled in-depth by Montalembert (1863, 6:169 ff.). Cf. also von Maurer (1870, 3:57 ff.).
232 For the later period, see in particular the work of F. Eulenburg (1904).
233 Santini (1887); see also Davidsohn's chapter "Türme in der Stadt" [Towers in the City] (1896a, 121).
234 Davidsohn (1896b, 1:554). Von Maurer (1870, 2:9 ff.) expatiates on the civic dwellings of the temporal lords in the *German* cities.
In *France*:

> "multi nobiles oppidani erant, qui magnorum possessores fundorum, in praecipuis baronibus nativae regionis pollebant, et multis magnae strenuitatis militibus, hereditario jure praeeminebant"

> [many nobles were townspeople, some of whom possessed land, they accompanied the principal barons native to that region, and the great vivacity of many of the soldiers was surpassed by hereditary right]

> From "Orderic Vital. IV" (for the year 1098), § 49, in Flach (1893, 2:368). — The list of the *hotels des grands* in Paris at the end of the 13th century is found in Géraud (1837, 627 f.).

235 Long before the forced *inurbamento* [urban migration], "the allures of comfort and sociability had caused individual families to settle in the city instead of in a tower on a lonely mountain peak" (Davidsohn 1896b, 1:343). For Venice, see R. Heynen (1905, 88).
236 With regards to the 'inurbamento della nobiltà' [the urban migration of some nobility], the information sought is found, for example, in Muratori (1739, 47); Bethmann-Hollweg (1846, 164 ff.); C. Bertagnolli (1881, 175); E. Poggi (1845, 2:163 ff.); and in the first edition of this

work (Sombart 1902, 1:313 ff.;2:198 f.).
237 See the first edition (Sombart 1902, 1:311 f.), and the literature mentioned there.
238 Bonifaccio (1744, 153).
239 Botero (1665, Lib. II, Cap. X, 112). (The work first appeared in Italian in 1589.)
240 "ils tirèrent leur subsistance de tout l'univers" [they drew their subsistence from the whole universe] (Montesquieu 1834, 3:110, Livre XX, Ch. V).
241 "extensive commerce checks itself, by raising the price of all labour and commodities" (Hume 1793, 2:207).
242 See the numbers underlying this calculation above on p. 174.
243 Lüneburg was in the year 1227 the most significant city of the duchy next to Brunswick (Heineken 1908, 21).
244 Ermisch (1891, 92). Cf. C. E. Leuthold (1889, 304 ff.).
245 Ermisch (1890, 148, 150).
246 Aronius (1902, 70 § 168).
247 "Mag. Adami gesta Hammenburgensis ecclesiae pontificum" in MGH SS (Vol. 7, Liber II, § 58, 326–327) (10th century).
248 Rietschel (1897, 36).
249 Dürr in Vol. 3 of A. Schmidt (1772, 3:190 ff., §§ 23-24).
250 Grandidier (1897, 363); cited in W. Kothe (1903, 36).
251 Kothe (1903, 123), op. cit., 123.
252 According to document No. 71 in Wiegand (1886, 46).
253 Henaux (1872, 200). Cf. M. L. Polain (1847).
254 Bücher (1886, 520).
255 Kallen (1907, 103). Cf. H. Schaefer (1903, 159 f.), and Kisky (1906).
256 Lethmate (1912, 34).
257 Stubbs (1874, 3:378).
258 G. Schmidt (1883, 2:550 §1594; 4:48ff. §2678).
259 Brackmann (1899, 69 f.).
260 MGH SS (Vol. 16, 253).
261 Rietschel (1905, 330).
262 See, for example, for Halle, Hertzberg (1889, 1:18 ff.). The garrison of Harzburg amounted to 300 men, that of Sachsenburg opposite, to 200. Source in Waitz (1844, 8:406). Why Waitz speaks in the text of "even 1,200", I do not know.
263 "orta est [...] inter vendentes et ementes [...] sedicio per scutarios regis in suburbio. Deinde clamor ingens tollitur, forenses campanae pulsantur."
[Discord has arisen between the buyers and sellers and the soldiers in a suburb. Next a great clamour is raised, and the city bells are tolled.]
"Udalrici Codex" §260 in Jaffé (1869, 445); cited in Rietschel (1905, 67).
264 Von Below (1892, 115).
265 Most of the material has been compiled by von Maurer (1862 Vol. I & II). Cf. also Waitz (1844, 6:323 ff.;7:302 ff.) regarding officials of the princes. But nowhere does one find figures.

266 We are informed about the government administration of the English kings, which was centralised early on (from the time of Henry I) in London, by Stubbs (1874, 1:406 ff.). The *curia regis* comprised the Exchequer, the supreme tribunal of the judicature, and the ministry of justice; in it sat the high dignitaries with a staff of officials.

267 "Thietmari chronicon" in MGH SS (Vol. 3, 744, Liber II § 2).

268 "opus construende urbis a circummanentibus illarum partium incolis nostro regio [...] iuri debitum."
[the work of building the city out of the surrounding area by residents of those parts was in our district [...] a legal obligation]
Document for 965 in MGH DD O I (No. 300, 416).

269 "eos qui ad civitatem vestram edificandam confluxerunt"
[they gathered those who were building your city]
From a Magdeburg customary law from the 13th century, cited in von Maurer (1870, 1:122).

270 "Wilhelmi Chronicon Andrensis monasterii" in MGH SS (Vol. 24, § 116, 724). See other instances in Waitz (1844, 8:210 ff.). For *England*, see Maitland (1907, 186 ff.).

271 See for *Germany*, for example, Damas (1879); one of the few writings from which one learns something about the history of *cities*. Bresslau (1884). Hauck (1904, 3:334 ff. (10th Century); 3:924 ff. (11th Century)). For individual cities, see Lesser (1888, 32 ff.); and Cardauns (1880, 142 ff.) for the later period.
A list of the large *French* church constructions of the 11th and 12th centuries is found in Levasseur (1900, 1:394 ff.). For *England*, Cunningham assumes that the significant development of construction activity in the 12th century caused a strong immigration, particularly of Flemish craftsmen. With good grounds against Ashley, see Cunningham (1895, 192 f.).

272 The *Tractus de laudibus Parisius* was written in the year 1323. Published in Le Roux de Lincy and Tisserand (1867). Cf. Boutié (1911, 333).

273 Rathgen (1881). Imbart de la Tour (1896).

274 Rietschel (1897, 39).

275 "salam [...] cum stationibus inibi banculas ante se habentibus"
[the hall [...] with stations therein and benches before the holdings themselves]
From MGH DD O I (No.145, 226), cited in Hartmann (1904b, 103).

276 Hence the expressions:

"cujus [...] *aedificandi et construendi* mercatum"

[of which [...] the building and construction of the market] (Baudi di Vesme, Desimoni, and Poggi 1873, 765 No. 442),

"mercatum *erigere* decrevimus"

[We decided to *erect* a market] (Janicke 1873, 1:6, §7),

which we encounter so often in the early medieval sources. Thus, however, also the donations of 'stationes' and their enjoyment, to which we

owe the frequent mention of this facility in the documents. See, for example, the documents which Schaube (1906, 9–11 and elsewhere) and Hartmann (1904b, 112) mention.
277 The *villani* of Aucklandshire had 18 boothes (*bothas*) to erect at the fair of St Cuthbert. See Seebohm (1883, 71).
278 "Johannes Ballard tenet mansum suum in Villa de Sancto Ivone juxta portam prioratus pro quo dat infirmario Ramesiae XX solidos per annum et *locat tempore nundinarum frontes et arreragia domorum suarum in eodem manso existentium*"
[Johannes Ballard tenants his dwelling in the monastery of Saint Ivone in the town of St Ives near the gate of the priory, for which he gives per year 20 solidos to the infirmary of Ramsey on condition that *they set up for the time of nine days in front and behind their houses in the same way as the existing dwelling*] (from 1251). (Hart and Lyons 1884, 1:286–87).
Of another farmer, it states:

"Et sustinet tres frontes in nundinis ad opus Abbatis"

[And he supports three fronts in the fair for the Abbot's need] (Hart and Lyons 1884, 1:291).

279 See references in R. Sohm (1890, 20). It is especially graphically described by F. V. Zillner (1890, 1:66 ff.).
280 "In eadem valle est vicus celeberrimus, Bristow nomine, in quo est portus navium ab Hibernia et Norvegia et ceteris transmarinis terris venientium *receptaculum*"
[In the same valley is the famous town of Bristol, in which is the port for ships coming from Ireland and Norway and other foreign countries, and *a place of shelter*] (12th century) (Hamilton 1870, 292 §154).
The *negotiatores* in Verdun had a:

"claustrum muro instar oppidi exstructum, ab urbe quidem Mose interfluente seiunctum, sed pontibus duobus interstratis ei annexum"

[a gate in the wall of the town built, the Moselle in fact flows in-between separating from the town, but the bridge connected it to the two roads]

From "Richeri historiarum" in MGH SS (Vol. 3, 629, Liber III, §103) (10th century).

Similar events in Magdeburg, see "Thietmari chronicon" in MGH SS (Vol. 3, 738, Liber I, §7), cited in Lamprecht (1885, 2:252).
281 Thus the houses in Münster which stand beside the market betray even today by their manner of construction "that they arose from the upgrading of market stalls" (Philippi 1894, 14).
282 Like the *negotiatores* who in the 11th century had migrated from Rouen and Caen to London in the wake of the conqueror. "No sooner had London submitted to the Norman Conqueror than we are told, 'many of the citizens of Rouen and Caen passed over thither, preferring to be dwell-

ers in that city'". According to the Vita S. Thomae (Giles 1845, 2:73) (cited in Gross (1890, 1:4) and Sharpe (1894, 1:30)). The traders from Bardowick moved to Lübeck, see Warncke (1912, 13).

283 The positive perquisites (like granting free land for building, etc.) will have exercised a somewhat larger influence on the decisions of dithering traders. See von Maurer (1870, 1:407); Waitz (1844, 8:388 ff.). In the same manner, he can be induced to remain constantly in one place through rules which tie perquisites expressly to *the condition of being settled*, as perhaps those of the Count of Flanders from the year 1127 in which he conferred customs duty privileges for St Omer:

> "omnes qui gildam eorum habent, et ad illam pertinent et infra cingulam ville sue manent, liberos omnes a teloneo facio ad portam Dichesmude et Graveningis"

> [all who have their guild, and they belong to it and they remain within the town belt, I make all free of tolls as far as the port of Diksmuide and Gravelines] (Gross 1890, 1:290)

But the key thing for the decision of our "merchant" always remains the outlook for a sufficient clientele.

284 From "Johannis Longi Chronica Sancti Bertini" in MGH SS (Vol. 25, 768).

285 Arnold (1854, 2:173) for Worms and Speyer; von Maurer (1870, 3:44) for Cologne, Basel, and Regensburg. The origin of the beguinages is in Belgium. Cf. in general, Uhlhorn (1882, 2:), and the thorough study of von Woikowsky-Biedau (1891).

286 Details over the number of benefices in the hospices of Lüneburg are given by Zechlin (1907, 48). They are, however, not complete for the Middle Ages. Nevertheless a few hundred are therein.

287 Bücher's work on the population of Frankfurt still contains the most and the best material. But even Bücher confesses to being an "ignoramus". Just like the only monograph known to me which deals with this phenomenon, the work of Kniecke (1893), which in consequence of the deficiency of factual material occupies itself with formal legal problems. Characteristically, in the giant arsenal of material which is called von Maurer's *Geschichte der Stadtverfassung*, the page which concerns itself with our problem (1870, 1:408) is about the only page in the entire work without notes. Cf. Otto (1893, 69 ff.) (15th century, worked according to Bücher's method); and Bungers (1896, 44 ff.) (13th century and subsequent, sourced from land registers).

288 "In metu erant omnes Saxionae civitates"
[All the Saxon communities existed in fear]
In the "Mag. Adami gesta Hammenburgensis ecclesiae pontificum" in MGH SS (Vol. 7, Liber 2, § 31, 317).

289 See "Ortliebi Zwifaltensis Chronicon" in MGH SS (Vol. 10, § 9, 77–78). We find the same stream of bonded serfs in other cities. For Constance, see Mone (1848, 1:140); for Basel, see Damas (1879, 43); for Florence, see Davidsohn (1896b, 1:607 f.). Pirenne tells us that the weavers from

the countryside were settling in the cities of Flanders and Brabant from the middle of the 11th century. Whether those were the "bonded" or the "free" country weavers remains to be seen. It is of course also quite indifferent for the economic effect (Pirenne 1910, 21). No sources are provided. Cf. also Kober (1908, 45 f.).

290 W. Wittich, for example, reports it with respect to the manumitted tenant farmers [*Laten*] in northwest Germany (1896, 329).

291 "la population de la France paraît avoir très notablement augmenté" [the population of France seems to have increased markedly] is the judgment over this period by such a good connoisseur as Levasseur (1900, 1:235).

The surplus of *German* population in the period from the 12th to the 13th century was so large that it sufficed to reconquer eastern Germany and fill the German cities, which in the 14th century had obtained a large part of the size which they then had until the 19th century. This is the outcome of the work of Püschel (1910).

292 For *Germany*, see Kniecke (1893, 61 ff. and elsewhere); the pointers to sources and literature are to be found there.
For *France*, see Stubbs (1874, 1:457); Flach (1893, 2:159 ff.; 2:208).
For *England*, see Gross (1890, 1:8); Green (1894, 1:174 f.).
For *Italy*, see Davidsohn (1896b, 1:608).

293 I forgo weighing down step by step with other literature or source evidence the depiction given in this chapter. It concerns in substance well-known things which I have only to classify in the context of my expositions. The particular way of seeing these things, which emerges perhaps here and there, naturally cannot, however, be established by "source evidence".

294 I think that one bars every path to understanding of the inner being of the medieval city when one equates them to the modern city and in contrast to the non-civic associations of the Middle Ages, as Paul Sander does (1906). As much as I applaud as correctly observed the contrast between the Middle Ages and modern times maintained by him (it is fundamentally that shown by Tönnies of community and association, organic and mechanical connectedness, traditional-empirical and rational formation, which also underlies my expositions everywhere), I consider it as much to be mistaken in attributing rational structures to the medieval city. Sander allots too determinant a significance to the circumstance of expansion (of large or small social circle) — *it depends on the spirit which dominates a group.*

295 In the introduction to the mining statute of the city of Goslar from the year 1494, Rammelsberg was usurped exclusively for the citizens and the city, and every intrusion of foreigners into the property and buildings of the mountain described as a "*depredation of the sustenance of the city*" (Wagner 1791, 1033 f.). Cf. in addition Neuberg (1892, 126).

296 This right of acquisition was allowed not only in 'smaller circumstances' to the citizens, as is suggested by Inama-Sternegg (1879, III.2:255). It applies in the largest city of the European Middle Ages as the so-called *droit de "part"* [right to a "share"] quite generally

(Boileau 1879, CXXXII). In England: "the right of Cavil" applied.
297 In the first edition, I argued extensively with the representatives of the conception of craftwork which deviates from my own. I now feel too strongly the pointlessness of such polemics to allot to them a part of the precious space in this work.
298 Which the French statutes express in a stereotyped form very nicely:

> "Quiconques veut estre de tel mestier, estre le puet poer tant qu'il sache le mestier et ait de coi."

> [Whoever wants to be in this occupation, to be the doer, he can as long as he knows the job and is quiet.]

[Tr.: above not cited by Sombart, but quoted in Demolins (1900, 284), and probably from Boileau (1879).]
299 Boehm (1876, 218; see also 45 f.). [Tr.: see also the "Reformation Kaiser Siegmunds" in MGH Staatsschriften (Vol. 6, 270).] In addition, Koehne (1906b). The asserted objections of Koehne against me and my use of the above quote from the named work are dealt with, I believe, by my remarks on page 63 ff.
300 Over the difference between the "craftsman" as economic subject in an economy organised on the basis of craftwork and the "craftsman" (in the technical sense) in the medieval economy of self-sufficiency or even in a modern capitalist enterprise, see the in-depth explanation in the first edition (Sombart 1902, 88 f.).
301 Since it does not involve here the verification of an empirical realisation of specific components of the craft-based organisation in history, no source evidence is required. Anyone who is interested in this is referred to the first edition (Sombart 1902), where it will be found in spades.
302 The idea of the production monopoly, which was originally conceived only for the craft as such without regard for the persons respectively forming the craft, then became nuanced with time so that the franchise confined itself to a specific number of masters — an idea which found its logical expression in the gradually more common "closing" of the craft.
303 Provisorischen Komitee des Zentralvereins zur Reorganisierung des Handwerkerstandes in Breslau (1848, 3). This expose also contains in addition a wealth of felicitous and subtle observations.
304 See the computations of J. G. Hoffmann (1839, 118) and the expositions based on it by Schmoller (1870, 338–39); also Schmoller (1895, 3:444-445) comes to similar results.
305 From a wood cutting of around 1600. Facsimile in Mummenhoff (1901, 94, picture #95).
306 See the rationale on page 229 ff.
307 Schrader (1890, 236 ff.).
308 Cf. Heideloff (1844, 16–18), and, in addition, von Maurer (1870, 2:483).

End Notes

309 I have in this section given here and there a few hints for the actual creation of sales conditions during the European Middle Ages in order to show that they were in fact favourable during this period for the craftwork-based organisation of economic life. In general, however, the "theoretical" character of the depiction is also preserved here.

310 As a result of the first Strasbourg town law, the furriers went themselves to Frankfurt for the purchase of the raw material. Cf. also von Below (1900a, 48).

311 An especially instructive example for the regulation of sales conditions for imported raw materials in favour of craftwork is offered by cotton, which was used by Basel's weavers of shirt material, see T. Geering (1886, 306 f.). Cf. also Hildebrand (1866, 224 f.).

312 Cf. Sidney and Beatrice Webb (1894, 25 f.).

313 In the year 1646, the Basel lace makers complained that those whom the council granted residence in Mönchenstein for two years behaved "contrary to all order", they "rushed through all the towns and villages with work" (Geering 1886, 600). It is described quite correctly even today honestly as a "maxim of craftwork" that the customer must seek out the producer. [Tr.: Sombart has the opaque reference "U. VI. 662" here.]

314 One can describe this competition as qualitative, and contrast it with the quantitative which is caused by the mere fact of the movement of a producer into the area.

315 Rogers (1884, 119 ff.). Based on wheat production.

316 Fabre (1893, 149 ff.). Based on an accounting over the Peter's pence [Tr.: an annual tax of one penny paid to Rome by every holder of land over a certain value.]

317 Levasseur (1889, 1:166 ff.; 1:288).

318 The criteria are: ca. 15,200 distinguished taxpayers in the *Registre de la Taille* (1292), and around 349 hectares and 61 ares [tr.: are = 100 m²] of cultivated land (Géraud 1837, 179 n. c; 471). I believe that accordingly a population of 60–70,000 heads represents the maximum. The space enclosed by the walls is somewhat greater than the total surface area of the fortress of Metz (1902/03 = 317.33 hectares). Metz had 68,598 residents in 1910. Cf. Leroux de Lincy and Tisserand (1867, 485 ff.).

319 According to the calculations of Topham (1785), whose method Rogers (1884, 118) makes his own. Based on tax lists which name every lay person over 14 years old.

320 Beloch (1895, 58). *Ypres*, according to a "credible" document, is supposed to have had 200,000 (!) residents in the 13th century (Vandenpeereboom 1878, 4:24). Documents from 1257 reduce the number to 40,000 (Pirenne 1899, 1:311).

321 Reisner (1903, 68; 78).

322 See the compilation under "Bevölkerungswesen" in the *Handwörterbuch der Staatswissenschaften* (Conrad et al. 1898, 2:663 f.), where for every number the sources from which they originate are named. The methods of investigation are handled by Jastrow (1886).

Cf. now Schmoller (1911, 167 ff.).
323 See note 319 on page 241.
324 Cf. Gross (1890, 73 n.4), where yet more pertinent literature is listed.
325 Rogers (1866, 1:55).
326 Eulenburg (1895, 448).
327 About 7 marks in present-day (1916) currency.
328 Vetter (1910, 63 ff.).
329 Schönberg (1879, 180–81).
330 Cf. the nice depiction in du Maroussem (1891, 2:29 ff.), where the clientele of a Parisian furniture maker in the 13th century is analysed.
331 For *England*, we hear occasionally of deliveries of larger quantities of clothing items to the poor, see Salzmann (1913, 137; 183): 1,000 ells of material; 150 pairs of shoes — 13th century. But those were surely rare exceptions.
332 First published by Géraud in Ser. I, Vol. 8 of the *Collection des documents inédits de l'histoire de France* (1837, 585 ff.), then by Scheler in Leipzig (1867). It would be a extraordinarily thankful task for an economic historian (with some spirit) to work on the *Dictionarius des Garlande* one day under a modern point of view. It contains an abundance of material, and it promises amply as much insight into medieval manufacturing existence as ten of the best guild statutes. — Another valuable source belonging to about the same period, from which we can extract interesting details over the quantity and type of wares offered for sale, are a few of the *fabliaux* [stories] of the 13th centuries; particularly "Le Dit des Marcheanz", which is printed in the second volume of the *Recueil des Fabliaux* published by Montaiglon and Raynaud (1872, 2:123 ff.). A precis is found in Hermann (1900, 36 f.).
333 Schmoller (1897, 372).
334 See what was noted above on page 165 f. about the strong agricultural element which even the larger cities had until deep into the Middle Ages.
335 While the Augsburg municipal law of 1276 expressly permitted the home slaughter of pigs, but forbade that of cattle, it surely concerned at the time only cattle raised by oneself. For no rational man would have thought to buy an ox at the market and slaughter it by himself at home!
336 "De Guillaume de S.-Germain, receveur de Berri, qu'il a livré pour la despense de l'ostel de mond. seigneur du froment des molins dud. seigneur à Raoulet de Ruelle, boulengier à Meun sur Yevre qui en a cuit et livré le pain pour lad. despense faicte à Meun sur Yevre ou mois d'aoust [mil] CCCLXXI."
[Guillaume St Germain, collector for de Berry, delivered for the expense of the house of the secular master of the wheat of the mill of the said master to Raoulet de Ruelle, baker at Meun-sur-Yèvre who cooked and delivered the bread for the expense of Meun-sur-Yèvre during the month of August 1371.] (Fagniez 1877, 166 n.2)
"... pro blado quod capitulum ipsum d. bolengario suo de quoquendo ministrat ..."

[... for corn which that very chapter managed through its baker for cooking ...] (Fagniez 1877, 166 n.3).

Fagniez's book is one of the best works on the history of manufacturing in the Middle Ages.

337 In the large (southern!) cities, there were, however, already also public cookshops like today's rotisseries in Italy. Thus we find in Paris in the 13th century the guild of "oyers hasteurs" [grillers of goose], of whom Boileau stipulated that they should only cook or roast good flesh.

338 For *German* cities, evidence in Inama-Sternegg (1879, III.2: 105); and Eulenburg (1896, 130). But even in *Paris*, one still had to bake at home at the end of the 13th century. I infer that from the fact that the millers had a double tariff: they received from the bakers 1 boisseau for every 2 setier, from the remaining clientele one for every setier; that is, however, the 'borgois' (Boileau 1879, 16 §V). It seems though as if the baking ovens, of which each of the better houses in Paris and other French cities had one ("les menus ménagiers de ladite ville [Melun], qui ne sont pas aisiés de cuire en leurs hostelz" [the household menus of the said town [Melun], which are not easy to cook in their lodgings] (Secousse 1734, 4:593)), were assigned only for the baking of smaller baked goods (not bread) and only came into use at specified times (for example, in years of high prices!) for baking bread. In comparison, both the large households of the rich lords and the religious institutes surely as a rule still baked in the 14th century, even in a big city like Paris, using their own baking ovens. See G. Fagniez (1877, 166 ff.) and the source cited above in footnote 336. The ordinariness of the numerous baking ovens themselves also speaks for the own-baking of the lords in the cities of the 13th and even part of the 14th centuries.

339 The tradition of brewing in turns [*Reihebrauen*] (in Regensburg 1230)! (Inama-Sternegg 1879, III.2:105). But there were already in the larger cities also wine and beer taverns which offered self-made or bought drinks — in 13th century Paris we find 56 "bufetiers vinetiers" [wine bars] and 37 "cervoisiers" [taverns].

340 See above note 335.

341 In Paris, the making of candles in the house was expressly permitted under the condition that a master candlemaker worked alongside. The housewife will of course have been irritated by the high payment which she gave the master (who was certainly entirely superfluous) and will have sought some passing candlemaker as help. But there the guild prohibition hits — no apprentice or journeyman (*valet*) without six years of apprenticeship behind him may help with the candlemaking in a private house. (Boileau 1879, 132 ff. § LXIV).

342 Schmoller (1897, 412); Inama-Sternegg (1879, III.2:125); Boileau (1879, 117 ff. § LVII).

343 Still even in Paris around the year 1400. Or is Poncete, the wife of Cardinot Auvry, who is described to us as "ligniere", and of whom we learn that she works sometimes in this house, sometimes that house (elle aloit aucune fois ouvrer par cy et par là [at any time she went here and there for work]), not a weaver? In the great Sachs-Villatte [Tr.:

German-French dictionary (1869-80)], under *linier* there is only the translation flax dealer, which obviously makes no sense. Was she a spinner? Did she prepare the flax so that the young women could then spin it? The source is: 22 October 1399, *Registre d'audience du Châtelet*, Y 5222, folio 142, cited in Fagniez (1877, 67 n.1).

344 In Heidelberg: Eulenburg (1896, 130); in Vienna: Eulenburg (1893, 282), and Zimmermann et al (1897, I.2:714); in Frankfurt am Main, "throughout": Bücher (1886, 230).

345 Bücher (1886, 230).

346 Thus the "magnans ou chaudronniers ambulants" [tinkers or itinerant copperworkers] — the mobile kettle menders in Paris (Boileau 1879, xc). Cf. also what is said below on page 255 about the pedlar craftwork of the Middle Ages.

347 Thus the wandering furniture menders, of whom mention appears in the 'Criées de Paris' [cries of Paris] of Guillaume de Villeneuve [Tr.: a 15th century French chronicler, see Crapelet and Villeneuve (1831, 137 ff.)].

348 See the compilation of source evidence in Inama-Sternegg (1879, III.2:78). In general, compare in this regard Bücher's various labours (1892; 1893). Bücher has rediscovered the 'Störer' for scholarship!

349 See for Lübeck, Hansen (1912, 56 ff., 142 f.). In the year 1579, 78.4% of all families had grain stores in the house. In Strasbourg (1473–77), of 26,198 residents, only 8,369 had no store of grain (Herzog 1909, 17).

350 For example, Herzog (1909, 19 ff.).

351 See evidence in Inama-Sternegg (1879, III.2:101); for Strasbourg see Herzog (1909, 38); for London (14th century), see Riley (1868, 129, 163); for Paris (14th century), see Fagniez (1877, 165), *Etudes*, 165; for Vienna (15th century), see Zimmermann et al (1897, II.2:694).

352 See Heideloff (1844); Janner (1876).

353 For example, Lamprecht (1885, 2:570 f., 2:613); and the works of D'Avenel (1894), Rogers (1884), etc., where building craftsmen's wages are found in excess.

354 For example, Rogers (1884, 103). — How a chapter tends to settle, by sending out a master builder and a chapter member in the possession of building materials for the building of their church, is described in an illustrative way for Xanten by Beissel (1885, 37 ff.).

355 For example, Fagniez for building glaziers (1898, 2:42 f., §21; 2:98 f., §42; 2:108 f., §51), and bell casting (1898, 2:128 ff., §59; 2:144 f., §61; 2:152 ff., §67); and Fagniez (1877, 359 ff., §XLII).

356 The London bricklayer's order of 1356 considers the "work in gross" (the undertaking of entire buildings by *one* building contractor) still as so unusual that with each undertaking of an entire building four or six masters had to stand guarantee. Cf. Brodnitz (1914, 28).

357 That the lime-burners and brickmakers in Venice were 'wage workers' up until the 14th century is accounted for by their statutes. It is, however, not evident whether they worked for the lime, brick, and stone dealers, or for the building owners. See their statutes in Monticolo (1896).

End Notes

358 Evidence in Fagniez (1877, 203; 359 ff., §XLII).
359 "Pro fabricando martellos" [hammers for construction] (Fagniez 1877, 359); "pro acuendo martelos" [hammers for sharpening] (Fagniez 1877, 204 n.3).
360 That surely formed the rule when the building was carried out in non-local places, like the rood screen in the cathedral at Troyes which Parisian masons executed (Fagniez 1877, 208).
361 "et une robe" [and a coat]; "aulne et demie de draps" [alder(?) and half a sheet]; and "une robe et unes chauces" [a coat and a stocking] are commonly recurring wage records (Fagniez 1877, 208 n.5).
362 An ample material for the history of "architects" and "building contractors" in the Middle Ages has been gathered by Fagniez (1877, 191 ff.). Also see the third volume of this work.
363 The linen yarn surely mostly, particularly in small cities; but even in Paris, where the weaver received the yarn either in strands or already in chains, "se aucuns ou aucune engagoit autrui file en pelote ou en chaine" [if they do not bind for others in a ball or a chain], (Boileau 1837, 390; Fagniez 1877, 229 n.2); and in Florence still in the 15th century (Sieveking 1906, 33). Likewise the woolen yarn, of which again it is reported for Paris that it was woven by hired weavers: "li mesme mestre doivent mettre en euvre le fil *come l'en leur baillera* à tistre les blans desus diz" [the same master must use the thread *that they will entrust to them* for weaving the white] (emphasis added) (Boileau 1837, 394; Fagniez 1877, 223 n.2). Occasionally the customer delivered to the weaver even the ingredients ("le suif et le son" [tallow and bran?] in Paris for the linen weaving (Fagniez 1877, 229)).
364 "si aliquem pannum ad chilendrandum datum fuerit" [if there was any cloth given to the calendrers] can be understood of the private citizen as well as of the cloth maker. See the Venetian guild statutes in Monticolo (1896, 142).
365 See for Bologna (13th century), Gaudenzi (1896, 133). Clear insights into the circumstances of the medieval tailoring business are given by the statutes of the tailors of Paris (Boileau 1879, 116 §LVI); for Venice in Monticolo (1896, 10–12); for Bologna in Gaudenzi (1896, 274 ff.).
There were men's and women's tailors in Paris (Boileau 1879, 15). The named statutes all originate from the 13th century.
366 Venice, see Monticolo (1896, 24).
367 *Statuts et ordonnances des marchands maîtres tailleurs d'habits, pourpointiers-chaussetiers de la ville, fauxbourgs, & banlieue de Paris* (France 1763). Cited in A. Franklin (1894, 89).
368 Boissonade (1900, 1:294).
369 See the sources in Fagniez (1877, 246 f.).
370 Zimmermann (1897, II.2:714).
371 For Venice: Monticolo (1896, 116); for Breslau: Eulenburg (1892, 73); for London: Riley (1868, 29), cited in Brodnitz (1914, 28).
372 For Osnabrück: Inama-Sternegg (1879, III.2:81).
373 See "Statuti della Società dei Ferratori" in Gaudenzi (1896, 186, 189).
374 For Lübeck (1454) see Inama-Sternegg (1879, III.2:81).

375 In Nuremberg's *Germanisches Nationalmuseum*. Now reproduced in the instructive work of Mummenhoff (1901, 40 ff.).
376 Boileau (1879, 7 § XX), and cf. in general Fagniez (1877, 108 f.).
377 Blümcke (1884, 210).
378 Boileau (1879, CXXXIV) and in the individual statutes therein.
379 In Vienna at the high market (13th century), where the shoemakers had their products for sale on market days. See Uhlirz's article in Zimmermann (1897, II.2:712).
380 In Zurich (14th century). See Fecht (1909, 29).
381 See the summary in von Below (1905, 57 ff.).
382 See, for example, Boileau (1879, 27 § IX, 29 § X). For the south German cities (Augsburg, Ulm, Strasbourg, Worms), see Eckert (1910).
383 A good idea is given of the half resident, half pedlar-like organisation of the retail business of such a *mercier* by a poem from the 14th century shared by Franklin (1894, 5 ff.); cf. Levasseur (1900, 1:332), and the statutes of the *merciers* from the year 1324 (Fagniez 1898, 2:58 § 27).
384 We are informed of their development in *Germany* by von Maurer (1870, 1:282 ff.); for *France*, see in particular P. Huvelin (1897, 604–17) for a detailed bibliography of the pertinent literature.
385 I have already given the following overview in substance in the first edition (Sombart 1902, 1:96-113). So as to preserve the picture's colourfulness, I will repeat it here with a few additions. I could easily augment to a considerable extent the evidence for the incidence of trade articles in inter-locale traffic during the Middle Ages, if I wanted to make use of the extremely diligent compilation which I now find in chapters III and IV of the stately work of J. G. van Dillen (1914); but I forbear from that and direct the patient reader to that work. The writer would like in connection to my efforts in the first edition to confute once more, and more thoroughly, the "theory" of Bücher on the "closed city economy". He has signalled, as a continuation of this volume comprising 224 closely printed large quarto pages, a second volume which shall occupy itself with the contrast, coined by myself, of the economy of satisfaction of needs [*Bedarfsdeckungswirtschaft*] with the acquisition economy [*Erwerbswirtschaft*]. Latterly, abundant material for the knowledge of international trade during the Middle Ages has been produced by Bugge (1914, 106 ff.).
386 Document from 1104. Cf. Lamprecht (1885, 2:313 f.).
387 Von Maurer (1870, 1:318-319); and von Below (1897, 236). Levying of market stall money from foreign cobblers as well in Nordhausen at the beginning of the 14th century (Falke 1869, 142).
388 Ashley (1896, 1:100).
389 Cf., for example, volume 4 of the *Zeitschrift für Geschichte des Oberrheins* (Franz Josef Mone 1853), and Schmoller (1897, 104, 110).
390 Even in the 11th century, we already find cloths as objects of international trade; thus in England according to Aelfric's colloquy (ca. 1000) in Thorpe (1834, 101–8), cited in Ashley (1896, 1:70; 1:114 n.9). And, in still earlier times, the trade returned with so-called "Friesian cloths" (Klumker 1899). It is, however, improbable that it involved the

End Notes

products of craftwork-based weaving before the 12th century. Cf. Kober (1908), and Häpke (1906).

391 A good idea of the great extent of the international cloth trade in the 14th and 15th centuries is given by the overview of the linen or cloth types which came to Danzig for sale in Hirsch (1858, 250 ff.).
392 See, over the linen trade in the Middle Ages in general, and that of Constance especially, the efforts of Schulte (1900, 1:112 ff.).
393 In Klöden (1841, 1:33).
394 Lewis (1908, 33 ff.).
395 Dunn (1844, 11 ff.). Salzmann (1913, 1 ff.) (on the basis of new handwritten materials).
396 Salzmann (1913, 125).
397 According to the oldest customs duty register from the world of the Alps, composed by Bishop Giso of Aosta in 900 (Schulte 1900, 1:68).
398 Heyd (1879, 1:424; 1:426; 1:437).
399 Kunze (1891, xlv).
400 Schulte (1900, 1:693 and elsewhere).
401 Höhlbaum (1876, 1:144 §432, and elsewhere).
402 Schaube (1897, 248).
403 Cunningham (1890, 1:184).
404 Hirsch (1858, 257 ff.).
405 Wehrmann (1864, 273).
406 Schulte (1900, 1:594).
407 Customs duty register of Bishop Giso of Aosta (Schulte 1900, 1:68).
408 Ashley (1896, 1:70) for Aelfric's colloquy (around 1000).
409 Customs duty privileges of the abbey of St Simeon from 1104 (Falke 1869, 139); customs duty privileges of the merchants of Dinant, conferred by the Senate of the city of Cologne (Ennen and Eckertz 1860, 1:563 f. § 80). See also Schreiber (1828, 1:5-6).
410 Falke (1869, 144).
411 Falke (1869, 146).
412 Höhlbaum (1876, 1:143 ff. § 432).
413 Kunze (1891, xlv; 334).
414 Wehrmann (1864, 272 ff.).
415 Hirsch (1858, 257 ff.).
416 Schulte (1900, 1:692 ff.).
417 Merchant regulations of the named cities in Klöden (1841, 1:31 ff. § 3).
418 Heyd (1879, 1:125-126). Schaube (1906, 23 f.).
419 Customs duty register of Bishop Giso of Aosta (960) (Schulte 1900, 1:68). In Schulte's opinion, it involves products of the Milanese weapons industry (1900, 1:69).
420 Beyer (1860, 1:467–469 § 409; 2:280–282 § 242). Falke (1869, 139). Von Below (1897, 148).
421 Kunze (1891, xlv).
422 Falke (1869, 144).
423 Frensdorff (1882, cxxxi n.6).
424 Hirsch (1858, 261).
425 Wehrmann (1864, 456).

426 Cf. Boeheim (1898, 171 ff.).
427 The Middle Ages had for them the description *minuta*, or *minuta mercimonia* [petty goods]. Cf. Kunze (1891, 49 § 56; 108 § 154; 346-353 § 374) regarding import articles for England during the 13th and 14th centuries. One also understands the same in many cases under *cromerey, merserie, mercimonia institoria*:

"*calibem et ferrum ac alia merc institoria*"

[peddler of firewood and iron and other merchandise]

(Höhlbaum 1876, 87 No. 224; 103 No. 251 Art. 11; 143 No. 343 Art. 11; 250 No. 610; 416 No. 965 Art. 1).
428 See, for example, the customs duties for passing through the city of Pirna (Falke 1869, 144). Numerous sorts of small steel implements were in the trader rolls of Anklam (1330) and Goslar (before 1359) (Klöden 1841, 1:31 ff.).
429 In Lübeck, the Nurembergers were consequently allowed to sell in open cellars wares finished by their craftsmen (15th century): locks, knives, forks, mirrors, wooden and lead paternosters, awls, tinplate, gauntlets, steel clamps, flutes, brass buckles, child's bells, pewter bowls, horse bridles, stirrups, spurs, spectacles, brass thimbles, lead buckles, tins, plates, and child bindings (Wehrmann 1864, intro., 107). We find moreover among products of the Nuremberg metal industries in the trade with Italy during the 14th and 15th centuries: altar candlesticks, writers' candlesticks, pendant lamps, brass bowls, carriages, enema syringes, compasses, barber bowls, shears, etc. (Schulte 1900, 1:719). Evidence for the extent of the Nuremberg exports is rendered by the extremely numerous *customs duty exemptions* which Nuremberg was able to obtain at various customs places. The schedule from 1332 lists no less than 69 places in which customs duty exemptions existed, and included the entire Kingdom of Arles (Schulte 1900, 1:658).
430 Customs duty register of Bishop Giso of Aosta (Schulte 1900, 1:68).
431 Schaube (1906, 24).
432 Von Below (1897, 152).
433 Falke (1859, 1:74).
434 Kunze (1891, xlv).
435 Register of customs duties for the Archbishop-governed Cochem (Lamprecht 1885, 2:311).
436 Hirsch (1858, 253).
437 Sneek's town records from 1456 (Hegel 1891, 2:290).
438 Original excerpt in Lamprecht (1885, 2:315).
439 Geering (1886, 141).
440 Hegel (1891, 1:99). Cf. Salzmann (1913, 174).
441 Hegel (1891, 1:280-281; 1:293).
442 Frensdorff (1882, cxvi).
443 Grünhagen (1884, 39).
444 Falke (1859, 1:135).
445 Falke (1859, 1:127).

446 Klöden (1841, 1:36).
447 Höhlbaum (1876, 1:144 f. No. 432).
448 Boissonnade (1900, 1:14).
449 According to Gross (1890, 1:46); Doren (1893, 150 n.3).
450 Von Below (1897, 153).
451 Schulte (1900, 1:74).
452 Frensdorff (1882, cxvi).
453 Verein für Geschichte und Alterthum Schlesiens (1857, 8:20).
454 Schulte (1900, 1:74).
455 Schulte (1900, 2:105).
456 Trader regulations of 1330 (Klöden 1841, 1:33).
457 Verein für Geschichte und Alterthum Schlesiens (1857, 8:19 f.).
458 Pauli (1847, 1:52).
459 Schreiber (1828, 1:6).
460 Schulte (1900, 2:105 Doc. 188).
461 Höhlbaum (1876, 1:144-147 No. 432).
462 Stieda (1894, 111).
463 Schulte (1900, 1:167).
464 "Dict. du mercier" in Crapelet & Villeneuve (1831).
465 Santini (1895, 190).
466 Wehrmann (1864, 272 ff., 286 f.).
467 Hirsch (1858, 256).
468 Hirsch (1858, 256).
469 Klöden (1841, 1:33, 1:53).
470 Verein für Geschichte und Alterthum Schlesiens (1857, 8:19 f.).
471 Hegel (1891, 1:407).
472 Schulte (1900, 1:706).
473 Stieda (1894, 111). Cf. also Höhlbaum (1876, 254 No. 621; 449 No. 1017 Art. 3; 452 No. 1018 Art. 8).
474 Sello (1884, 12).
475 Forestié (1890, lii ff.).
476 Nirrnheim (1895, lviii).
477 Schulte (1900, 1:718).
478 Geering (1886, 233).
479 See Kitchins introduction to the charters of Edward III for the St Giles Fair (1886).
480 Evidence for *England*: Green (1894, 2:40); for *France*: Fagniez (1877, 184); for *Strasbourg*: Herzog (1909, 60 f.).
481 Ubiquities in the sense of Alfred Weber (1912, 1:51; 1929, 51).
482 See the excerpts in Rogers (1884, 105 f.).
483 See, for example, Schulte (1900, 1:112).
484 Geering (1886, 308). A good overview of the extensive development of specialities in the *cloth trade* is given by the poem from 12th century Flanders "Conflictus ovis et lini" [the dispute between sheep and flax], lines 169–212 (Haupt 1859, 220 f.).
485 Cf., alongside the already named works of Böheim, perhaps even van Duyse (1897, 65 f.).
486 For example, Chatillon-Plessis (1894, 225).

487 Bücher (1886, 1:148 ff.).
488 Eulenburg (1896, 112).
489 See the calculations in Fagniez (1877, 6 ff.).
490 Schmoller (1897, 92).
491 Eulenburg (1893, 286).
492 See for *France*, Levasseur (1900, 1:500); for *Italy*, Kowalewsky (1895, 414 ff.); for *England*, Cunningham (1890, 1:306 f.).
493 Over the sparseness of the sources, see Inama-Sternegg (1899).
494 Lamprecht (1885, 1:164).
495 Schmoller (1871, 299–300).
496 Cunningham (1890, 1:170). Denton (1888, 128–31). Rogers (1898, 46 f.).
497 Levasseur (1889, 1:140 ff.).
498 De Borchgrave (1865, 37).
499 Vanderkindere (1879, 135 ff.).
500 Over the high child mortality in the Middle Ages, see Bücher (1886, 45 f.).
501 "Following on the hardship, one can almost say, were always great illnesses of the people; *mortalitas* and *pestilentia* are inseparable companions of every famine." (Curschmann 1900, 60).
502 For the famines, see Curschmann (1900). With it, cf. Denton (1888, 91 ff.): "famine [...] was so common in England, that all attempts to specify the years of scarcity would only mislead" (1888, 92); Creighton (1891, 15–52) (a good depiction for the period from 679 to 1322), and Levasseur (1900, 1:523), who assumes 19 years of famine for France in the 14th century, and 16 in the 15th century. — Over the *plague*, cf. in addition to the well-known work of Hecker & Hirsch (1865):
 - for *Germany*: Hoeniger (1882); Lechner (1884);
 - for *France*: Levasseur (1900, 1:521 ff.; 1889, 1:176), and the literature cited therein;
 - for *Italy*: the great work of Corradi (1865), (up to 1500) also covers the famines; and Kowalewsky (1895, 406);
 - for the *Netherlands*, especially for *Belgium*: the comprehensive work of Torfs (1839);
 - for *England*: Creighton (1891). In England, the problem has experienced an especially in-depth treatment. The most important writings are assembled and discussed in the historical introduction by Petit-Dutaillis to Réville (1898, xxx ff.).
503 Rogers assumes ⅓, Cunningham ½, and Denton even more.
504 D'Avenel (1894, 1:273 ff.).
505 Rogers (1866, 1:24 ff.). Seebohm (1883, 33 f., 54).
506 See the work of Borchgrave cited in note 498 to page 271.
507 Cunningham (1895, 177 ff.).
508 Shared in Liesegang (1897, 644 n.1).
509 Document from 19 April 1399 in Fagniez (1898, 2:167 f. No.70).
510 Boissonade (1900, 1:370).
511 Förster (1869, 3:130 f.; 4:69 f.).
512 Semper (1878, 2:514).

End Notes

513 Bücher (1886, 1:116 f.).
514 "C'est que mille inégalités naturelles empêchaient l'uniformité, à laquelle tendaient les règlements"
[It was because a thousand natural inequalities prevented the uniformity to which the rules were directed] (Fagniez 1877, 120).
515 Schönberg (1879, 180–81).
516 Eulenburg (1895, 457). "It has absolutely not been proven that at the time a middling estate formed the norm, [...] we observe rather amongst the civic population the greatest(?) contrasts of rich and poor" (Eulenburg 1895, 459).
517 Eulenburg (1895, 460). [Tr.: quote marks added as this paragraph is word for word from Eulenburg.]
518 Bücher (1886, 1:91).
519 According to the figures of the Ulnagers Accounts for 1395 which are provided from the handwritten sources by Salzmann (1913, 157 f.). Cf. below on pages 278 and 283.
520 Mone (1865, 15, 19).
521 Document from 1415 in Fagniez (1898, 203 No. 108).
522 Boileau (1879, 93 ff. § L).
523 Salzmann (1913, 157 f.).
524 As, for example, Schanz does in his otherwise meritorious book, *Zur Geschichte der deutschen Gesellenverbände* (1877).
525 Text in Schanz (1881, 2:598-600).
526 Master Tönnies Evers in Lübeck (16th century) had at times 12 journeymen and seven apprentices in service. The guild, however, enforced their dismissal (Warncke 1912, 87).
527 Fagniez treats the Parisian mills of the 13th and 14th centuries most in-depth in his *Etudes* (1877, 156 ff.).
528 Schmoller (1897, 110).
529 Cf. the detailed description of the Aachen cloth making in Thun (1879, 1:8 ff.), and that of the Black Forest locales in Gothein (1892, 531). From both works I have obtained the impression that the purely craftwork-based character even of the export cloth making remained preserved until far into the so-called modern period. Until deep into the 18th century craftwork-based organisation was also a part of the *English* and *French* cloth making industries. I will speak about that in-depth in this work in a later volume with the depiction of the essence of early capitalist manufacturing.
530 Cf. the graphic description of those struggles in Vanderkindere (1879, 147 ff.).
531 Espinas & Pirenne (1906).
532 Doren (1901, 1:27).
533 Again, the depiction in a later volume of this work is to be referred to.
534 Sieveking (1897, 101 ff.).
535 Sandi (1755, 2.1:247, 256); cited in Smith (1776, Bk. III, Ch. 3).
536 "Che ciascun mercadante testor abbia libertà di poter tessere al suo propio con un solo tellar con le sue man proprie potendo tuor un garzon e non più per aida quel tellar"

[That each merchant weaver has the freedom to be able to weave for himself with a single loom with his own hands, since he can no longer be an apprentice for that loom] (Broglio d'Ajano 1893, 49 f.).
537 Tommasi (1847, 397 ff.); cited in Sieveking (1897, 129).
538 Geering (1886, 465 f.).
539 Geering (1886, 306 f.).
540 See the thorough bibliography in the next volume, and Chapter 29.
541 Beck (1884, 1:945 ff.; 2:177 ff. and elsewhere). See also the next volume.
542 Thun (1879, 2:8 ff.). Cf. Boeheim (1897), and Beck (1884, 2:342 ff.; 2:987 ff.).
543 Schoenlank (1894, 48). Cf. also Falke (1859, 1:125 f.).
544 Cf. for their characteristics also Roth (1800, 3:).
545 Frankenstein (1887, 48).
546 Beckmann (1777, 10:148).
547 "Trade must according to its nature be practised capitalistically." (Ehrenberg 1901, 123).
548 Stephan (1869).
549 Doren (1901, 1:68).
550 The licences amounted (1277/78) to 4,235 sacks (Kunze 1891, 332 No. 366).
551 Doren (1901, 1:54).
552 Over the incompetence of the Middle Ages for statistics, see Lamprecht (1885, 2:6 ff.).
553 Stieda (1887, lvi, lvii). Stieda's Introduction to this edition belongs undoubtedly to the most valuable publications over medieval trade. Cf. also Wendt (1902).
554 Naudé (1889); in addition, see *my* review of the book (1890, 312 f.). I have attempted there to obtain in a mathematical way and through comparison with modern circumstances a more exact idea of the extent of the grain trade of Hamburg and Stettin in their prime.
555 That was perhaps two thirds of the total exports according to the calculations of Schaube on page 68 of the essay cited on page 320.
556 Kunze (1891, 332 No. 366). The numbers mentioned relate to the licences issued, and thus depict the *maximum* exports, which was mostly not reached.
557 A well-known chronicler writes around 1500 that there were townsmen who in one year probably shipped 400 lasts of grain (Naudé 1889, 32). That was thus a wonder. In 1580, the Stettin merchants petitioned that one would prefer, instead of imposing an oath on them, prescribing how much grain — 60 or 100 lasts — the merchant may buy as a maximum according to the opportunity of the time. Within an entire year (?), it would almost appear unbelievable. But if 400 lasts was something special, then 100 lasts are unexceptional, and as the result of an enforced limit, not even so little. In the same year (1580), the guild brothers complained, "it is for pity that 6, 8, or at most 11 or 12 persons would have the grain turnover exclusively in their hands" (Naudé 1889, 73). It was thus already in a state which was felt to be unhealthy, so

that we must assume for the earlier period a much larger number of dealers.
558 Bücher (1893, 119 n.23).
559 Simonsfeld (1887, 2:10; 2:18 ff.; 2:112). "A peculiarity of the Middle Ages is the strong emergence of the mercantilistic officials and clerical elements (brokers, public measurers, weighers, etc.)."
560 As a symptom of low turnover which is likewise still of a general nature, the long procrastination with the actual silver standard could be mentioned. The first gold coins were minted in Germany in 1325 (Schulte 1900, 1:329); in England in 1344 (Rymer 1727, 5:403).
561 Rehme (1894). Cf. also Pauli (1847, 1:140 ff.).
562 From the literature over *commenda* and similar relationships, which has also surely been completely worked over by Goldschmidt, the following stand out: Lastig (1879); Lattes (1899, 154 ff.); and Max Weber (1889). Cf. also the works cited on page 323 f.
563 Schönberg (1879, 180–81).
564 Hartung (1895a; 1895b). The wealth tax amounted to ½% for real estate, ¼% for chattels; we do not know how the wealth was distributed over the two categories, since we only know the total tax paid by a person. I have assumed an equal relationship between the two categories of wealth. That 6,000 fl. would thus be equal to 4,000 fl. in real estate or 8,000 fl. in chattels. The tax is 10 fl. [Tr.: Sombart's arithmetic is flawed here.]
565 Regarding this, see von Below (1900a, 42 ff.), and cf. my depiction in a later volume of this work.
566 Rogers (1884, 124).
567 The calculation is found in Rymer's *Foedera*. It is printed in Jacob (1838, 1:222). [Tr.: the quoted text and figures are from the last-named. Quote marks were omitted by Sombart.]
568 Stieda (1887, lxix).
569 Hirsch (1858, 264). "In that time, it lay in the interest of sea captains to run as shallow draughted vessels as possible, because they could sail with these into shallow harbours most comfortably. Nobody probably thought of dredging work in larger measure, or of deepening the mouth", is remarked of Stettin in the 14th century by Theodor Schmidt (1859, 8). Cf. Siewert (1897, 207 ff.). The drawings of Willy Stöwer portray very graphically the various types of Hanseatic ship in the 14th and 15th century. They are in fact punts [*Nachen*] in the modern sense, like those which only rarely still frequent the German rivers for economic purposes. See the table in the Helmolt edited *Weltgeschichte* (1899, VII:36-37).
570 Printed by Tafel and Thomas (1856, 3:403-448).
571 Stieda (1887, lxxxviii ff.). Cf. Stieda (1884, 77 ff.).
572 Kunze (1891, 340 ff. No. 372).
573 Cf. Häpke (1905, 1079).
574 Heynen (1905, 91).
575 Davidsohn (1896a, 3:123 No. 623; 3:125 No. 635; 3:158 No. 770; 3:193 No. 974).

576 Sieveking (1906, 17 f.).
577 Schulte (1900, 1:116).
578 See "Chronik des Burkard Zink 1368-1468" in Frensdorff et al (1865, 2:128, 132).
579 Schulte (1900, 2:105 Doc. 188).
580 Geering (1886, 145). For comparison, one calls perhaps on Riga's article of grievance towards England from the year 1406, in which the wares of three sunken trading ships and their owners were listed. Here it also concerns hundreds of small traders, of whom every single one had as many wares on the ship as a pack carrier today carries on his back or at all events a "travelling hawker" pushes in his cart. The documents are printed in Kunze (1891, 241 ff. No. 326).
581 Häpke (1908, Appendix).
582 Geering (1887, 43). Printed also as Supplement VIII to Inama-Sternegg (1899, III.2:523).
583 "Von Kaufshandlung und Wucher" in Luther (1899, 15:296).
584 "Trade" is "honest", "when it happens [...] for an honest, similar and real act as especially for sustaining his house and his children and servants according to his status"; it is "dishonest" and "ungodly", "first of all through the rampant, discontinuous, inordinate stinginess of a man". As per the excerpts from the writing of Christian Kuppener over usury in Neumann (1865, 594-595 D6 & E1). An entirely craftwork-based spirit is expressed also by the "Regeln frommer Kaufmannschaft" [Rules of Pious Trade] (Neumann 1865, 606 F3v), whose No. 4 states that the profit of the trading business should not be taken from avarice, but as compensation for the work expended.
585 Thus Heinrich von Langenstein describes the merchant next to the farmer and craftsman as a man who provides "*the necessary livelihood for himself and others in the sweat of his brow through physical work*" in contrast to the spiritual workers and the idlers to whom the contracting usurers belonged. From the "Tractatus de contractibus emtionis et venditionis" in the Appendix of the Cologne Edition (1483) of Johannes Gerson's works (1483, 4:185 f.), cited in Janssen (1874, 1:480).
586 See for this the summation in Schmoller (1899, 1055 ff.), and Gengler (1882, 456 ff.). Much material is in Klöden (1841), particularly volumes 2 and 3, and Falke (1869, 197 ff.). From the newer literature are highlighted: Doren (1893), and Des Marez (1901, 75 ff.). It is also to be recalled at this point that the concept of "trade" originally in many cases coincided with that of "change", transportation, or movement. This has been explained convincingly by Schrader (1886, 63, 79, and elsewhere).
587 Von Maurer (1870, 1:403 ff.).
588 Höhlbaum (1876, 1:244 No. 692).
589 Geering (1886, 412).
590 In my view, von Below in his often referred to essay, "Grosshändler und Kleinhändler im deutschen Mittelalter" (1900a, 1 ff.), completely succeeds in proving that up into the 16th century an independent "wholesale trade" (in Germany) did not exist, rather all importers and

exporters also particularised, that is, were "chandlers" or "tailors".
591 Geering (1886, 240–42).
592 Philippe (1858, 89 ff.).
593 Of 69 representatives who signed the document from 960 concerning the prohibition of trade with slaves, only 35 write their names in their own hand; in the document from 971 concerning trade in wood and weapons with Saracens, of 81 only 18; with the remaining names there is "signum manus" [sign of the hand] (Tafel and Thomas 1856, 12:22 ff; 12:28 ff.). Cf. now Heynen (1905, 81 f.).
594 Von Rem himself in his diary (Rem 1861, 5) relates how he came to Venice to learn the abacus, ie. calculating: "there I learnt to calculate in just 5½ months". Other examples of Germans who learnt to calculate in Venice are provided by Simonsfeld (1887, 2:39-40).
595 Geering (1886, 212).
596 See, for example, Sattler (1887, 8), or the introduction of Koppmann to "Tölners Handlungsbuch" (Tölner 1885, xviii f.), or the tax lists for Paris from the year 1292 (Géraud 1837, v): "La plupart des additions sont inexactes" [Most of the additions are inexact].
597 Sieveking (1902, 215). Cf. von Slaski (1905, 21 f.).
598 Cf. the good accomplishments now in Luschin von Ebengreuth's article in Zimmermann et al (1897, II.2:847 ff.), and in Sander (1906, 107 ff.).
599 "The idea of quota-like joint regulation absolutely did not emerge during the existence of the community as a measure of the rights of the individuals; their needs were rather, be they large or small [...] covered from the joint fund without accounting for the weights of the individuals, in which on the other hand — which is likewise especially characteristic — the overall purchases of the individual, be they large or small, were thrown to his personal disposal without any charge." (M. Weber 1889, 45–46).
600 Lastig (1879, 400–414).
601 "stock-in-trade there undoubtedly was, but no Capital as we now use the term." (1890, 1:4). Cf. what is said in the postscript to this chapter.
602 The commonly recurring form of corporative trading concerns, however, finds furthermore its explanation also in that, as we know, still strongly distributed *opportunistic trade* of all earlier times. Even those "distinguished" people, who thanks to their wealth were the earliest in a position to practise an extended trade, were able to or wanted to do this in many cases only in the form of engaging a professional (craftsman-) trader to do it, with whom they then obviously entered into a relationship of profit sharing. Cf. also von Below (1900a, 38 ff.).
603 Over the pre-capitalist shipping companies, see Goldschmidt (1891, 336 ff.), and in addition the especially instructive "Tabula de Amalfa" which is edited and annotated by Laband (1864, 305 ff.).
604 Schulte (1900, 1:281).
605 Fagniez (1898, 1:110 No. 135; 1:161 No. 167; 1:166 No. 171). Cf. the introduction to it (Fagniez 1898, 1:xlv ff.).
606 See the extraordinarily interesting place in Boileau (1879, 93 Tit. L Art. VI). Cf. also my book, *Die Juden und das Wirtschaftsleben* (1911, 60 ff.;

1962, 61 ff.).
607 The prohibition on consignment business was still pronounced in 1417 at the courts in Lübeck: "Nobody shall buy herring before it is caught, grain before it is grown, garments before they are made" (Neumann 1865, 37). Prohibition of all credit businesses were still in the German municipal laws of the 15th century (Neumann 1865, 88 ff.).
608 "Le cambiali a scadenza protatta, il deposito a interesse fermo, il nome stesso di banchieri, le fiere dei cambi, i banchi pubblici, operazioni ed istituti che s' incardiano sopra l' uso generale e costante del mutuo feneratizio appartengono tutte all' età moderna."
[The promissory notes with deadlines, the deposit at fixed interest, the very name of banker, the exchange fairs, the public banks, operations and institutes that are based on the general and constant use of the mutual loan, all belong to the modern age .] (Toniolo 1895, 571).
609 What I say here about the canonical prohibition of interest is in substance already contained in the first edition. It retains its force for the Early and in part still the High Middle Ages. That in the Late Middle Ages the canonical prohibition of interest was limited to consumer credit and no longer applied to the profits of capital is something I have shown in my *Der Bourgeois* (1913a).
610 "Are then the Jews," Geiler von Kaiserberg asked, "better than the Christians, in that they *do not want to work with the work of their hands*? Do they not stand under God's command: in the sweat of thy face shalt thou earn bread? *Practising usury with money means not working, but maltreating others in idleness.*" [Tr.: not referenced by Sombart.]
611 "huiusmodi homines *pro intentione lucri*, quam habent, cum omnis usura et superabundantia prohibentur in lege, iudicandi sunt male agere."
[such people, as far as they have *intentionally profited*, with all interest and excess forbidden in law, are judged to have acted poorly]
(Emphasis added.) From "Decretalium Gregorii papae IX compilationis" in Richter and Friedberg (1879, 2:814 Cap. X) (from 1186).
Further evidence for the scorning of *usuraria voluntas* [disposition towards usury] in Neumann (1865, 95 f.).
612 An illustrative description of the life of the German merchant in foreign lands has been drawn up by Falke (1859, 1:200 ff.).
613 It is hardly necessary to mention evidence that the *idea of sustenance* also dominated the regulations of the traders' guilds. Especially instructive are the circumstances of the *English* traders' guilds as they are described to us by Gross (1890). For a general orientation, Doren (1893, 60, 97, 147) is also suitable. See also Kießelbach (1860, 206). For *France*, the following in particular are to be compared: Levasseur (1900), Fagniez (1877; 1898), and Pigeonneau (1887). The pedlars "are disturbers of the fixed local *sustenance* of the retailers." (Ersch et al. 1828, 2.3 Harrich-Hebung:186).
614 "It was time here to break off the competition of the Constance salesmen (ie. of linen) amongst each other and to strengthen the renown of

the Constance body of merchants" (Schulte 1900, 1:163).

615 The statute for Novgorod designates that nobody shall turnover (or have in stock?) more than 1,000 marks in a year, be it his own or a stranger's property (that he has on *sendeve* contract [Tr.: a commission business where the merchant takes a fixed salary and the client bears all the risk]) or company property.

616 Statute of the Ribe [Tr.: town in Jutland] and Danish travellers to Stade (14th century):

> "Vorthmer dat yement in der kumpenye deme anderen dar vorekop dede, de schal der kumpenye dat beteren mit veer olden groten"

> [Further that someone in the partnership preempts the others, they shall insure the partnership with 4 old groschen(?)] (Höhlbaum 1876, 3:90 No. 183 § 7).

617 "The gildsman was generally under obligation to share all purchases with his brethren, that is to say, if he bought a quantity of a given commodity, any other gildsmen could claim a portion of it at the same price at which he purchased it." (Gross 1890, 1:49). Evidence in Gross (1890, 2:46, 150, 161, 185, 218, 219, 226, 290, 352). The statutes of the guild of Saint-Omer contain the regulation (in § 2):

> "si quis vero guildam habens mercatum aliquid non ad victum pertinens valens V gr. s. et supra taxaverit et alius gildam habens supervenerit si voluerit in mercato illo porcionem habebit"

> [if someone, however, of the guild making some trade pertinent to their livelihood of the value 5 groschens (?) and valued higher and another of the guild having come upon it, if he wishes he will have his portion of the trade] (Doren 1893, 60).

The regulations frequently also state that a buyer is obligated, as long as the sale is not perfect, to allow any other member of the association to take part on demand for half of the purchase. Cf. Conze (1889, 16 f.).

618 The only thing which Beckmann cites against me is the fact that the smallness of the ships proves nothing for the tiny extent of the trade, because often a "remarkably large number" of ships were placed in the service of trading enterprises. That I doubt for *one* trading enterprise. Beckmann seems to mean the departure together of several ships. On *one* ship — as small as it was — we find mostly an entire mob of merchants present in person or represented by their wares.

www.ingramcontent.com/pod-product-compliance
Lightning Source LLC
Chambersburg PA
CBHW021141240426
43661CB00075B/1598